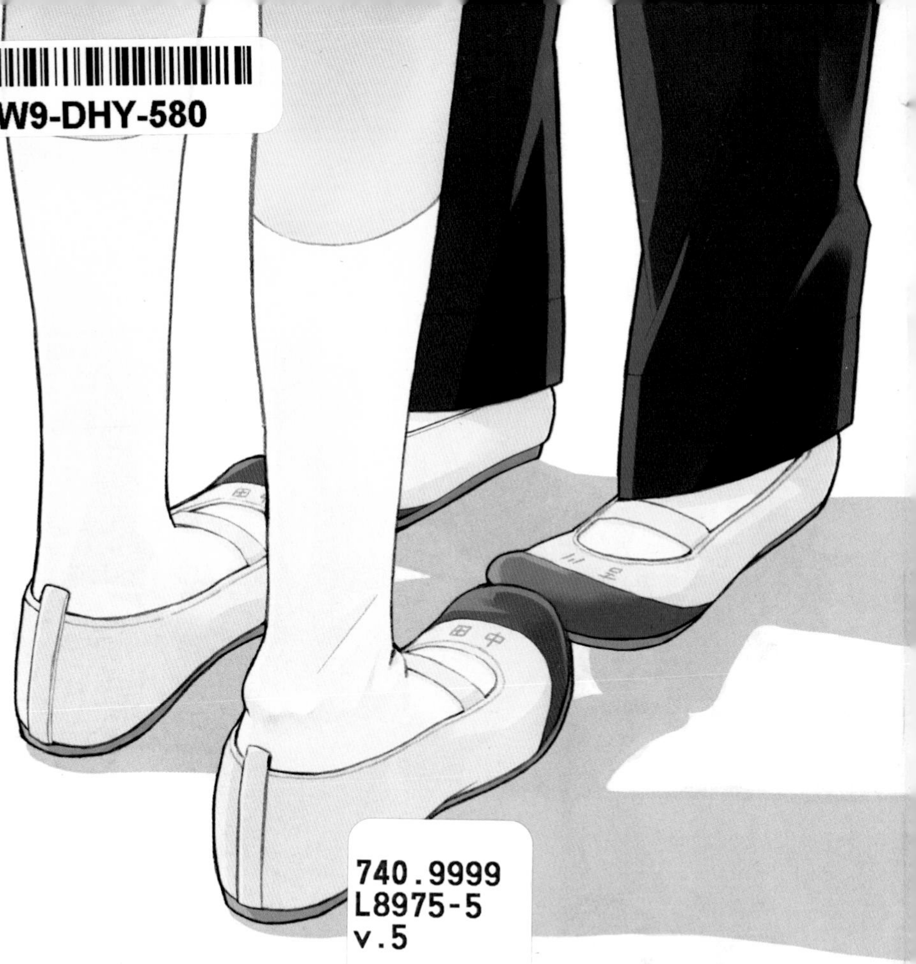
田中

Love at Fourteen

Fuka Mizutani

5

SHOES: TANAKA/YOSHIKAWA

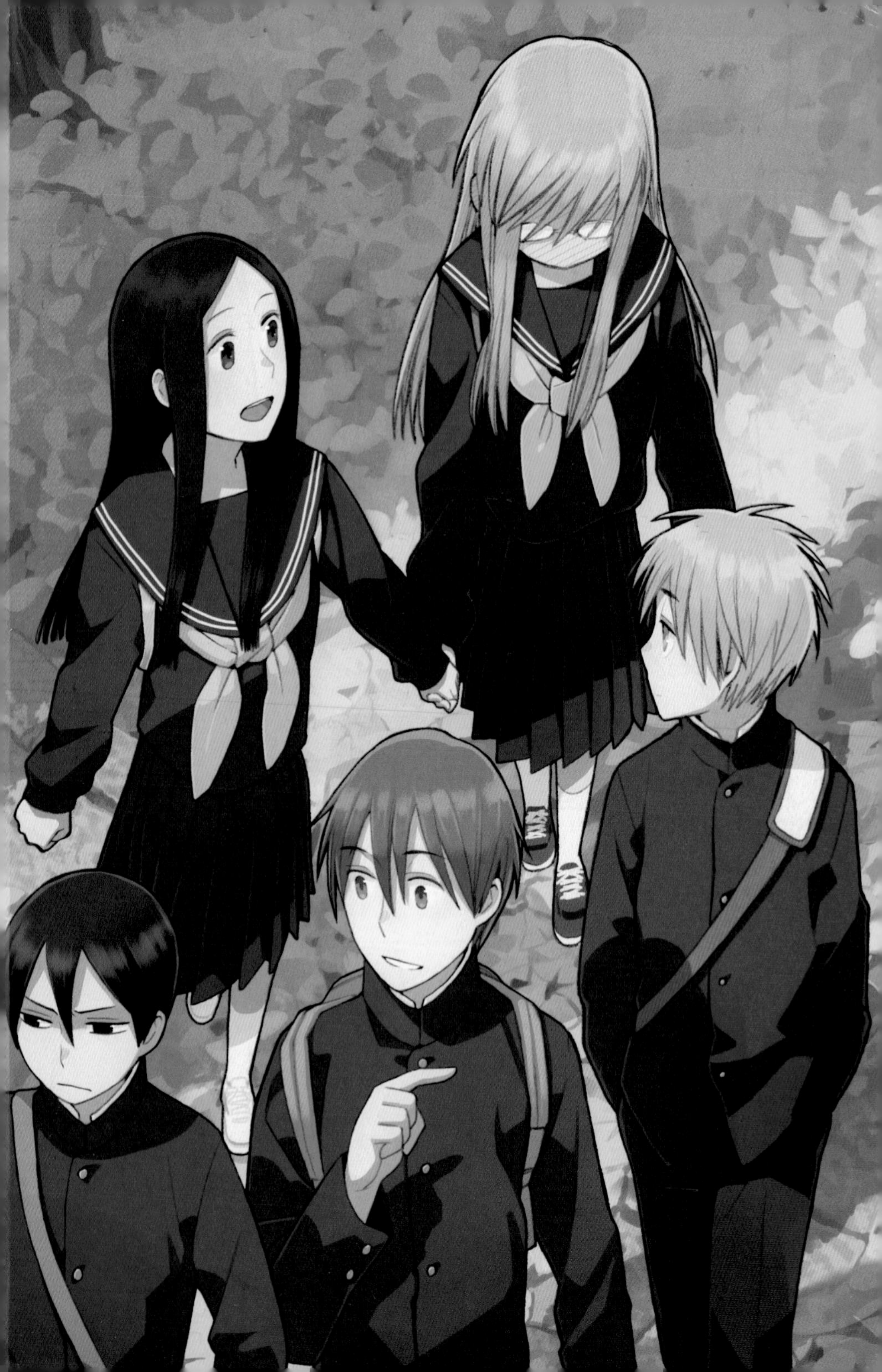

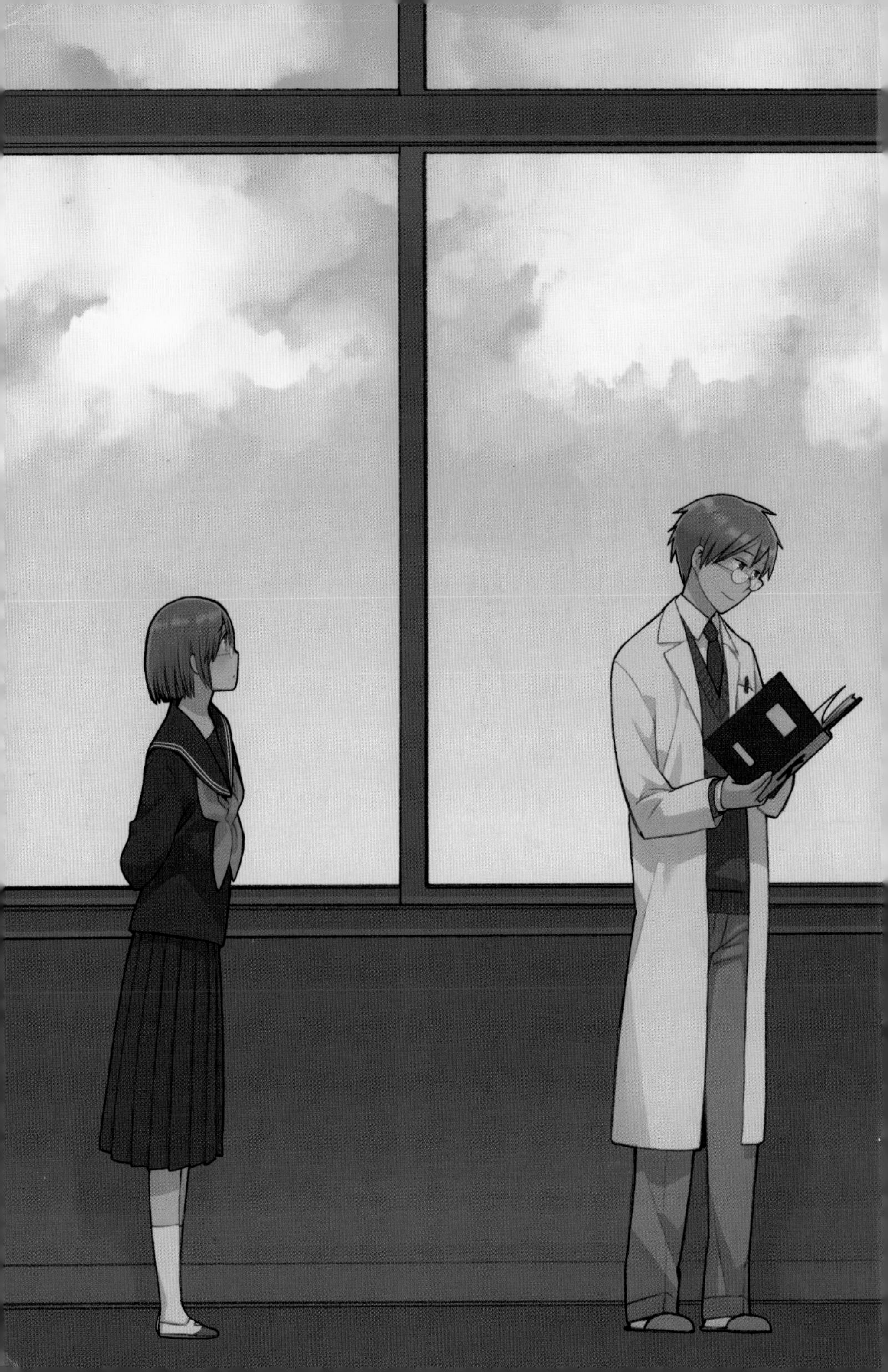

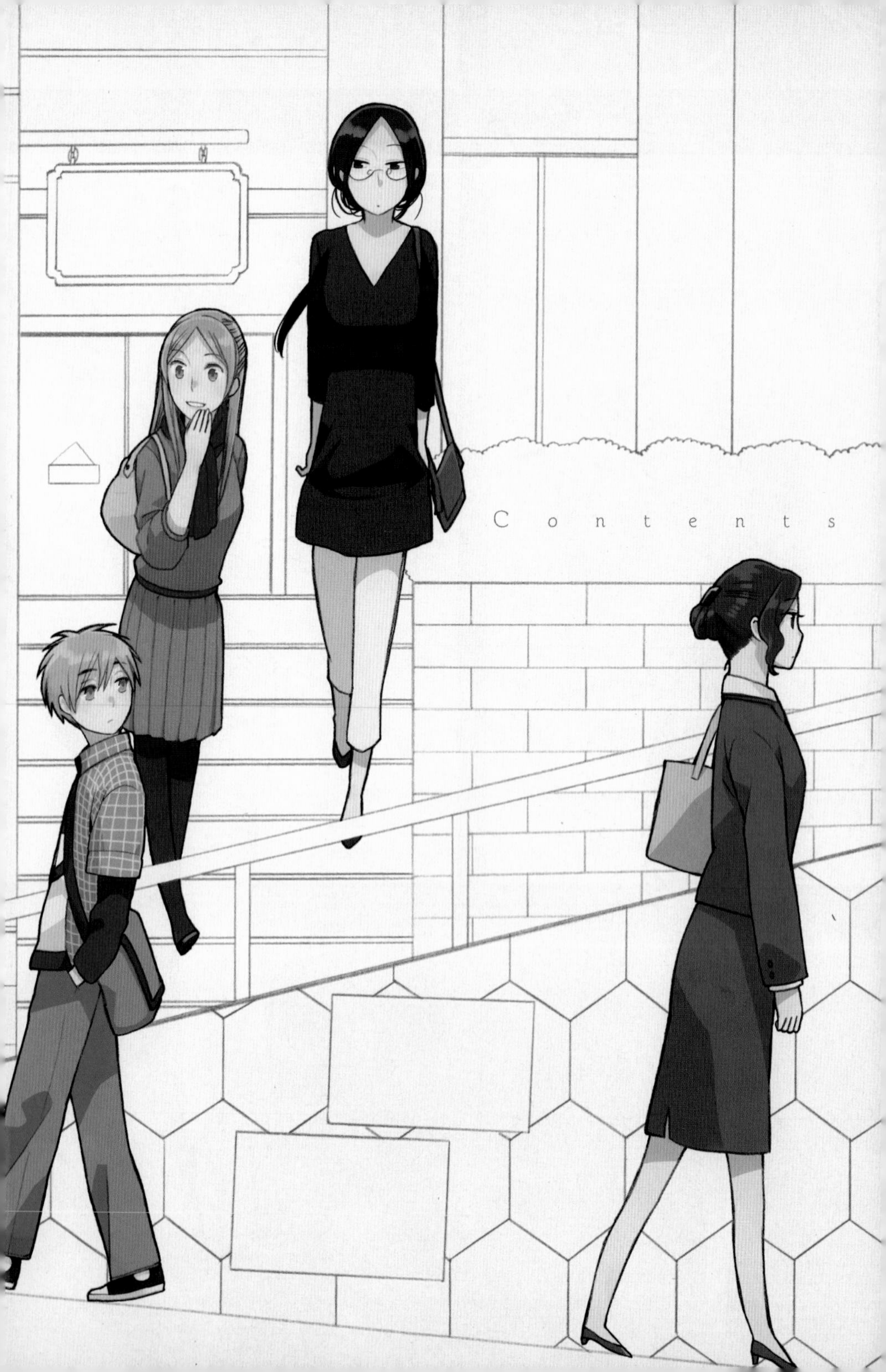

Contents

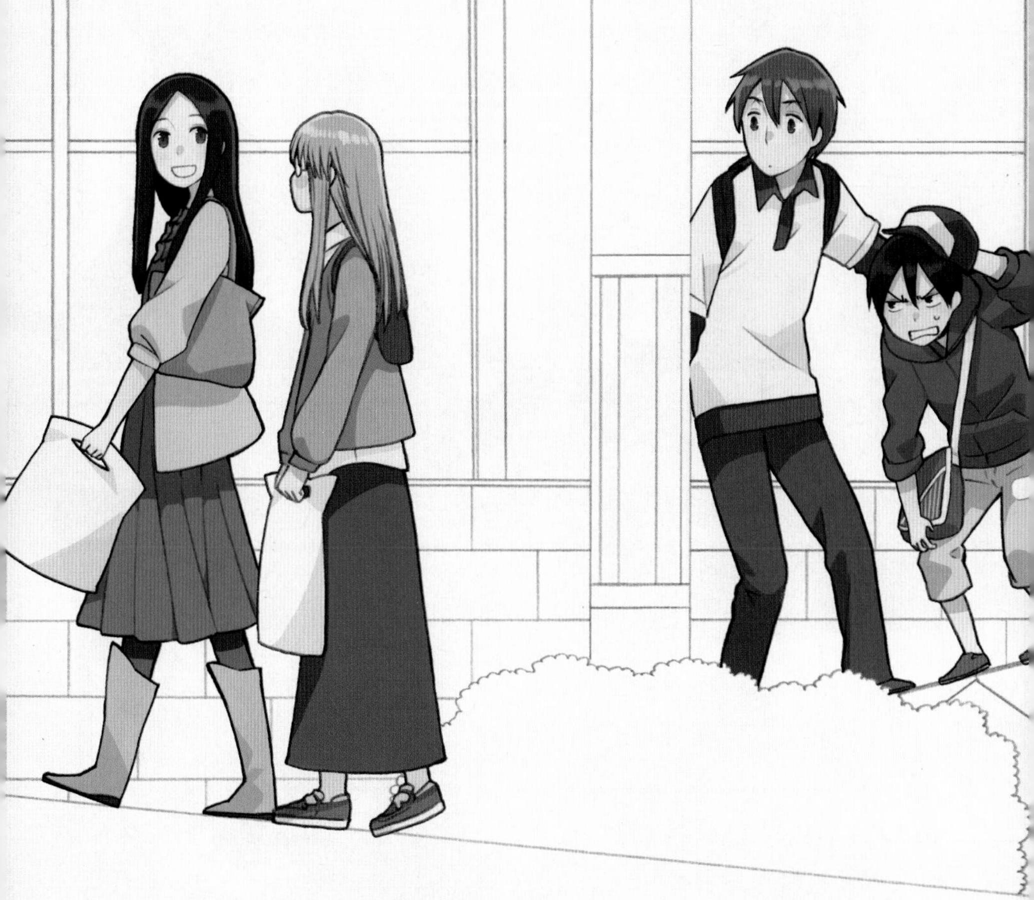

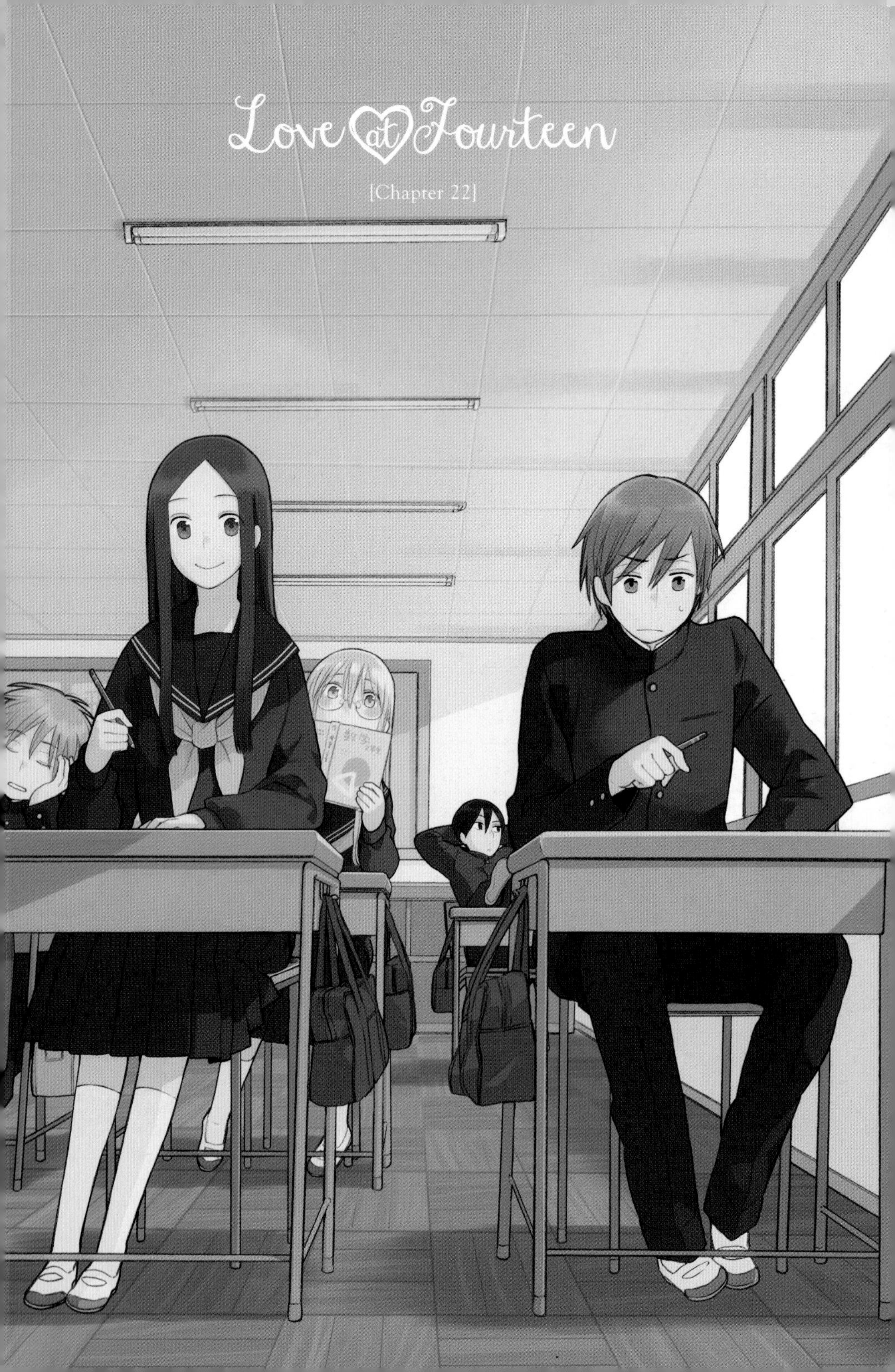
Love at Fourteen
[Chapter 22]

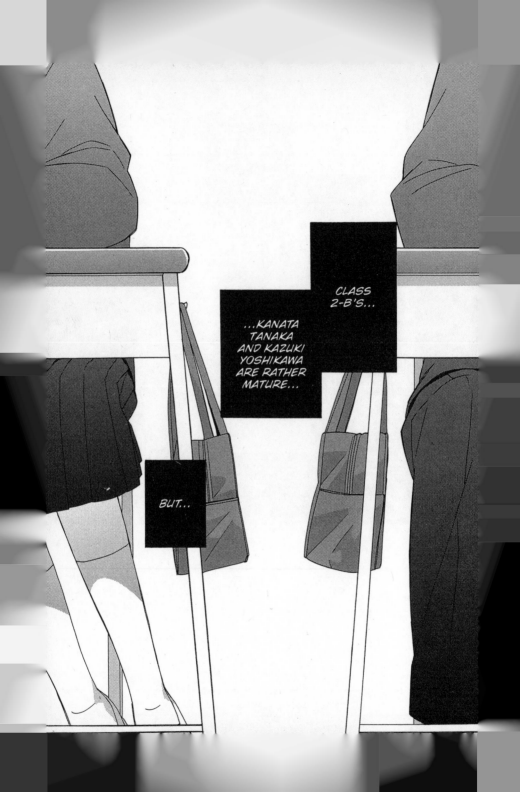

CLASS 2-B'S...

...KANATA TANAKA AND KAZUKI YOSHIKAWA ARE RATHER MATURE...

BUT...

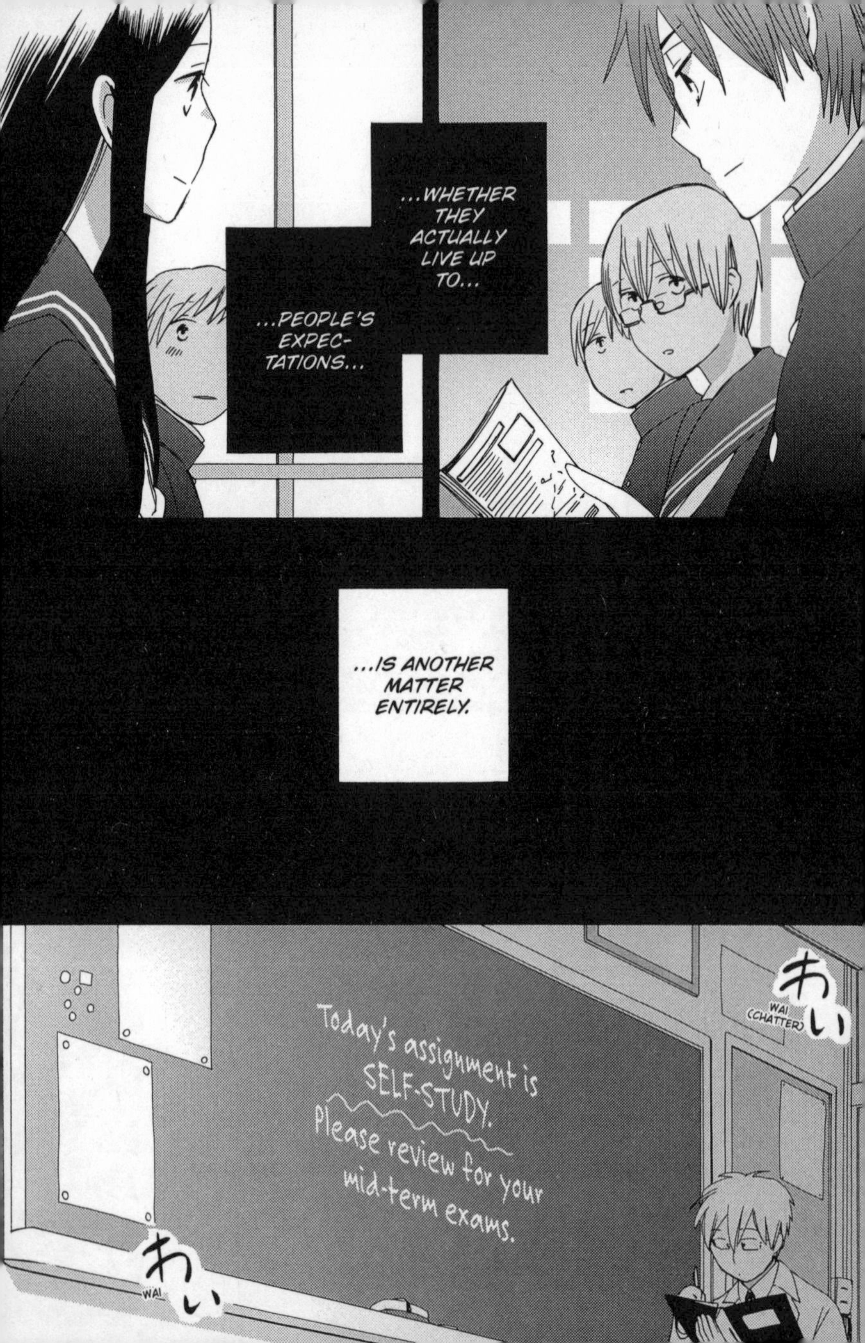
...WHETHER THEY ACTUALLY LIVE UP TO...
...PEOPLE'S EXPECTATIONS...
...IS ANOTHER MATTER ENTIRELY.
わい
WAI (CHATTER)
Today's assignment is SELF-STUDY. Please review for your mid-term exams.
わい
WAI

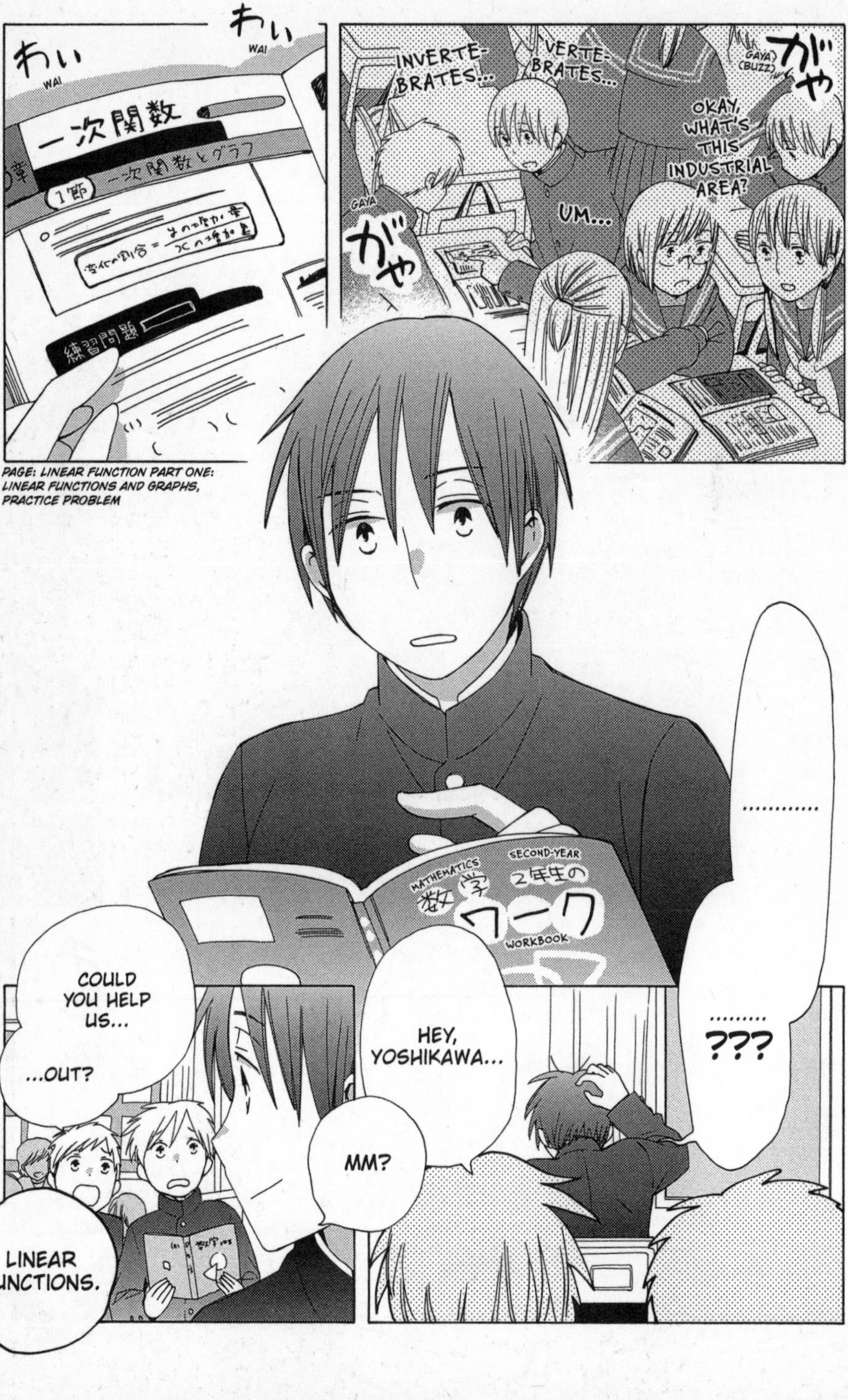
がや
GAYA (BUZZ)
VERTE-BRATES...
OKAY, WHAT'S THIS INDUSTRIAL AREA?
INVERTE-BRATES...
UM...
GAYA
がや
わい
WAI
わい
WAI
一次関数
1節 一次関数とグラフ
練習問題
PAGE: LINEAR FUNCTION PART ONE: LINEAR FUNCTIONS AND GRAPHS, PRACTICE PROBLEM
....
SECOND-YEAR
2年生の
MATHEMATICS
数学
ワーク
WORKBOOK
....
???
HEY, YOSHIKAWA...
MM?
COULD YOU HELP US...
...OUT?
LINEAR FUNCTIONS.

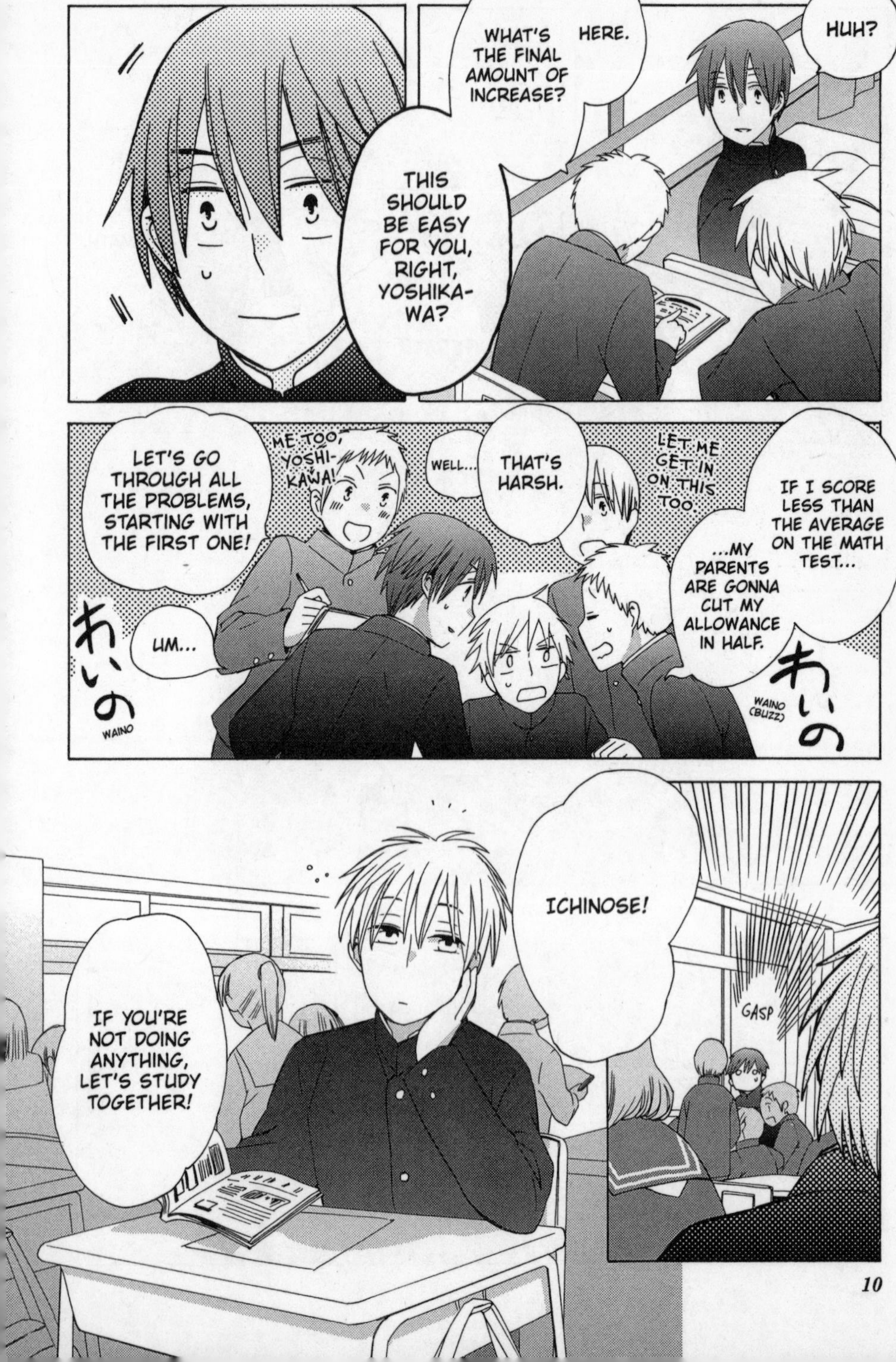
HUH?
WHAT'S THE FINAL AMOUNT OF INCREASE? HERE.
THIS SHOULD BE EASY FOR YOU, RIGHT, YOSHIKAWA?
IF I SCORE LESS THAN THE AVERAGE ON THE MATH TEST...
...MY PARENTS ARE GONNA CUT MY ALLOWANCE IN HALF.
わいの
WAINO (BUZZ)
LET ME GET IN ON THIS TOO.
THAT'S HARSH.
WELL...
ME TOO, YOSHIKAWA!
LET'S GO THROUGH ALL THE PROBLEMS, STARTING WITH THE FIRST ONE!
UM...
わいの
WAINO
ICHINOSE!
GASP
IF YOU'RE NOT DOING ANYTHING, LET'S STUDY TOGETHER!

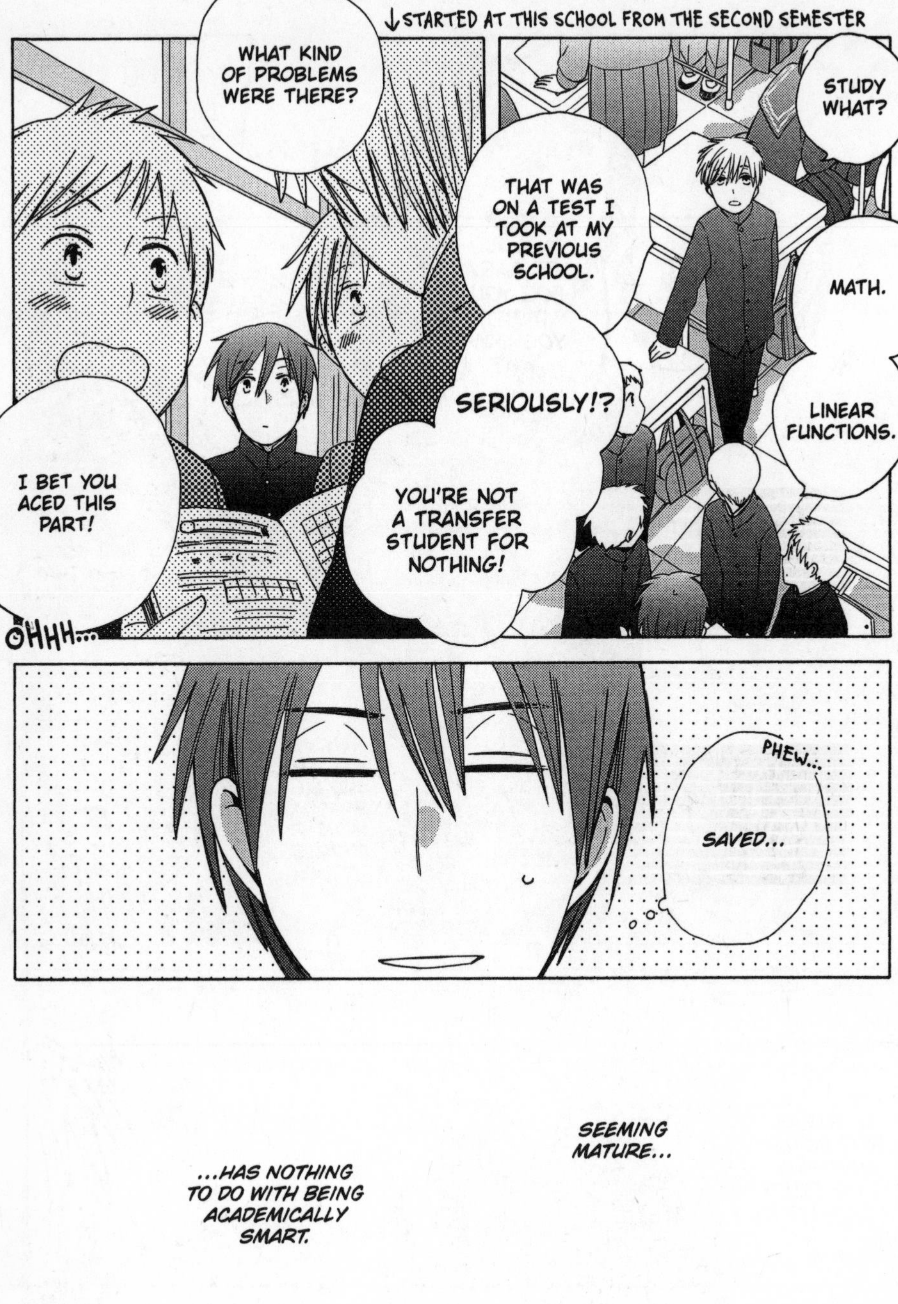
↓STARTED AT THIS SCHOOL FROM THE SECOND SEMESTER
STUDY WHAT?
MATH.
LINEAR FUNCTIONS.
THAT WAS ON A TEST I TOOK AT MY PREVIOUS SCHOOL.
WHAT KIND OF PROBLEMS WERE THERE?
SERIOUSLY!?
YOU'RE NOT A TRANSFER STUDENT FOR NOTHING!
I BET YOU ACED THIS PART!
OHHH...
PHEW...
SAVED...
SEEMING MATURE...
...HAS NOTHING TO DO WITH BEING ACADEMICALLY SMART.

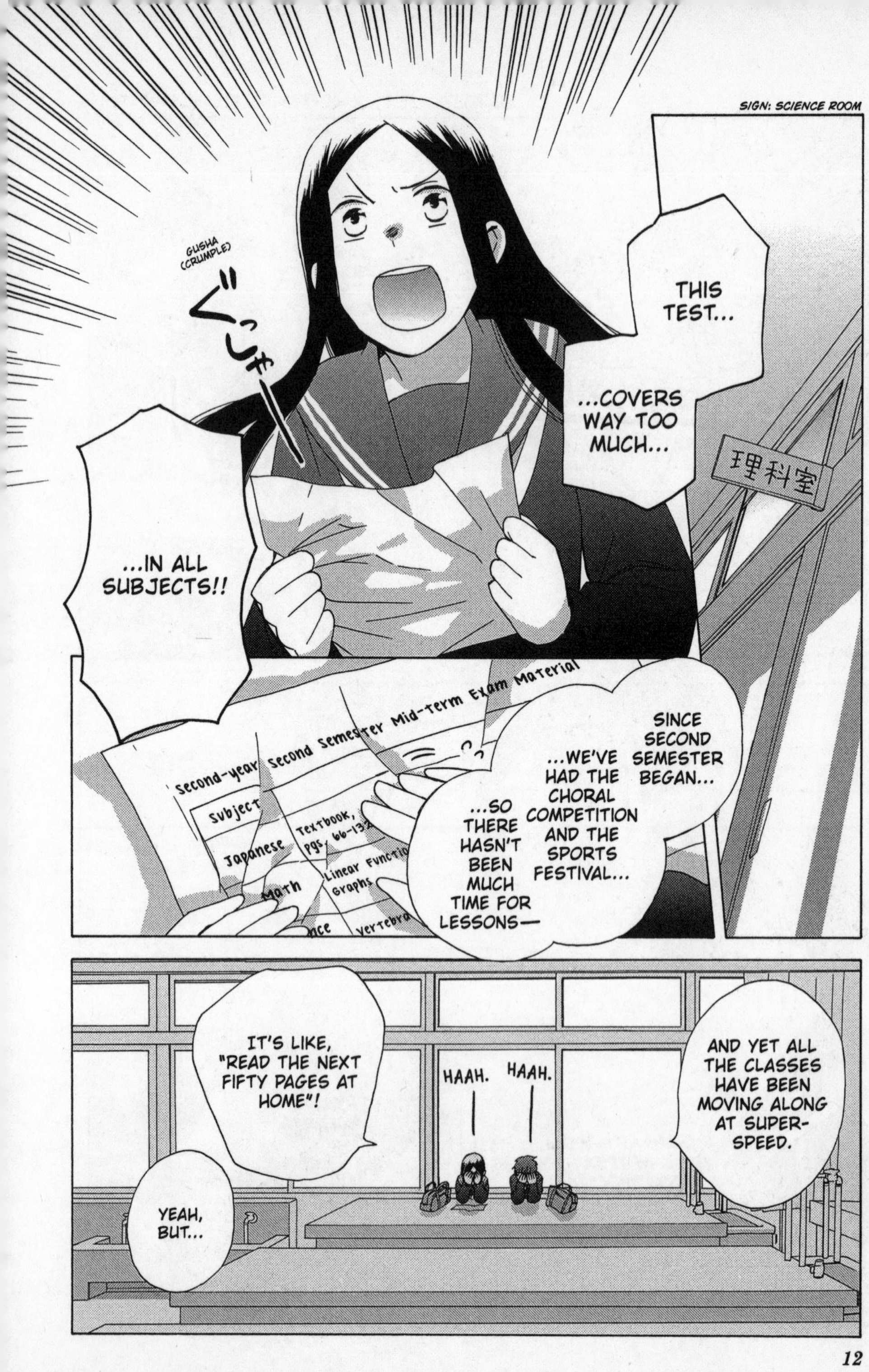
SIGN: SCIENCE ROOM
THIS TEST...
...COVERS WAY TOO MUCH...
理科室
GUSHA (CRUMPLE)
ぐっしゃー
...IN ALL SUBJECTS!!
Second-year Second Semester Mid-term Exam Material
Subject
Japanese
Textbook, pgs. 66-13
Math
Linear Functio
Graphs
Vertebra
SINCE SECOND SEMESTER BEGAN...
...WE'VE HAD THE CHORAL COMPETITION AND THE SPORTS FESTIVAL...
...SO THERE HASN'T BEEN MUCH TIME FOR LESSONS—
AND YET ALL THE CLASSES HAVE BEEN MOVING ALONG AT SUPER-SPEED.
HAAH.
HAAH.
IT'S LIKE, "READ THE NEXT FIFTY PAGES AT HOME"!
YEAH, BUT...

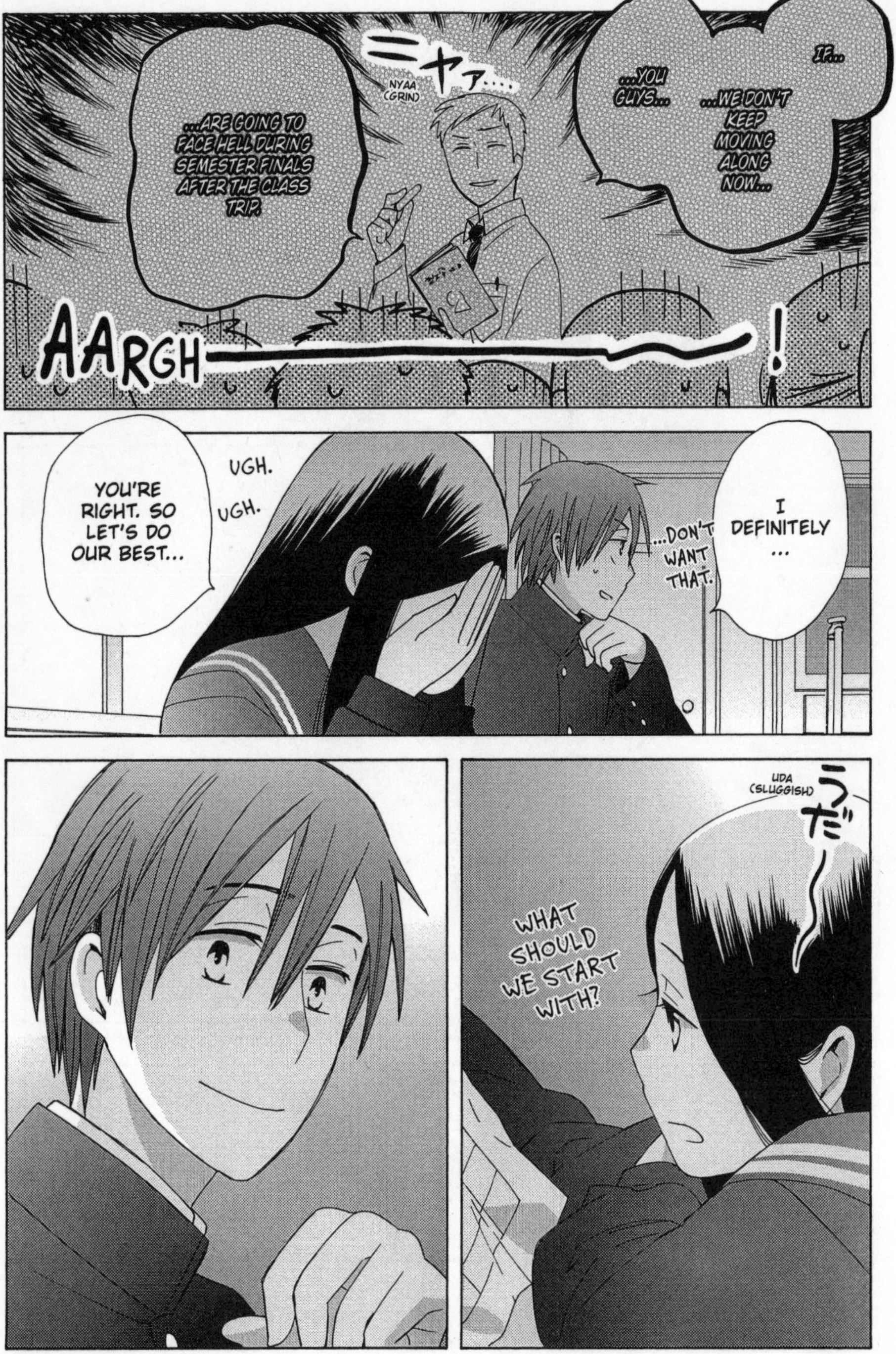
IF...
...WE DON'T KEEP MOVING ALONG NOW...
...YOU GUYS...
ニヤァ....
NYAA (GRIN)
...ARE GOING TO FACE HELL DURING SEMESTER FINALS AFTER THE CLASS TRIP.
AARGH—!
I DEFINITELY ...
...DON'T WANT THAT.
UGH.
UGH.
YOU'RE RIGHT. SO LET'S DO OUR BEST...
うだ～
UDA (SLUGGISH)
WHAT SHOULD WE START WITH?

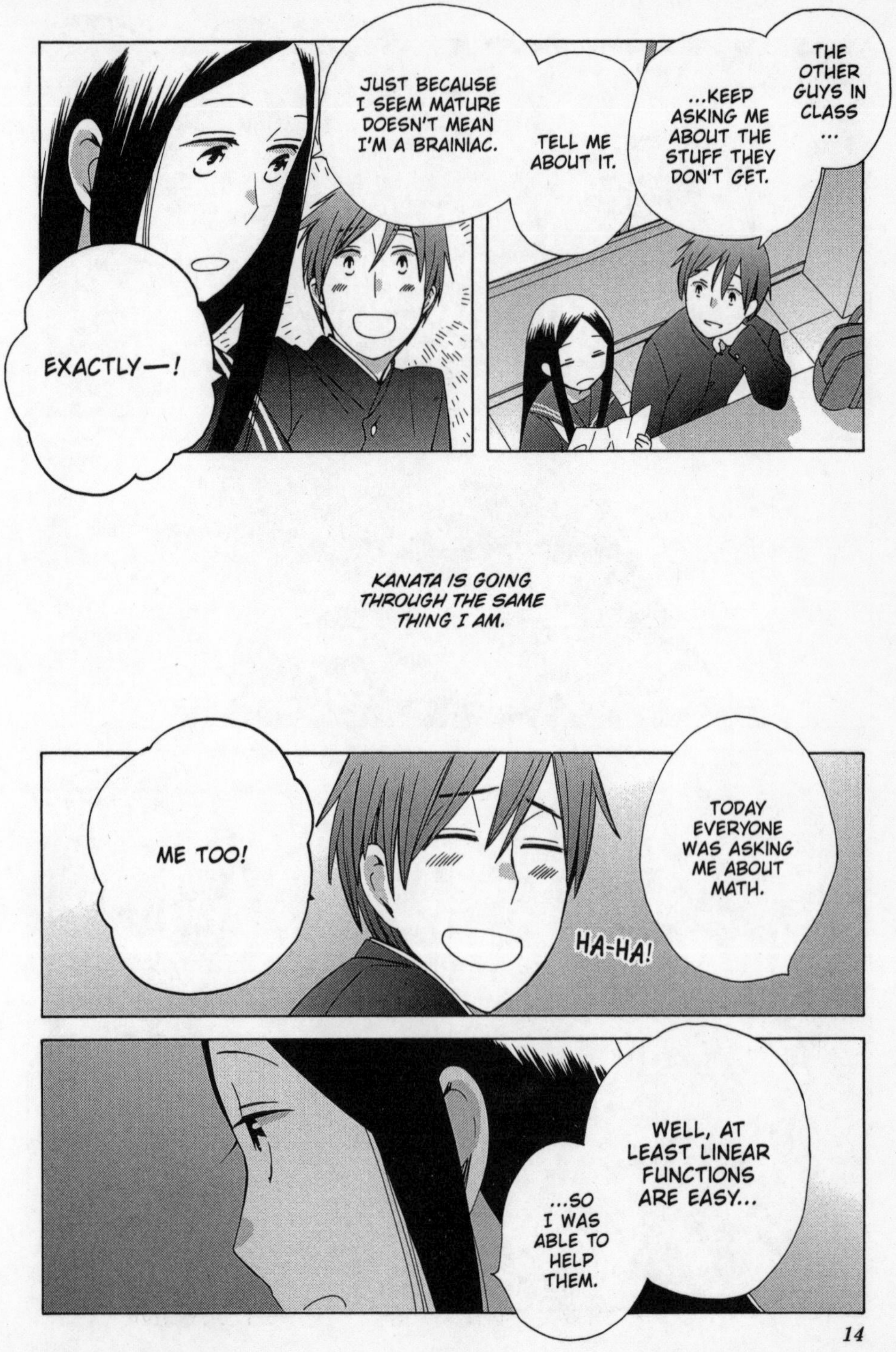
THE OTHER GUYS IN CLASS ...
...KEEP ASKING ME ABOUT THE STUFF THEY DON'T GET.
TELL ME ABOUT IT.
JUST BECAUSE I SEEM MATURE DOESN'T MEAN I'M A BRAINIAC.
EXACTLY—!
KANATA IS GOING THROUGH THE SAME THING I AM.
TODAY EVERYONE WAS ASKING ME ABOUT MATH.
HA-HA!
ME TOO!
WELL, AT LEAST LINEAR FUNCTIONS ARE EASY...
...SO I WAS ABLE TO HELP THEM.

KANATA...

...IS GOING...

...THROUGH THE
SAME THING...

?

RIGHT?

YEAH.

SURE.

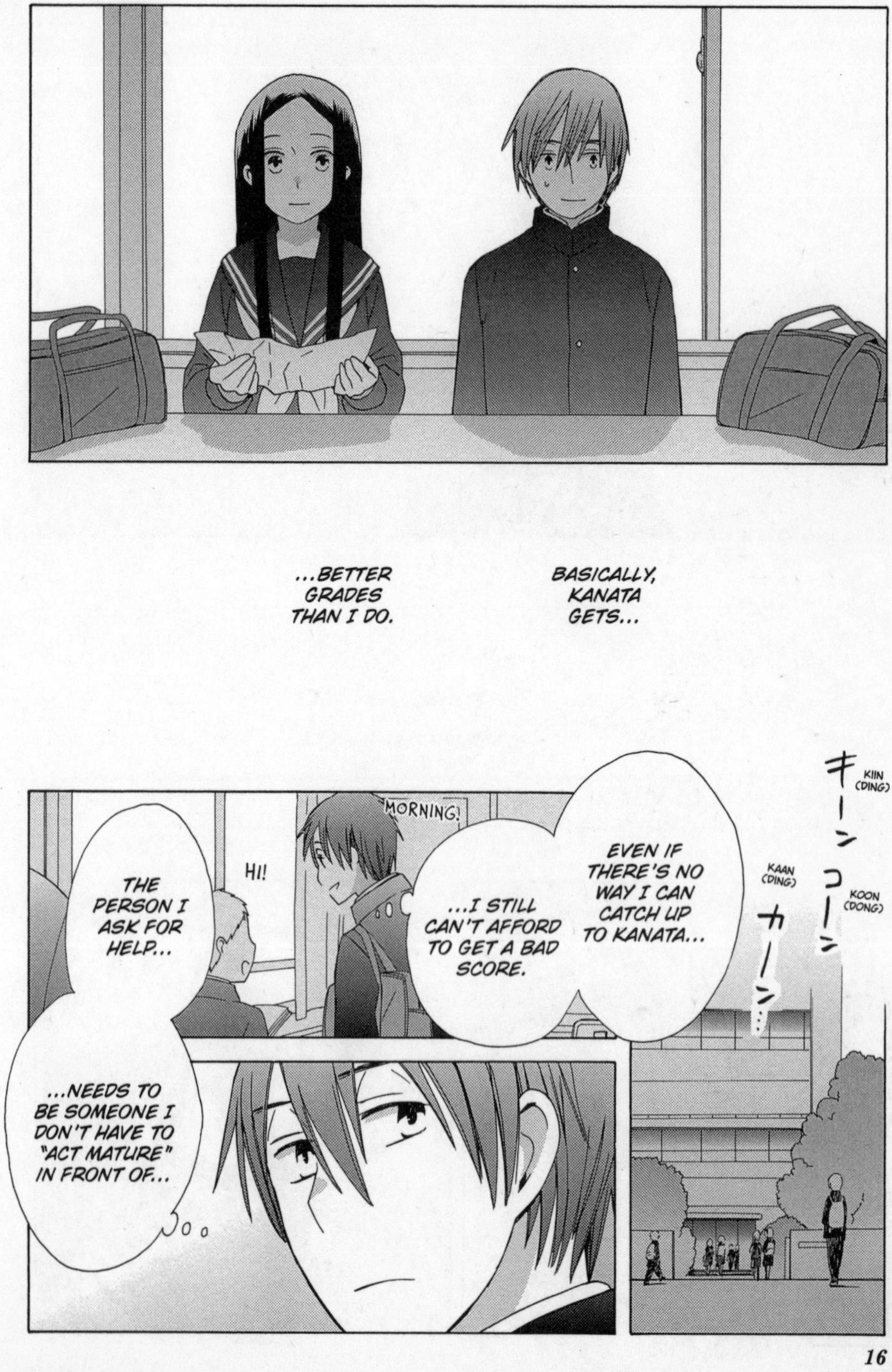
BASICALLY, KANATA GETS...
...BETTER GRADES THAN I DO.
キーン KIIN (DING)
コーン KOON (DONG)
カーン... KAAN (DING)
EVEN IF THERE'S NO WAY I CAN CATCH UP TO KANATA...
...I STILL CAN'T AFFORD TO GET A BAD SCORE.
MORNING!
HI!
THE PERSON I ASK FOR HELP...
...NEEDS TO BE SOMEONE I DON'T HAVE TO "ACT MATURE" IN FRONT OF...

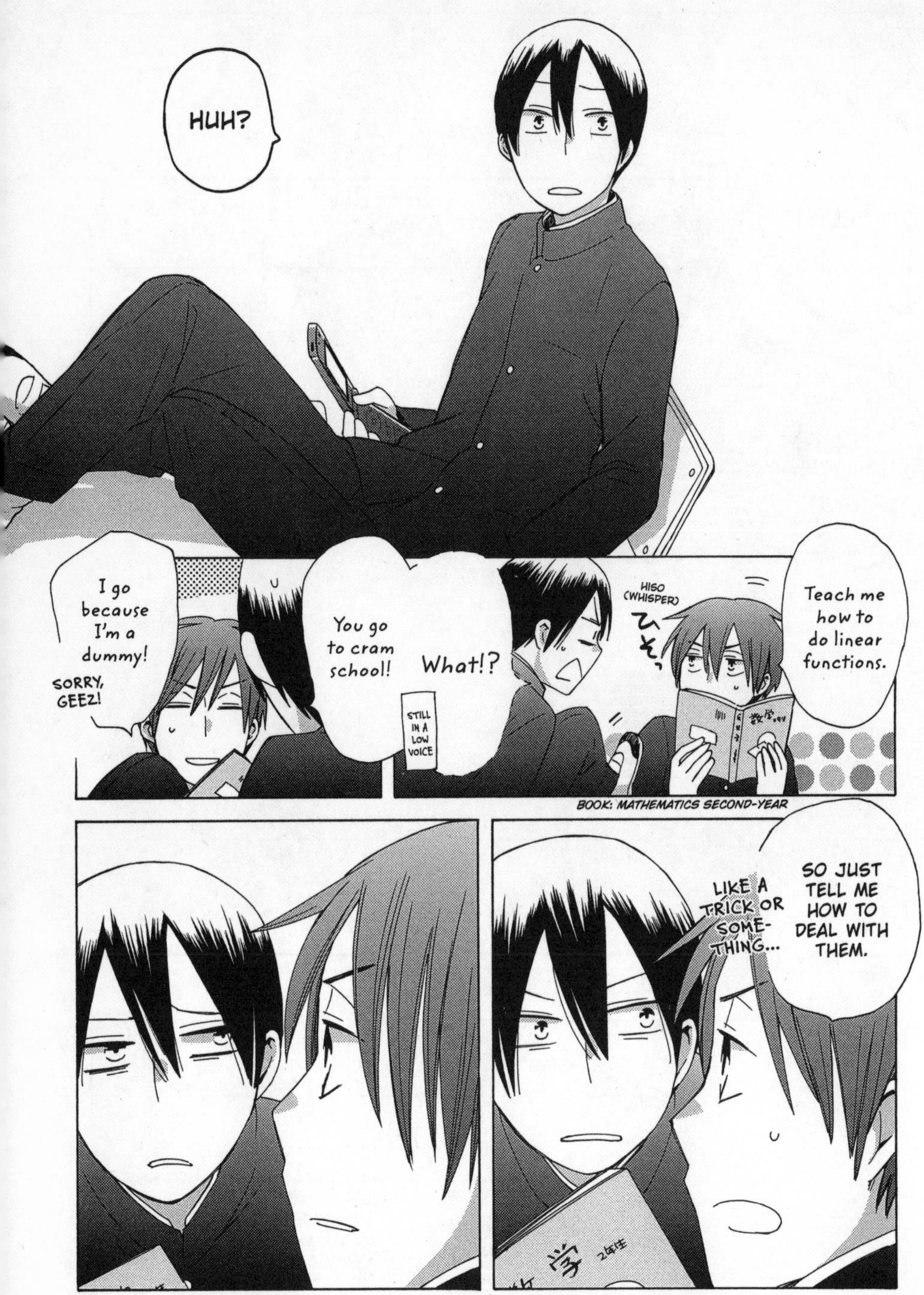
HUH?
Teach me how to do linear functions.
HISO (WHISPER)
BOOK: MATHEMATICS SECOND-YEAR
What!?
STILL IN A LOW VOICE
You go to cram school!
I go because I'm a dummy!
SORRY, GEEZ!
SO JUST TELL ME HOW TO DEAL WITH THEM.
LIKE A TRICK OR SOME-THING...

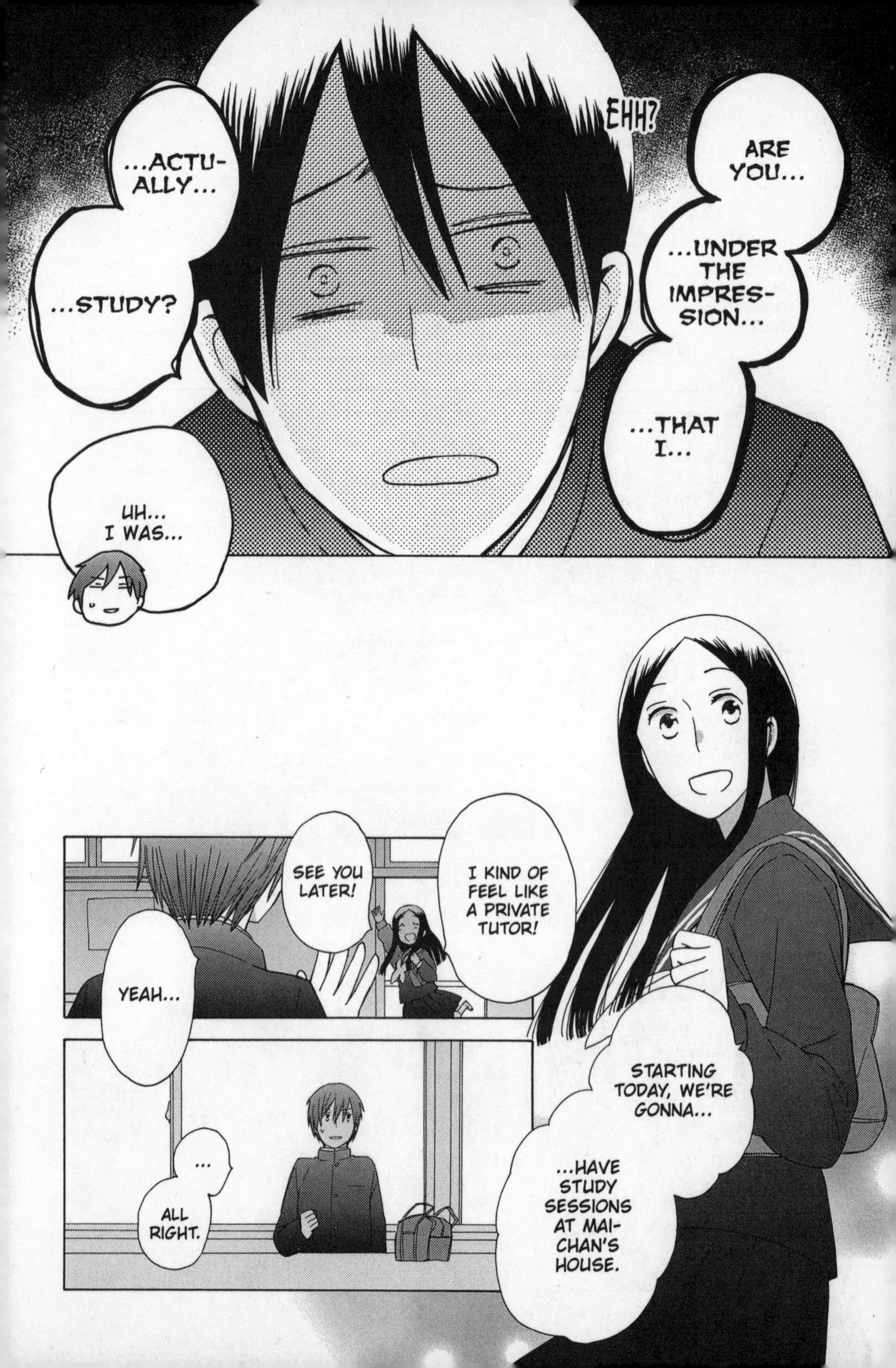
EHH?
ARE YOU...
...UNDER THE IMPRESSION...
...THAT I...
...ACTUALLY...
...STUDY?
UH... I WAS...
STARTING TODAY, WE'RE GONNA...
...HAVE STUDY SESSIONS AT MAI-CHAN'S HOUSE.
I KIND OF FEEL LIKE A PRIVATE TUTOR!
SEE YOU LATER!
YEAH...
...
ALL RIGHT.

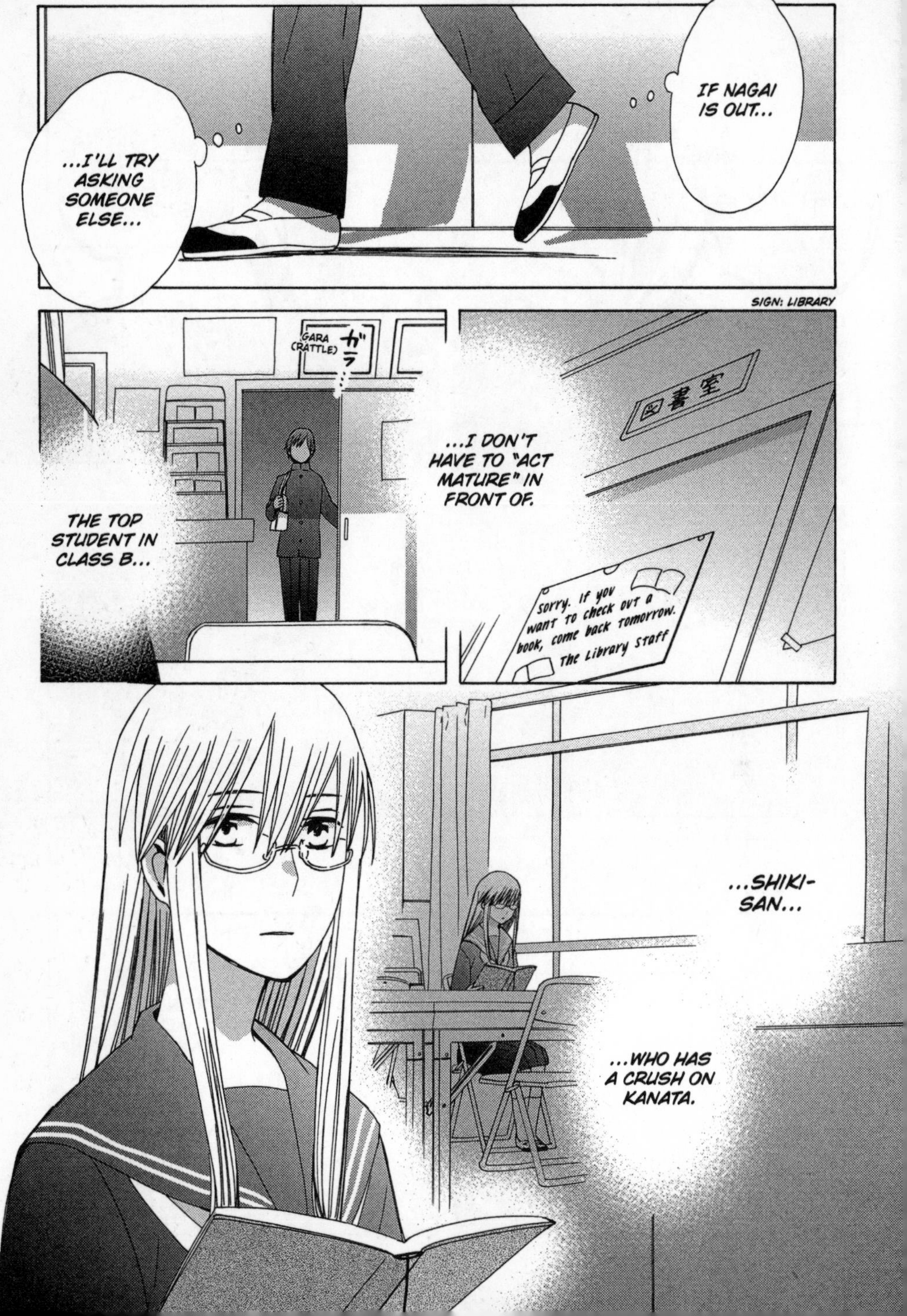
IF NAGAI IS OUT...
...I'LL TRY ASKING SOMEONE ELSE...
SIGN: LIBRARY
図書室
Sorry. If you want to check out a book, come back tomorrow.
The Library Staff
GARA (RATTLE)
ガラ...
...I DON'T HAVE TO "ACT MATURE" IN FRONT OF.
THE TOP STUDENT IN CLASS B...
...SHIKI-SAN...
...WHO HAS A CRUSH ON KANATA.

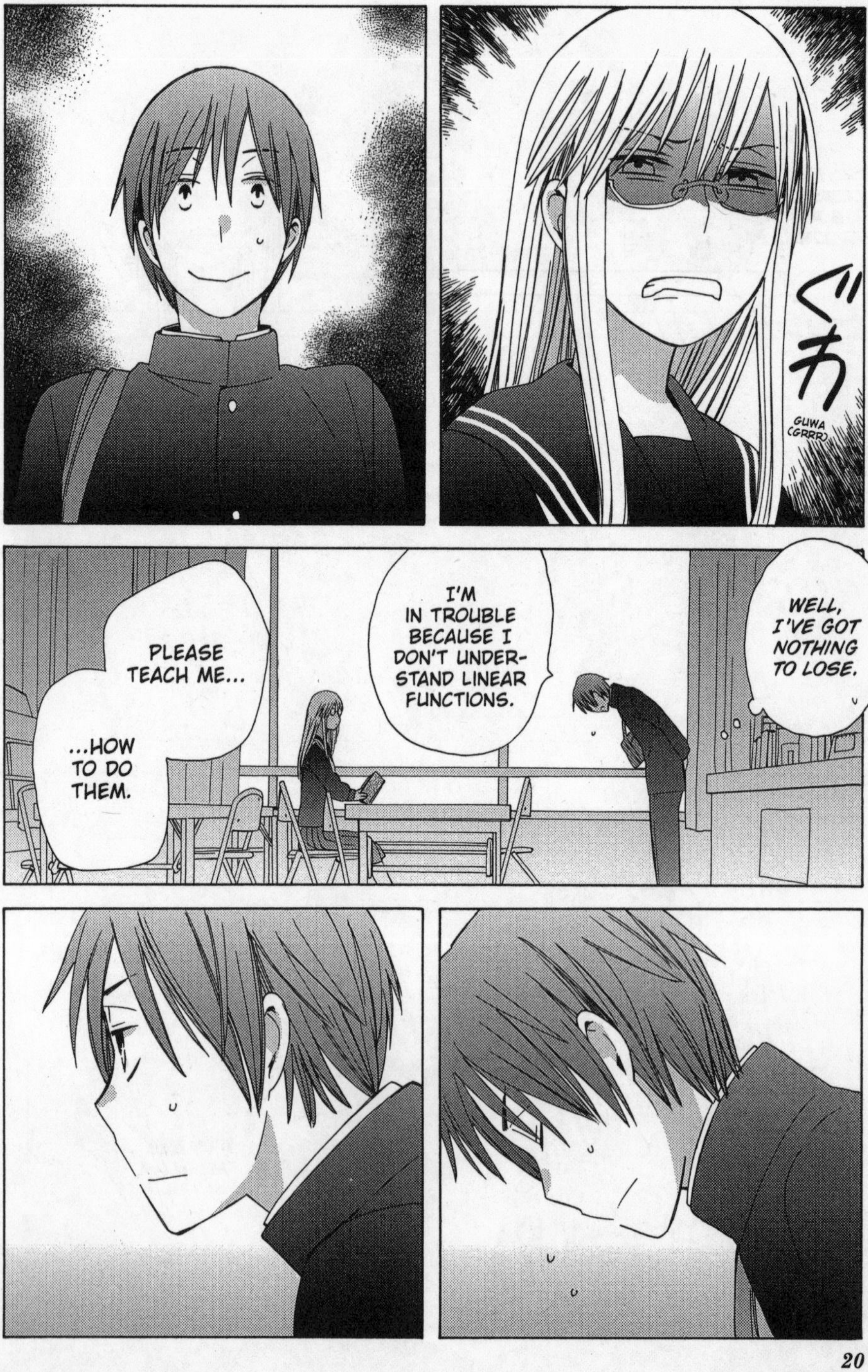
ぐわ
GUWA (GRRR)
WELL, I'VE GOT NOTHING TO LOSE.
I'M IN TROUBLE BECAUSE I DON'T UNDER-STAND LINEAR FUNCTIONS.
PLEASE TEACH ME...
...HOW TO DO THEM.

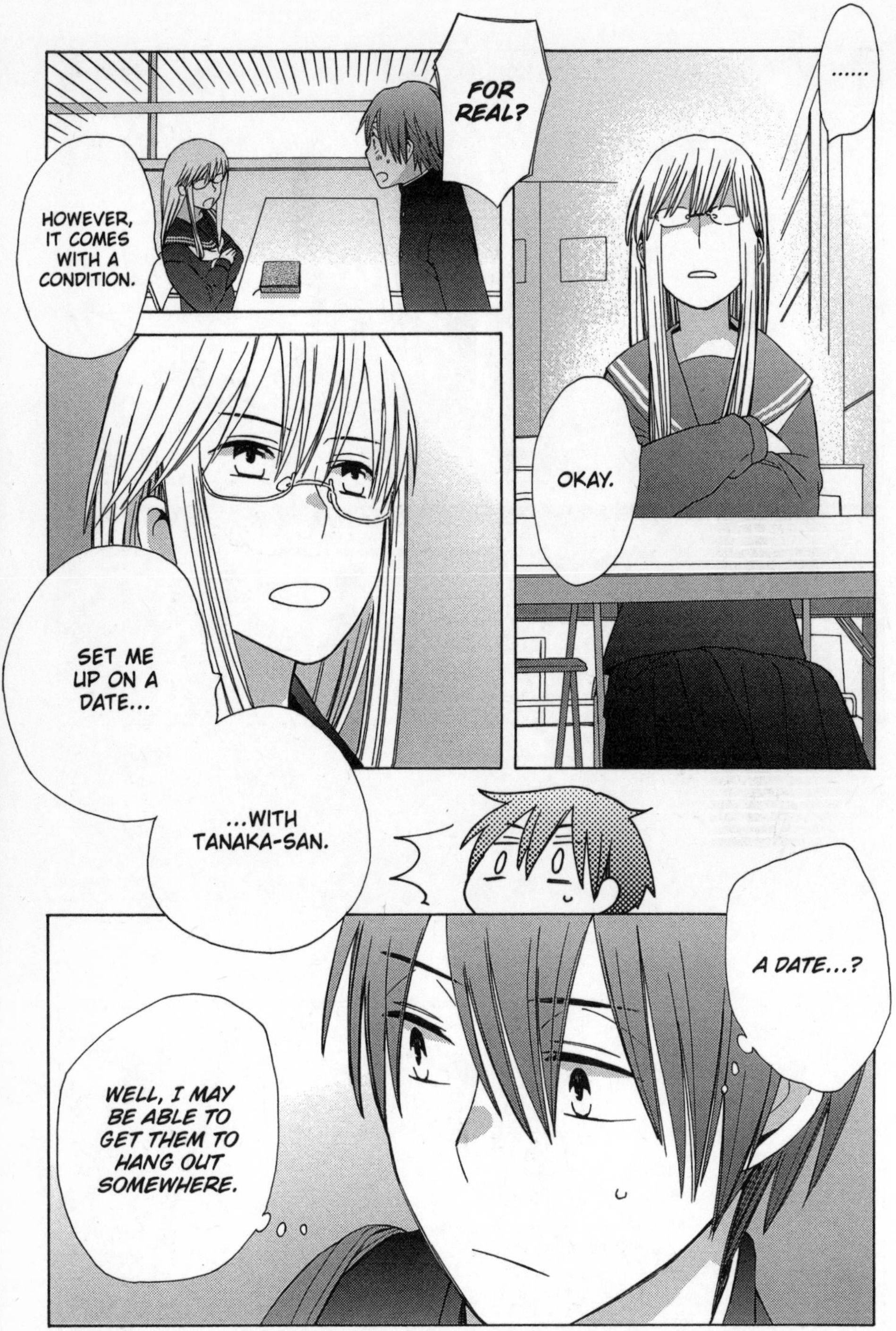
......
OKAY.
FOR REAL?
HOWEVER, IT COMES WITH A CONDITION.
SET ME UP ON A DATE...
...WITH TANAKA-SAN.
A DATE...?
WELL, I MAY BE ABLE TO GET THEM TO HANG OUT SOMEWHERE.

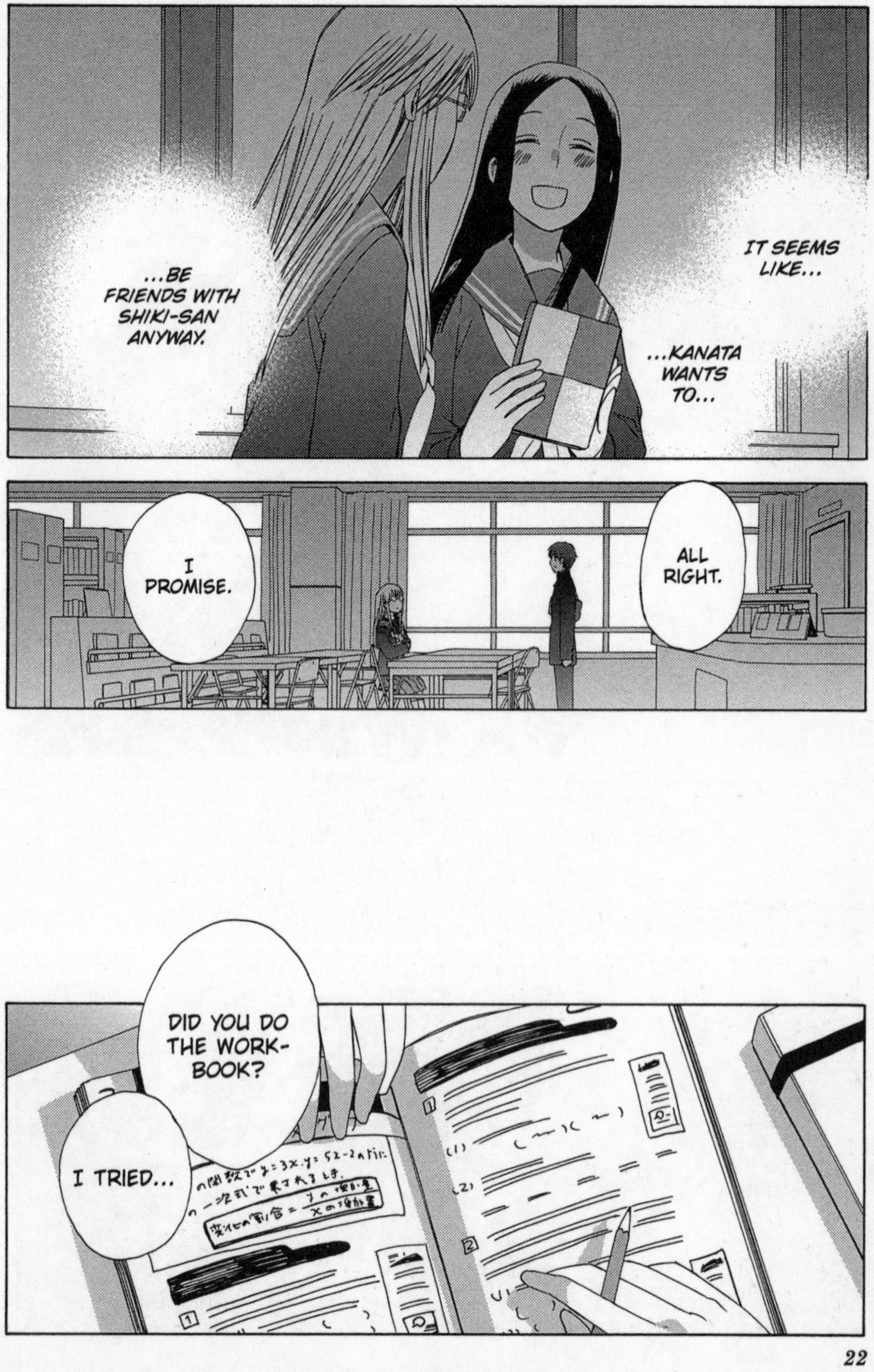
IT SEEMS LIKE...
...KANATA WANTS TO...
...BE FRIENDS WITH SHIKI-SAN ANYWAY.
ALL RIGHT.
I PROMISE.
DID YOU DO THE WORK-BOOK?
I TRIED...

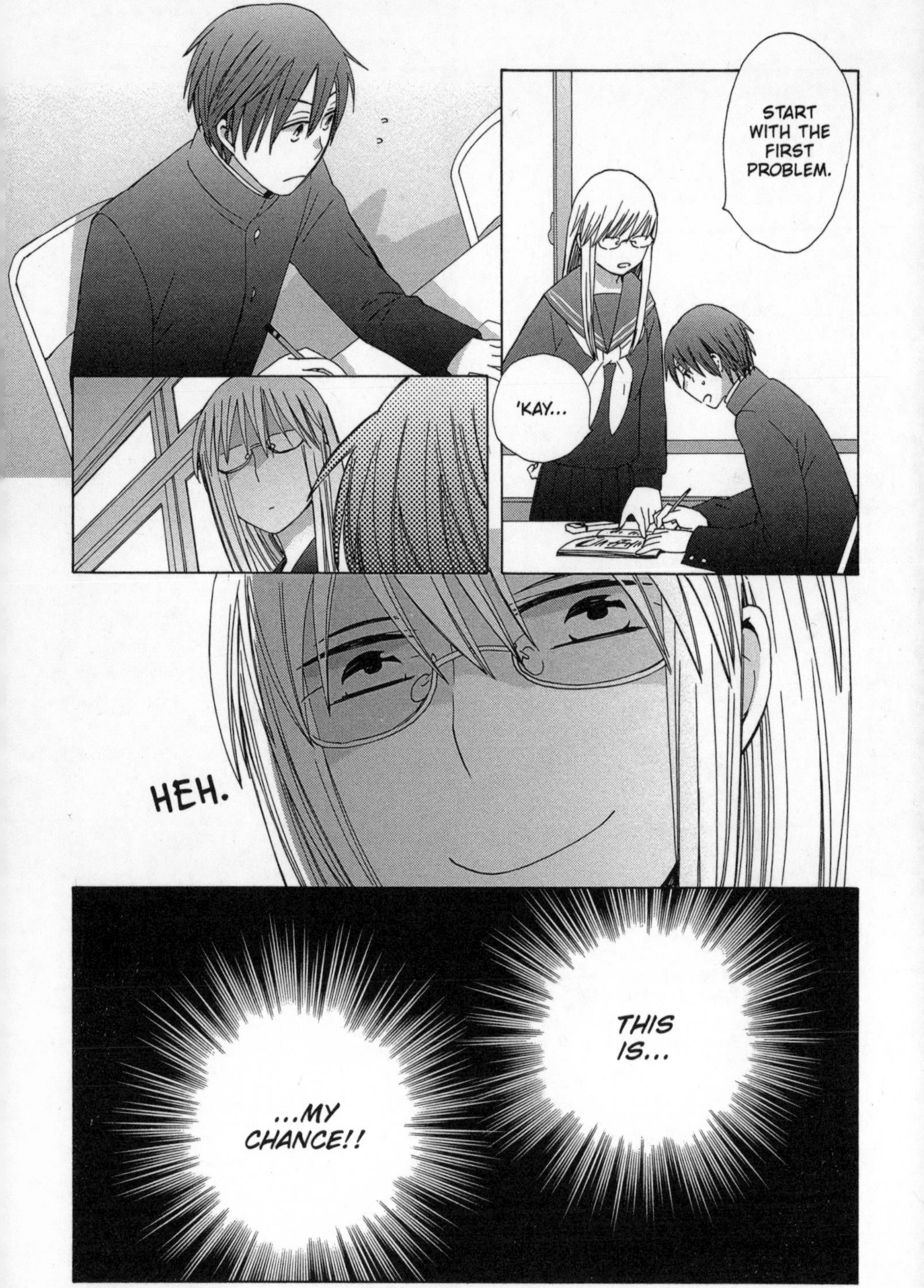
START WITH THE FIRST PROBLEM.
'KAY...
HEH.
THIS IS...
...MY CHANCE!!

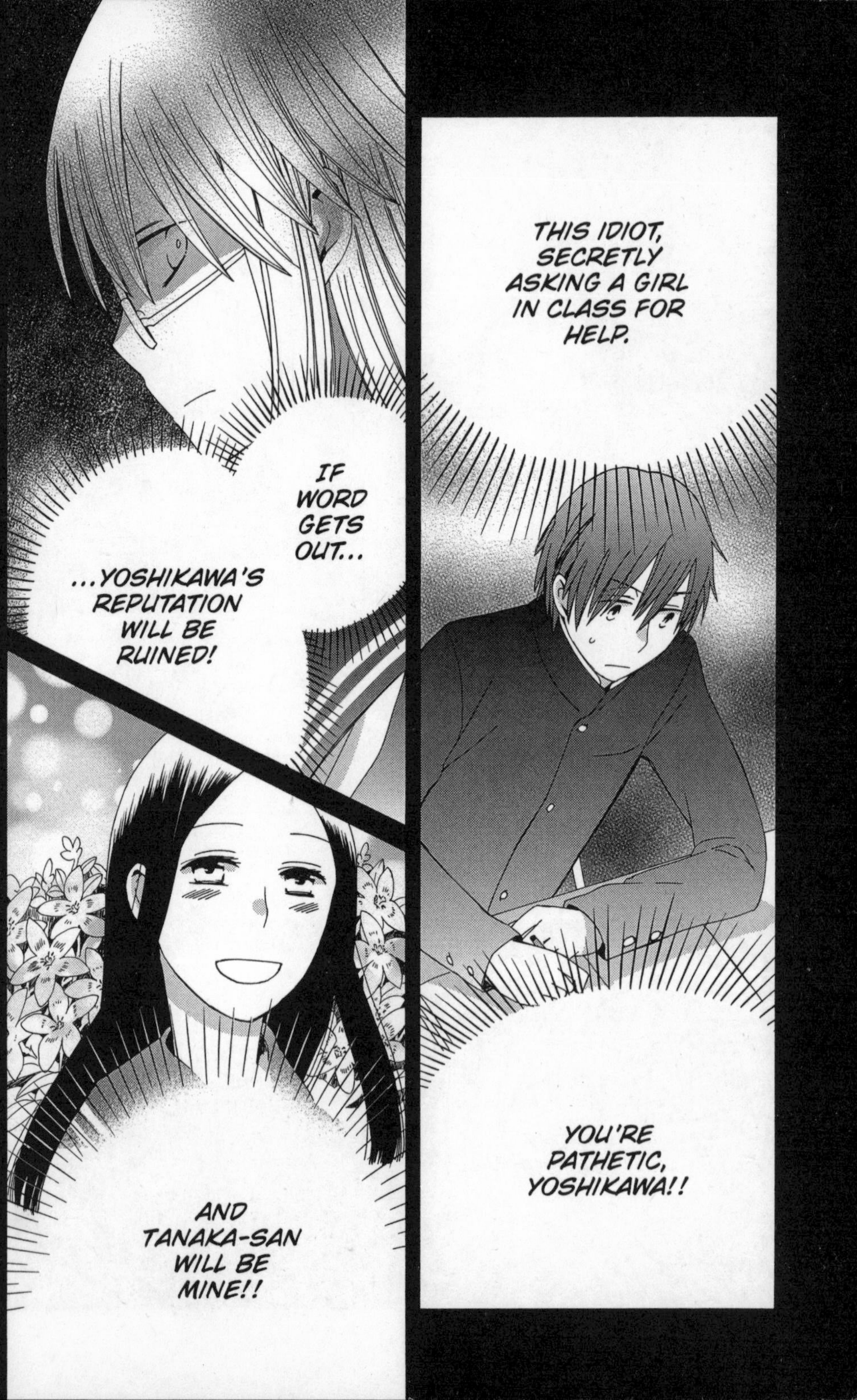
THIS IDIOT, SECRETLY ASKING A GIRL IN CLASS FOR HELP.
YOU'RE PATHETIC, YOSHIKAWA!!
IF WORD GETS OUT...
...YOSHIKAWA'S REPUTATION WILL BE RUINED!
AND TANAKA-SAN WILL BE MINE!!

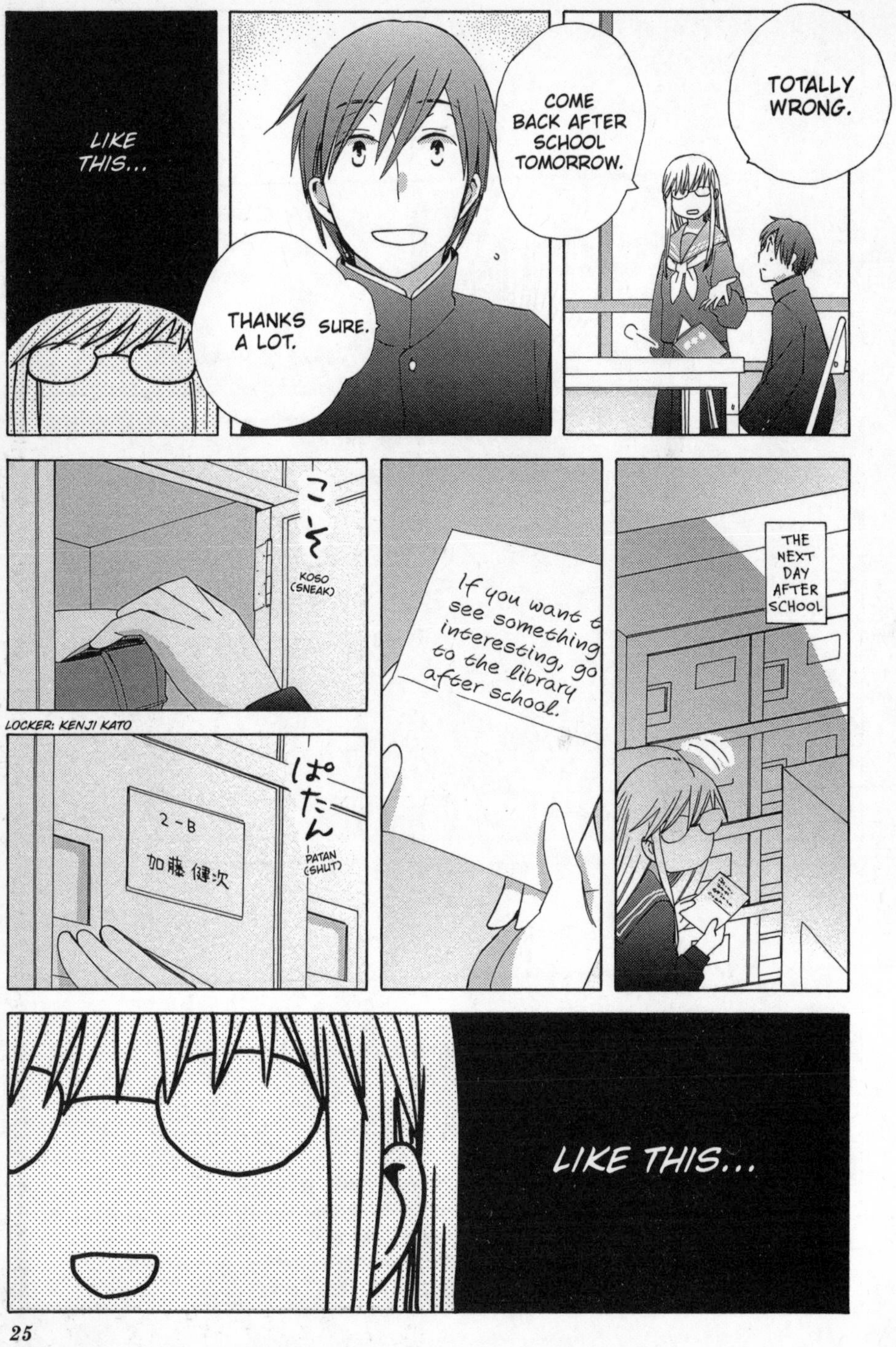
TOTALLY WRONG.
COME BACK AFTER SCHOOL TOMORROW.
SURE.
THANKS A LOT.
LIKE THIS...
THE NEXT DAY AFTER SCHOOL
If you want t
see something
interesting, go
to the library
after school.
こそ
KOSO (SNEAK)
LOCKER: KENJI KATO
ぱたん
PATAN (SHUT)
2-B
加藤 健次
LIKE THIS...

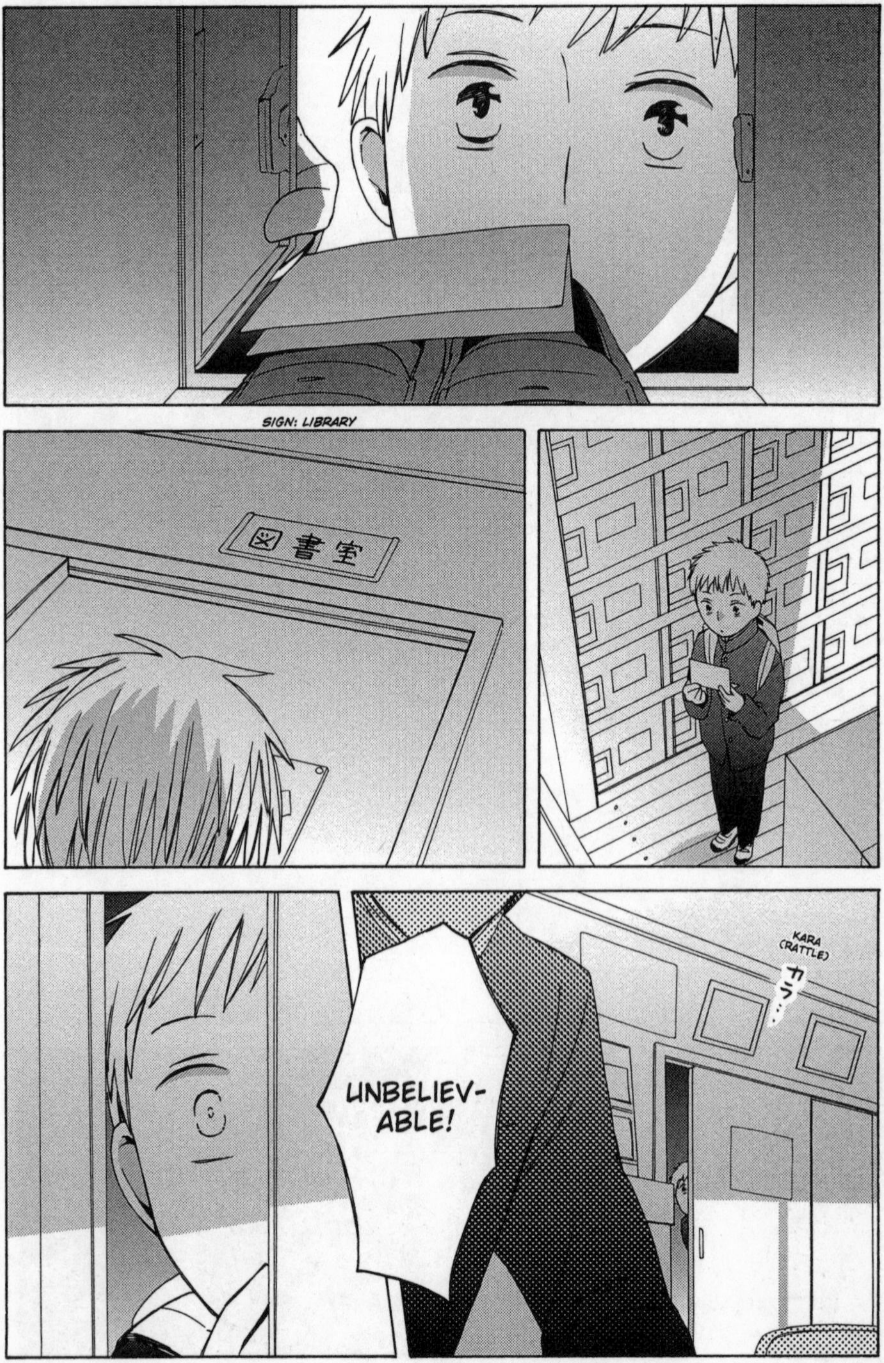
SIGN: LIBRARY
図書室
KARA (RATTLE)
カラ…
UNBELIEV-ABLE!

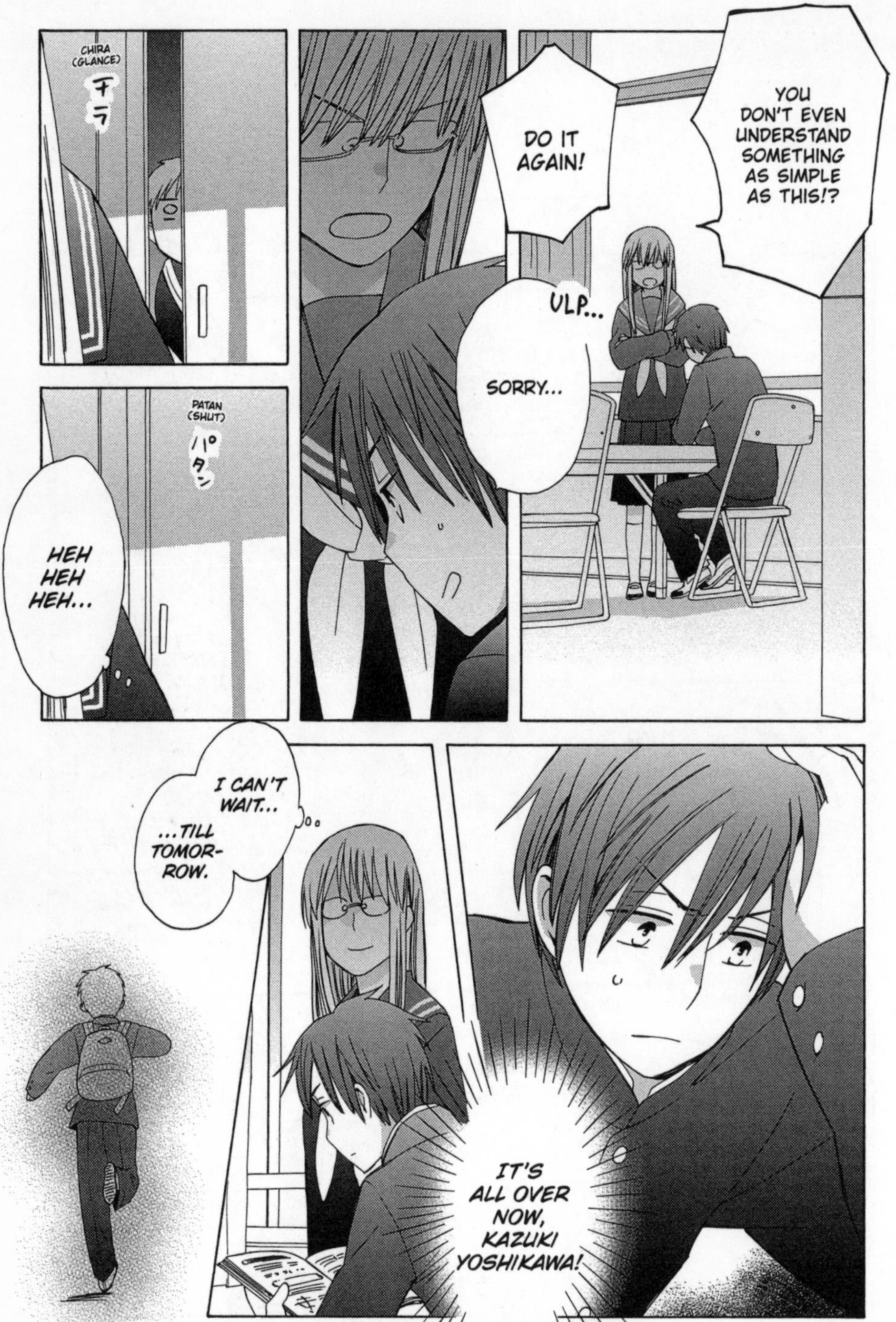
YOU DON'T EVEN UNDERSTAND SOMETHING AS SIMPLE AS THIS!?
DO IT AGAIN!
ULP...
SORRY...
CHIRA (GLANCE)
チラ
PATAN (SHUT)
パタン
HEH HEH HEH...
IT'S ALL OVER NOW, KAZUKI YOSHIKAWA!
I CAN'T WAIT...
...TILL TOMORROW.

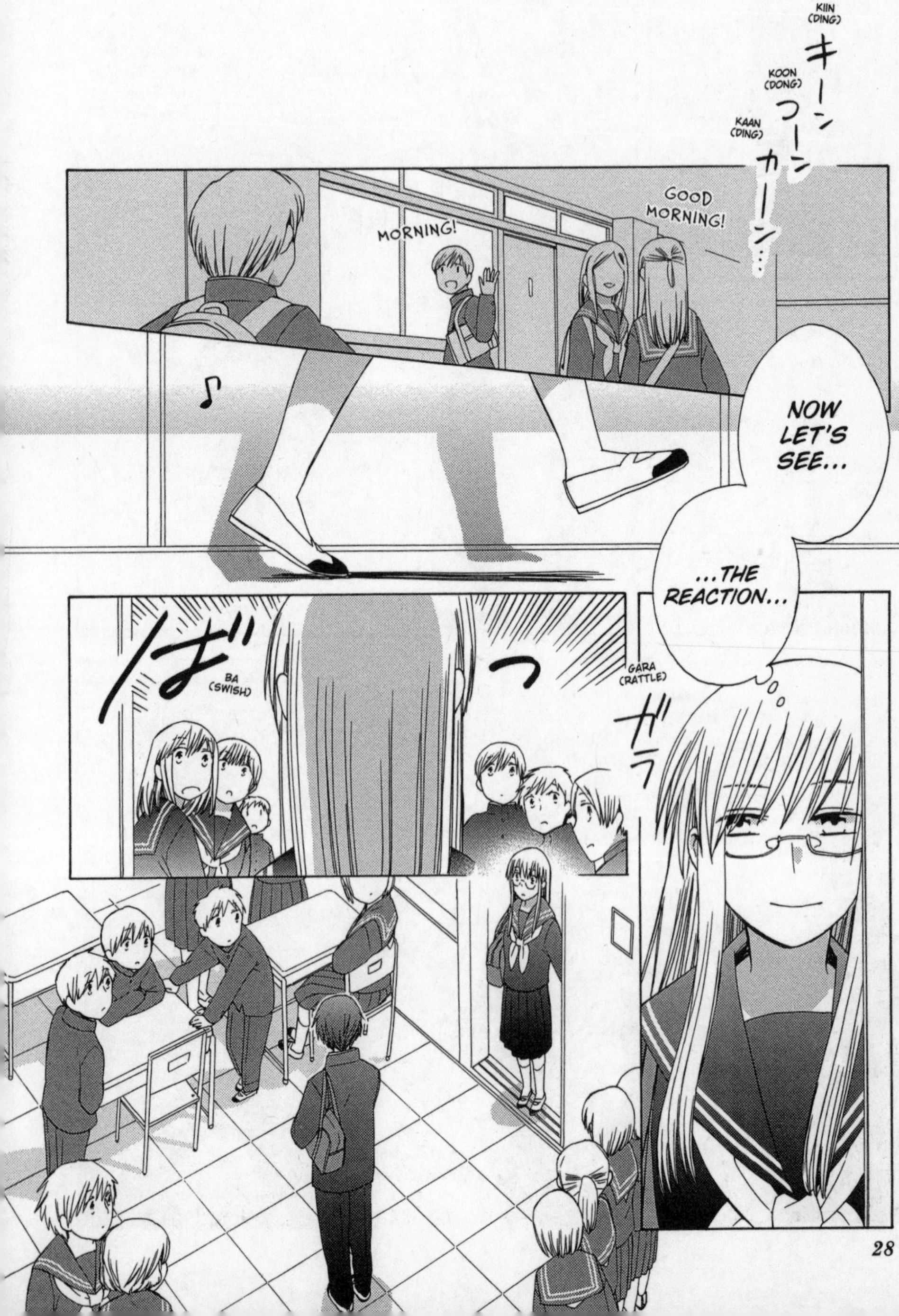
KIIN (DING)
キーン
KOON (DONG)
コーン
KAAN (DING)
カーン…
GOOD MORNING!
MORNING!
♪
NOW LET'S SEE...
...THE REACTION...
GARA (RATTLE)
ガラ
BA (SWISH)
ばっ

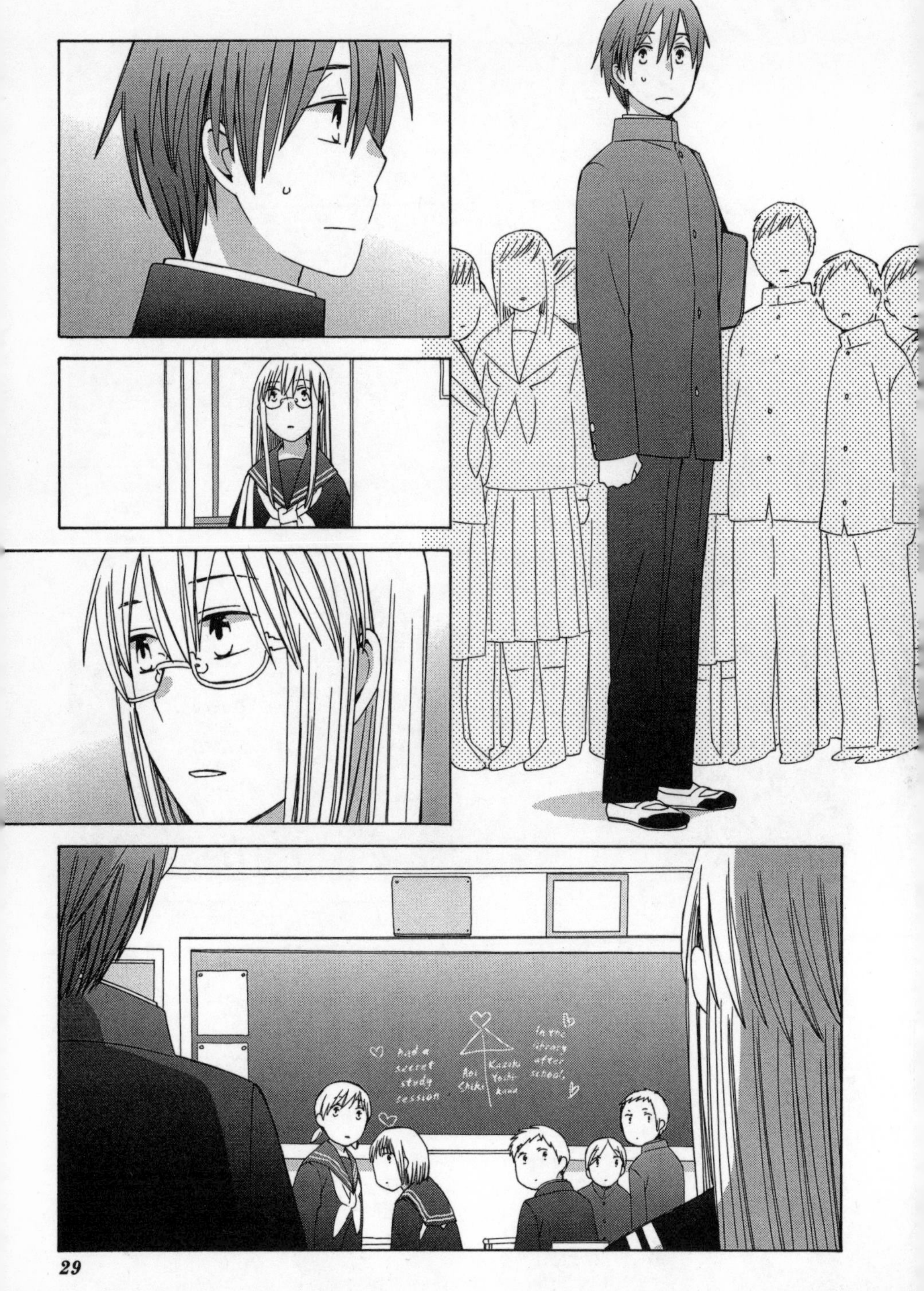
had a secret study session
Aoi Chiki
Kazuki Yoshikawa
in the library after school.

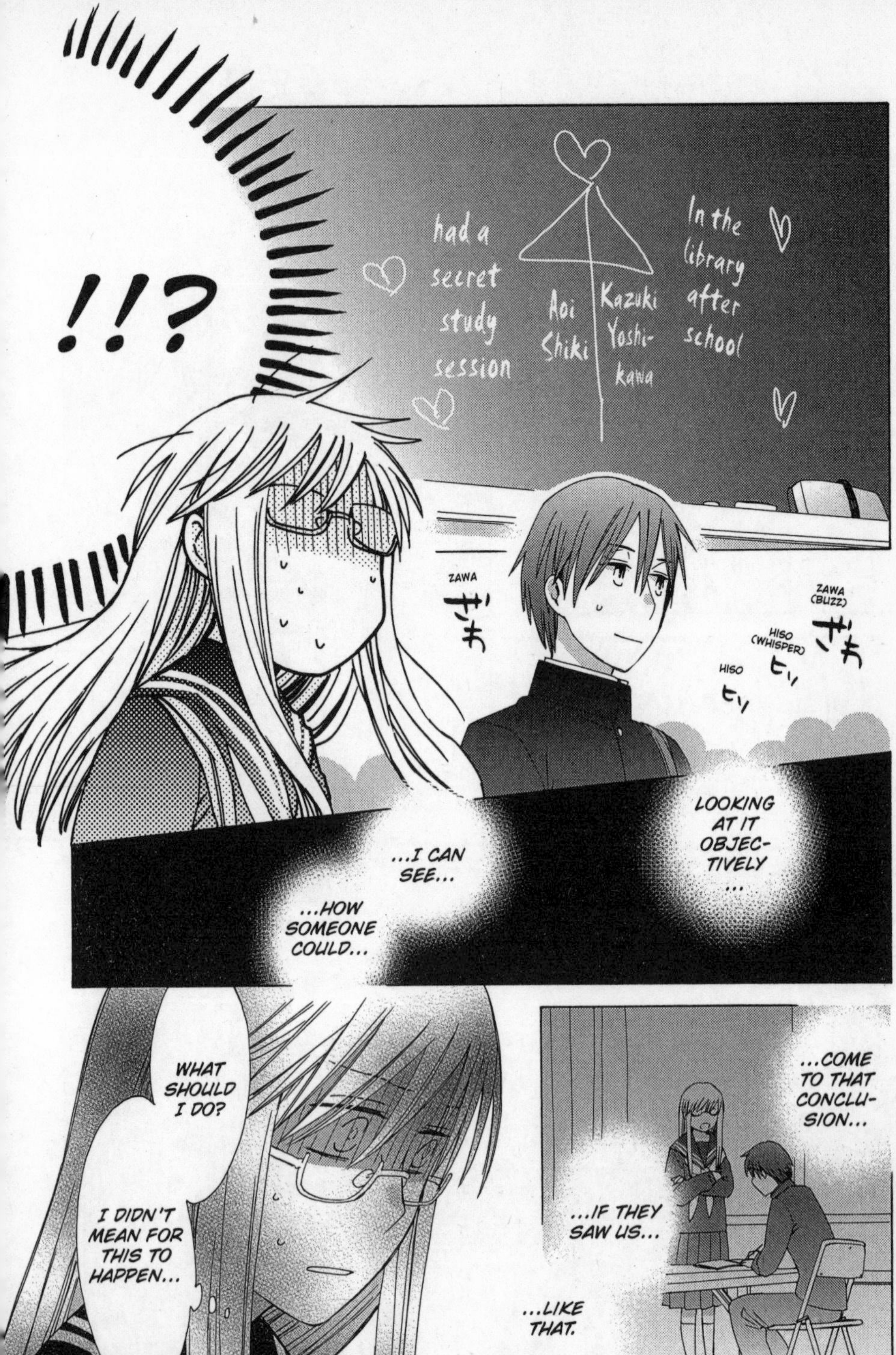
In the library after school
Kazuki Yoshikawa
Aoi Shiki
had a secret study session
ZAWA (BUZZ)
HISO (WHISPER)
HISO
ZAWA
!!?
LOOKING AT IT OBJECTIVELY...
...I CAN SEE...
...HOW SOMEONE COULD...
...COME TO THAT CONCLUSION...
...IF THEY SAW US...
...LIKE THAT.
WHAT SHOULD I DO?
I DIDN'T MEAN FOR THIS TO HAPPEN...

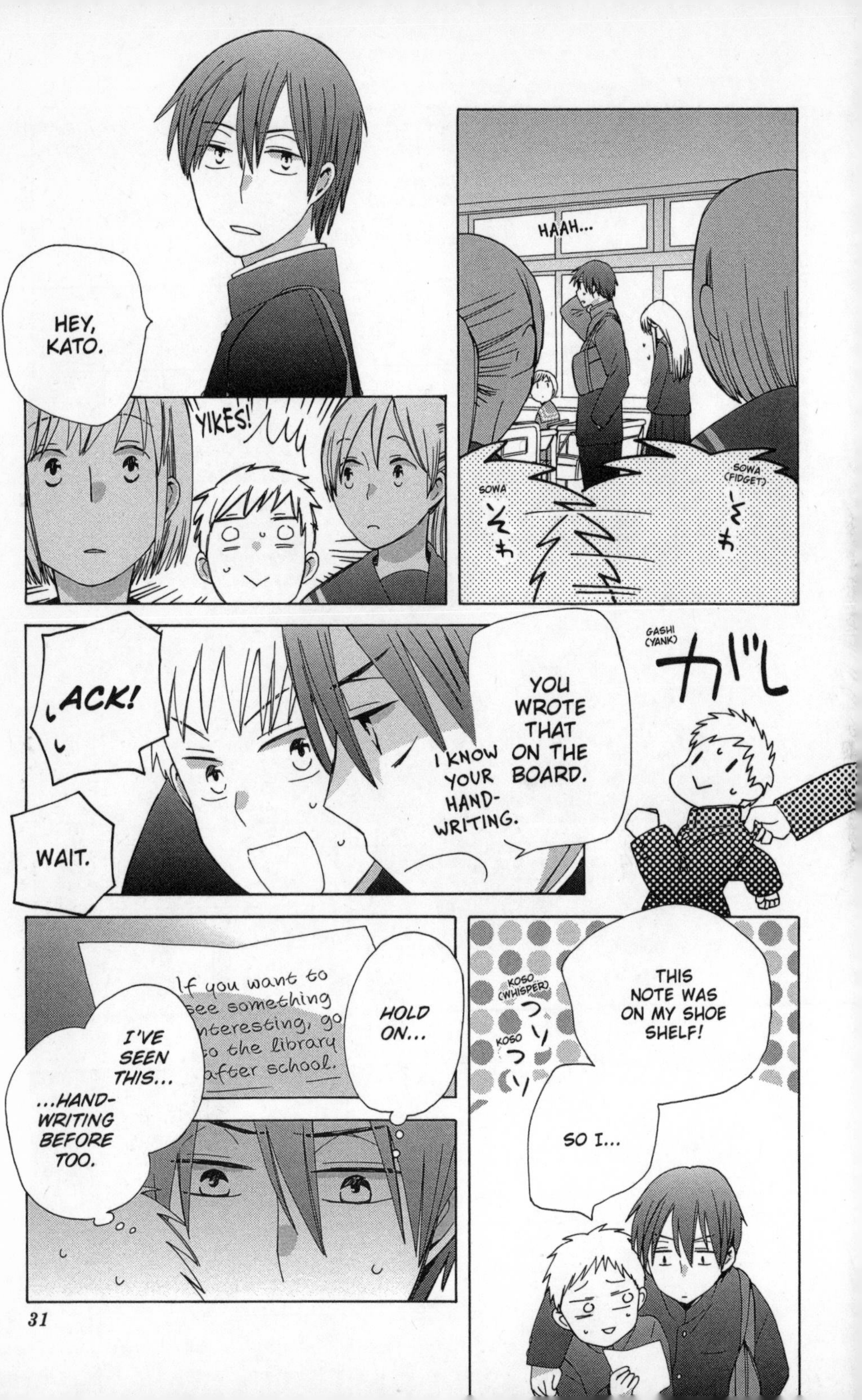
HAAH...
SOWA (FIDGET)
そわ
SOWA
そわ
HEY, KATO.
YIKES!
GASHI (YANK)
がし
YOU WROTE THAT ON THE BOARD.
I KNOW YOUR HAND-WRITING.
ACK!
WAIT.
THIS NOTE WAS ON MY SHOE SHELF!
KOSO (WHISPER)
こそ
KOSO
こそ
SO I...
If you want to see something interesting, go to the library after school.
HOLD ON...
I'VE SEEN THIS...
...HAND-WRITING BEFORE TOO.

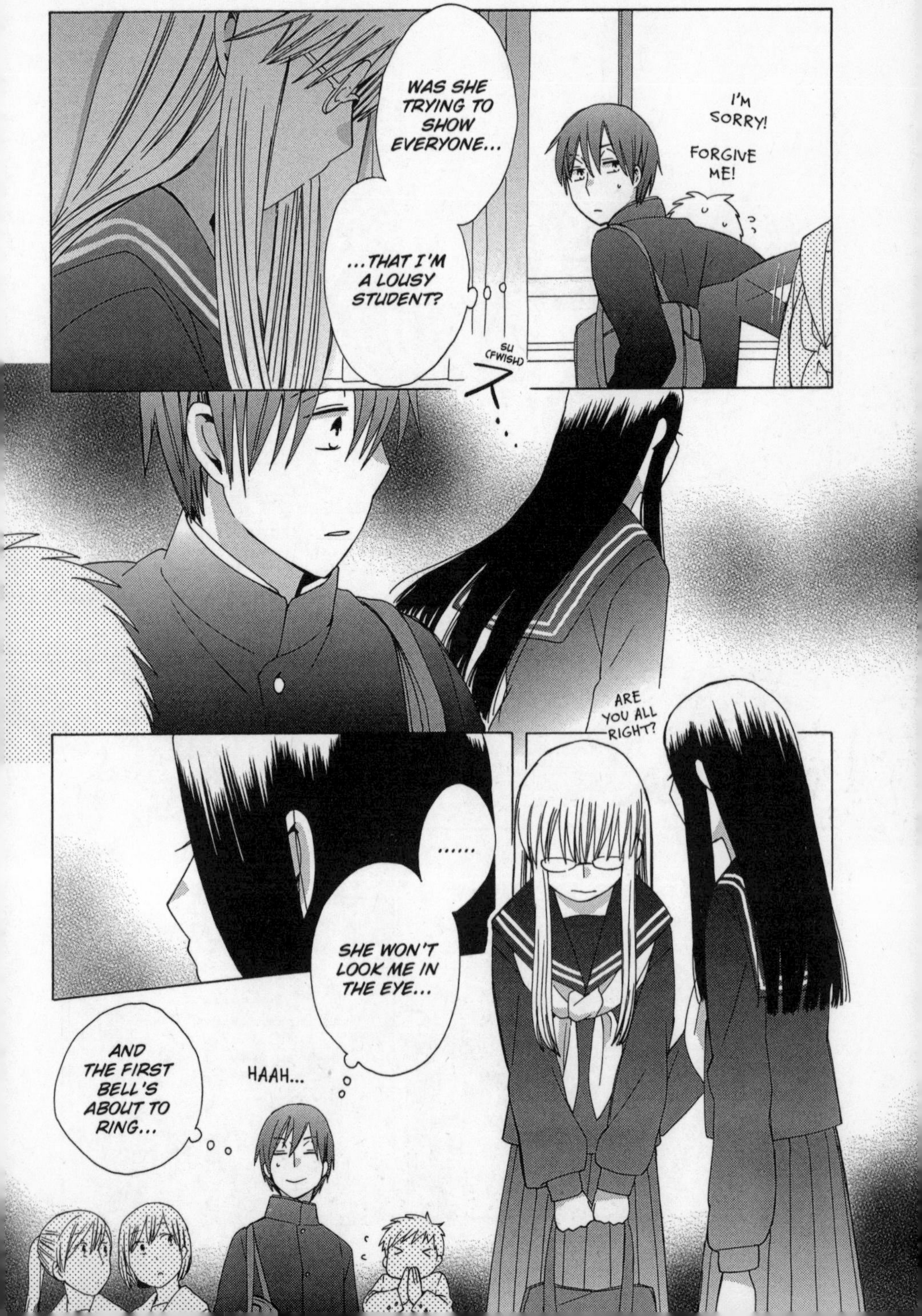
I'M SORRY!
FORGIVE ME!
WAS SHE TRYING TO SHOW EVERYONE...
...THAT I'M A LOUSY STUDENT?
SU (FWISH)
ARE YOU ALL RIGHT?
......
SHE WON'T LOOK ME IN THE EYE...
HAAH...
AND THE FIRST BELL'S ABOUT TO RING...

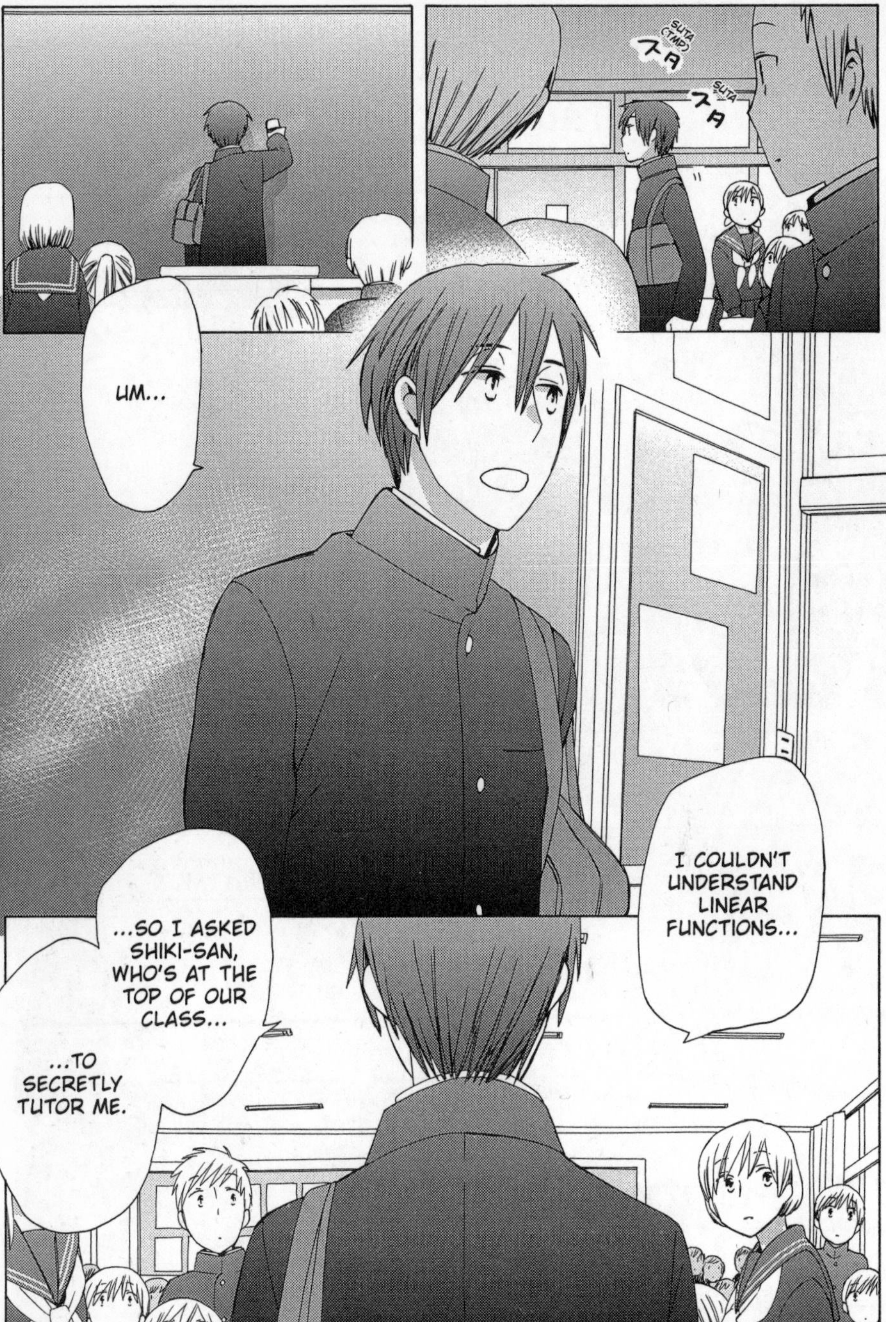
SUTA (TMP)
スタ
SUTA
スタ
UM...
I COULDN'T UNDERSTAND LINEAR FUNCTIONS...
...SO I ASKED SHIKI-SAN, WHO'S AT THE TOP OF OUR CLASS...
...TO SECRETLY TUTOR ME.

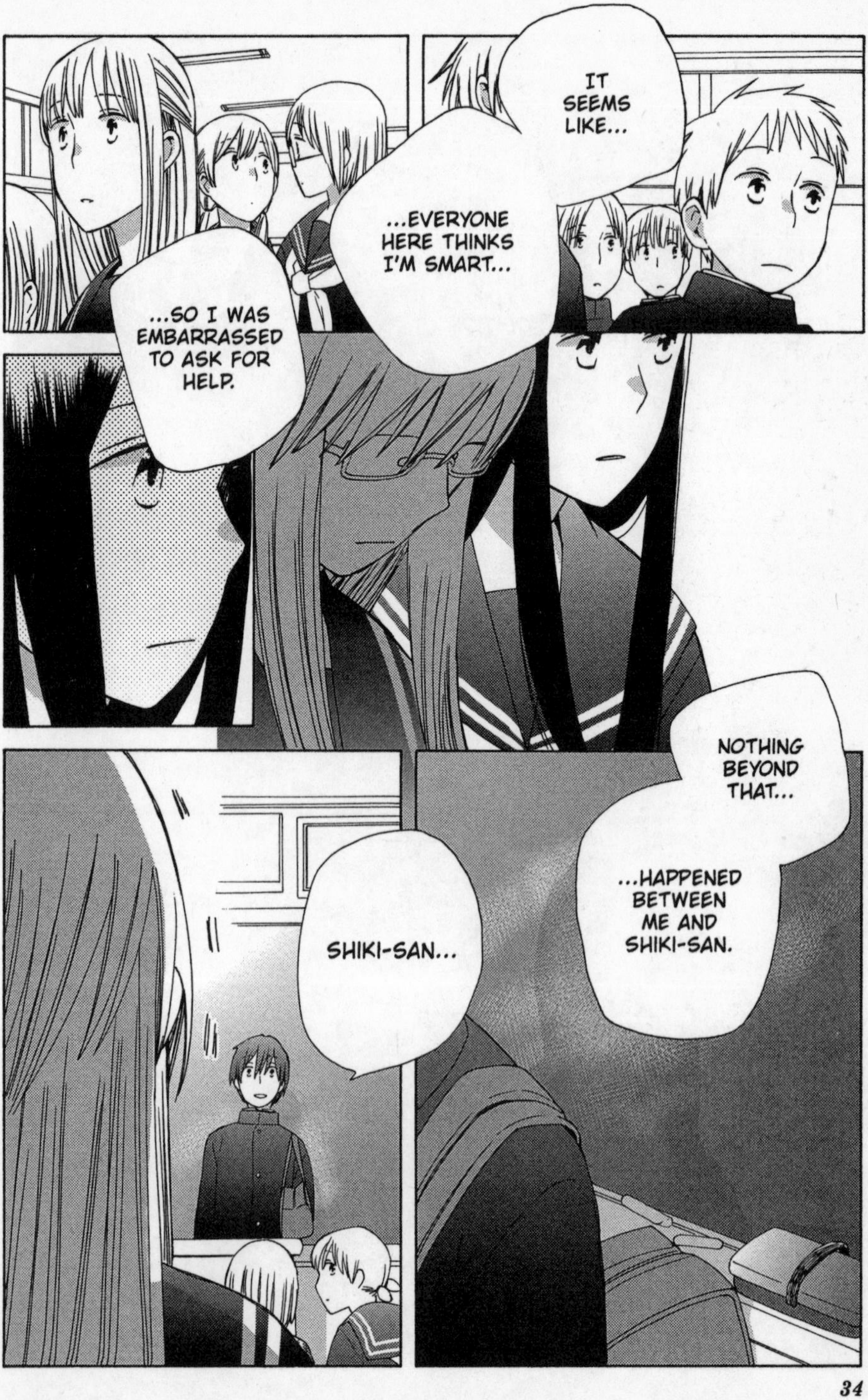
IT SEEMS LIKE...
...EVERYONE HERE THINKS I'M SMART...
...SO I WAS EMBARRASSED TO ASK FOR HELP.
NOTHING BEYOND THAT...
...HAPPENED BETWEEN ME AND SHIKI-SAN.
SHIKI-SAN...

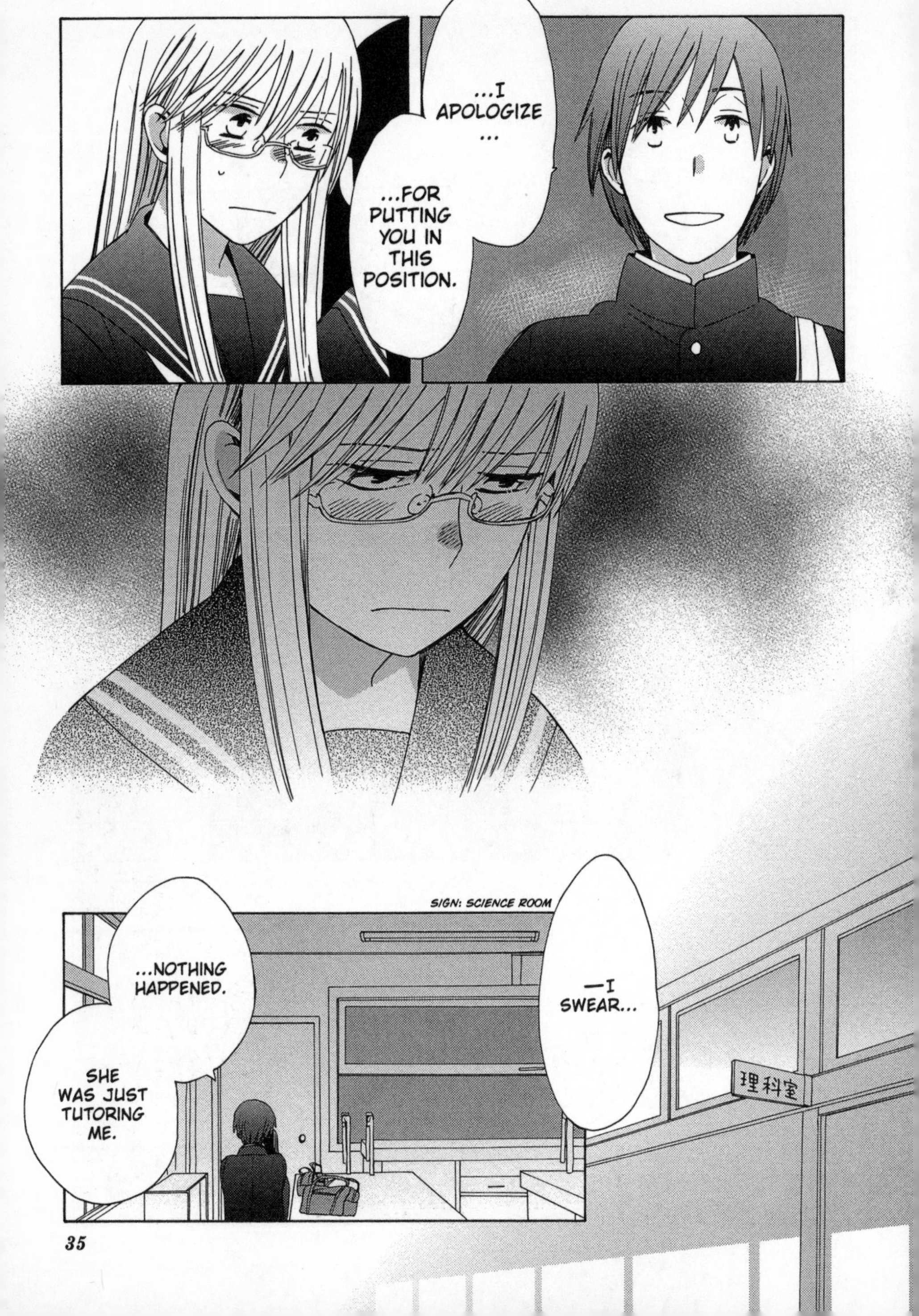
...I APOLOGIZE ...
...FOR PUTTING YOU IN THIS POSITION.
SIGN: SCIENCE ROOM
理科室
—I SWEAR...
...NOTHING HAPPENED.
SHE WAS JUST TUTORING ME.

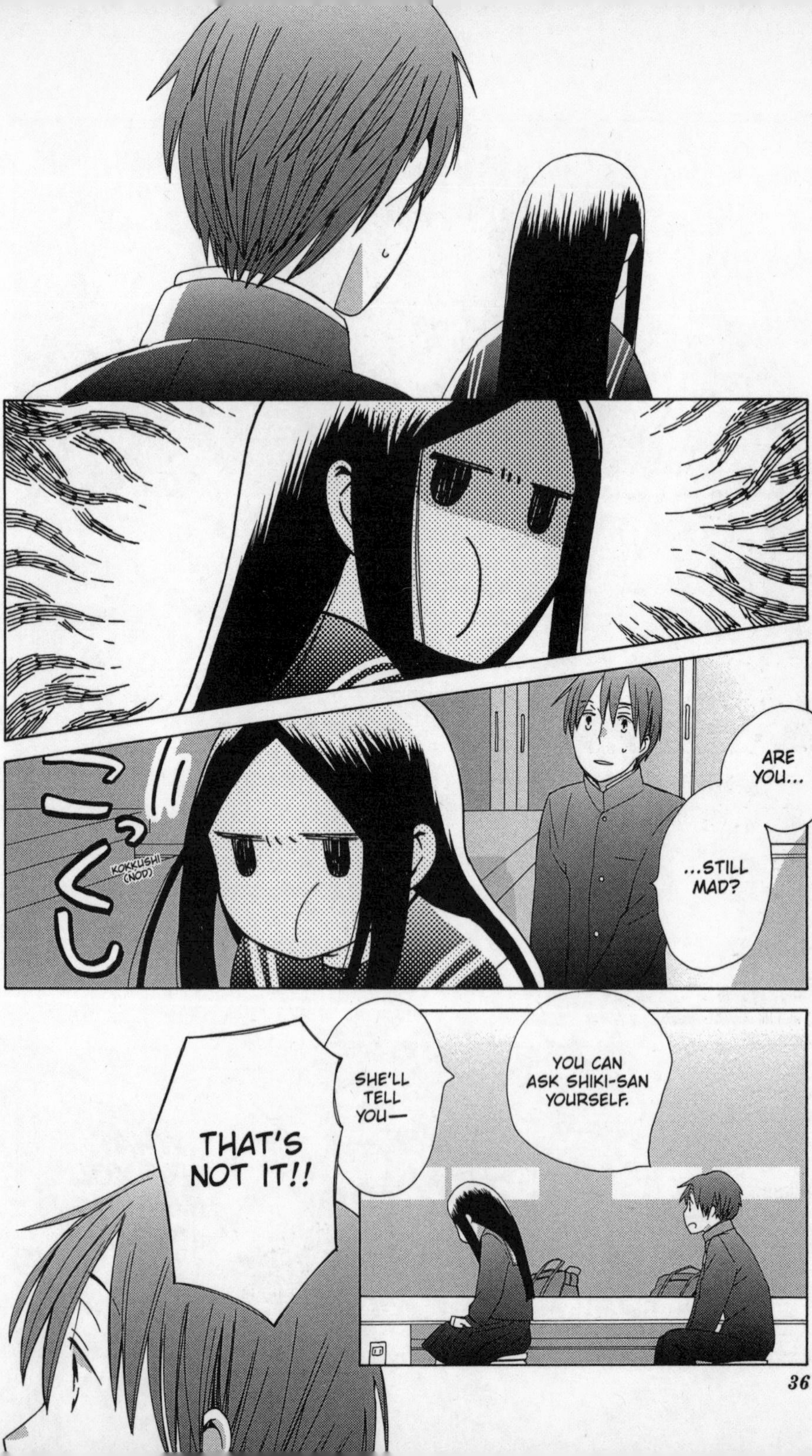
ARE YOU...
...STILL MAD?
KOKKUSHI (NOD)
YOU CAN ASK SHIKI-SAN YOURSELF.
SHE'LL TELL YOU—
THAT'S NOT IT!!

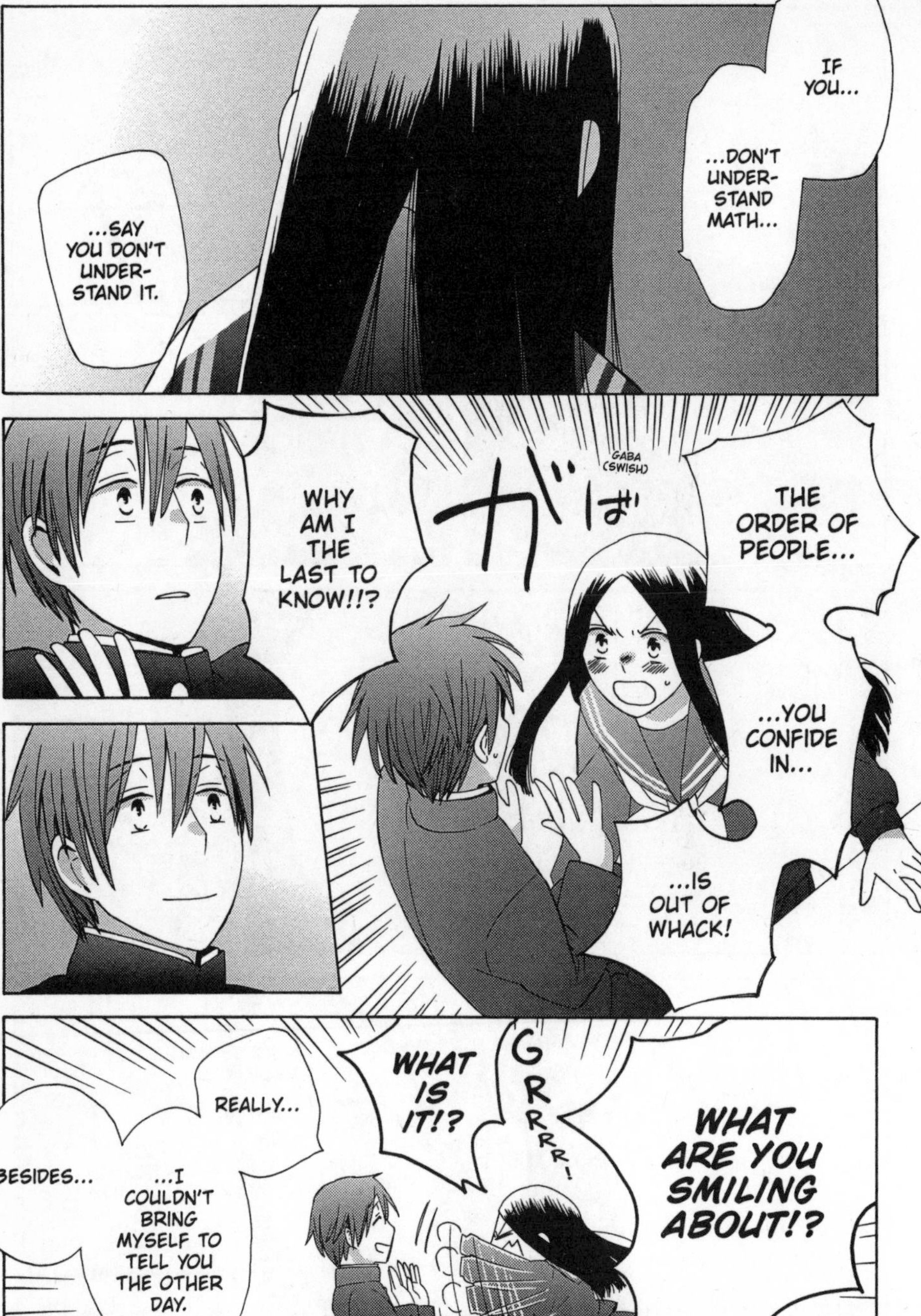
IF YOU...
...DON'T UNDER-STAND MATH...
...SAY YOU DON'T UNDER-STAND IT.
THE ORDER OF PEOPLE...
GABA (SWISH)
WHY AM I THE LAST TO KNOW!!?
...YOU CONFIDE IN...
...IS OUT OF WHACK!
WHAT ARE YOU SMILING ABOUT!?
GRRRR!
WHAT IS IT!?
REALLY...
BESIDES...
...I COULDN'T BRING MYSELF TO TELL YOU THE OTHER DAY.

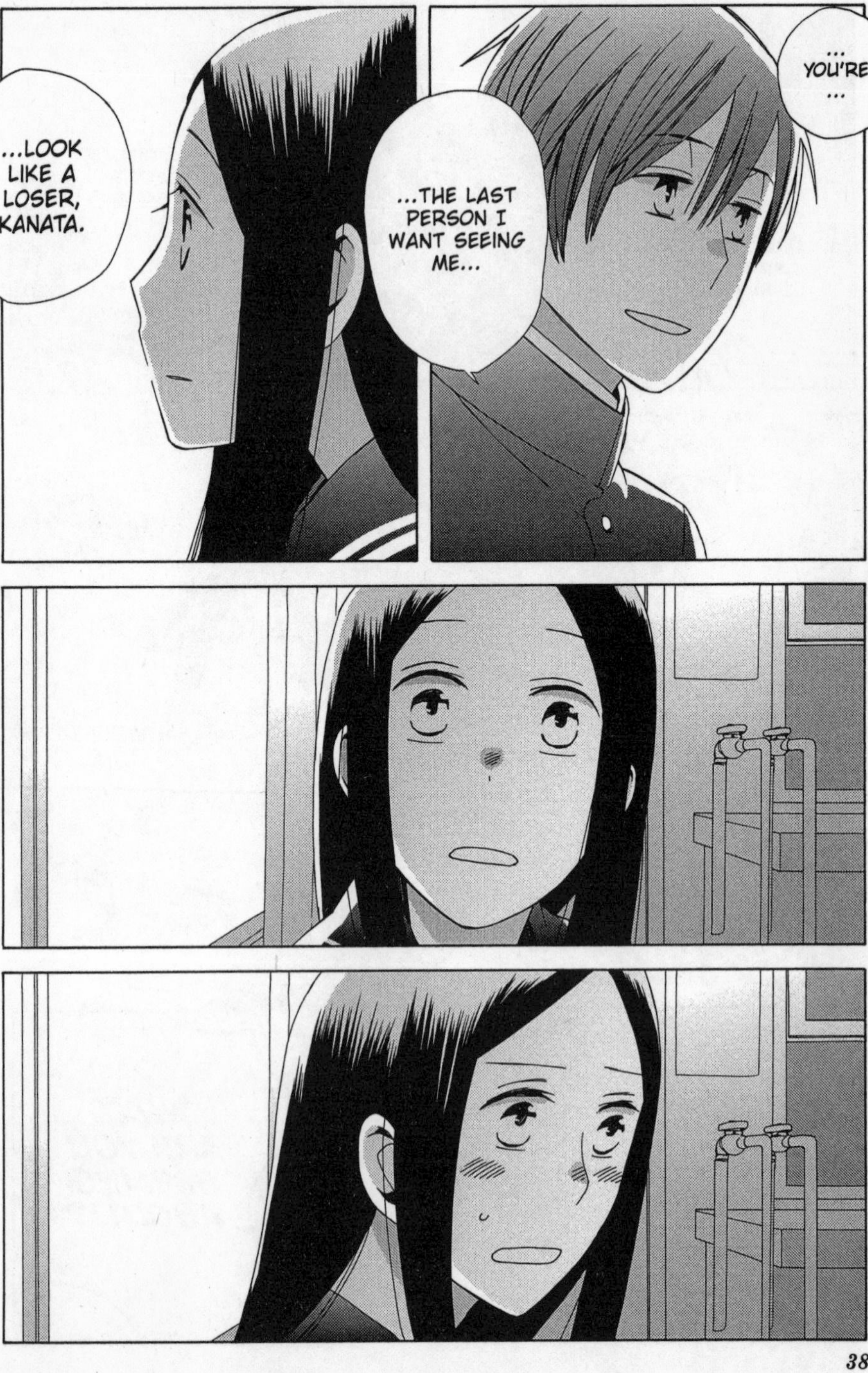
...YOU'RE ...
...THE LAST PERSON I WANT SEEING ME...
...LOOK LIKE A LOSER, KANATA.

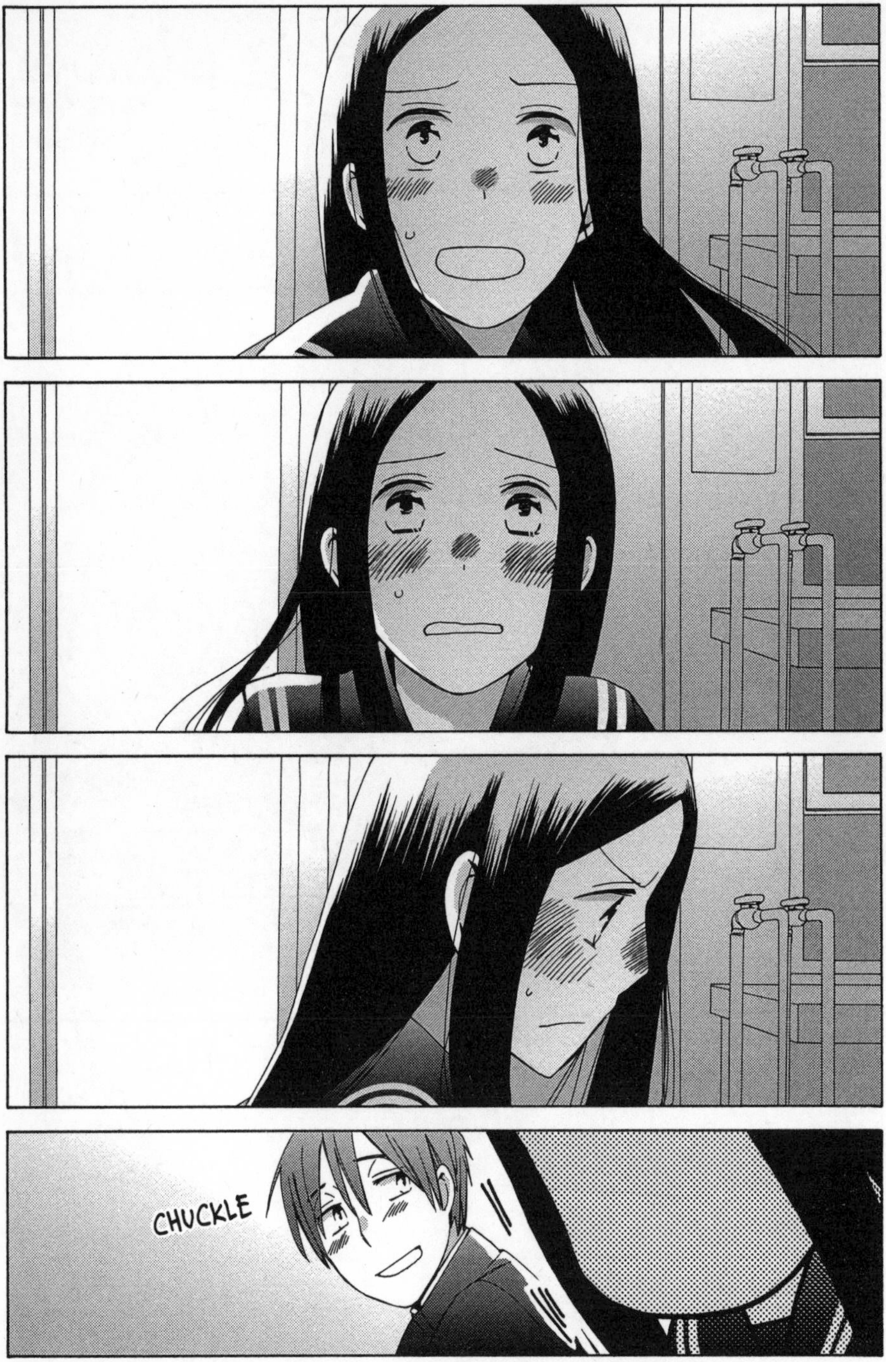
CHUCKLE

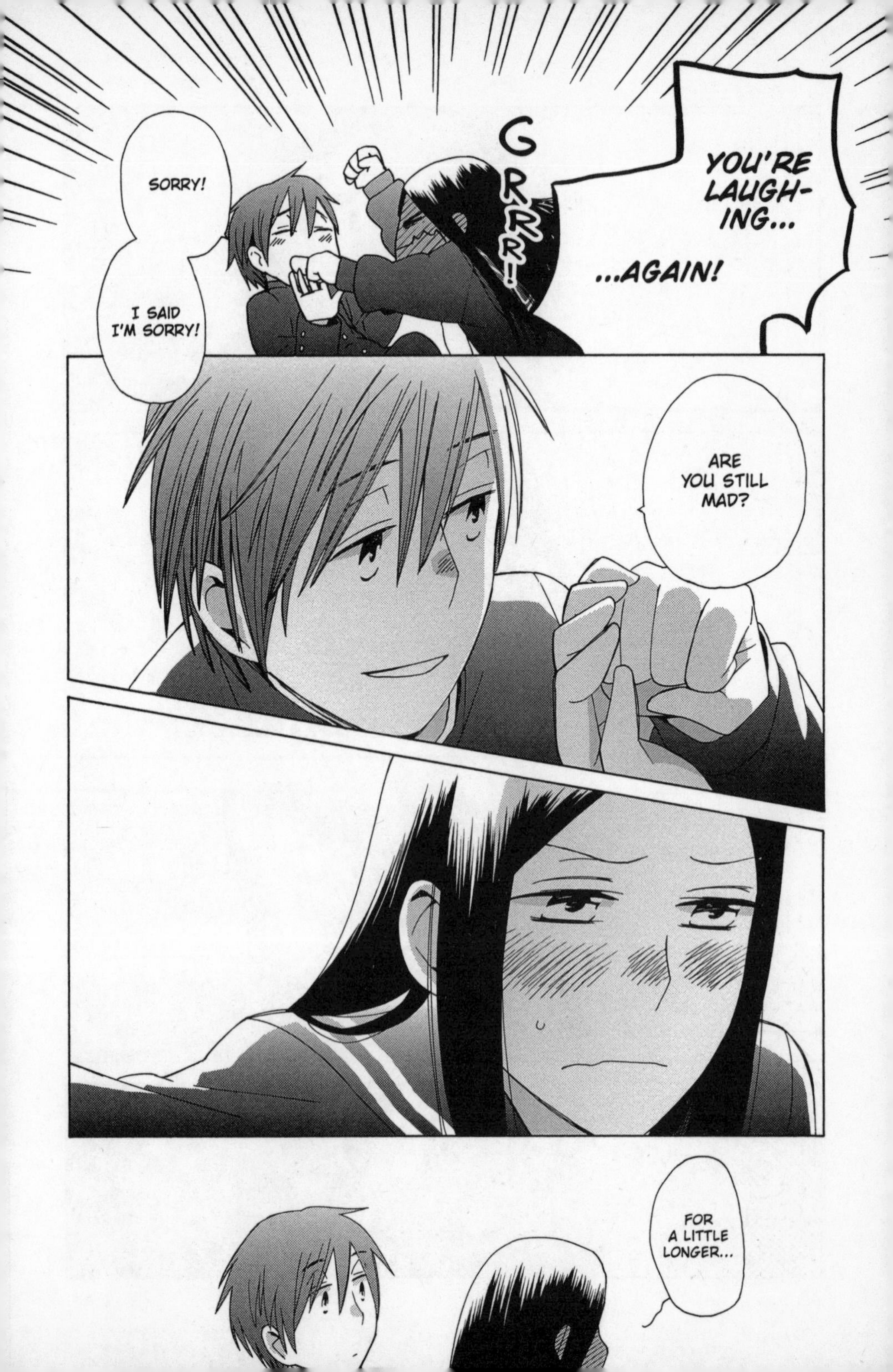
YOU'RE LAUGH-ING...
...AGAIN!
GRRR!
SORRY!
I SAID I'M SORRY!
ARE YOU STILL MAD?
FOR A LITTLE LONGER...

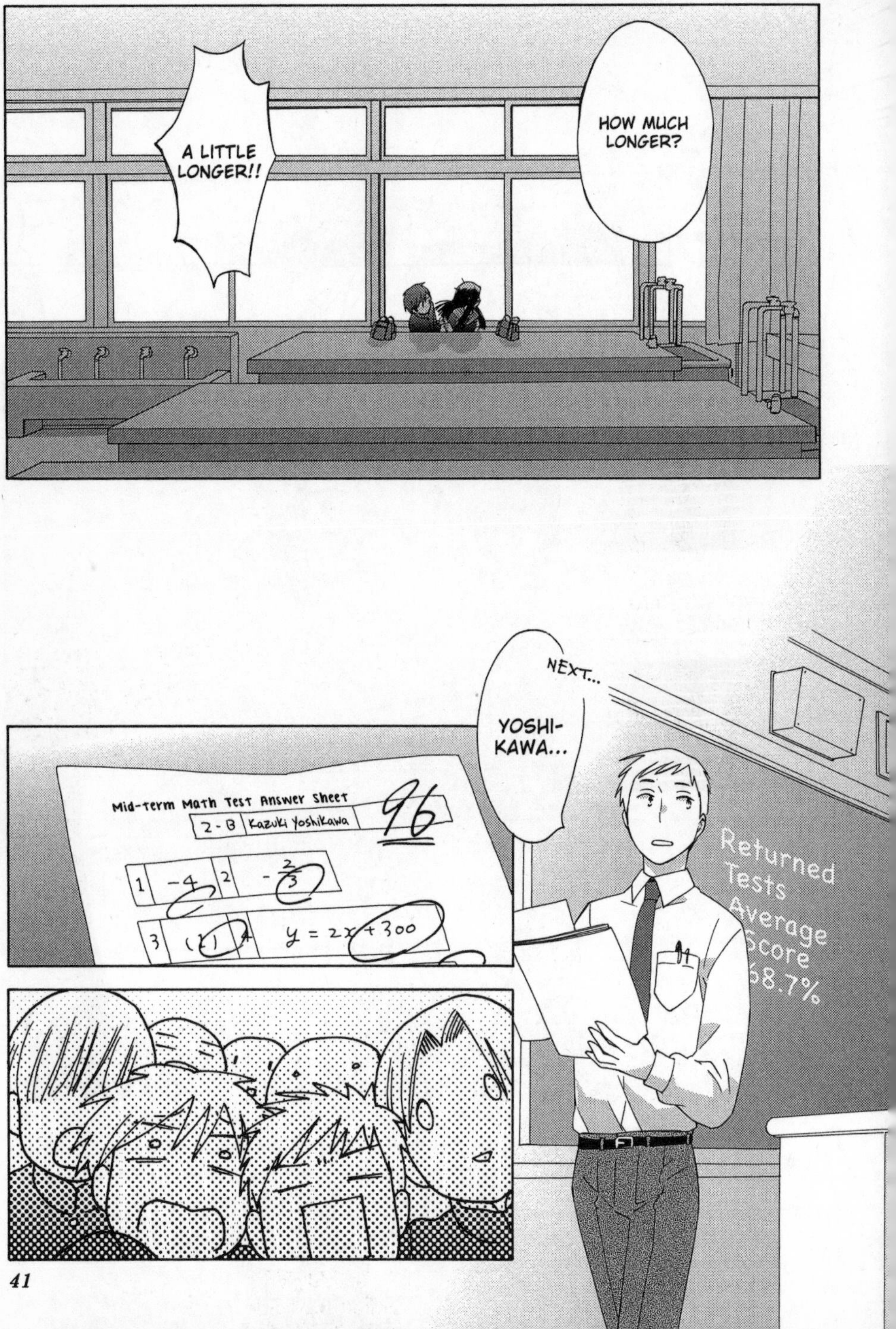
HOW MUCH LONGER?
A LITTLE LONGER!!
NEXT...
YOSHI-KAWA...
Returned Tests Average Score 68.7%
Mid-term Math Test Answer Sheet
2 - B
Kazuki Yoshikawa
96
1 -4
2 -2/3
3 (2)
4 y = 2x + 300

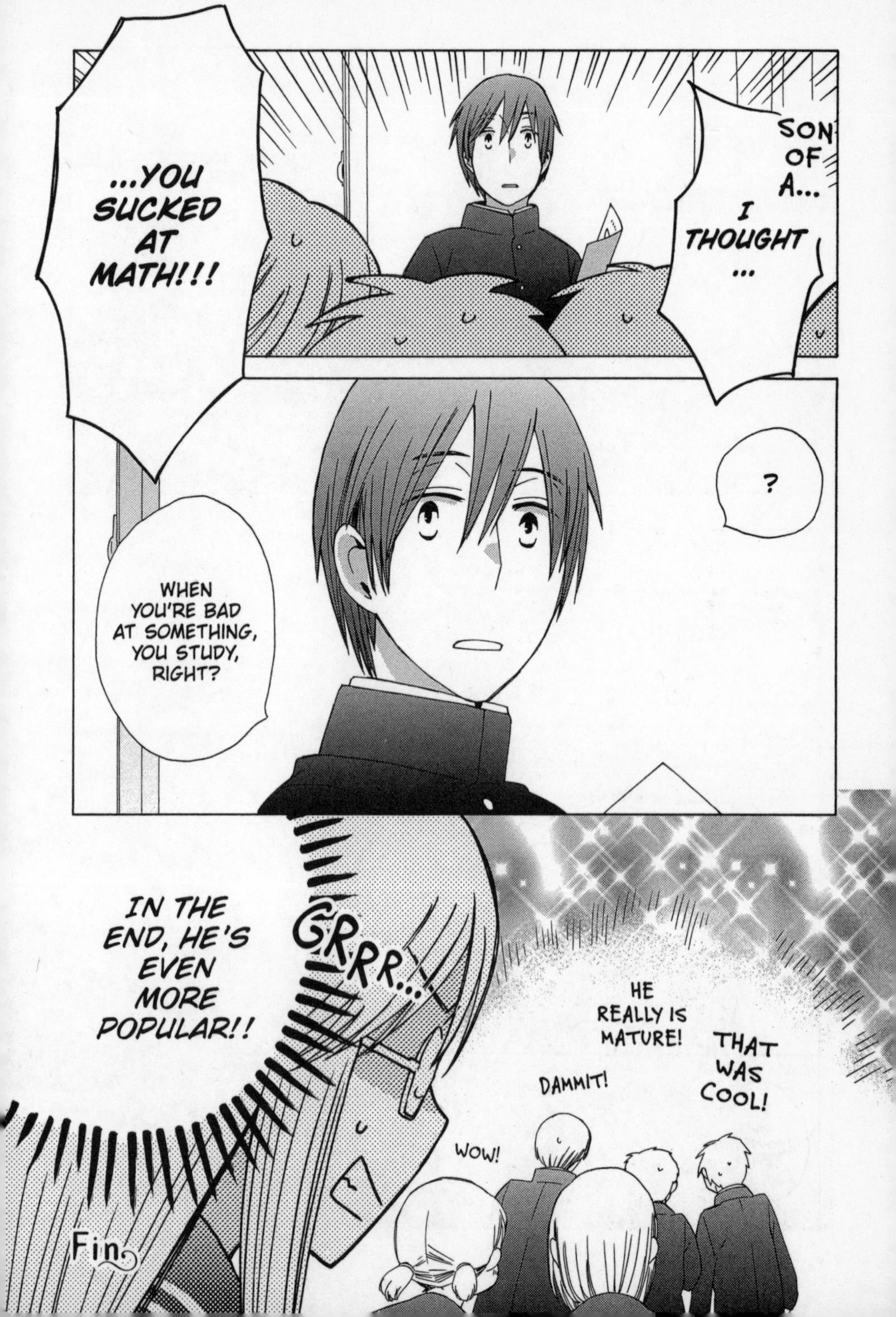
SON OF A... I THOUGHT...
...YOU SUCKED AT MATH!!!
?
WHEN YOU'RE BAD AT SOMETHING, YOU STUDY, RIGHT?
HE REALLY IS MATURE!
THAT WAS COOL!
DAMMIT!
GRRR...
IN THE END, HE'S EVEN MORE POPULAR!!
WOW!
Fin.

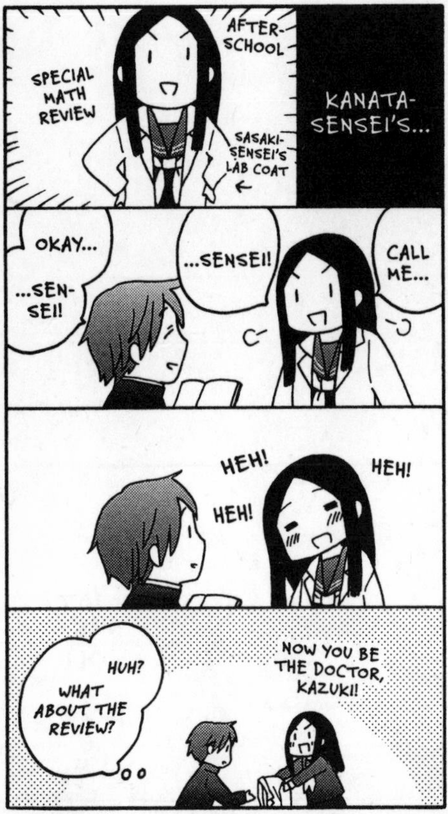
KANATA-SENSEI'S...
AFTER-SCHOOL
SPECIAL MATH REVIEW
SASAKI-SENSEI'S LAB COAT
CALL ME...
...SENSEI!
OKAY...
...SEN-SEI!
HEH!
HEH!
HEH!
NOW YOU BE THE DOCTOR, KAZUKI!
HUH? WHAT ABOUT THE REVIEW?

Love at Fourteen

Fuka Mizutani

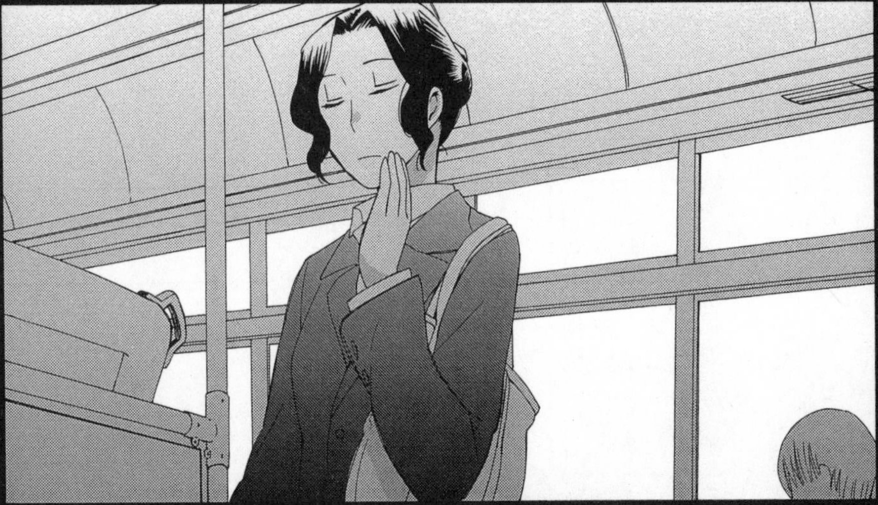

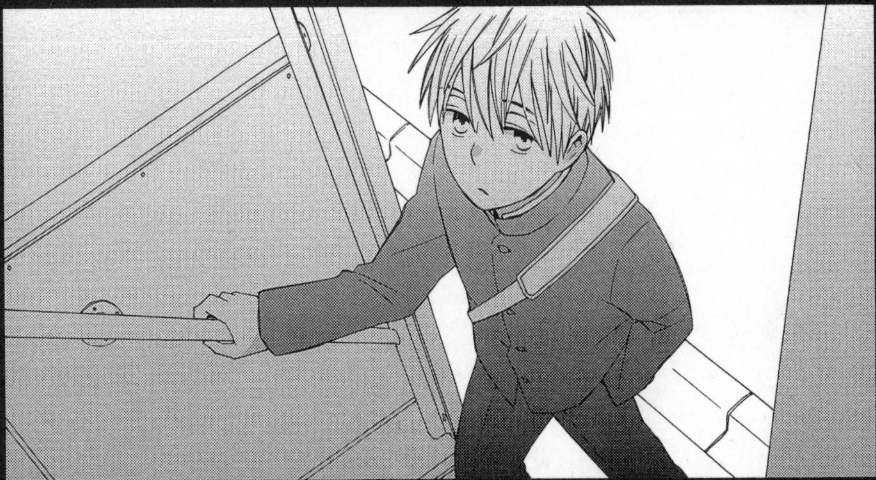

Love at Fourteen

No Way

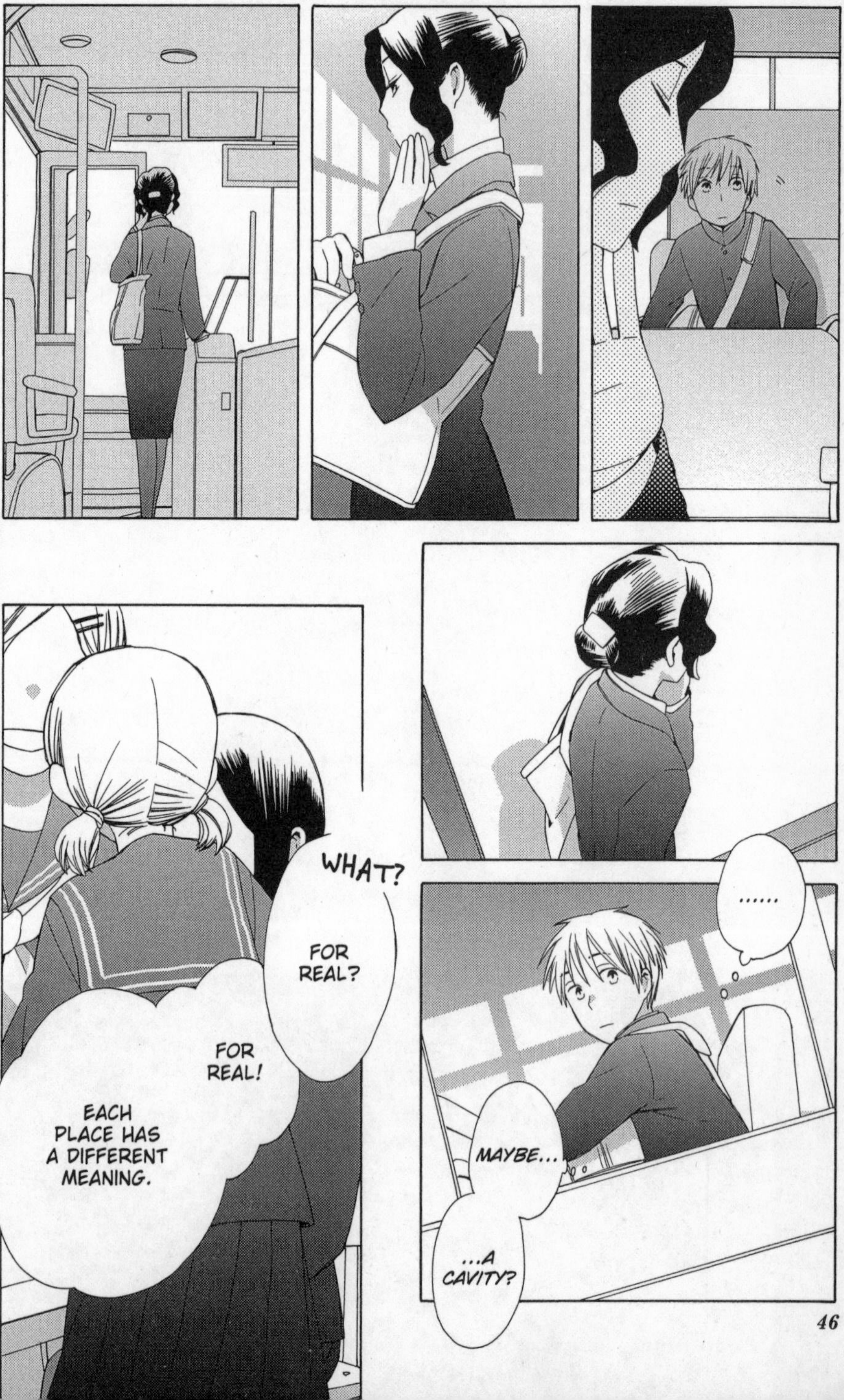
......
MAYBE...
...A CAVITY?
WHAT?
FOR REAL?
FOR REAL!
EACH PLACE HAS A DIFFERENT MEANING.

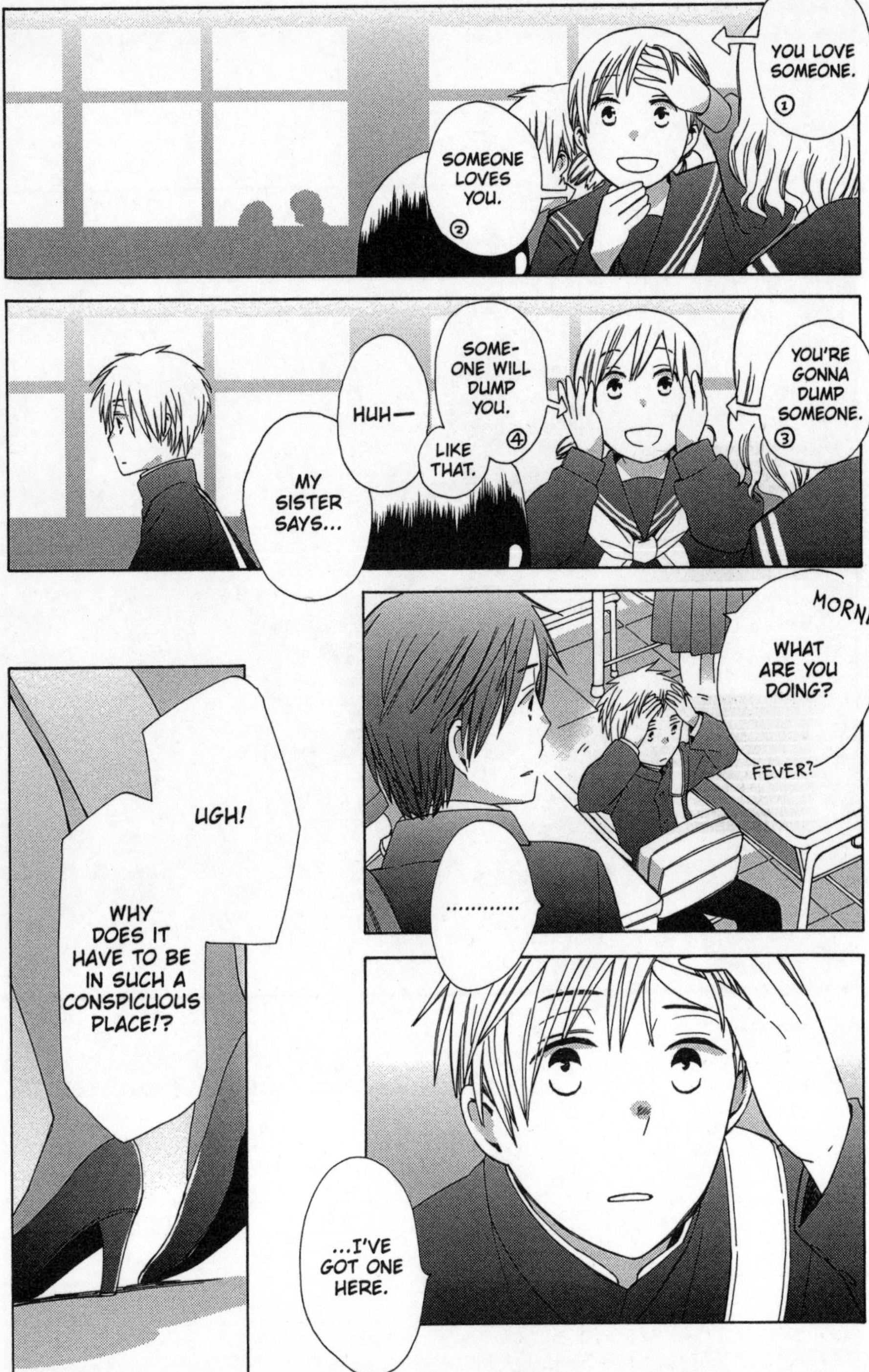
YOU LOVE SOMEONE. ①
SOMEONE LOVES YOU. ②
YOU'RE GONNA DUMP SOMEONE. ③
SOME-ONE WILL DUMP YOU. ④
LIKE THAT.
HUH—
MY SISTER SAYS...
MORNING!
WHAT ARE YOU DOING?
FEVER?
....
...I'VE GOT ONE HERE.
UGH!
WHY DOES IT HAVE TO BE IN SUCH A CONSPICUOUS PLACE!?

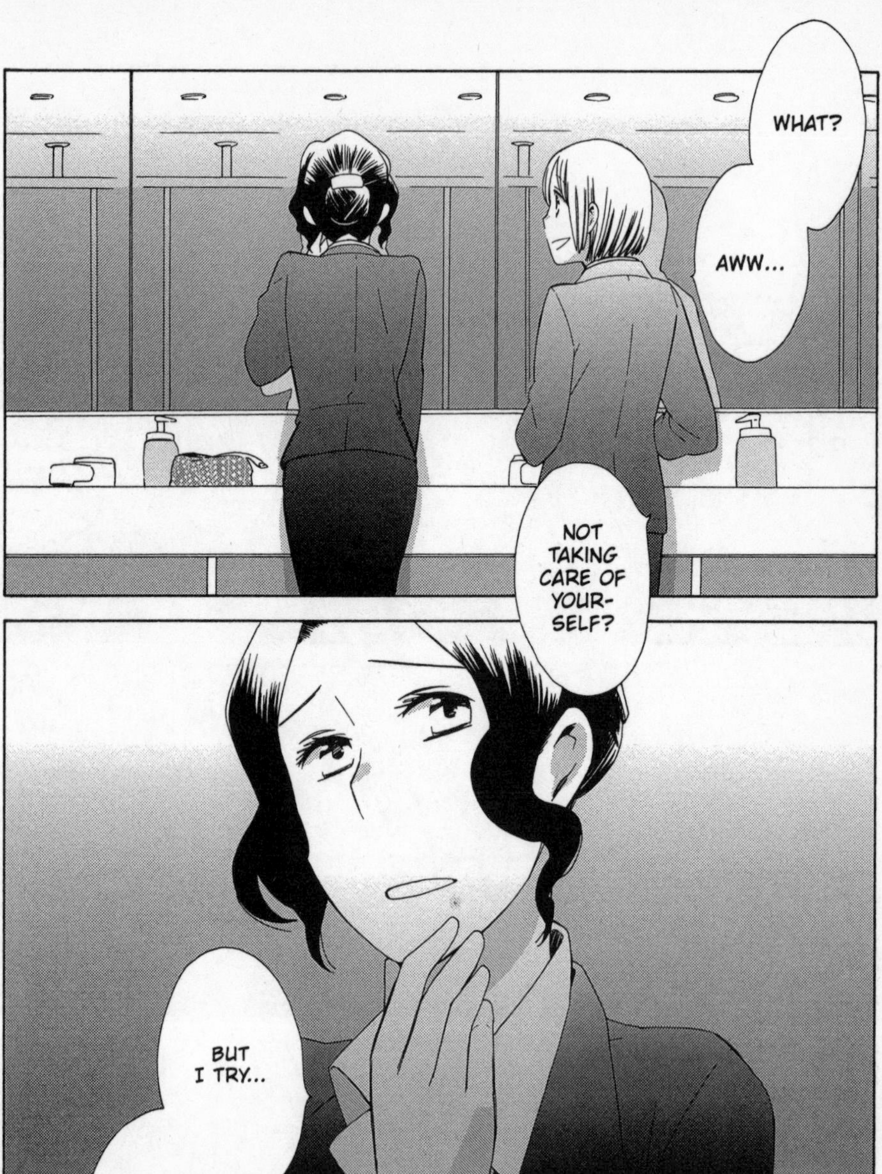
WHAT?
AWW...
NOT TAKING CARE OF YOUR-SELF?
BUT I TRY...
...TO TAKE CARE OF MYSELF.

Fin

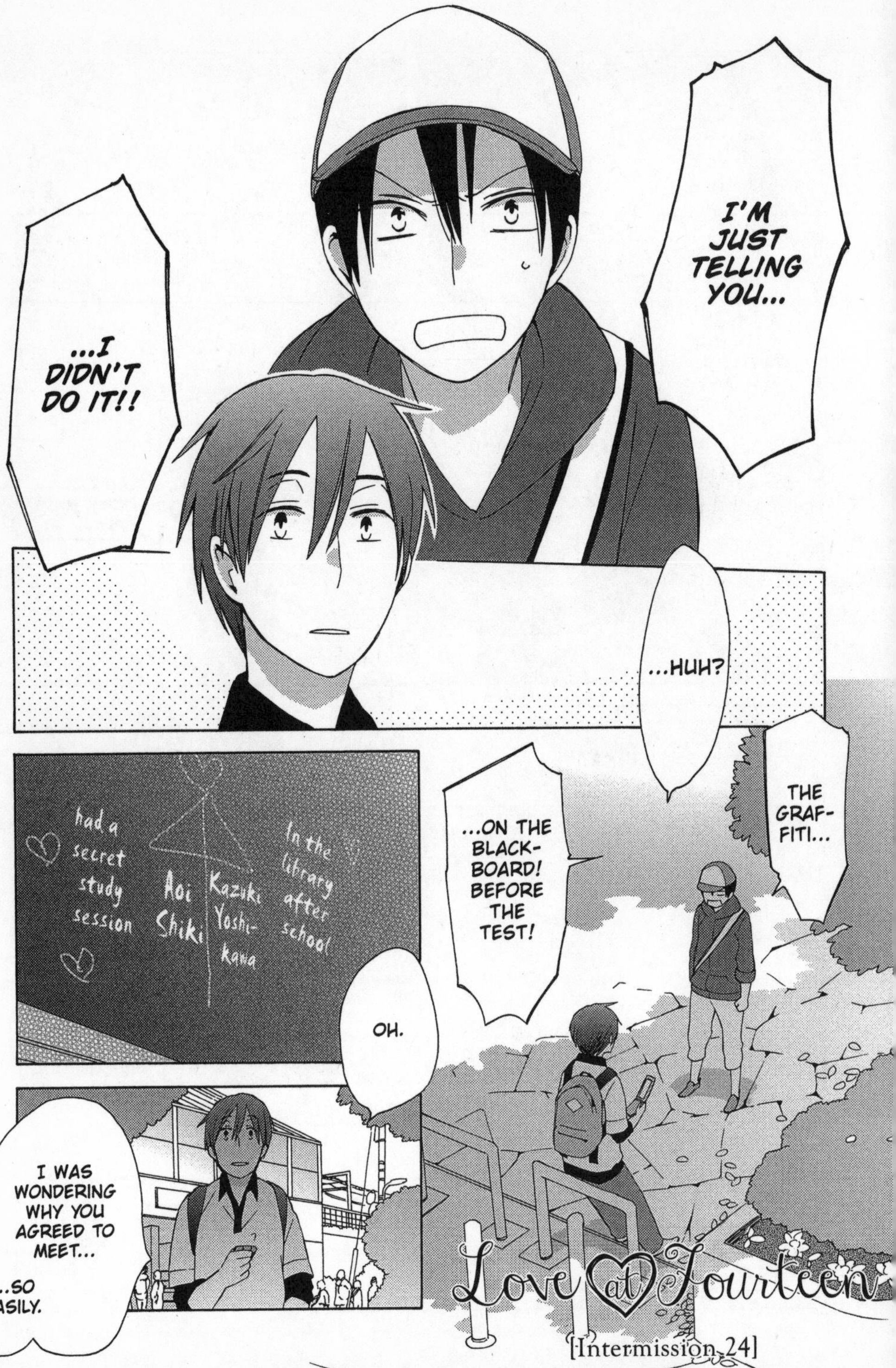
I'M JUST TELLING YOU...
...I DIDN'T DO IT!!
...HUH?
THE GRAF-FITI...
...ON THE BLACK-BOARD! BEFORE THE TEST!
OH.
had a secret study session
Aoi Shiki
Kazuki Yoshi-kawa
In the library after school
I WAS WONDERING WHY YOU AGREED TO MEET...
...SO EASILY.
Love at Fourteen
[Intermission 24]

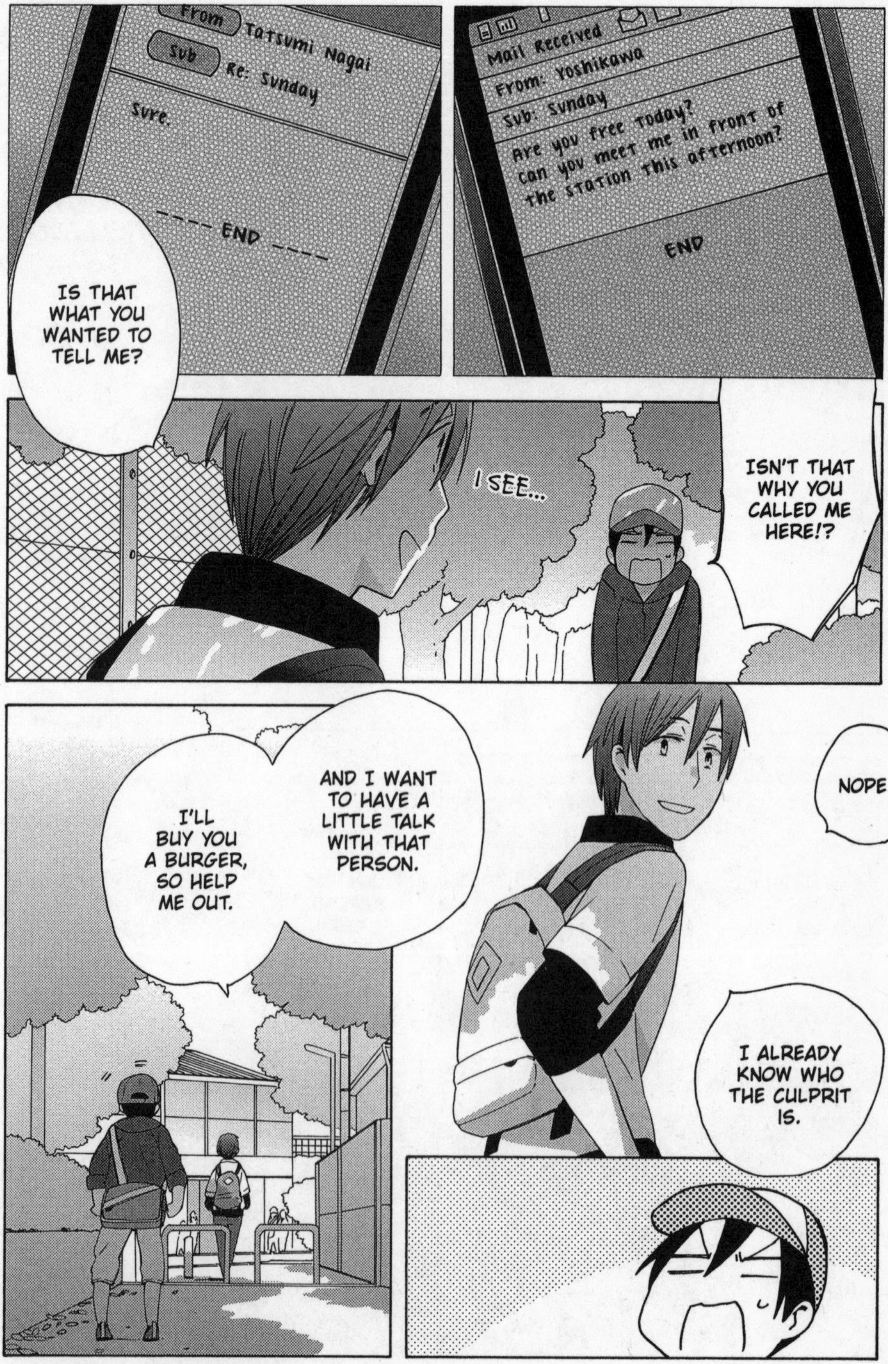
Mail Received
From: Yoshikawa
Sub: Sunday
Are you free today? Can you meet me in front of the station this afternoon?
END
From Tatsumi Nagai
Sub Re: Sunday
Sure.
---- END ----
IS THAT WHAT YOU WANTED TO TELL ME?
I SEE...
ISN'T THAT WHY YOU CALLED ME HERE!?
NOPE.
I ALREADY KNOW WHO THE CULPRIT IS.
AND I WANT TO HAVE A LITTLE TALK WITH THAT PERSON.
I'LL BUY YOU A BURGER, SO HELP ME OUT.

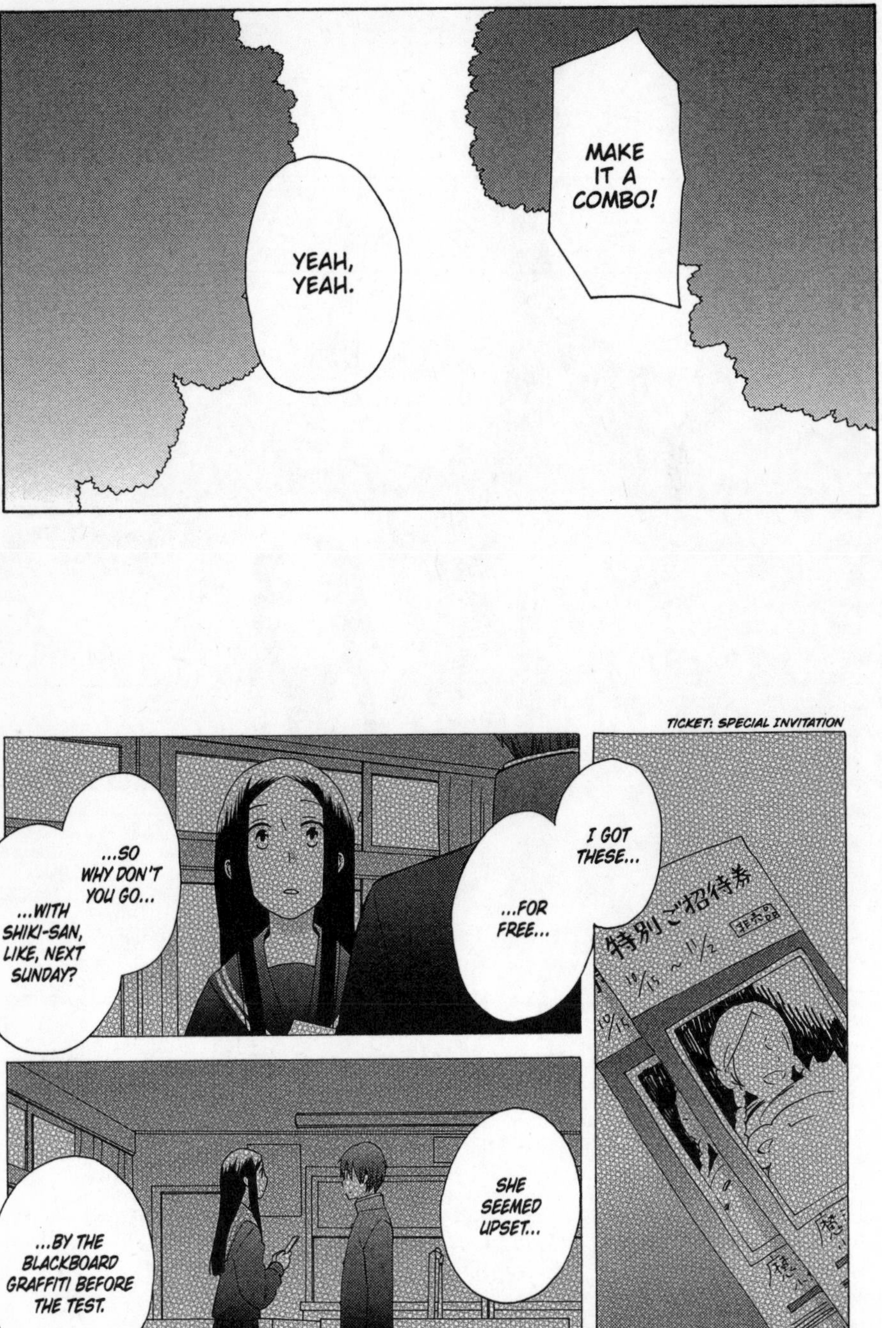
MAKE IT A COMBO!
YEAH, YEAH.
TICKET: SPECIAL INVITATION
特別ご招待券
10/15 ~ 11/2
I GOT THESE...
...FOR FREE...
...SO WHY DON'T YOU GO...
...WITH SHIKI-SAN, LIKE, NEXT SUNDAY?
SHE SEEMED UPSET...
...BY THE BLACKBOARD GRAFFITI BEFORE THE TEST.

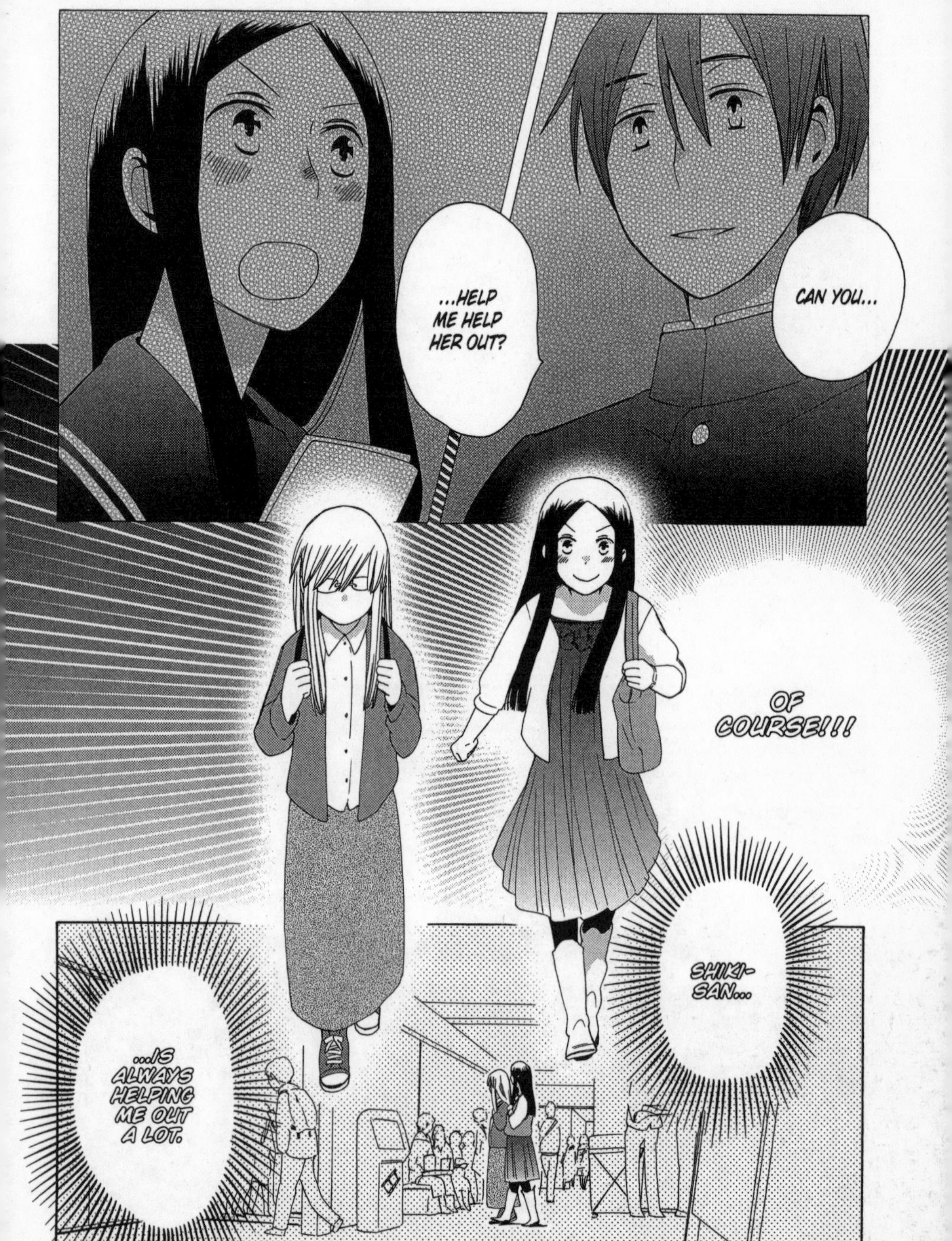
CAN YOU...
...HELP ME HELP HER OUT?
OF COURSE!!!
SHIKI-SAN...
...IS ALWAYS HELPING ME OUT A LOT.

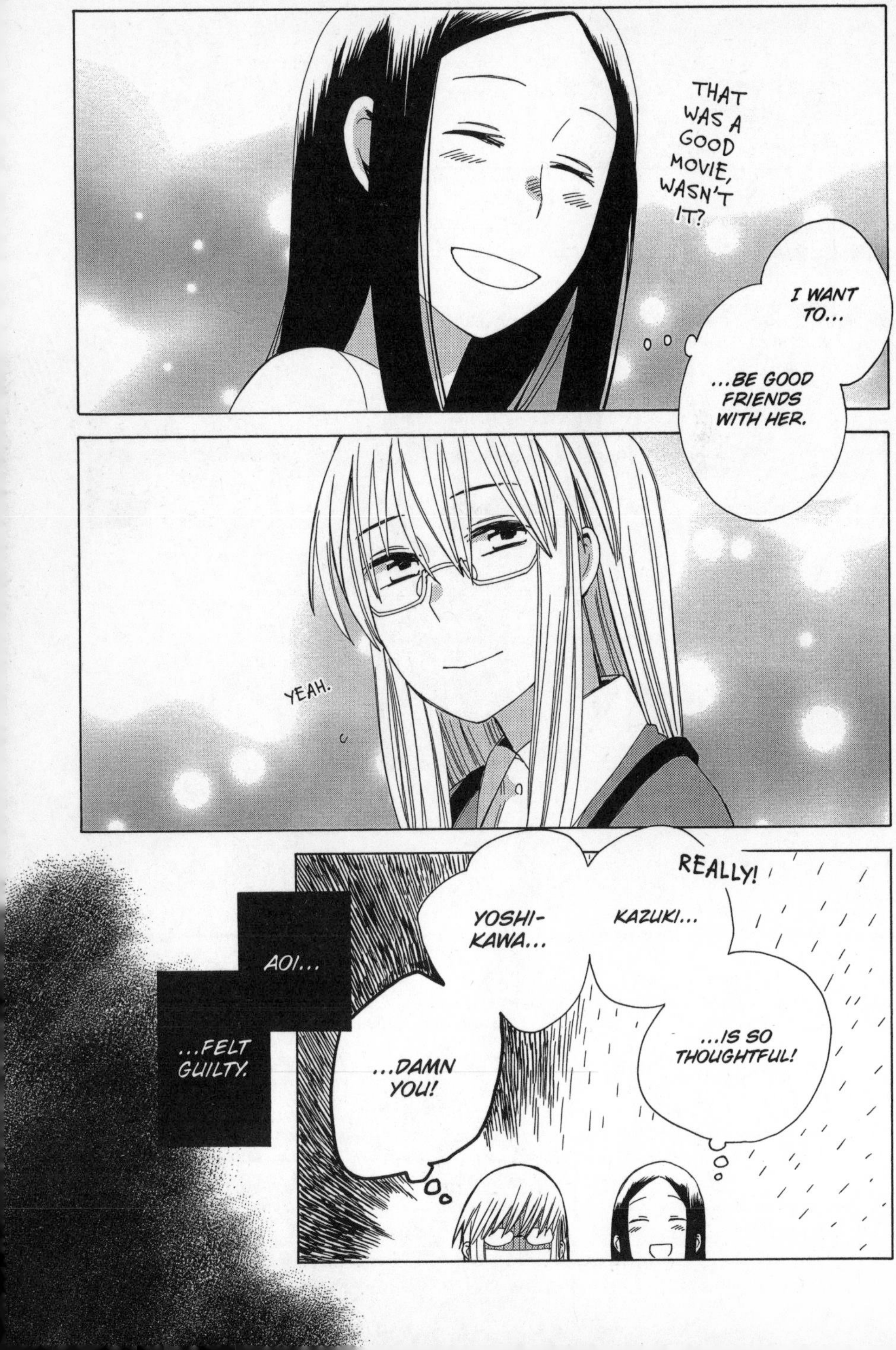
THAT WAS A GOOD MOVIE, WASN'T IT?
I WANT TO...
...BE GOOD FRIENDS WITH HER.
YEAH.
REALLY!
KAZUKI...
...IS SO THOUGHTFUL!
YOSHI-KAWA...
...DAMN YOU!
AOI...
...FELT GUILTY.

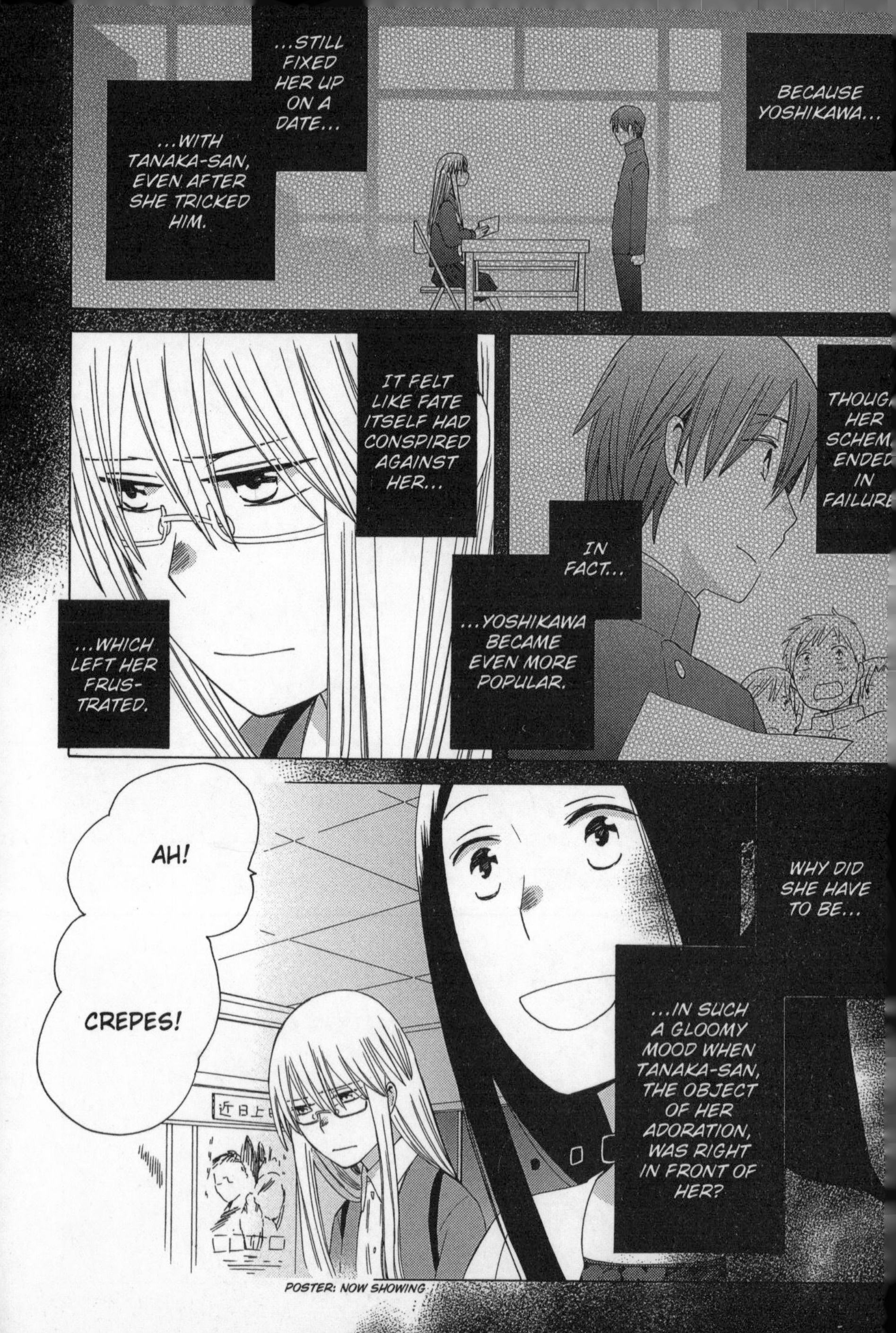
BECAUSE YOSHIKAWA...
...STILL FIXED HER UP ON A DATE...
...WITH TANAKA-SAN, EVEN AFTER SHE TRICKED HIM.
THOUG HER SCHEM ENDED IN FAILURE
IN FACT...
...YOSHIKAWA BECAME EVEN MORE POPULAR.
IT FELT LIKE FATE ITSELF HAD CONSPIRED AGAINST HER...
...WHICH LEFT HER FRUS-TRATED.
WHY DID SHE HAVE TO BE...
...IN SUCH A GLOOMY MOOD WHEN TANAKA-SAN, THE OBJECT OF HER ADORATION, WAS RIGHT IN FRONT OF HER?
AH!
CREPES!
POSTER: NOW SHOWING

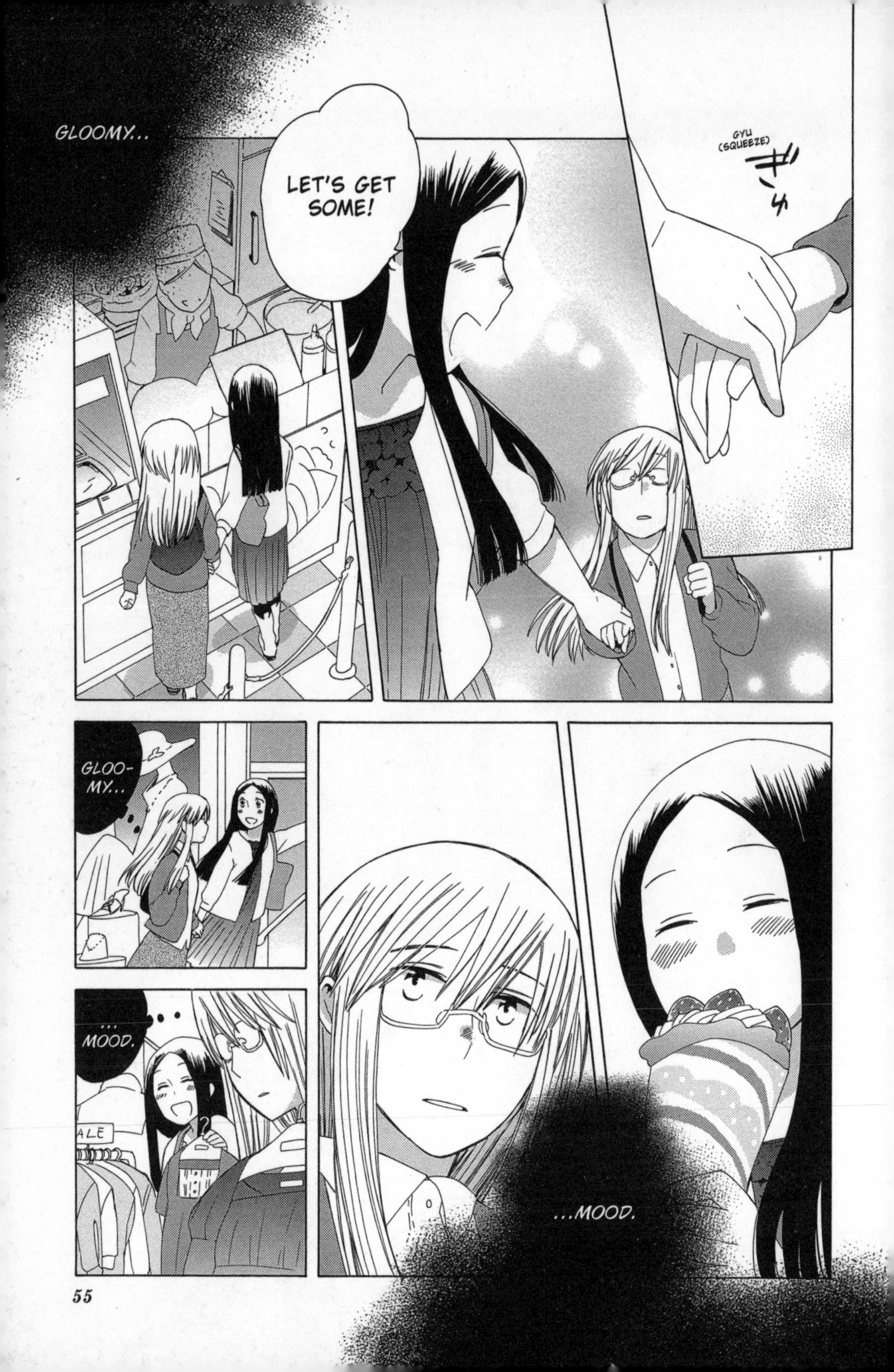
GYU (SQUEEZE)
ぎゅ
LET'S GET SOME!
GLOOMY...
...MOOD.
GLOO-MY...
...
...MOOD.
ALE

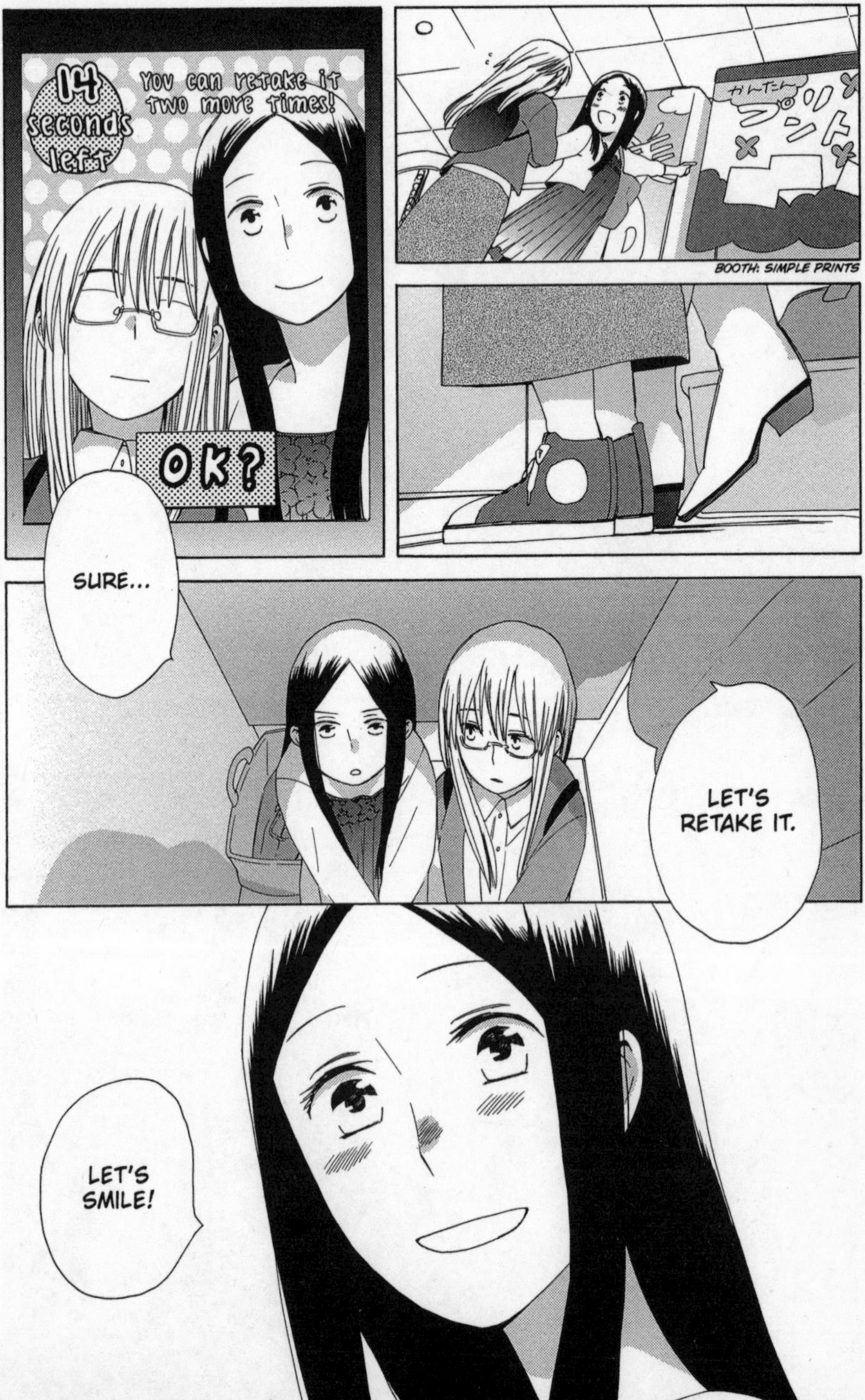
かんたん
プリント
BOOTH: SIMPLE PRINTS
14 seconds left
You can retake it two more times!
OK?
SURE...
LET'S RETAKE IT.
LET'S SMILE!

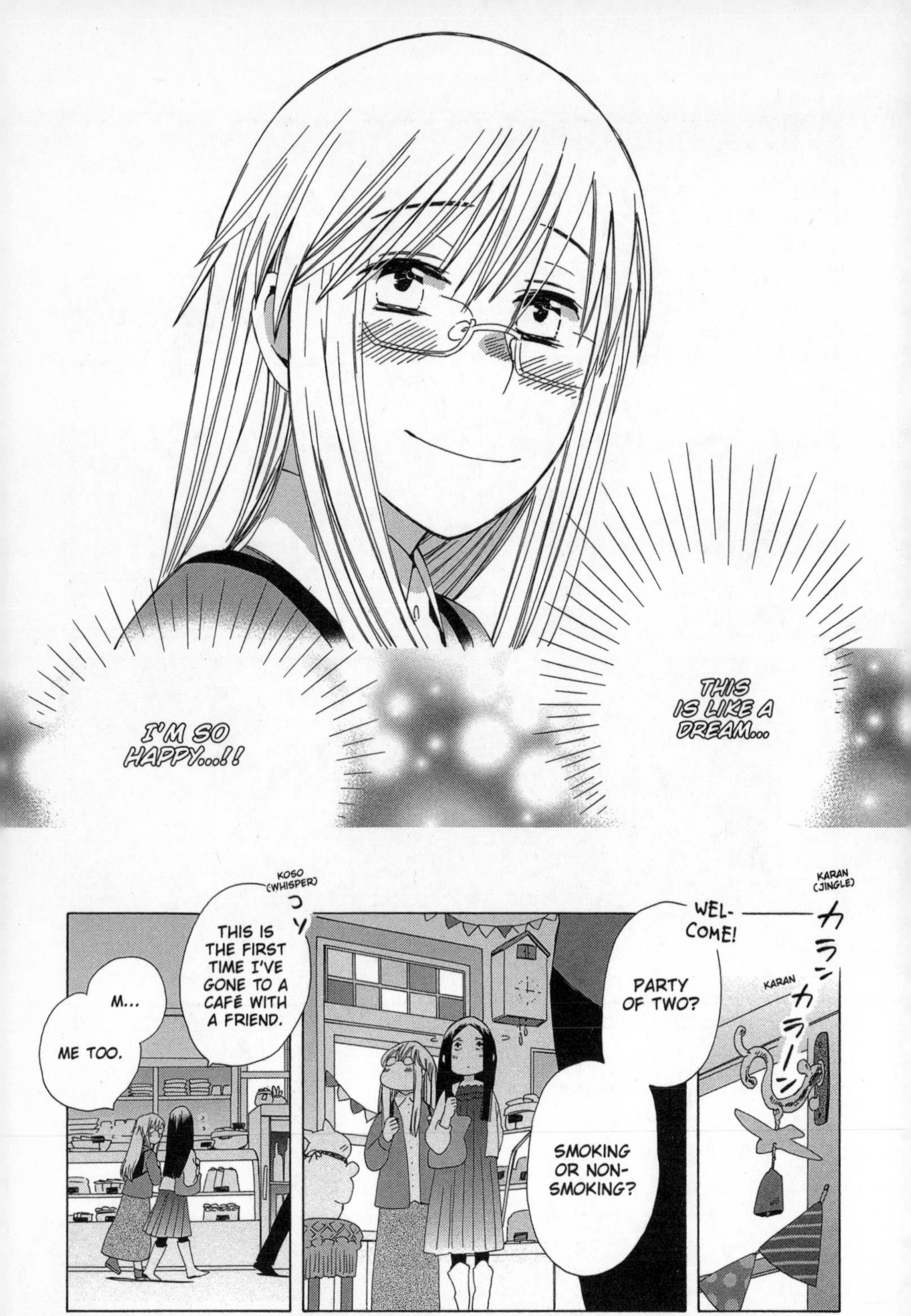
THIS IS LIKE A DREAM...
I'M SO HAPPY...!!
KARAN (JINGLE)
カラン
KARAN
カラーン
WEL-COME!
PARTY OF TWO?
SMOKING OR NON-SMOKING?
KOSO (WHISPER)
コソ
THIS IS THE FIRST TIME I'VE GONE TO A CAFÉ WITH A FRIEND.
M...
ME TOO.

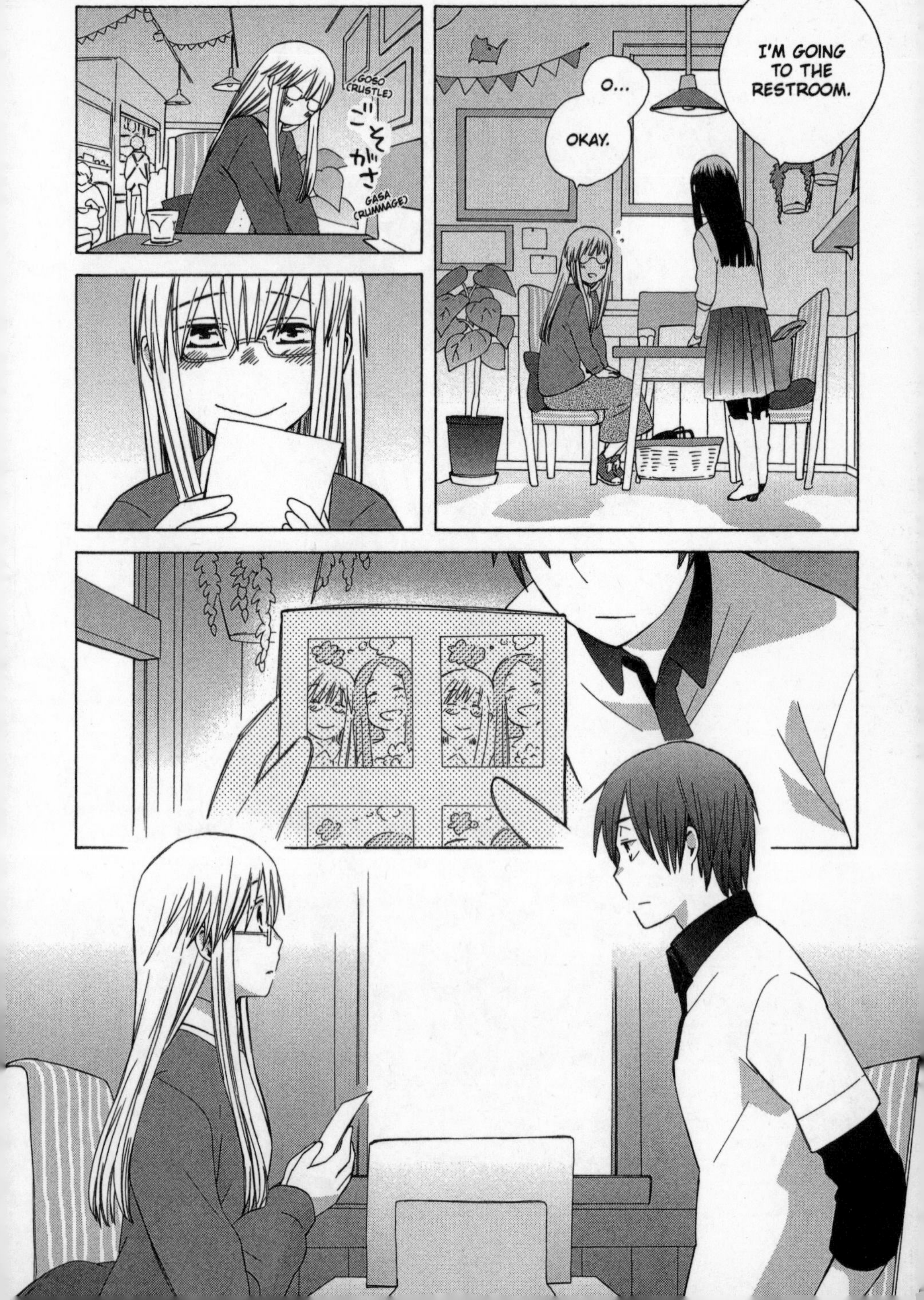
I'M GOING TO THE RESTROOM.
O...
OKAY.
GOSO (RUSTLE)
ごそがさ
GASA (RUMMAGE)

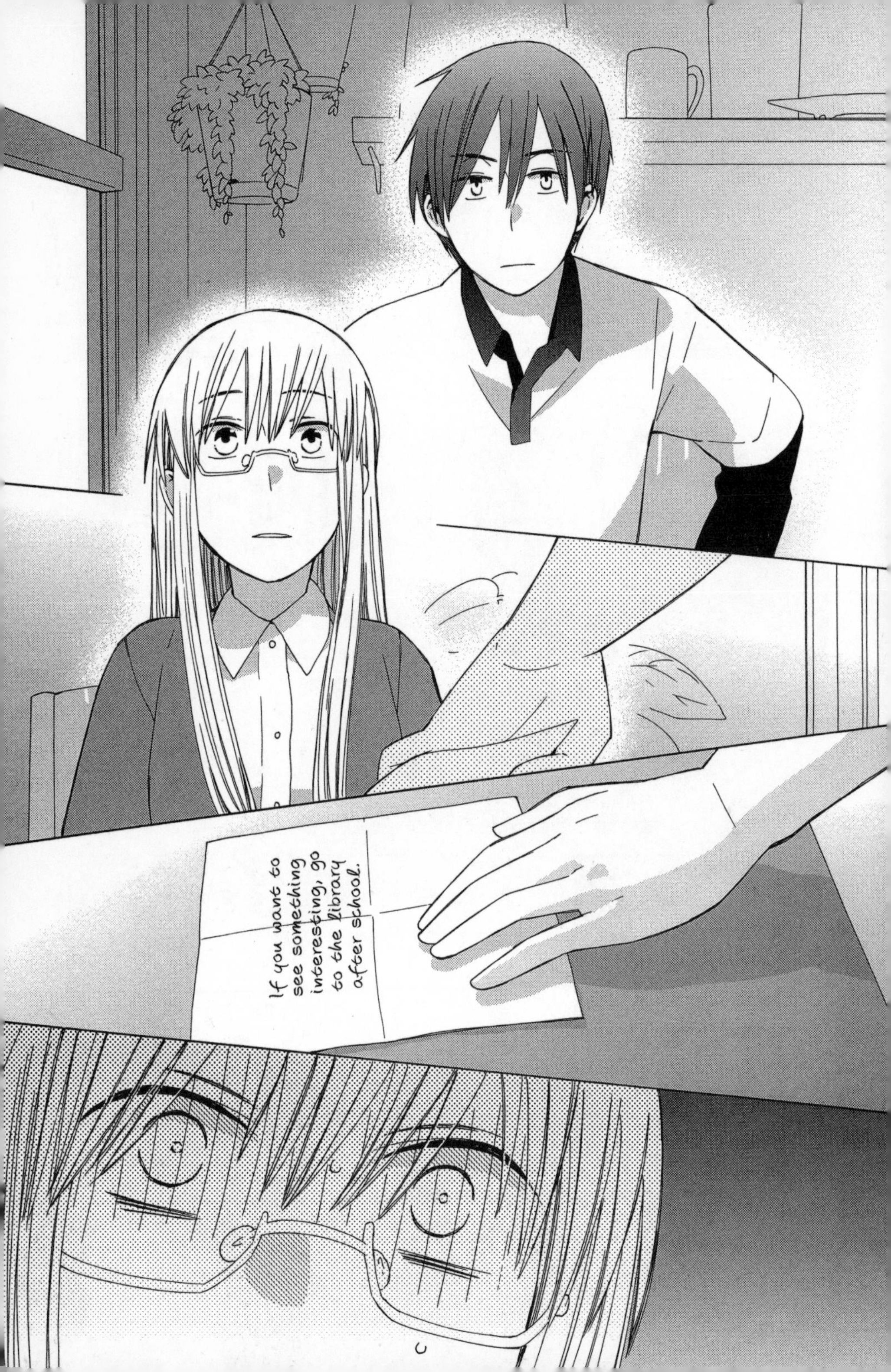
If you want to see something interesting, go to the library after school.

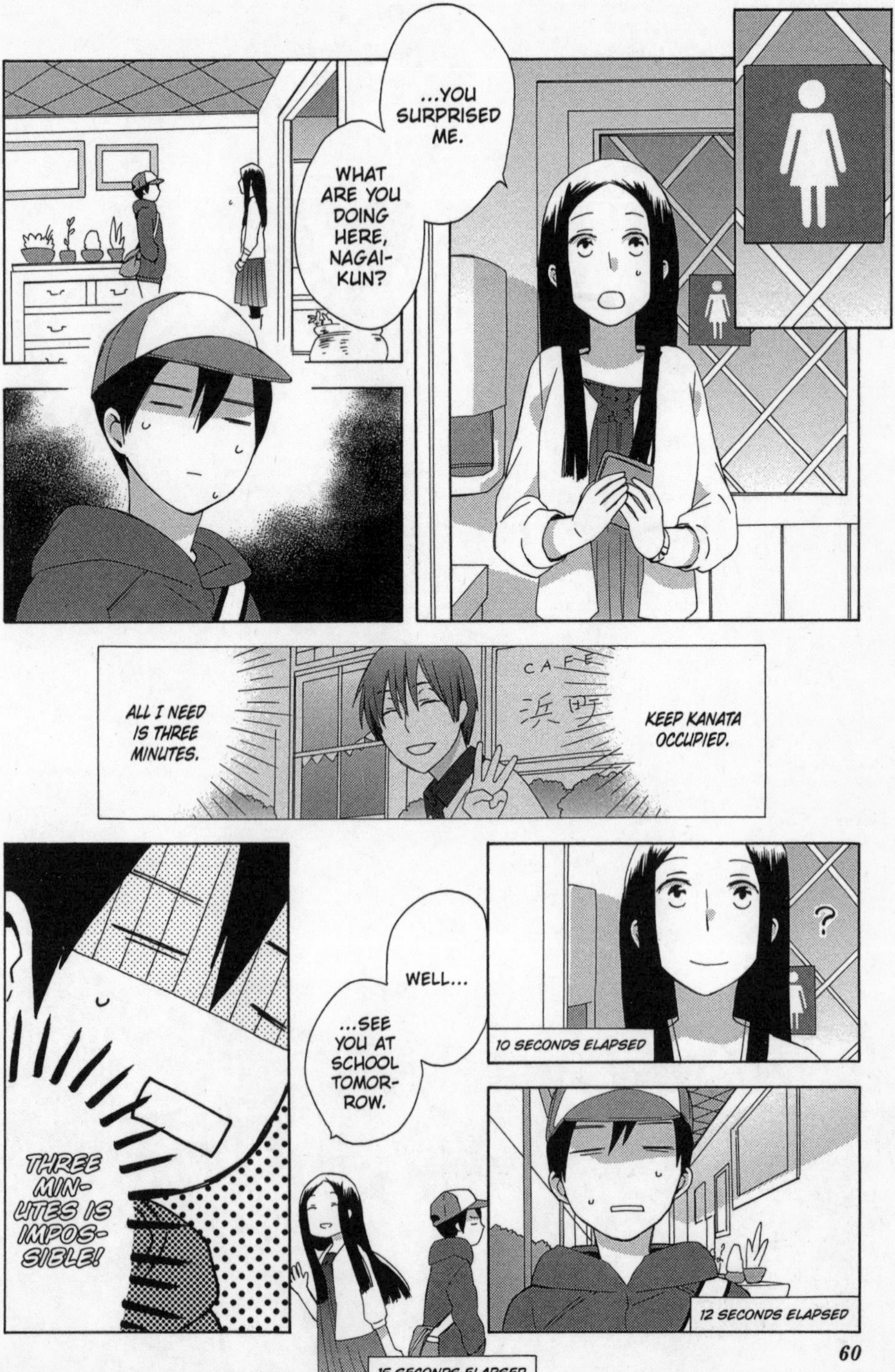
...YOU SURPRISED ME.
WHAT ARE YOU DOING HERE, NAGAI-KUN?
CAFE
KEEP KANATA OCCUPIED.
ALL I NEED IS THREE MINUTES.
?
10 SECONDS ELAPSED
WELL...
...SEE YOU AT SCHOOL TOMOR-ROW.
12 SECONDS ELAPSED
THREE MIN-UTES IS IMPOS-SIBLE!
15 SECONDS ELAPSED

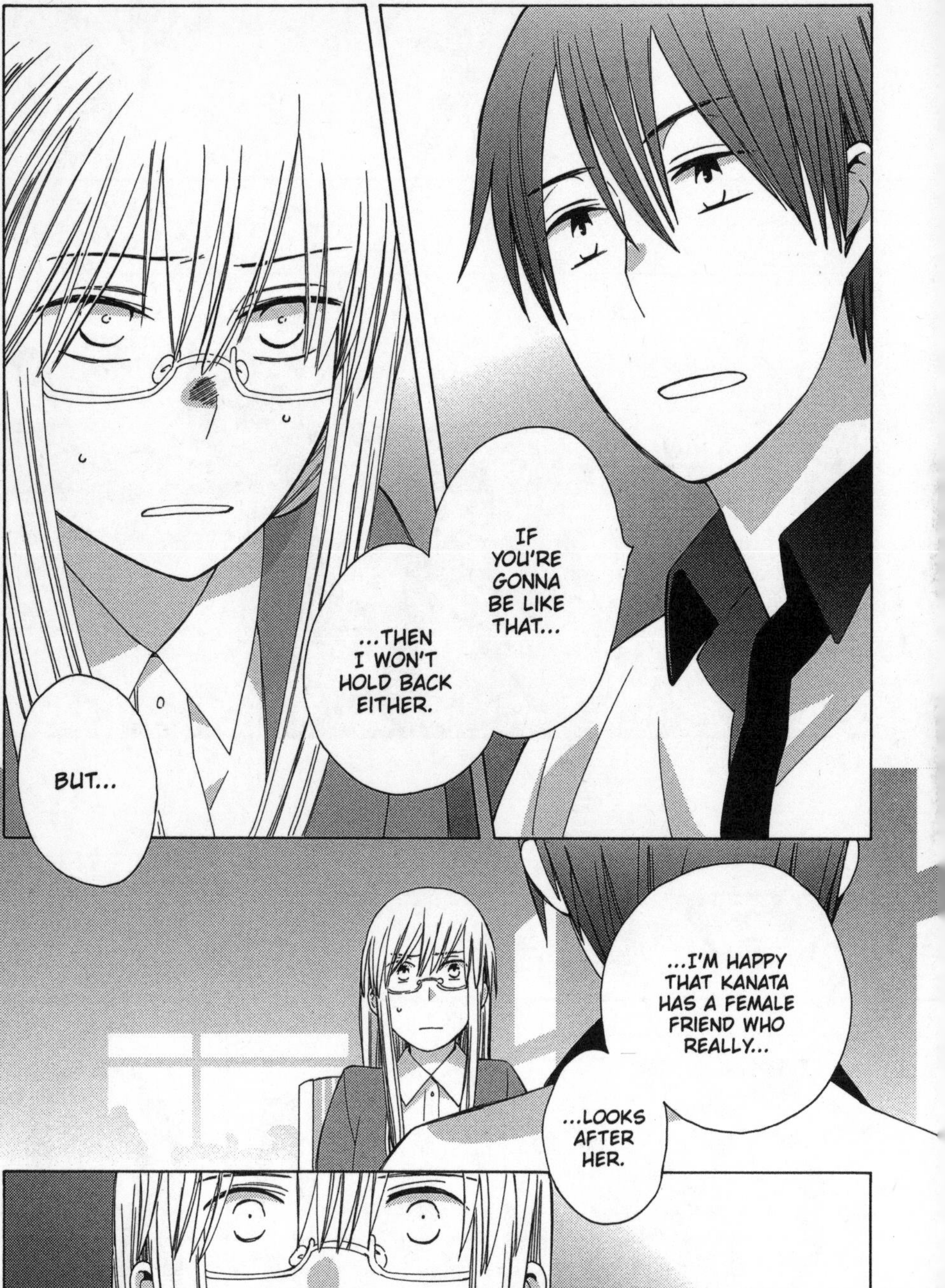
IF YOU'RE GONNA BE LIKE THAT...
...THEN I WON'T HOLD BACK EITHER.
BUT...
...I'M HAPPY THAT KANATA HAS A FEMALE FRIEND WHO REALLY...
...LOOKS AFTER HER.

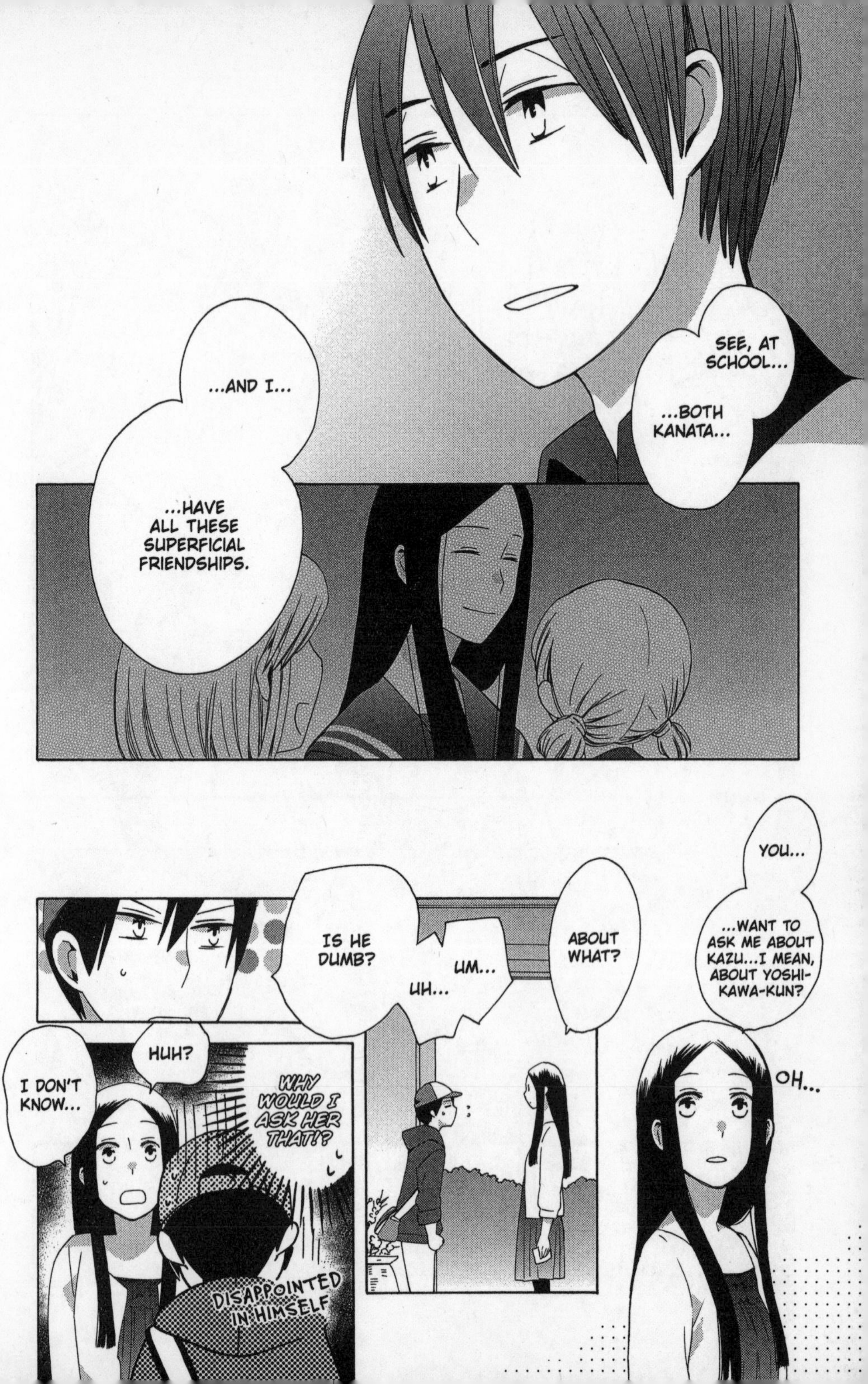
SEE, AT SCHOOL...
...BOTH KANATA...
...AND I...
...HAVE ALL THESE SUPERFICIAL FRIENDSHIPS.
YOU...
...WANT TO ASK ME ABOUT KAZU...I MEAN, ABOUT YOSHI-KAWA-KUN?
OH...
ABOUT WHAT?
UM...
UH...
IS HE DUMB?
HUH?
I DON'T KNOW...
WHY WOULD I ASK HER THAT!?
DISAPPOINTED IN HIMSELF

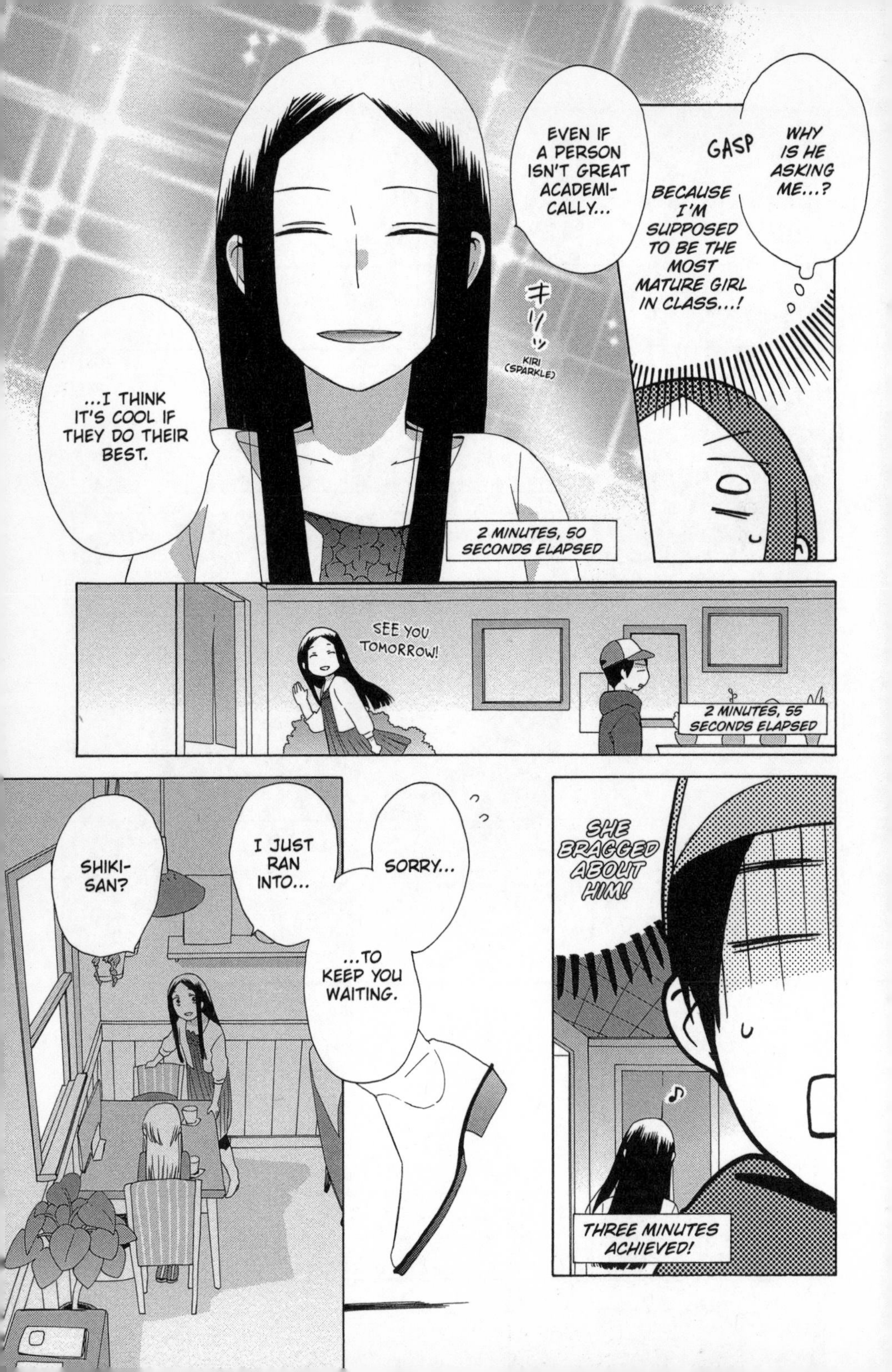
GASP
WHY IS HE ASKING ME...?
BECAUSE I'M SUPPOSED TO BE THE MOST MATURE GIRL IN CLASS...!
EVEN IF A PERSON ISN'T GREAT ACADEMI-CALLY...
KIRI (SPARKLE)
...I THINK IT'S COOL IF THEY DO THEIR BEST.
2 MINUTES, 50 SECONDS ELAPSED
2 MINUTES, 55 SECONDS ELAPSED
SEE YOU TOMORROW!
SHE BRAGGED ABOUT HIM!
THREE MINUTES ACHIEVED!
SORRY...
I JUST RAN INTO...
...TO KEEP YOU WAITING.
SHIKI-SAN?

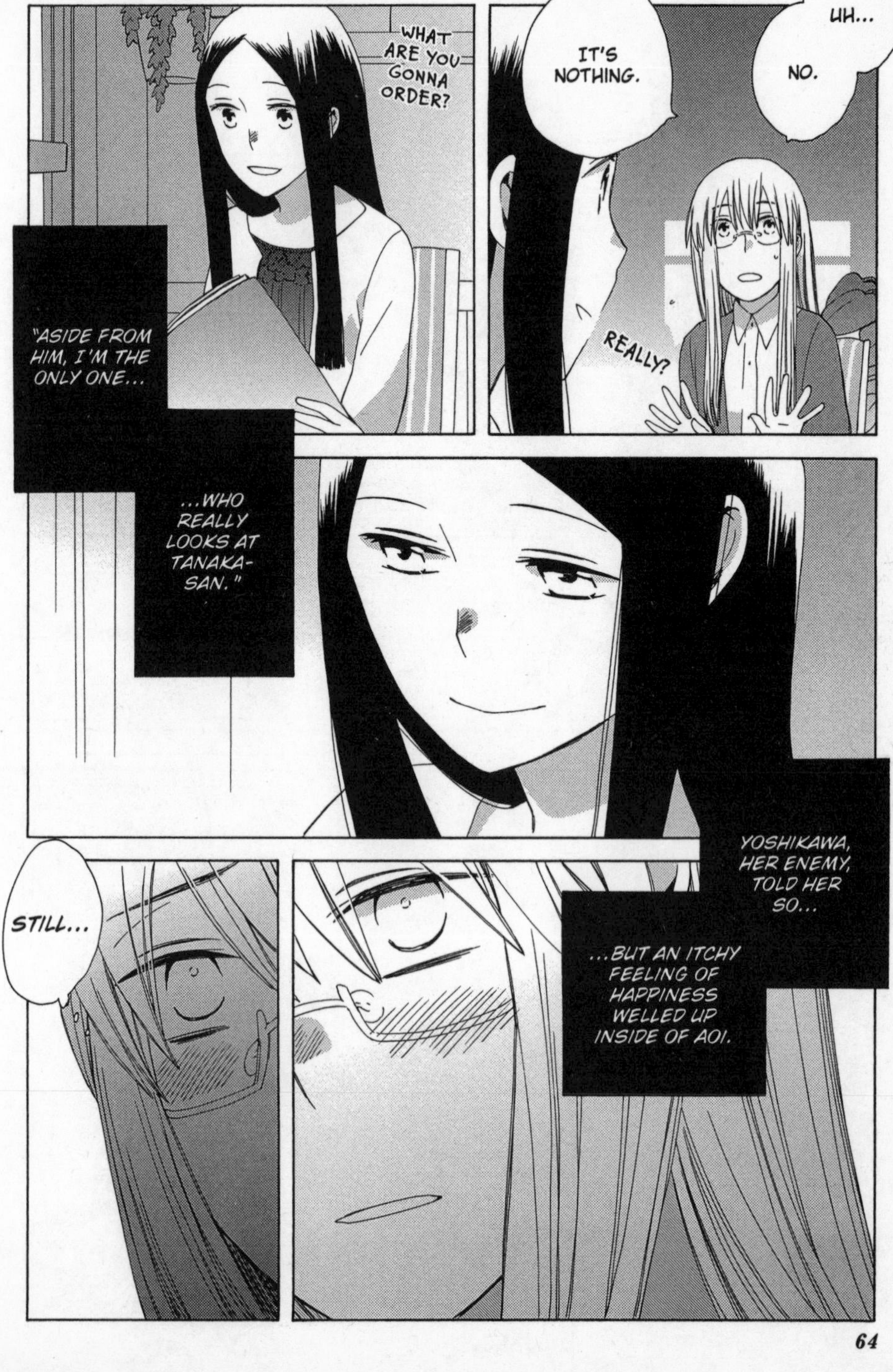
UH...
NO.
IT'S NOTHING.
REALLY?
WHAT ARE YOU GONNA ORDER?
"ASIDE FROM HIM, I'M THE ONLY ONE...
...WHO REALLY LOOKS AT TANAKA-SAN."
YOSHIKAWA, HER ENEMY, TOLD HER SO...
...BUT AN ITCHY FEELING OF HAPPINESS WELLED UP INSIDE OF AOI.
STILL...

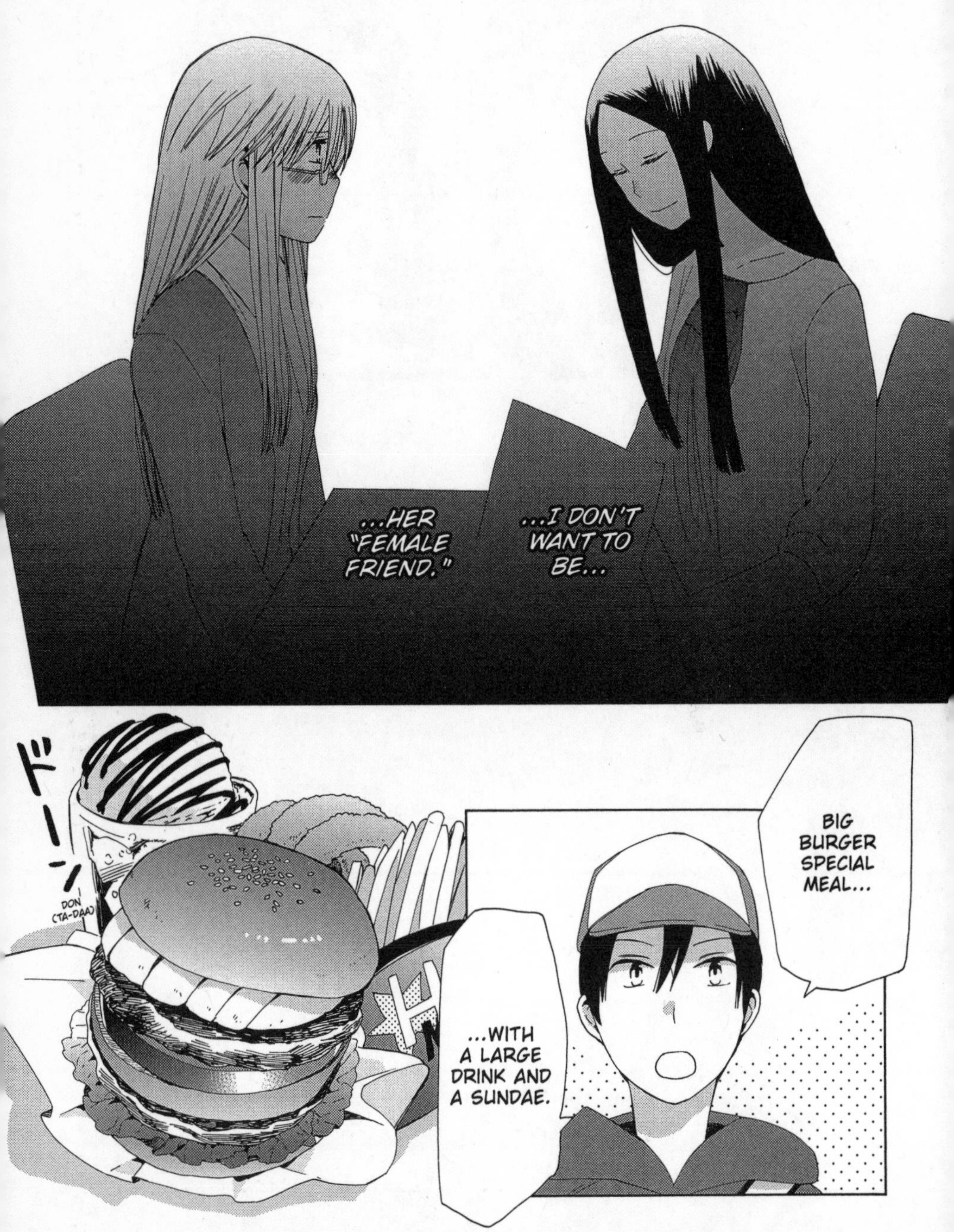
...I DON'T WANT TO BE...
...HER "FEMALE FRIEND."
BIG BURGER SPECIAL MEAL...
...WITH A LARGE DRINK AND A SUNDAE.
ドーン
DON (TA-DAA)

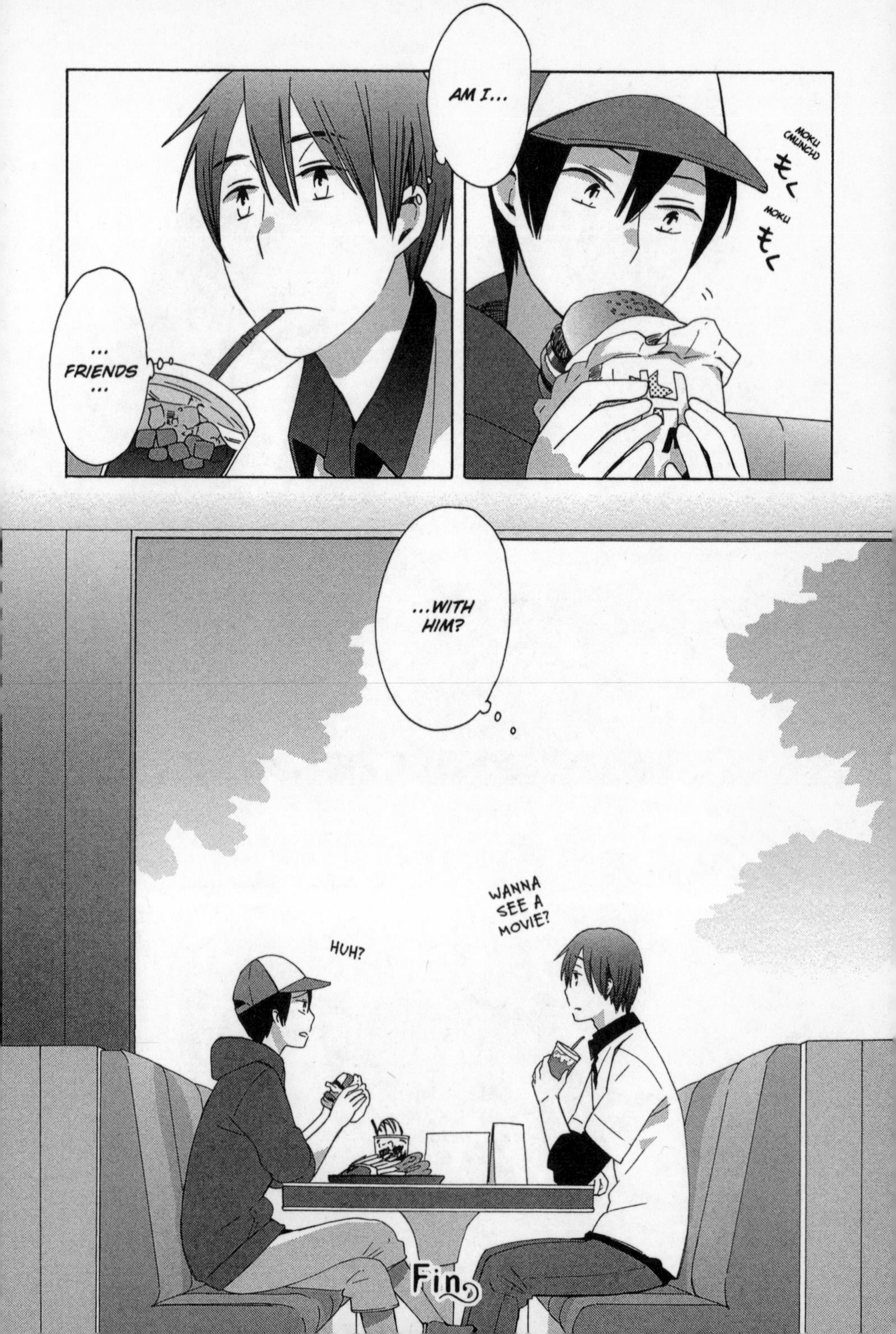
AM I...
MOKU (MUNCH) もく
MOKU もく
...FRIENDS...
...WITH HIM?
WANNA SEE A MOVIE?
HUH?
Fin

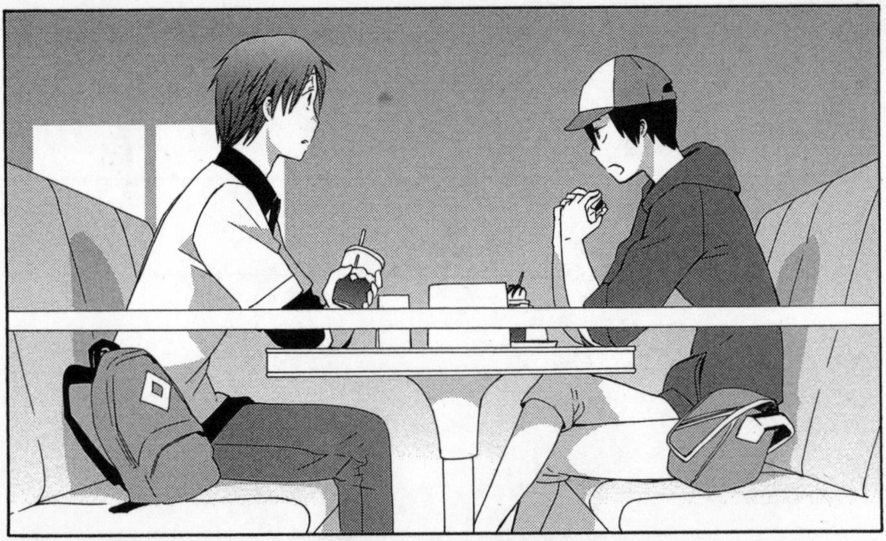

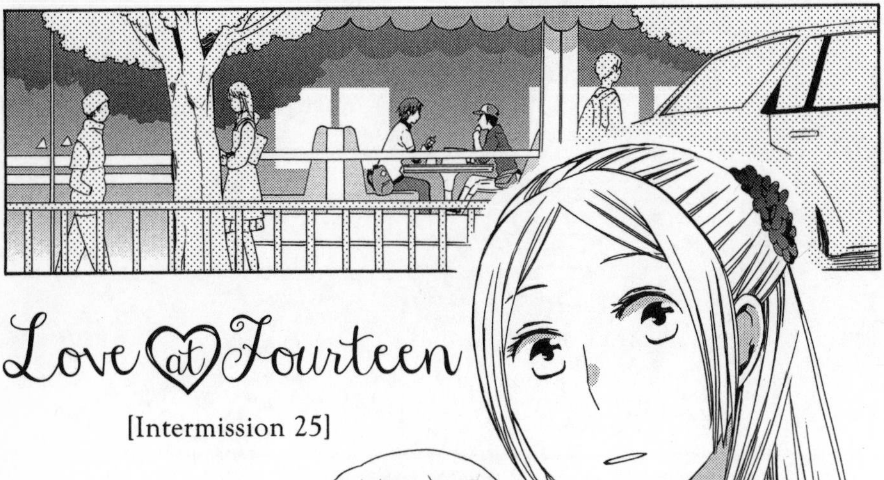

Love at Fourteen

[Intermission 25]

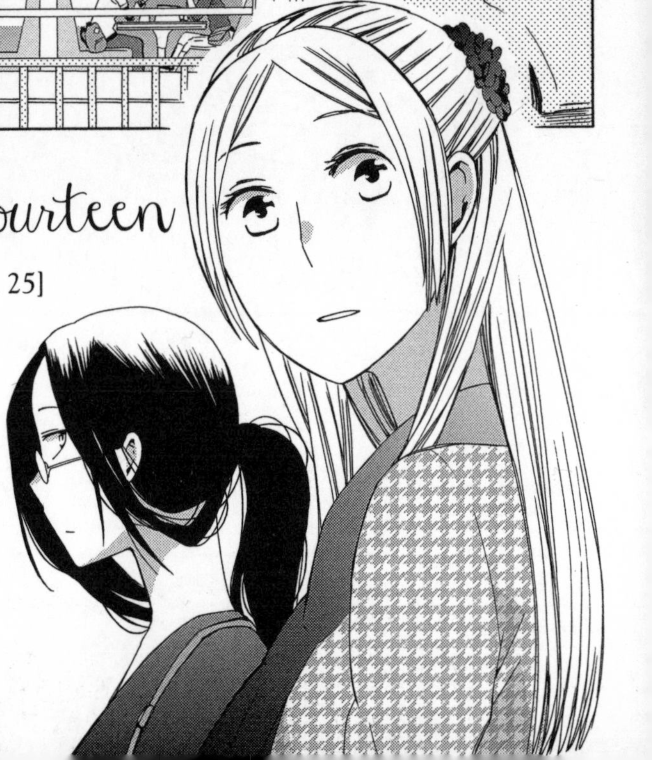

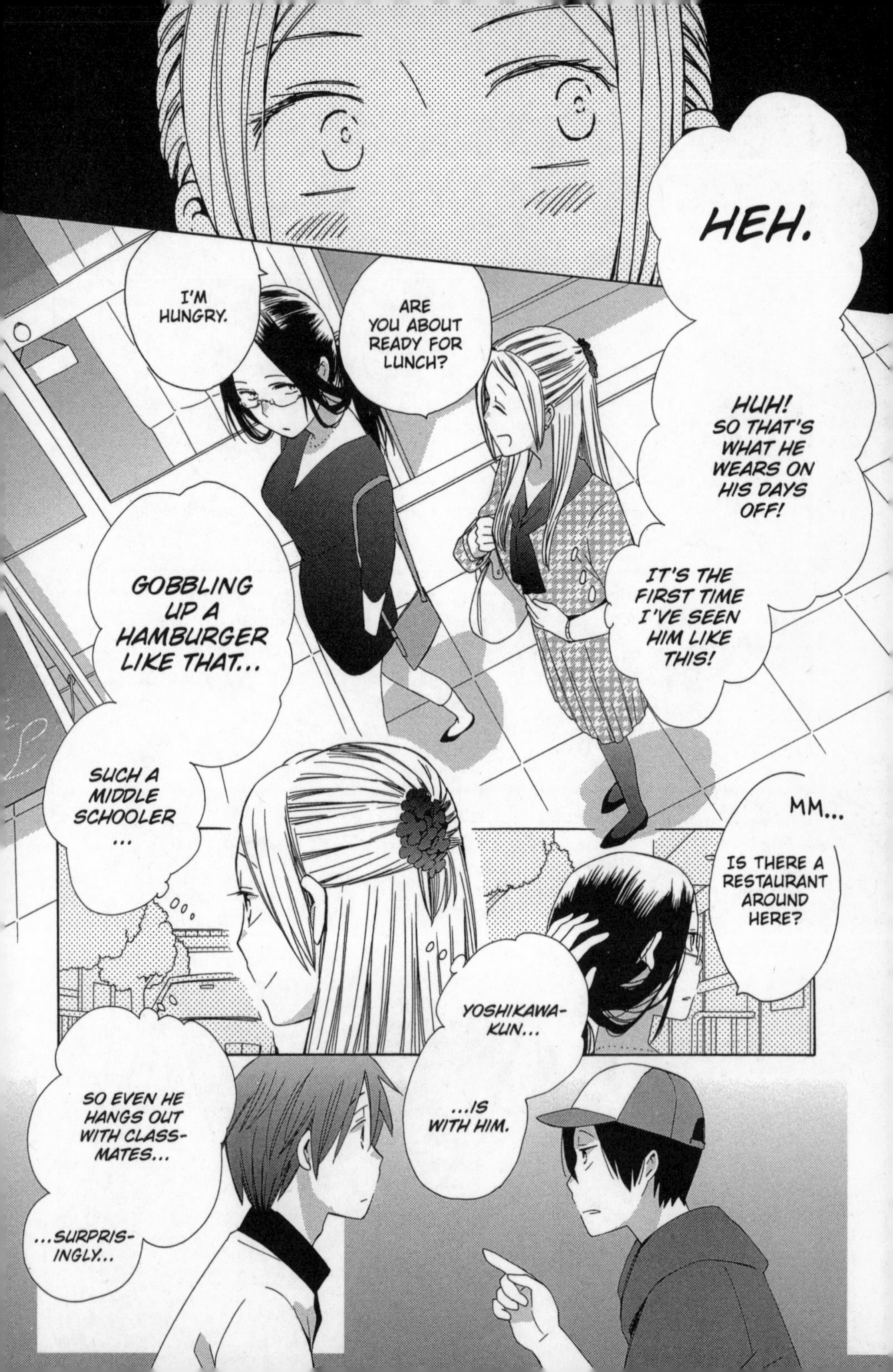
HEH.
HUH! SO THAT'S WHAT HE WEARS ON HIS DAYS OFF!
IT'S THE FIRST TIME I'VE SEEN HIM LIKE THIS!
ARE YOU ABOUT READY FOR LUNCH?
I'M HUNGRY.
GOBBLING UP A HAMBURGER LIKE THAT...
SUCH A MIDDLE SCHOOLER ...
MM...
IS THERE A RESTAURANT AROUND HERE?
YOSHIKAWA-KUN...
...IS WITH HIM.
SO EVEN HE HANGS OUT WITH CLASSMATES...
...SURPRISINGLY...

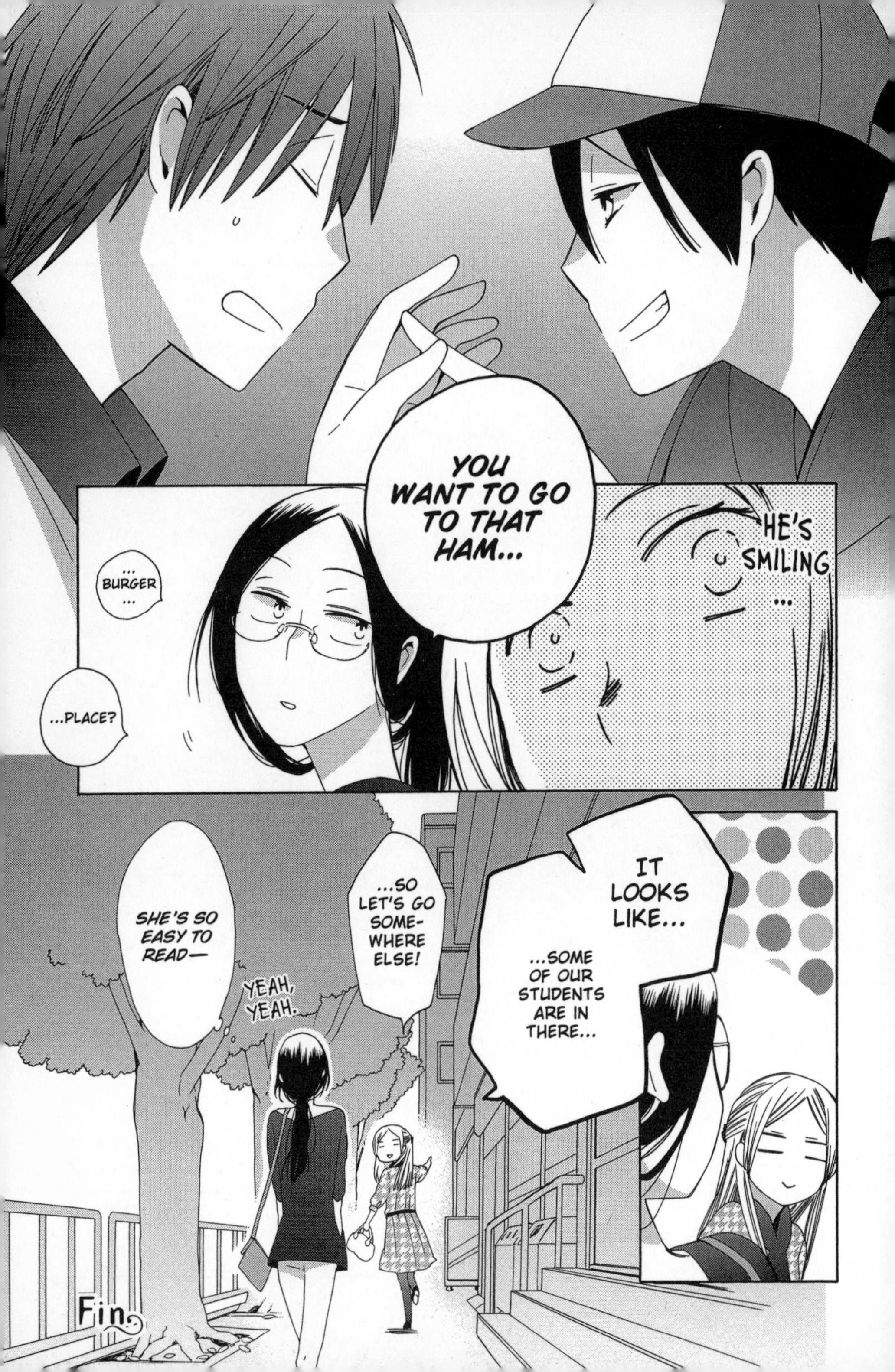
YOU WANT TO GO TO THAT HAM...
HE'S SMILING...
...BURGER...
...PLACE?
IT LOOKS LIKE...
...SOME OF OUR STUDENTS ARE IN THERE...
...SO LET'S GO SOME-WHERE ELSE!
YEAH, YEAH.
SHE'S SO EASY TO READ—
Fin.

Love at Fourteen

Fuka Mizutani

Love ♡ at Fourteen

What thing?

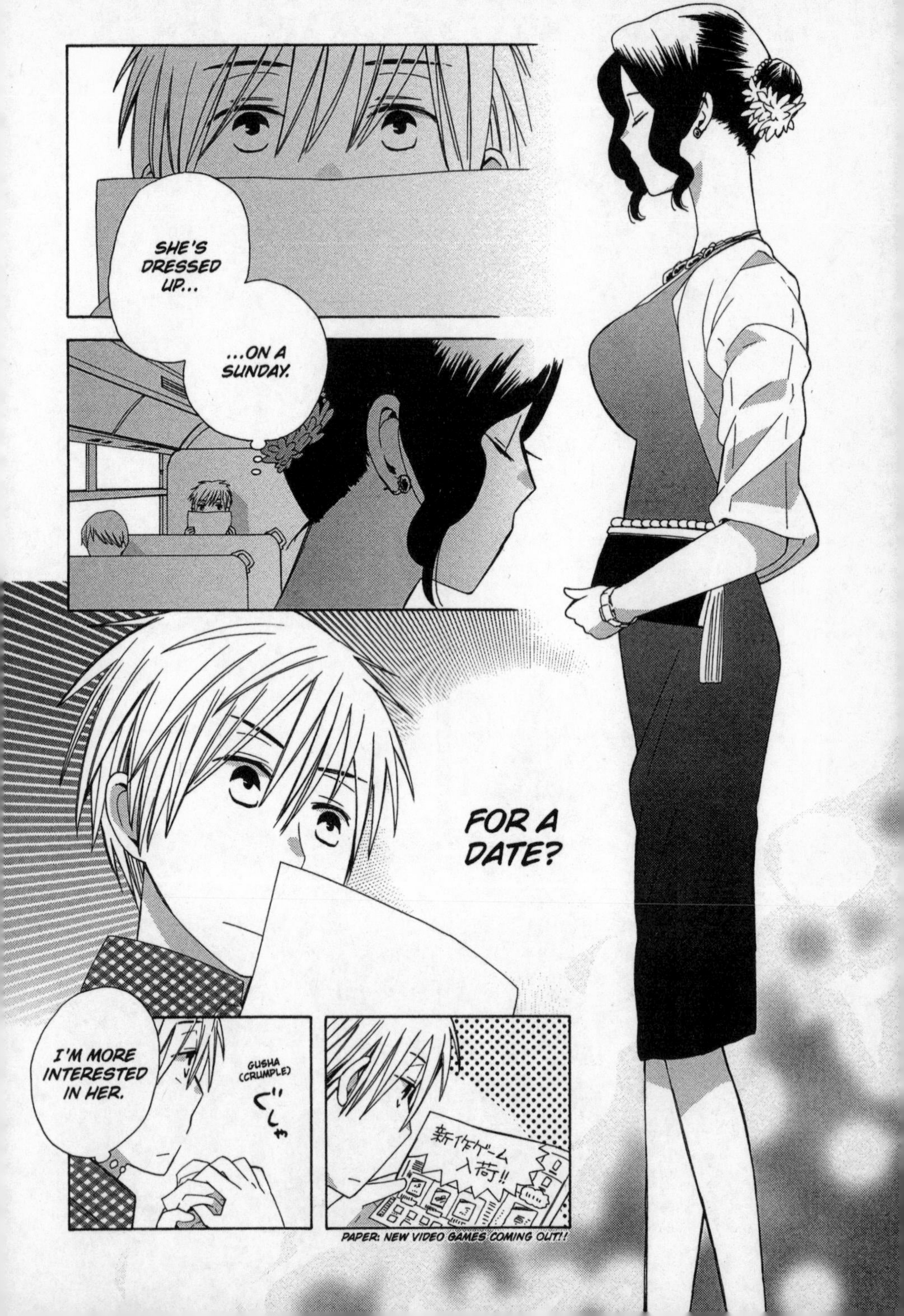
SHE'S DRESSED UP...
...ON A SUNDAY.
FOR A DATE?
新作ゲーム入荷!!
I'M MORE INTERESTED IN HER.
GUSHA (CRUMPLE)
ぐしゃ
PAPER: NEW VIDEO GAMES COMING OUT!!

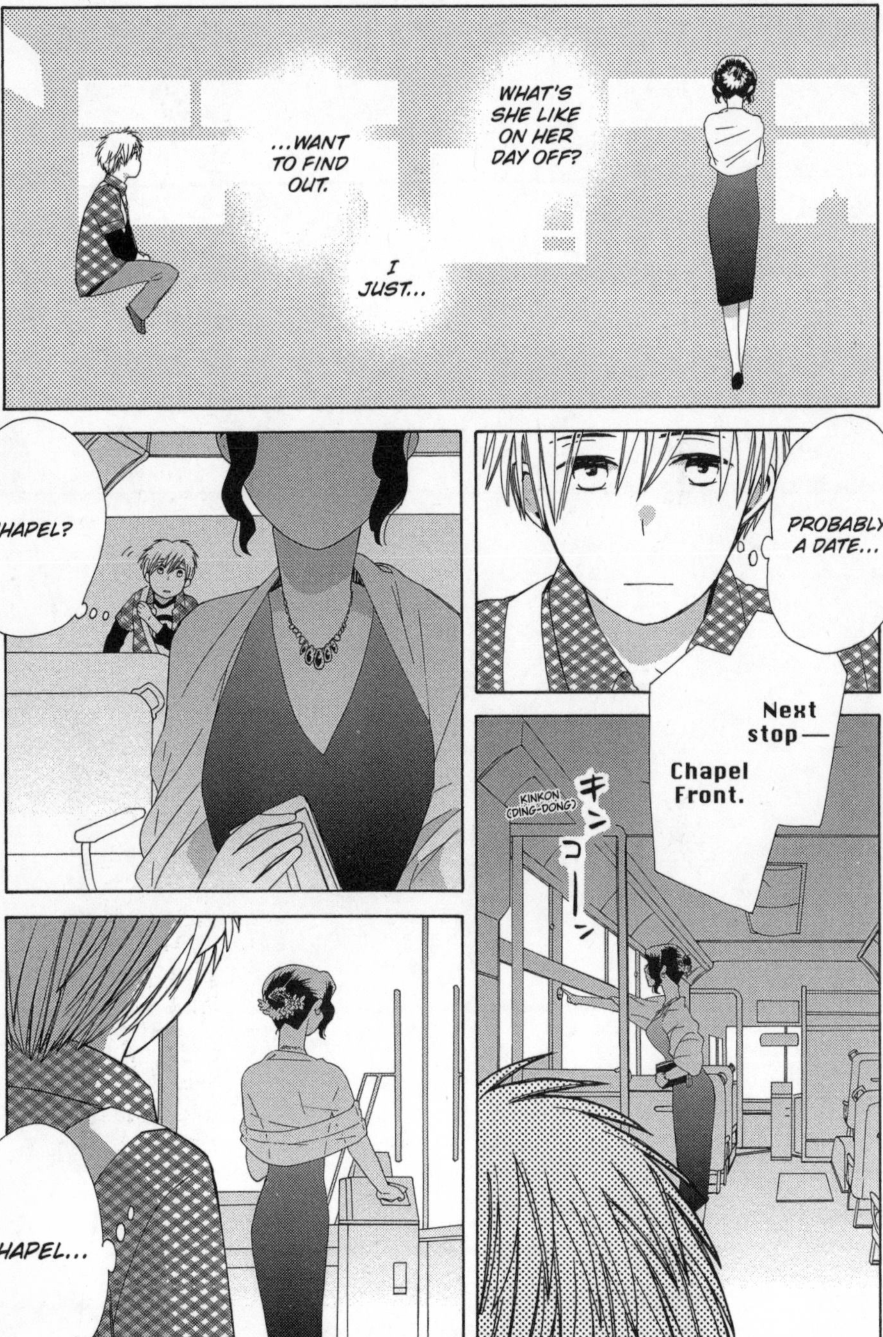
WHAT'S SHE LIKE ON HER DAY OFF?
I JUST...
...WANT TO FIND OUT.
PROBABLY A DATE...
CHAPEL?
Next stop— Chapel Front.
キンコーン
KINKON (DING-DONG)
CHAPEL...

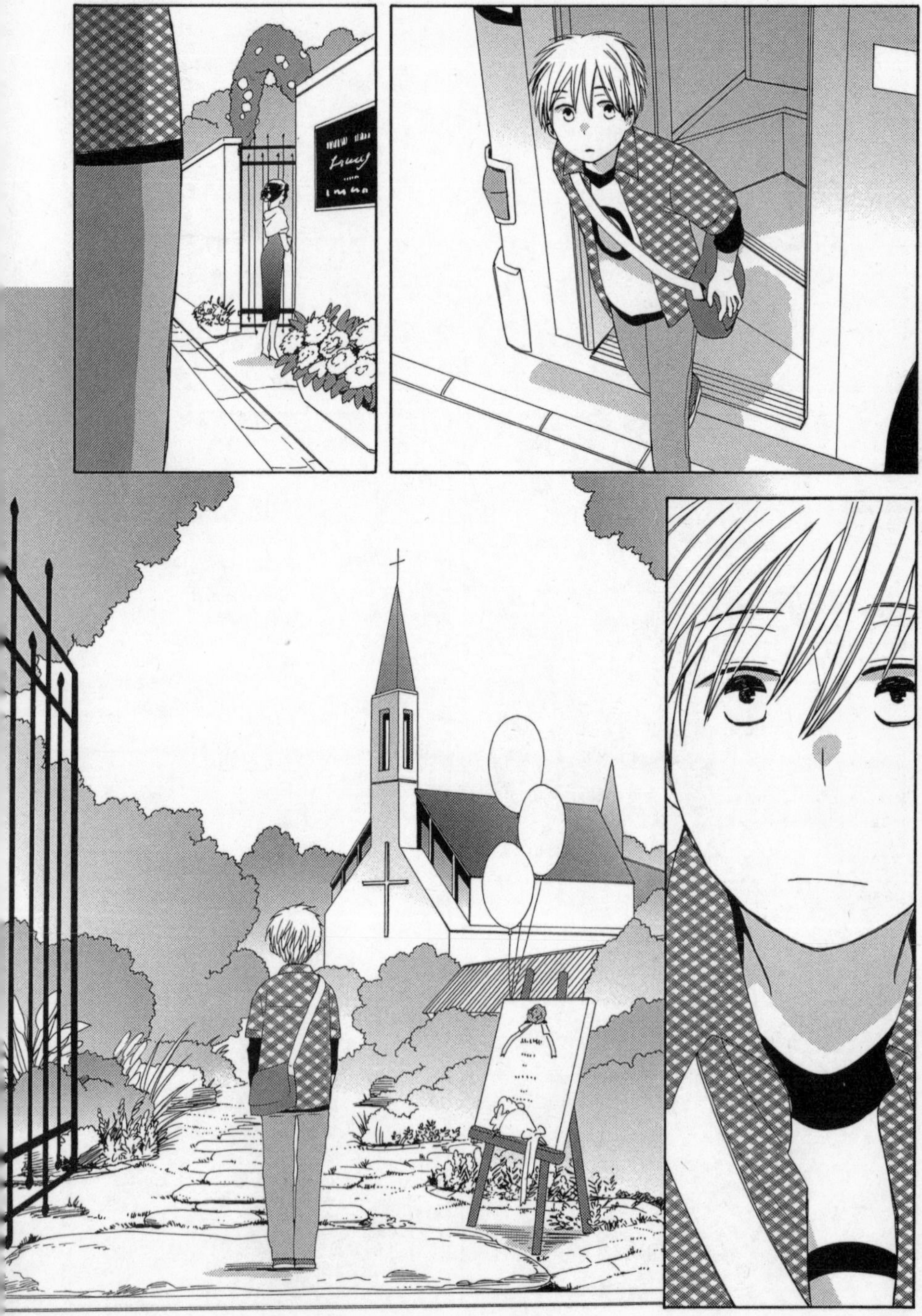

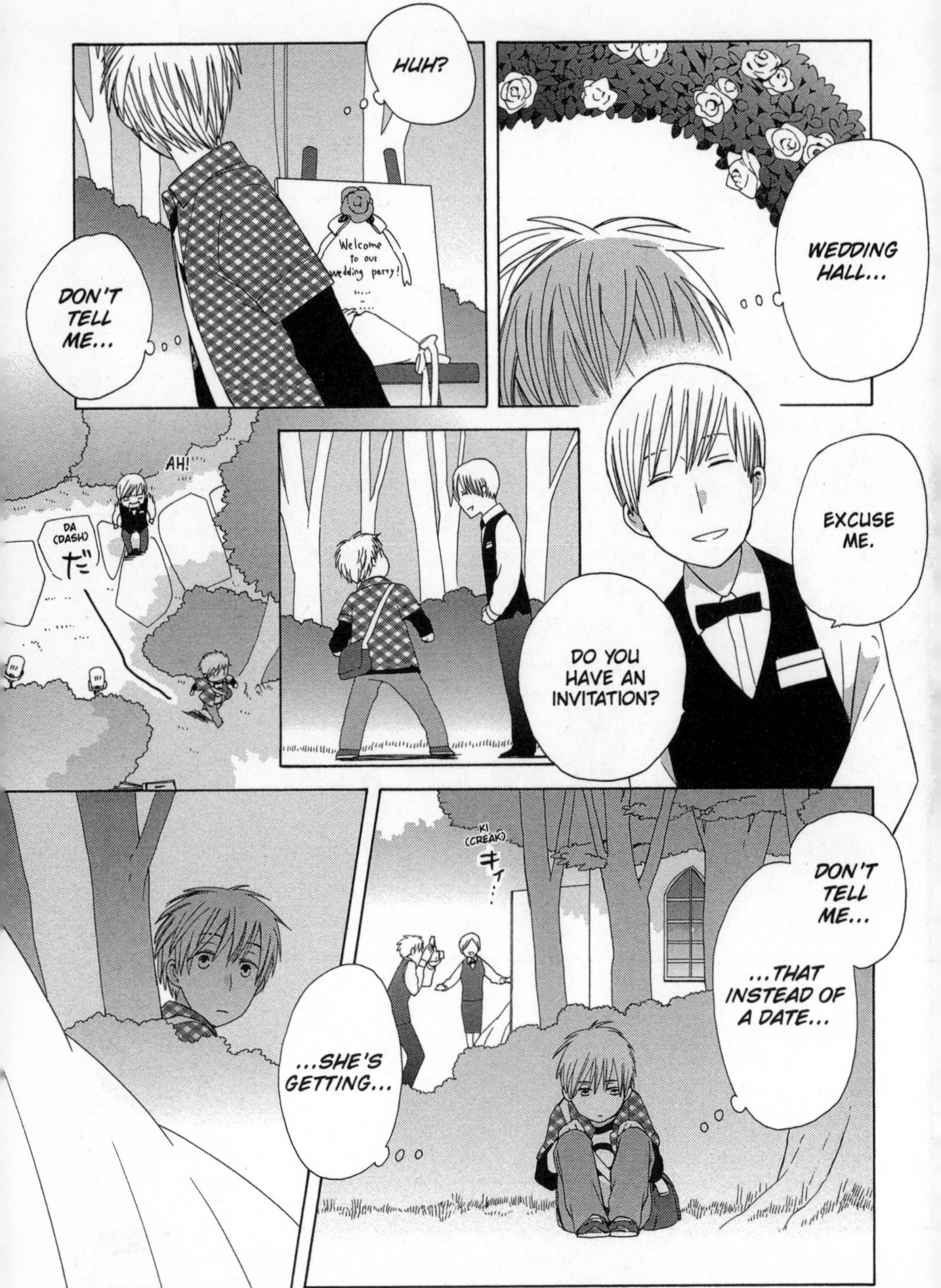
WEDDING HALL...
HUH?
Welcome to our wedding party!
DON'T TELL ME...
EXCUSE ME.
DO YOU HAVE AN INVITATION?
AH!
DA (DASH) だ
KI (CREAK) キィ...
DON'T TELL ME...
...THAT INSTEAD OF A DATE...
...SHE'S GETTING...

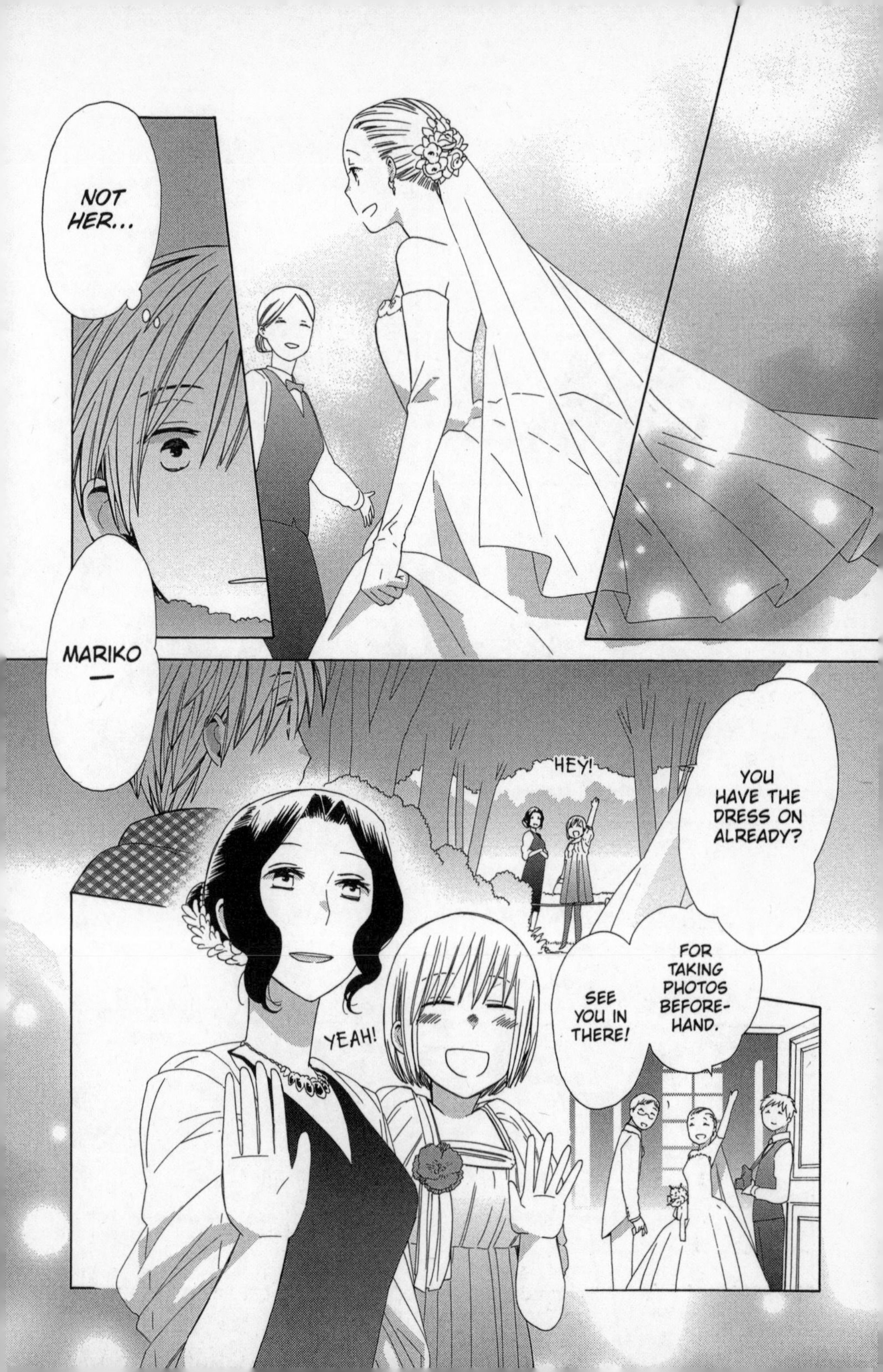
NOT HER...
MARIKO —
YOU HAVE THE DRESS ON ALREADY?
HEY!
FOR TAKING PHOTOS BEFORE-HAND.
SEE YOU IN THERE!
YEAH!

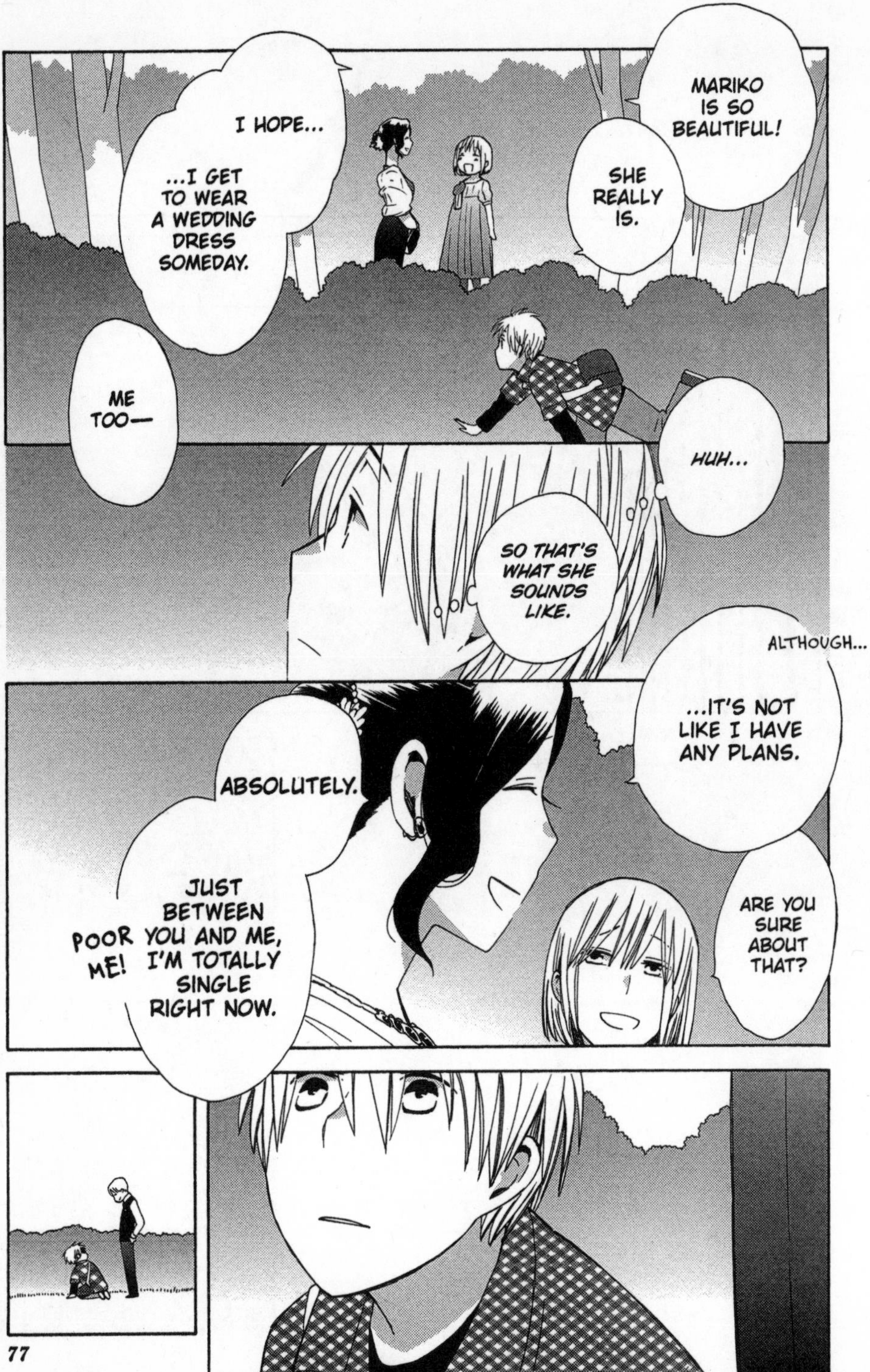

MARIKO IS SO BEAUTIFUL!
SHE REALLY IS.
I HOPE...
...I GET TO WEAR A WEDDING DRESS SOMEDAY.
ME TOO—
HUH...
SO THAT'S WHAT SHE SOUNDS LIKE.
ALTHOUGH...
...IT'S NOT LIKE I HAVE ANY PLANS.
ARE YOU SURE ABOUT THAT?
ABSOLUTELY.
JUST BETWEEN YOU AND ME, I'M TOTALLY SINGLE RIGHT NOW.
POOR ME!

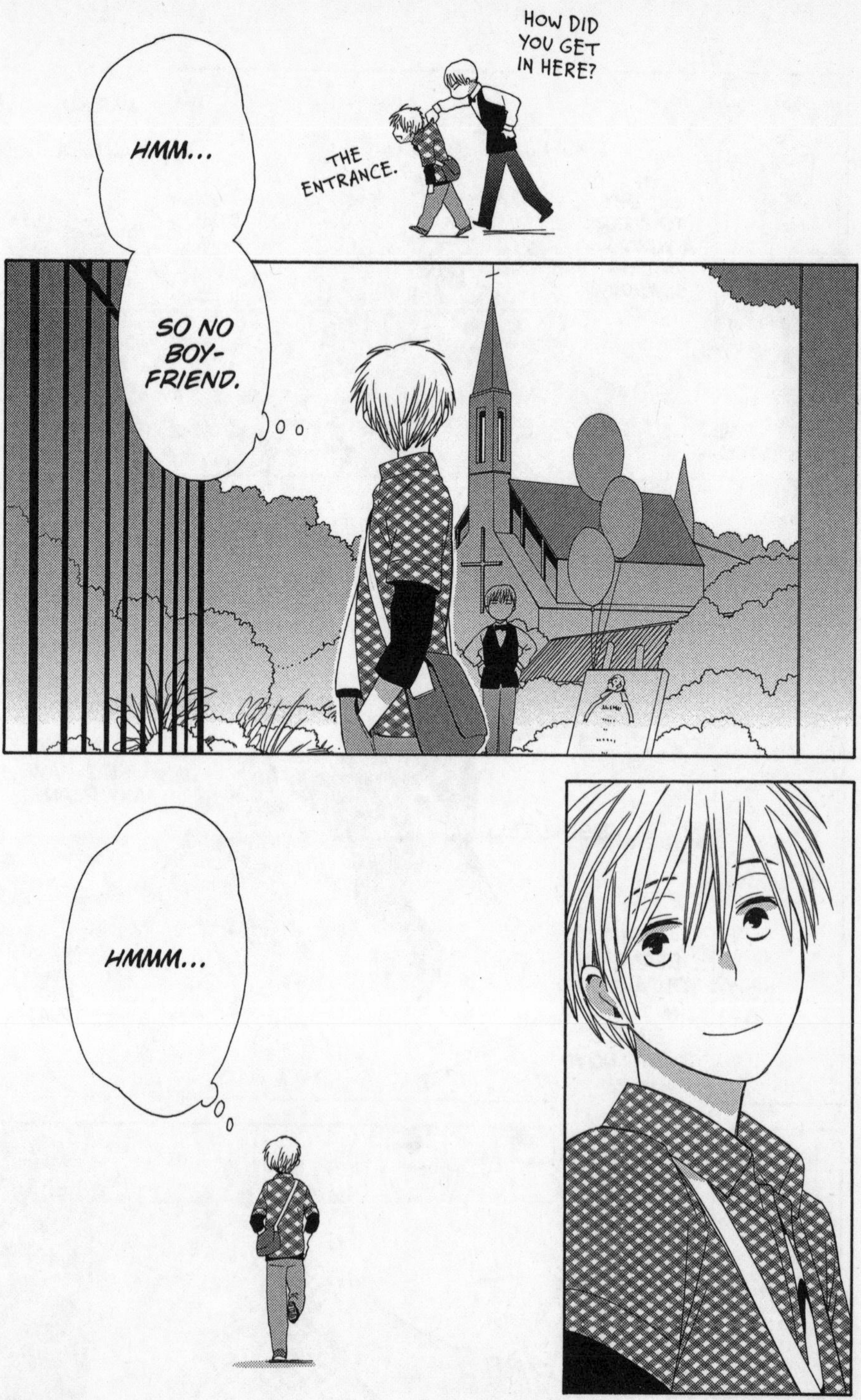
HOW DID YOU GET IN HERE?
THE ENTRANCE.
HMM...
SO NO BOY-FRIEND.
HMMM...

Fin

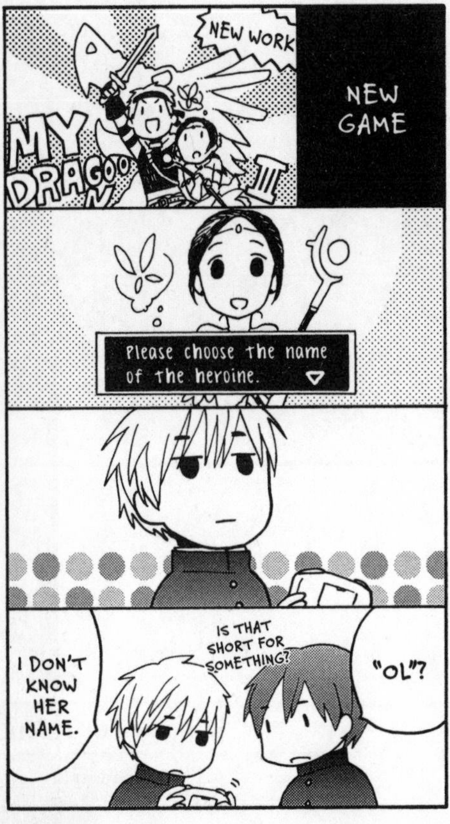
NEW GAME
NEW WORK
MY DRAGOON III
Please choose the name of the heroine.
"OL"?
IS THAT SHORT FOR SOMETHING?
I DON'T KNOW HER NAME.

Love at Fourteen

Fuka Mizutani

Love at Fourteen

[Chapter 23]

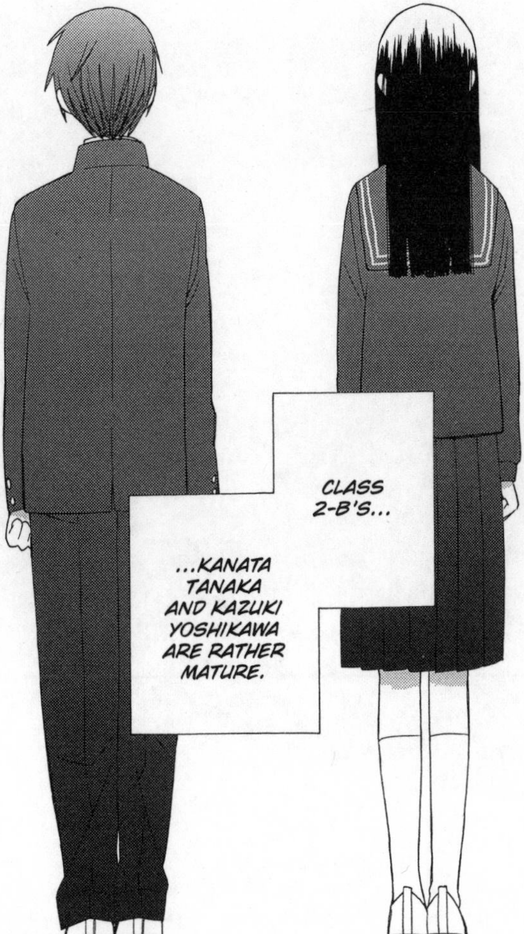
CLASS 2-B'S...
...KANATA TANAKA AND KAZUKI YOSHIKAWA ARE RATHER MATURE.

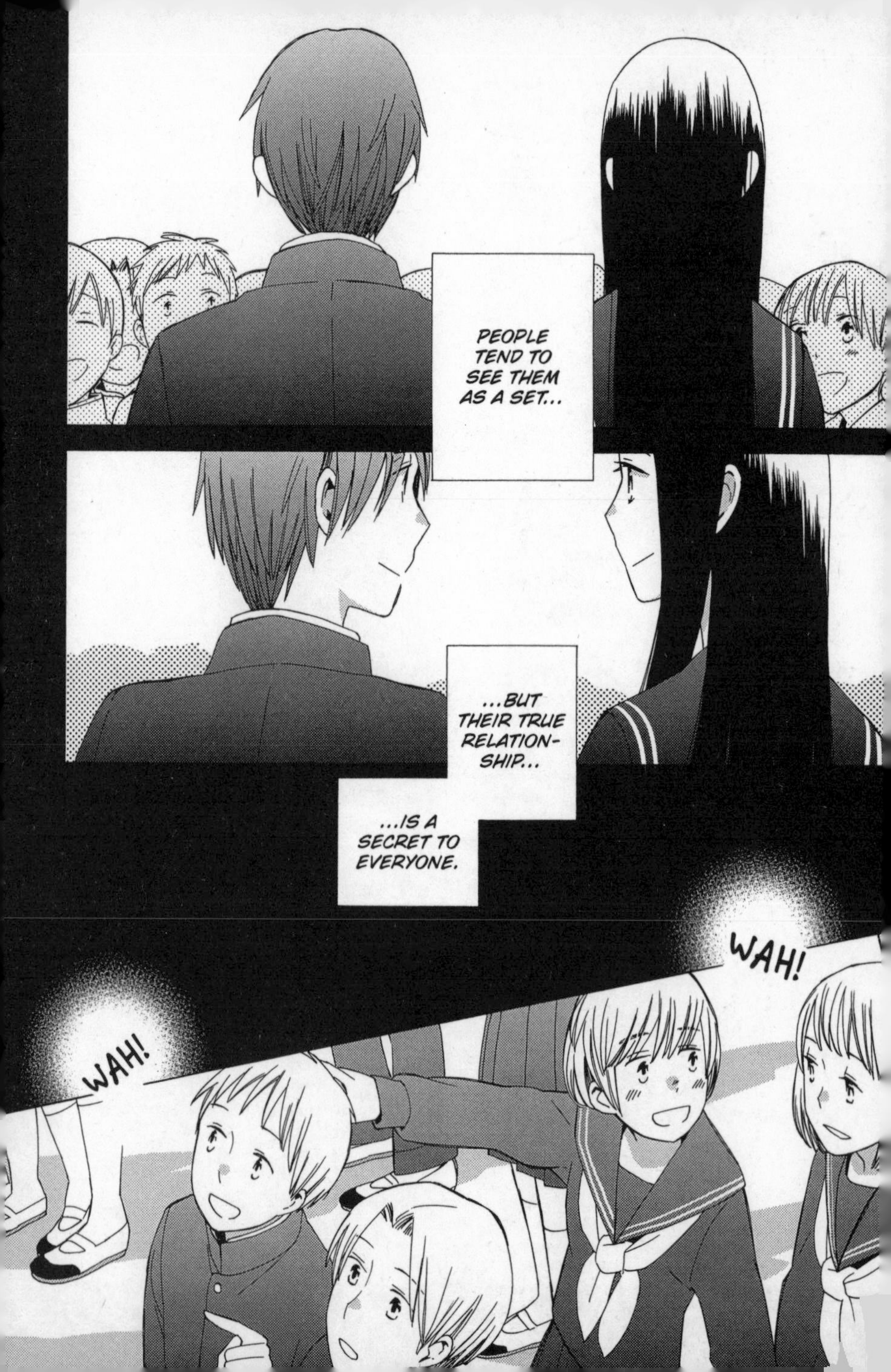
PEOPLE TEND TO SEE THEM AS A SET...
...BUT THEIR TRUE RELATION-SHIP...
...IS A SECRET TO EVERYONE.
WAH!
WAH!

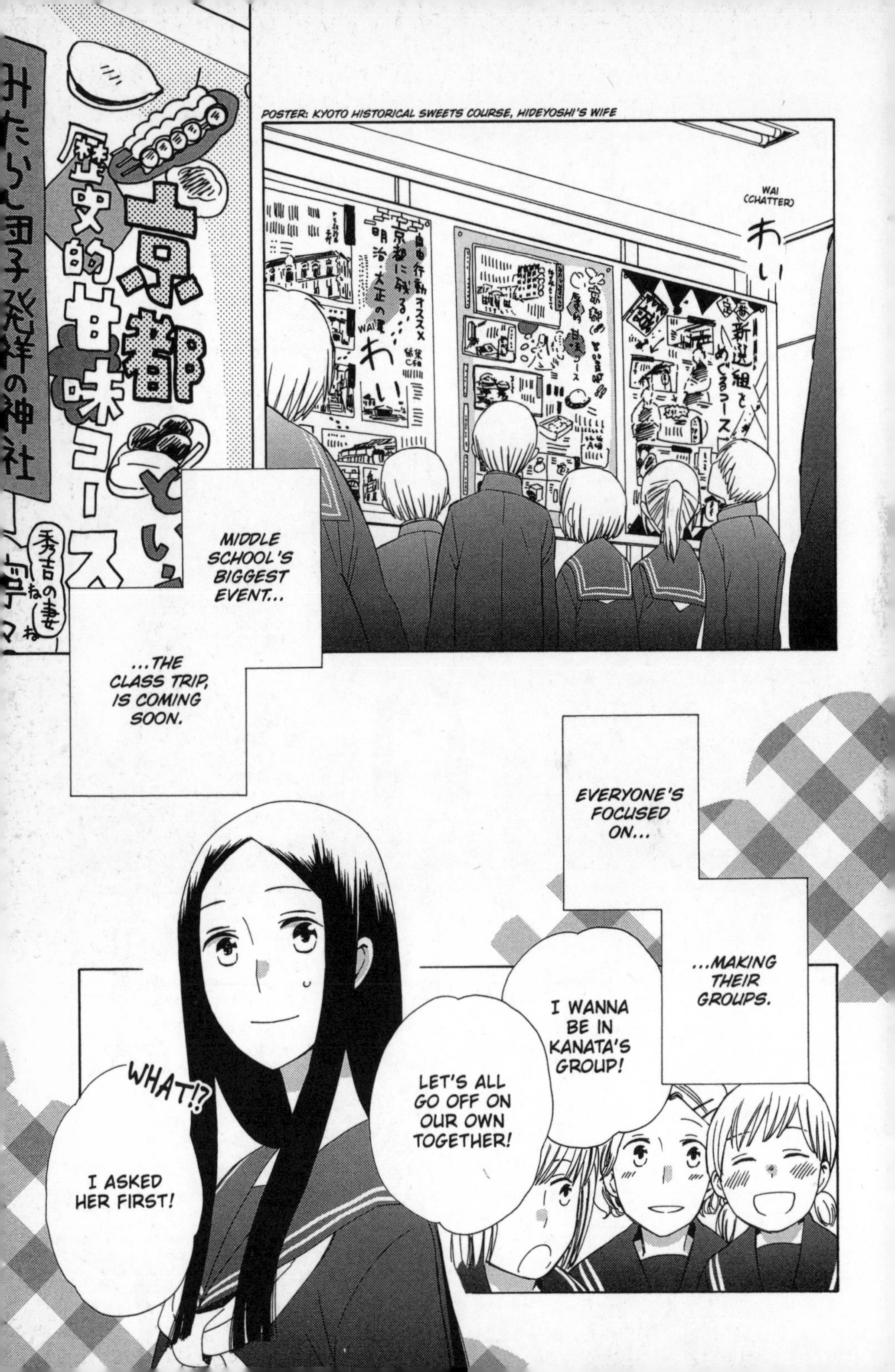
WAI (CHATTER)
わい
WAI
わい
新選組をめぐるコース
MIDDLE SCHOOL'S BIGGEST EVENT...
...THE CLASS TRIP, IS COMING SOON.
POSTER: KYOTO HISTORICAL SWEETS COURSE, HIDEYOSHI'S WIFE
京都歴史的甘味コース
秀吉の妻ねね
EVERYONE'S FOCUSED ON...
...MAKING THEIR GROUPS.
I WANNA BE IN KANATA'S GROUP!
LET'S ALL GO OFF ON OUR OWN TOGETHER!
WHAT!?
I ASKED HER FIRST!

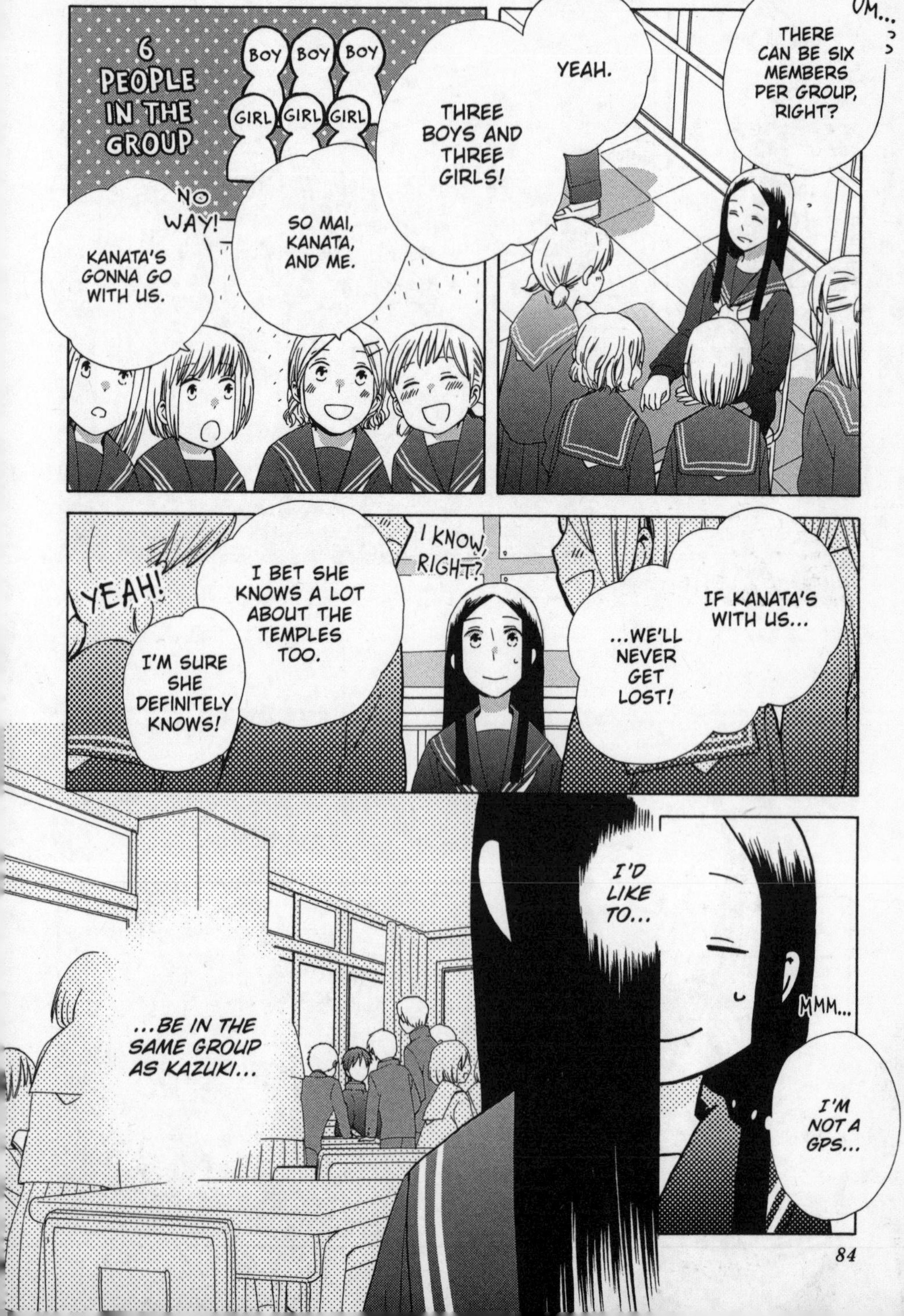
UM...?
THERE CAN BE SIX MEMBERS PER GROUP, RIGHT?
YEAH.
THREE BOYS AND THREE GIRLS!
6 PEOPLE IN THE GROUP
BOY BOY BOY
GIRL GIRL GIRL
SO MAI, KANATA, AND ME.
NO WAY!
KANATA'S GONNA GO WITH US.
IF KANATA'S WITH US...
...WE'LL NEVER GET LOST!
I KNOW, RIGHT?
I BET SHE KNOWS A LOT ABOUT THE TEMPLES TOO.
YEAH!
I'M SURE SHE DEFINITELY KNOWS!
MMM...
I'M NOT A GPS...
I'D LIKE TO...
...BE IN THE SAME GROUP AS KAZUKI...

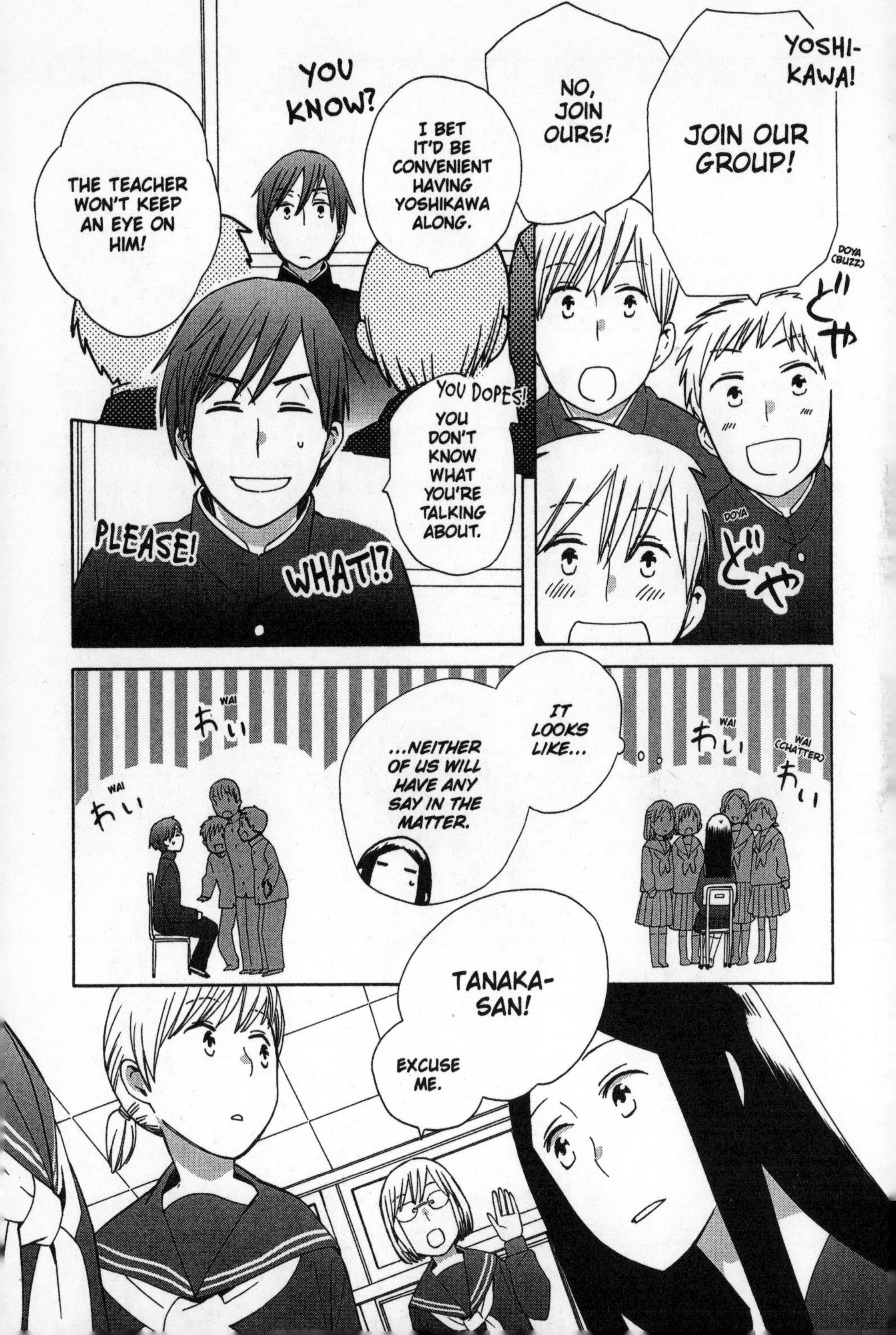
YOSHI-KAWA!
JOIN OUR GROUP!
DOYA (BUZZ)
NO, JOIN OURS!
DOYA
I BET IT'D BE CONVENIENT HAVING YOSHIKAWA ALONG.
YOU KNOW?
THE TEACHER WON'T KEEP AN EYE ON HIM!
YOU DOPES!
YOU DON'T KNOW WHAT YOU'RE TALKING ABOUT.
WHAT!?
PLEASE!
WAI (CHATTER)
WAI
IT LOOKS LIKE...
...NEITHER OF US WILL HAVE ANY SAY IN THE MATTER.
WAI
WAI
TANAKA-SAN!
EXCUSE ME.

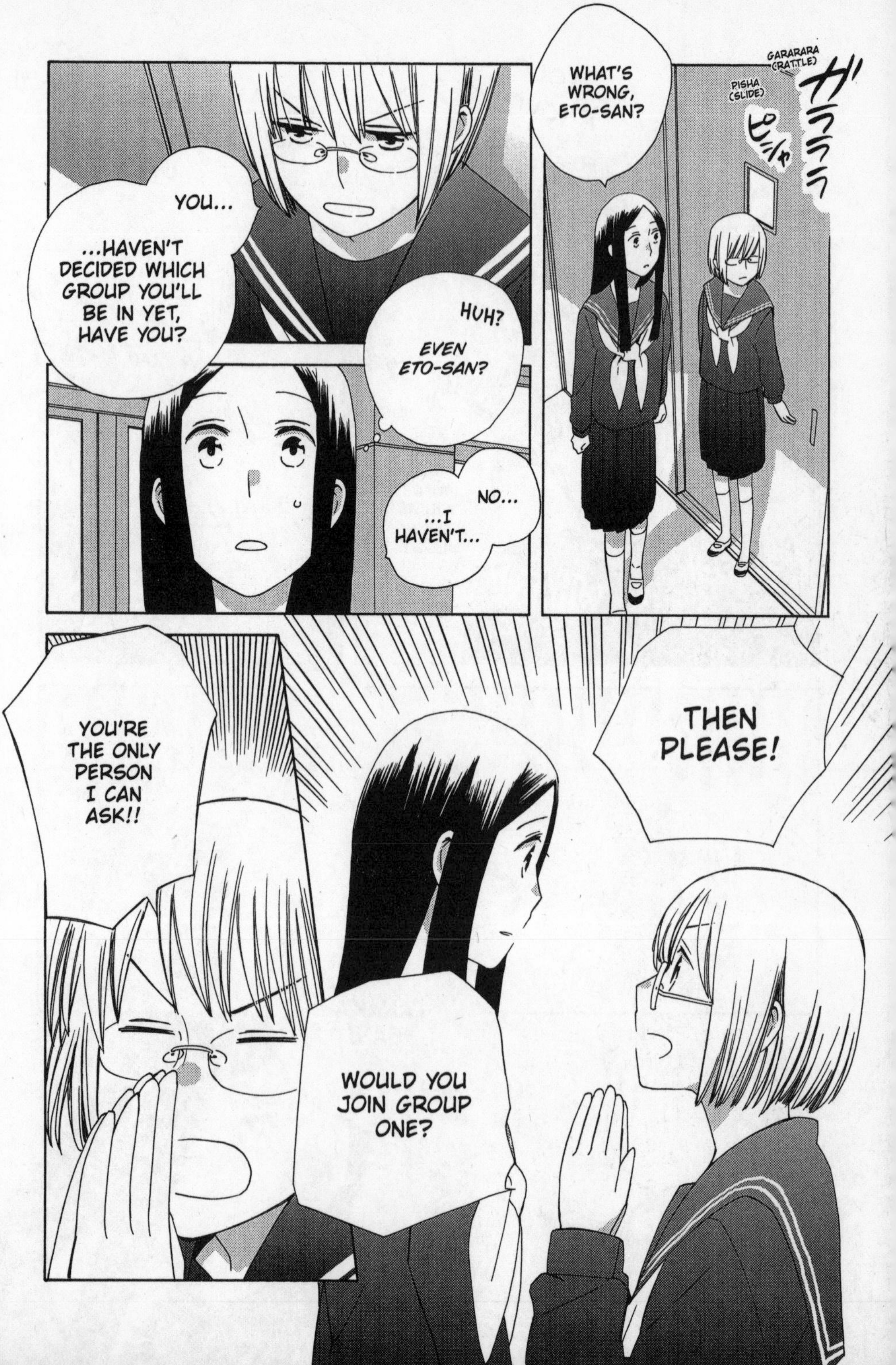

GARARARA (RATTLE)
ガラララ
PISHA (SLIDE)
ピシャ
WHAT'S WRONG, ETO-SAN?
YOU...
...HAVEN'T DECIDED WHICH GROUP YOU'LL BE IN YET, HAVE YOU?
HUH?
EVEN ETO-SAN?
NO...
...I HAVEN'T...
THEN PLEASE!
YOU'RE THE ONLY PERSON I CAN ASK!!
WOULD YOU JOIN GROUP ONE?

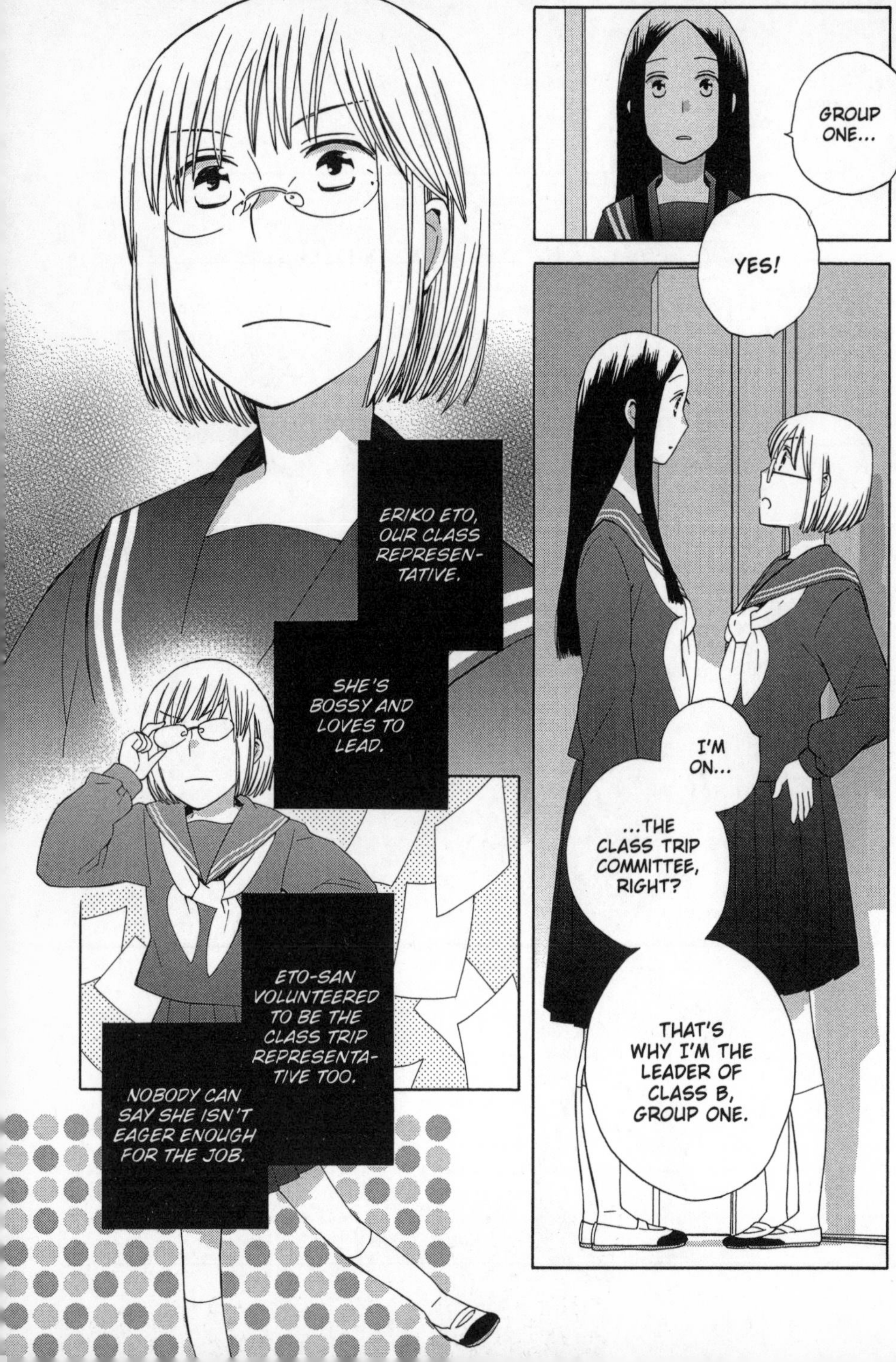
GROUP ONE...
YES!
I'M ON...
...THE CLASS TRIP COMMITTEE, RIGHT?
THAT'S WHY I'M THE LEADER OF CLASS B, GROUP ONE.
ERIKO ETO, OUR CLASS REPRESEN-TATIVE.
SHE'S BOSSY AND LOVES TO LEAD.
ETO-SAN VOLUNTEERED TO BE THE CLASS TRIP REPRESENTA-TIVE TOO.
NOBODY CAN SAY SHE ISN'T EAGER ENOUGH FOR THE JOB.

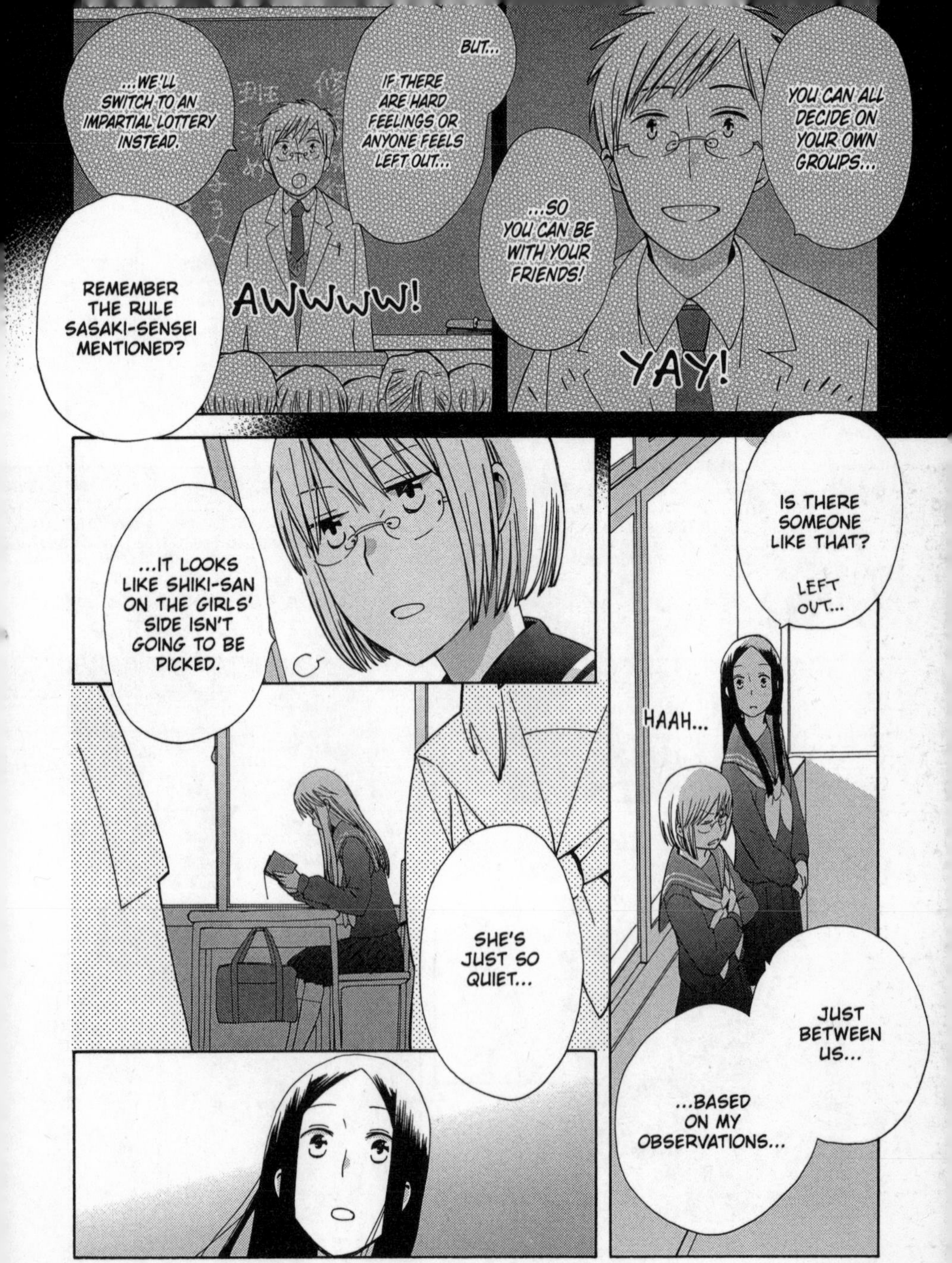
YOU CAN ALL DECIDE ON YOUR OWN GROUPS...
...SO YOU CAN BE WITH YOUR FRIENDS!
YAY!
BUT...
IF THERE ARE HARD FEELINGS OR ANYONE FEELS LEFT OUT...
...WE'LL SWITCH TO AN IMPARTIAL LOTTERY INSTEAD.
AWWWW!
IS THERE SOMEONE LIKE THAT?
LEFT OUT...
HAAH...
JUST BETWEEN US...
...BASED ON MY OBSERVATIONS...
REMEMBER THE RULE SASAKI-SENSEI MENTIONED?
...IT LOOKS LIKE SHIKI-SAN ON THE GIRLS' SIDE ISN'T GOING TO BE PICKED.
SHE'S JUST SO QUIET...

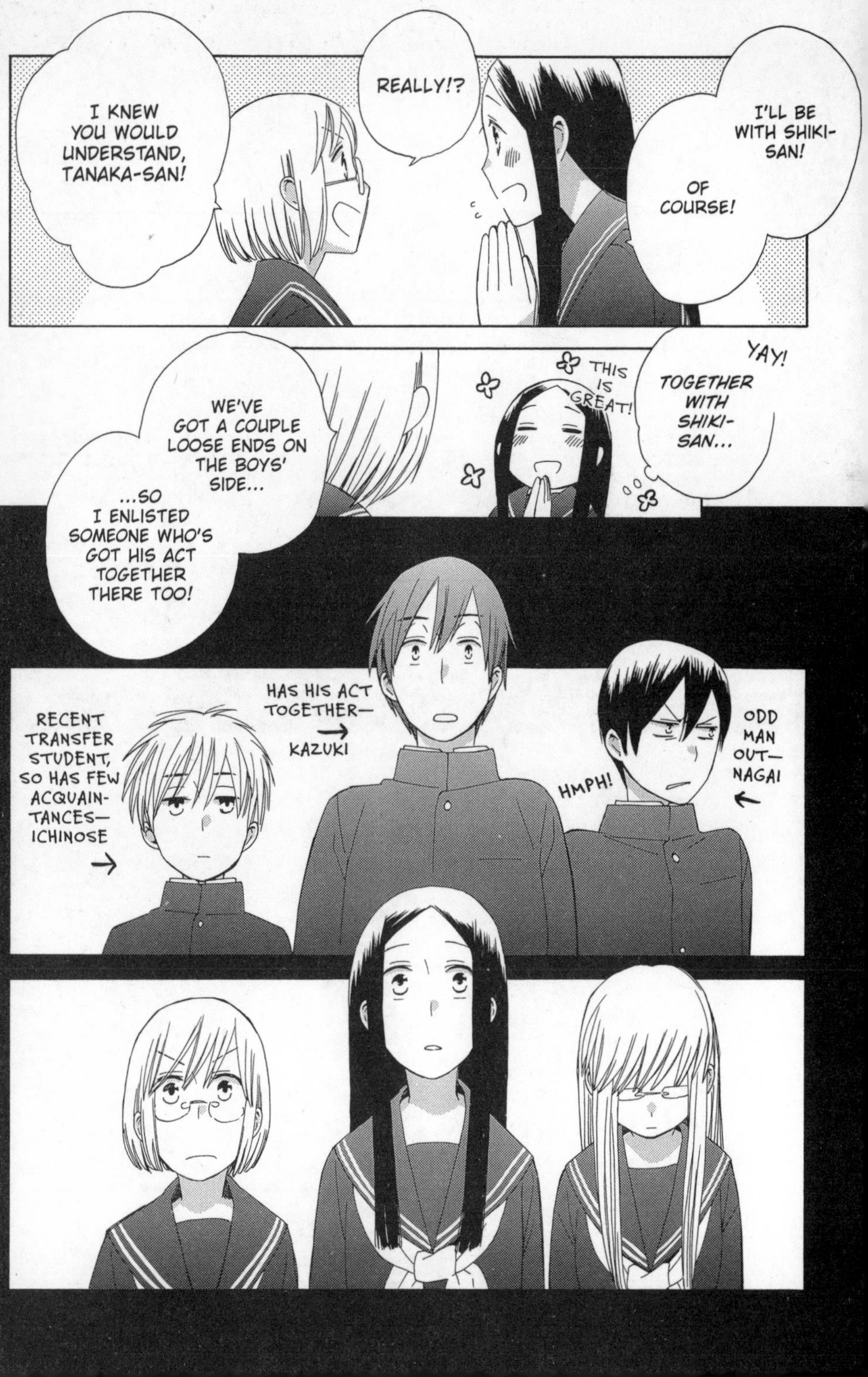
I'LL BE WITH SHIKI-SAN!
OF COURSE!
REALLY!?
I KNEW YOU WOULD UNDERSTAND, TANAKA-SAN!
YAY!
TOGETHER WITH SHIKI-SAN...
THIS IS GREAT!
WE'VE GOT A COUPLE LOOSE ENDS ON THE BOYS' SIDE...
...SO I ENLISTED SOMEONE WHO'S GOT HIS ACT TOGETHER THERE TOO!
ODD MAN OUT—NAGAI
HMPH!
HAS HIS ACT TOGETHER—KAZUKI
RECENT TRANSFER STUDENT, SO HAS FEW ACQUAINTANCES—ICHINOSE

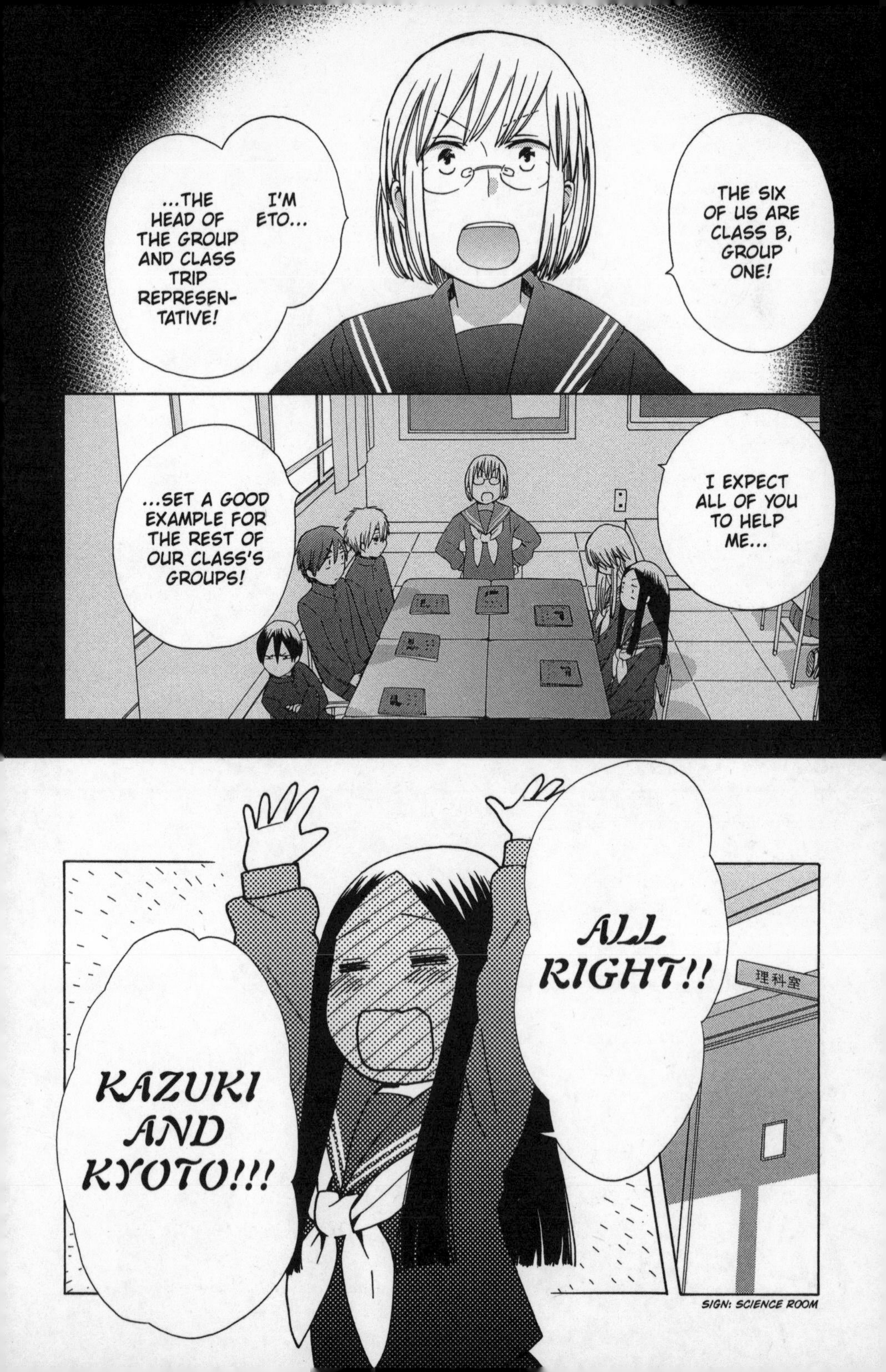
THE SIX OF US ARE CLASS B, GROUP ONE!
I'M ETO...
...THE HEAD OF THE GROUP AND CLASS TRIP REPRESEN-TATIVE!
I EXPECT ALL OF YOU TO HELP ME...
...SET A GOOD EXAMPLE FOR THE REST OF OUR CLASS'S GROUPS!
ALL RIGHT!!
KAZUKI AND KYOTO!!!
理科室
SIGN: SCIENCE ROOM

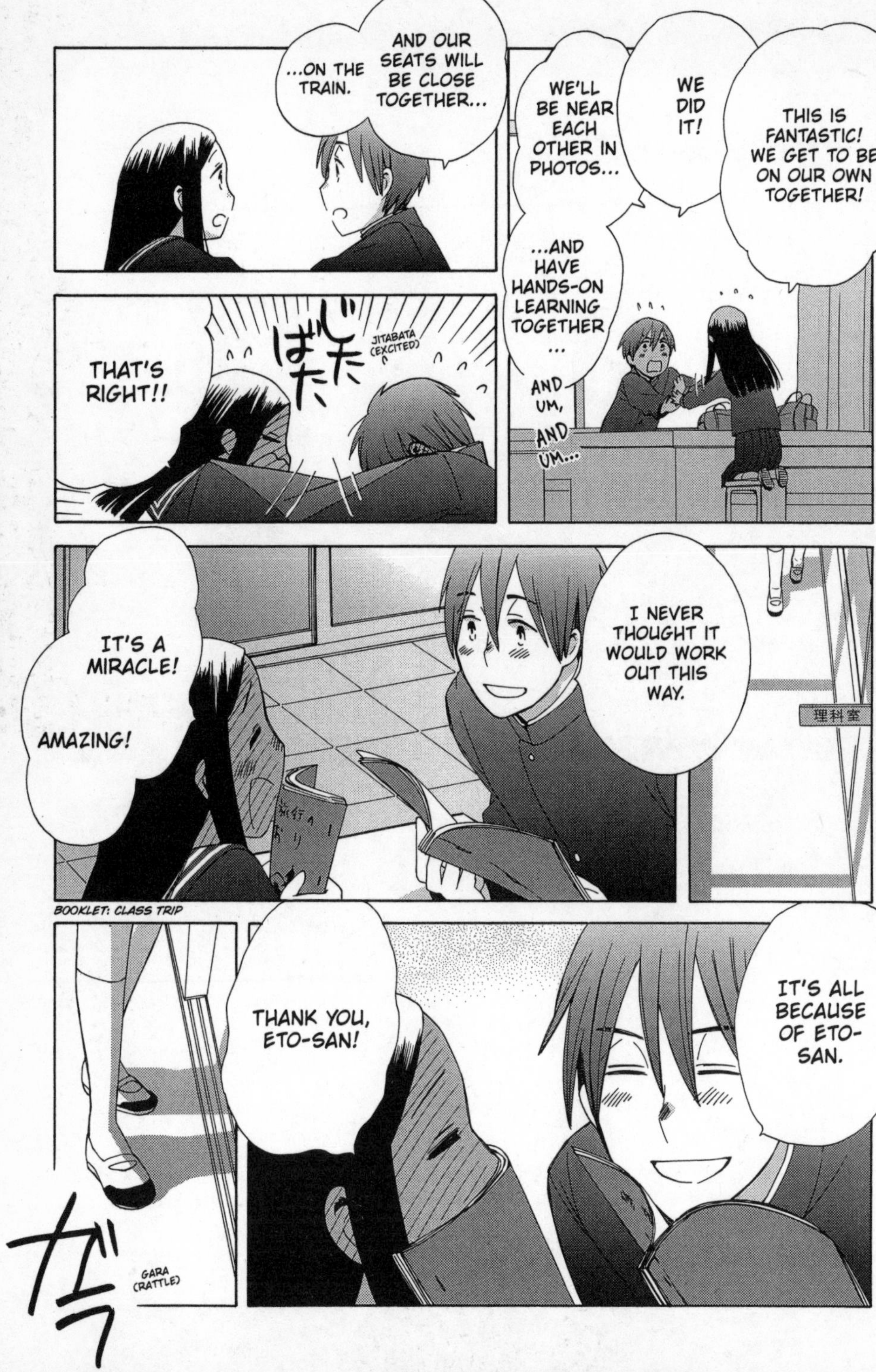
THIS IS FANTASTIC! WE GET TO BE ON OUR OWN TOGETHER!
WE DID IT!
WE'LL BE NEAR EACH OTHER IN PHOTOS...
...AND HAVE HANDS-ON LEARNING TOGETHER ...
AND UM, AND UM...
AND OUR SEATS WILL BE CLOSE TOGETHER...
...ON THE TRAIN.
じたばた
JITABATA (EXCITED)
THAT'S RIGHT!!
I NEVER THOUGHT IT WOULD WORK OUT THIS WAY.
理科室
IT'S A MIRACLE!
AMAZING!
BOOKLET: CLASS TRIP
IT'S ALL BECAUSE OF ETO-SAN.
THANK YOU, ETO-SAN!
ガラ
GARA (RATTLE)

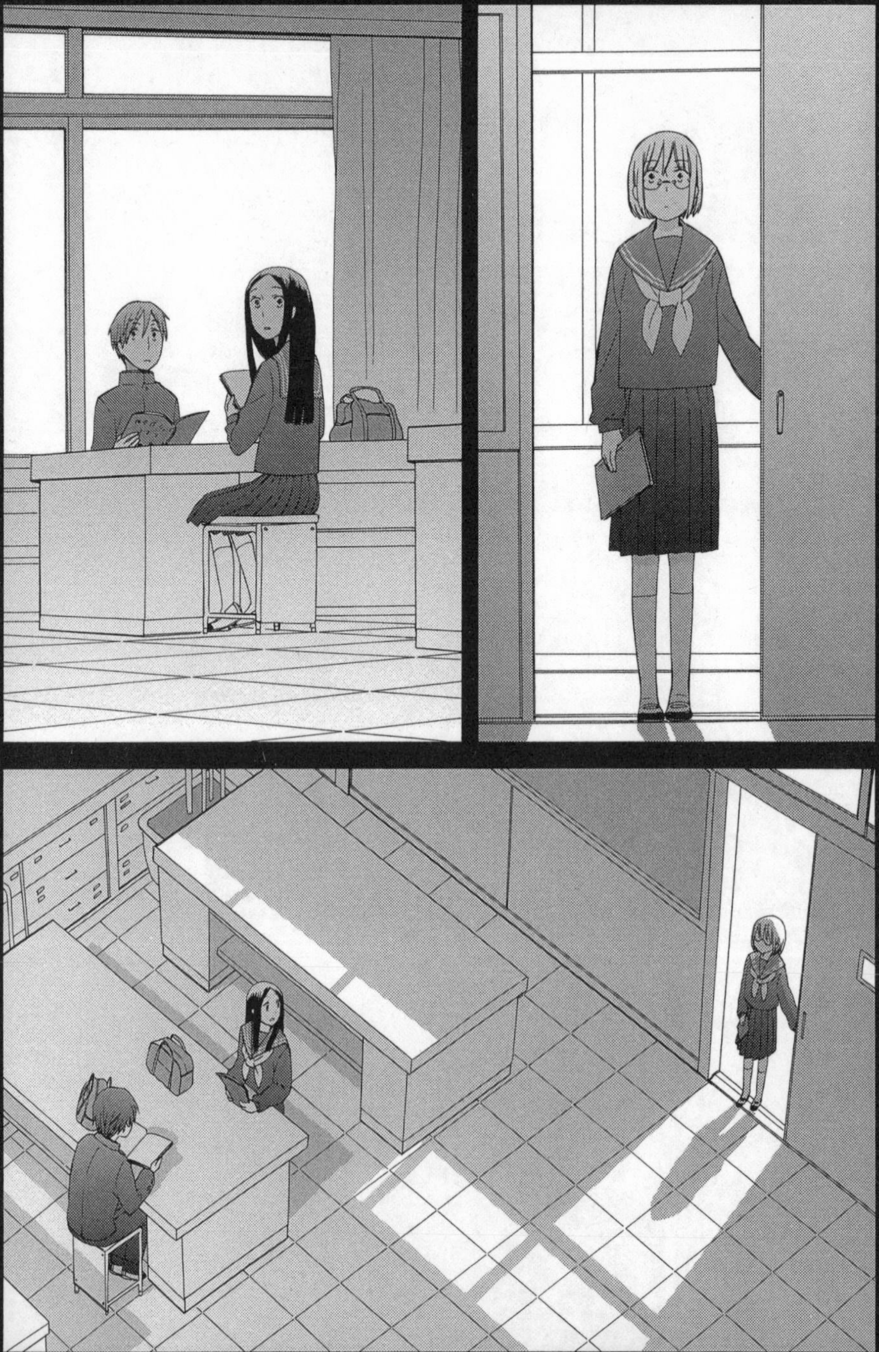

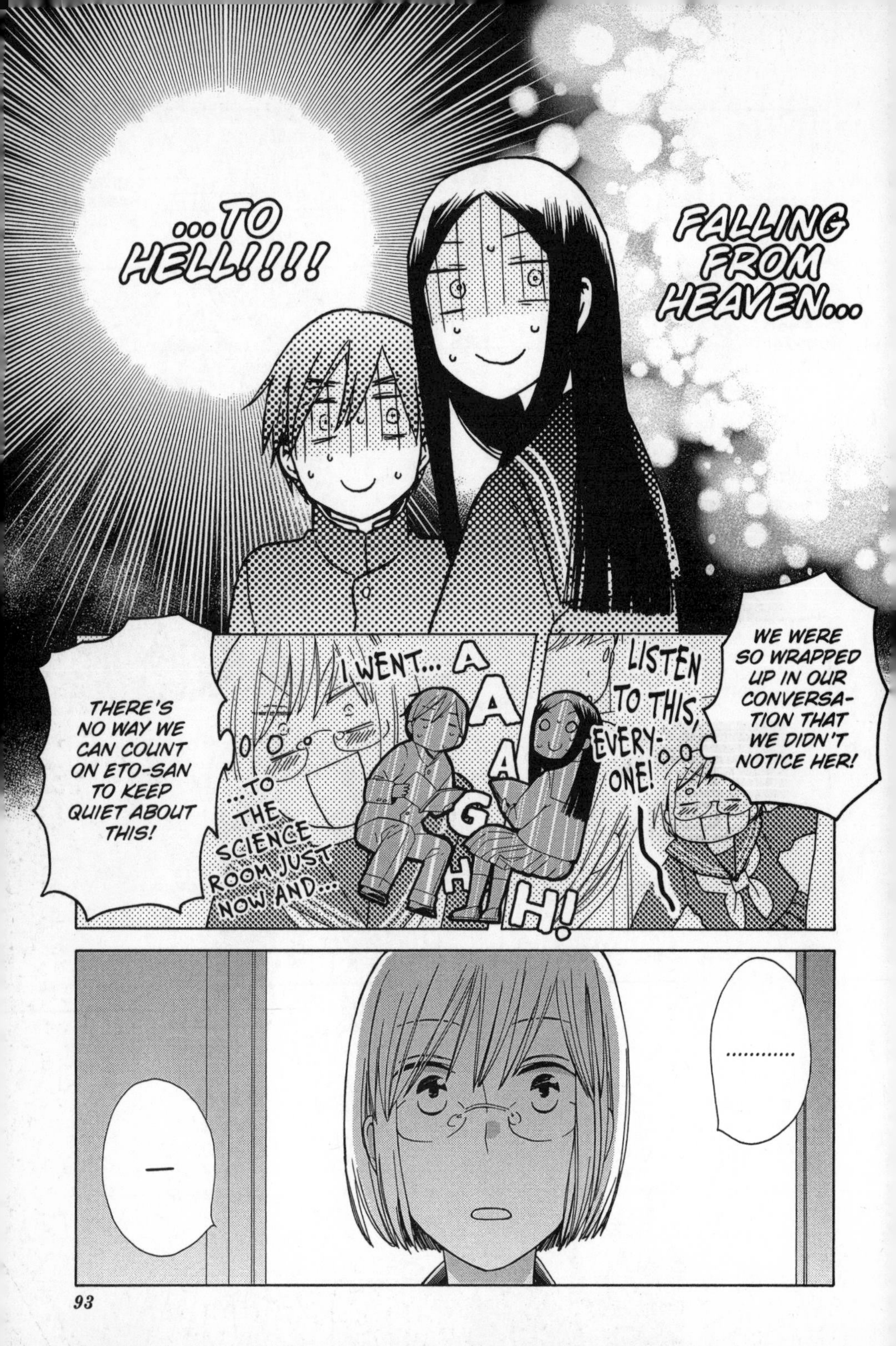
FALLING FROM HEAVEN...
...TO HELL!!!!
WE WERE SO WRAPPED UP IN OUR CONVERSA-TION THAT WE DIDN'T NOTICE HER!
LISTEN TO THIS, EVERY-ONE!
I WENT... ...TO THE SCIENCE ROOM JUST NOW AND...
AAAGHH!
THERE'S NO WAY WE CAN COUNT ON ETO-SAN TO KEEP QUIET ABOUT THIS!
....
—

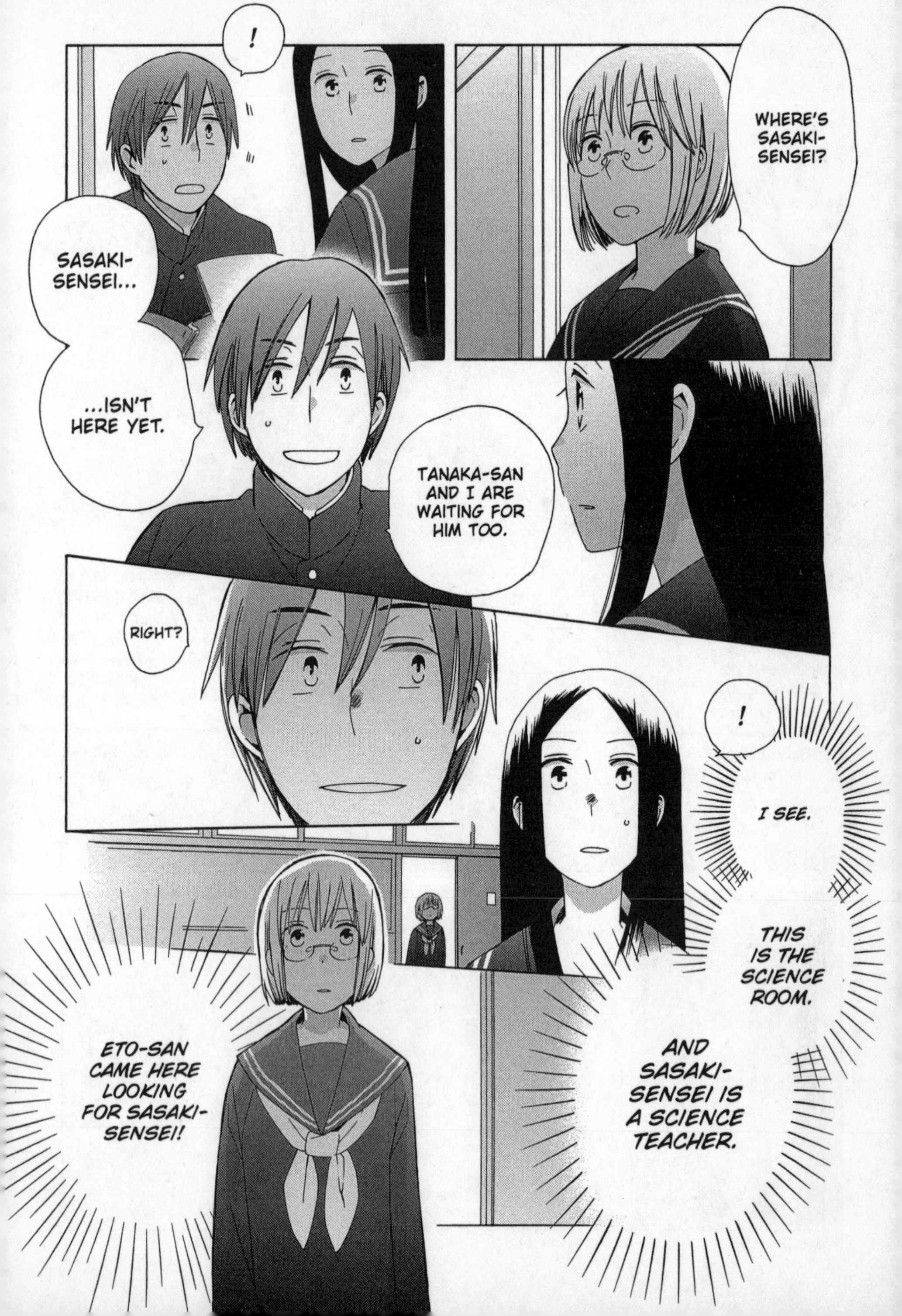
WHERE'S SASAKI-SENSEI?
!
SASAKI-SENSEI...
...ISN'T HERE YET.
TANAKA-SAN AND I ARE WAITING FOR HIM TOO.
RIGHT?
!
I SEE.
THIS IS THE SCIENCE ROOM.
AND SASAKI-SENSEI IS A SCIENCE TEACHER.
ETO-SAN CAME HERE LOOKING FOR SASAKI-SENSEI!

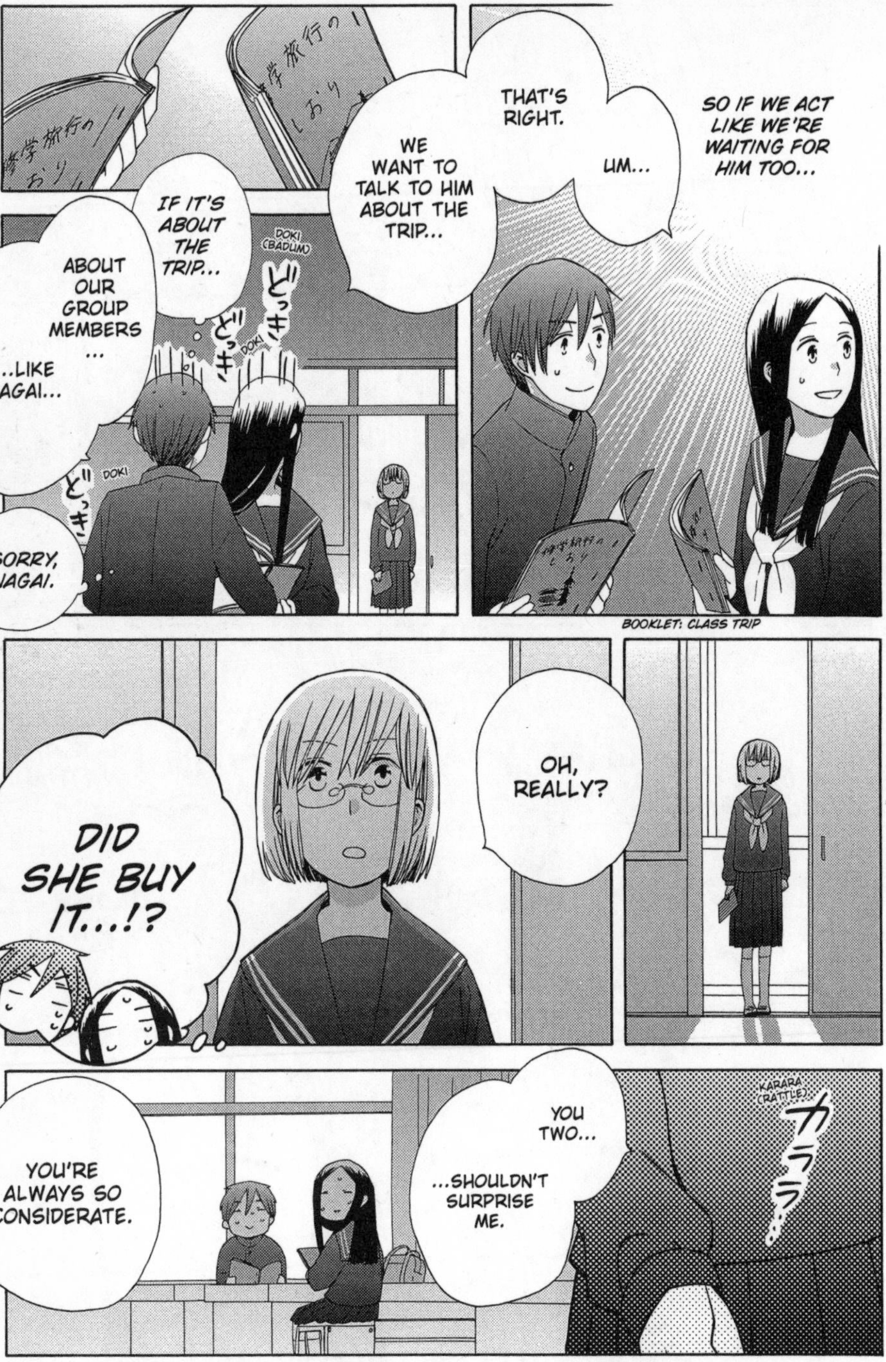
SO IF WE ACT LIKE WE'RE WAITING FOR HIM TOO...
UM...
THAT'S RIGHT.
WE WANT TO TALK TO HIM ABOUT THE TRIP...
BOOKLET: CLASS TRIP
IF IT'S ABOUT THE TRIP...
DOKI (BADUM)
DOKI
ABOUT OUR GROUP MEMBERS ...
...LIKE NAGAI...
DOKI
SORRY, NAGAI.
OH, REALLY?
DID SHE BUY IT...!?
KARARA (RATTLE)
YOU TWO...
...SHOULDN'T SURPRISE ME.
YOU'RE ALWAYS SO CONSIDERATE.

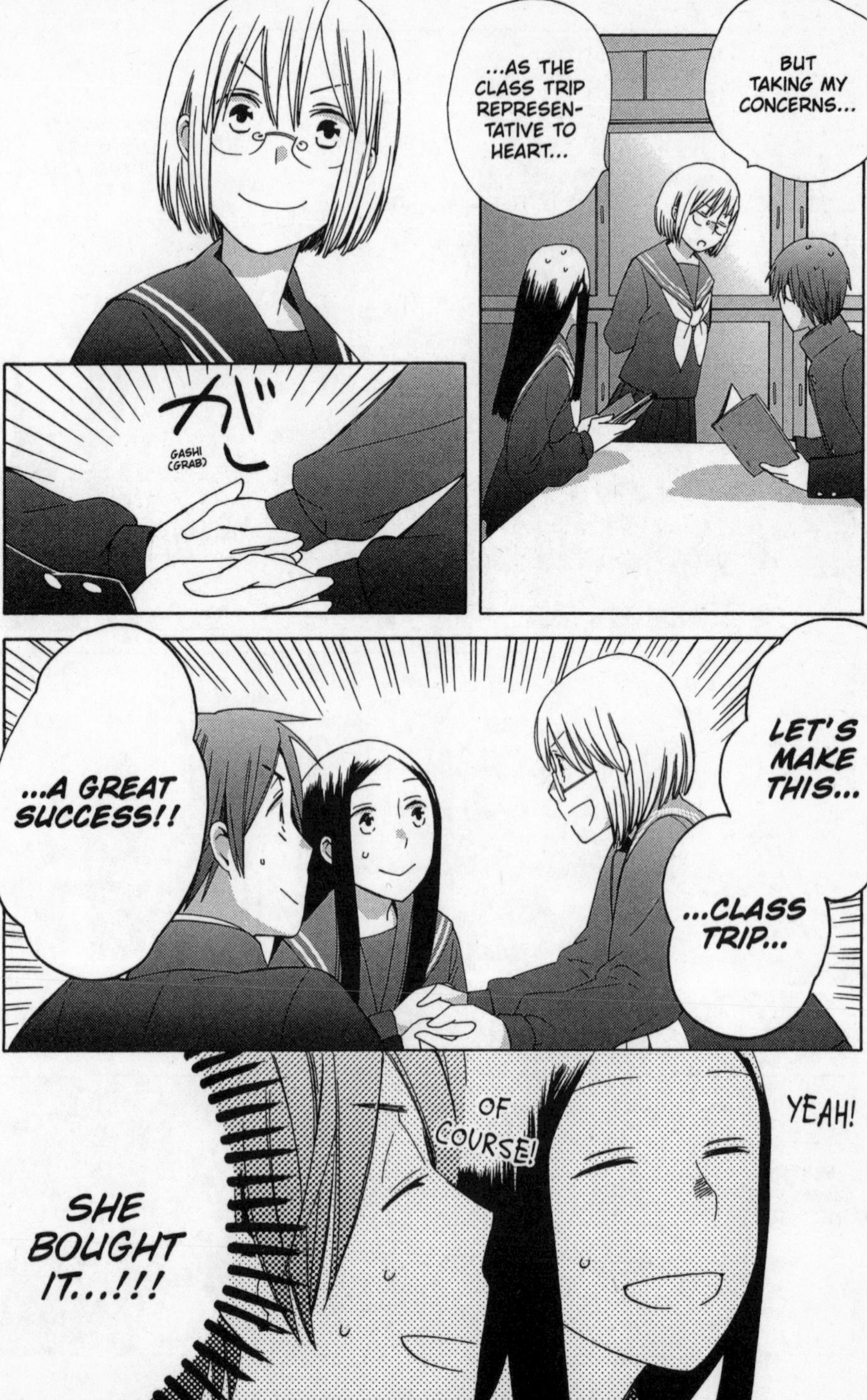
BUT TAKING MY CONCERNS...
...AS THE CLASS TRIP REPRESEN-TATIVE TO HEART...
がし
GASHI (GRAB)
LET'S MAKE THIS...
...CLASS TRIP...
...A GREAT SUCCESS!!
YEAH!
OF COURSE!
SHE BOUGHT IT...!!!

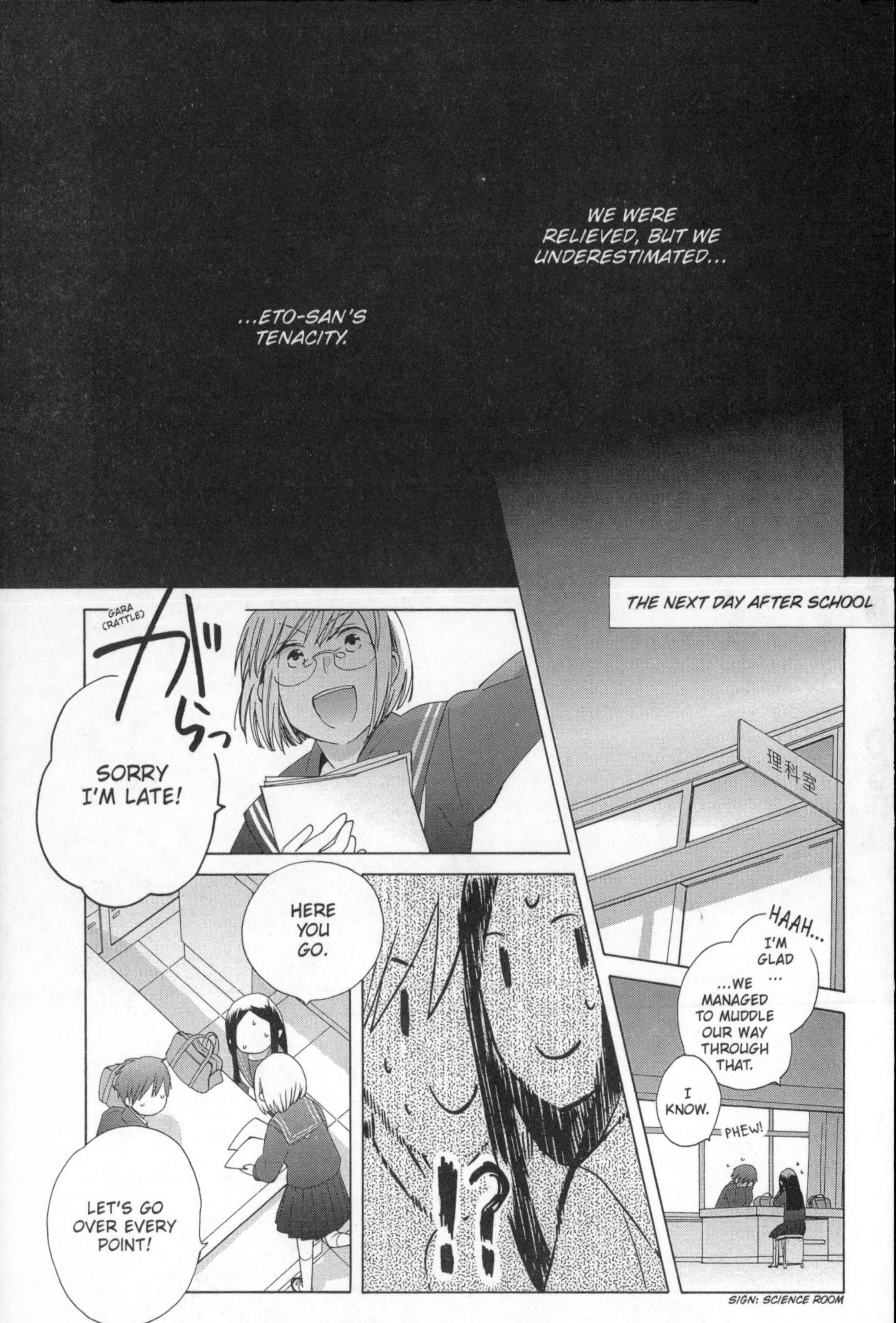
WE WERE RELIEVED, BUT WE UNDERESTIMATED...
...ETO-SAN'S TENACITY.
THE NEXT DAY AFTER SCHOOL
理科室
HAAH...
I'M GLAD...
...WE MANAGED TO MUDDLE OUR WAY THROUGH THAT.
I KNOW.
PHEW!
がらっ
GARA (RATTLE)
SORRY I'M LATE!
!?
HERE YOU GO.
LET'S GO OVER EVERY POINT!

SIGN: SCIENCE ROOM

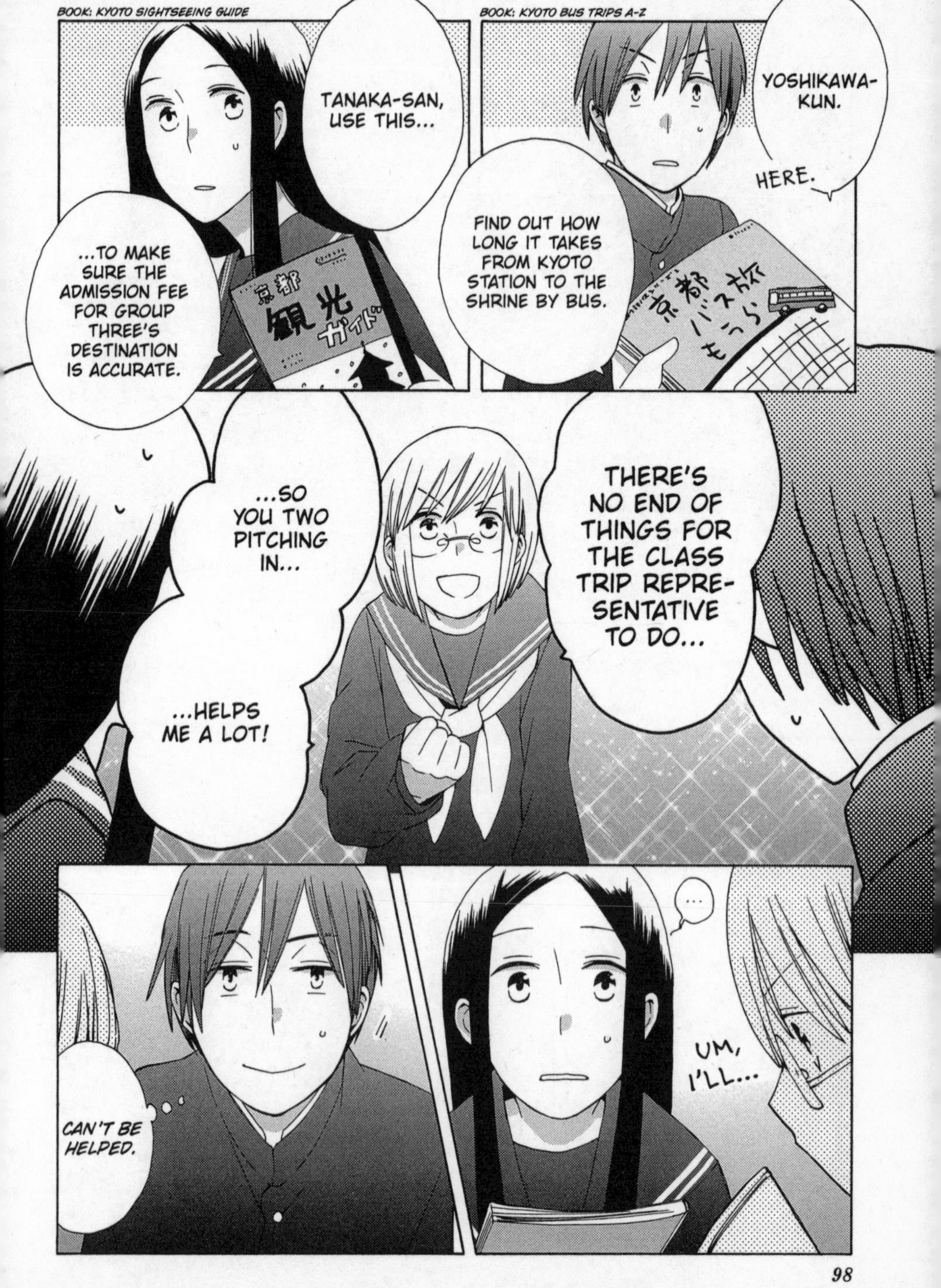
BOOK: KYOTO BUS TRIPS A-Z
YOSHIKAWA-KUN.
HERE.
FIND OUT HOW LONG IT TAKES FROM KYOTO STATION TO THE SHRINE BY BUS.
BOOK: KYOTO SIGHTSEEING GUIDE
TANAKA-SAN, USE THIS...
...TO MAKE SURE THE ADMISSION FEE FOR GROUP THREE'S DESTINATION IS ACCURATE.
THERE'S NO END OF THINGS FOR THE CLASS TRIP REPRESENTATIVE TO DO...
...SO YOU TWO PITCHING IN...
...HELPS ME A LOT!
...
UM, I'LL...
CAN'T BE HELPED.

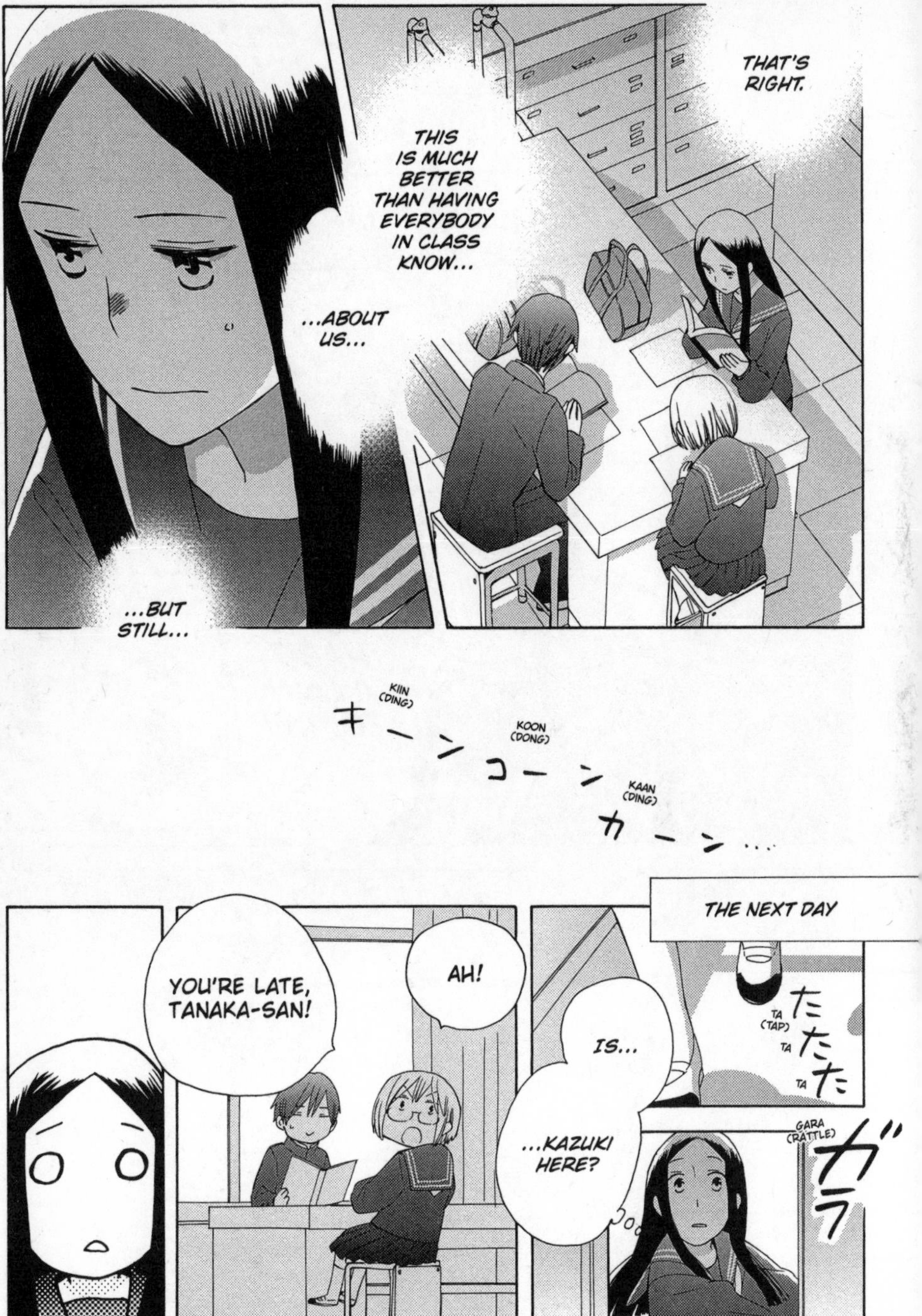
THAT'S RIGHT.
THIS IS MUCH BETTER THAN HAVING EVERYBODY IN CLASS KNOW...
...ABOUT US...
...BUT STILL...
KIIN (DING) キーン
KOON (DONG) コーン
KAAN (DING) カーン...
THE NEXT DAY
TA (TAP) TA TA たたた
GARA (RATTLE) ガラ
IS...
...KAZUKI HERE?
AH!
YOU'RE LATE, TANAKA-SAN!

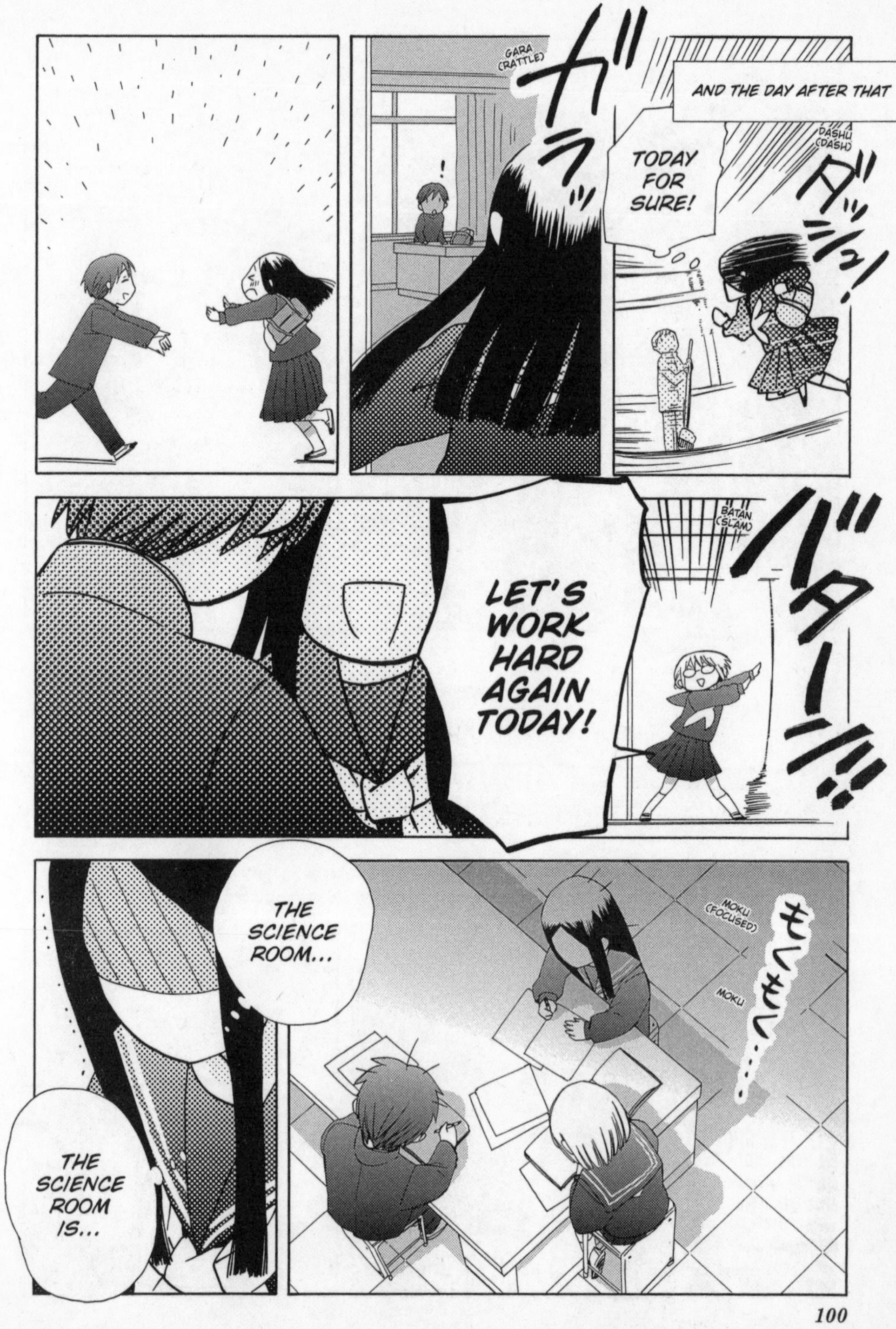
AND THE DAY AFTER THAT
TODAY FOR SURE!
DASHU (DASH)
ダッシュ!
GARA (RATTLE)
ガラッ
!
BATAN (SLAM)
バターン!!
LET'S WORK HARD AGAIN TODAY!
MOKU (FOCUSED)
もくもく…
MOKU
THE SCIENCE ROOM...
THE SCIENCE ROOM IS...

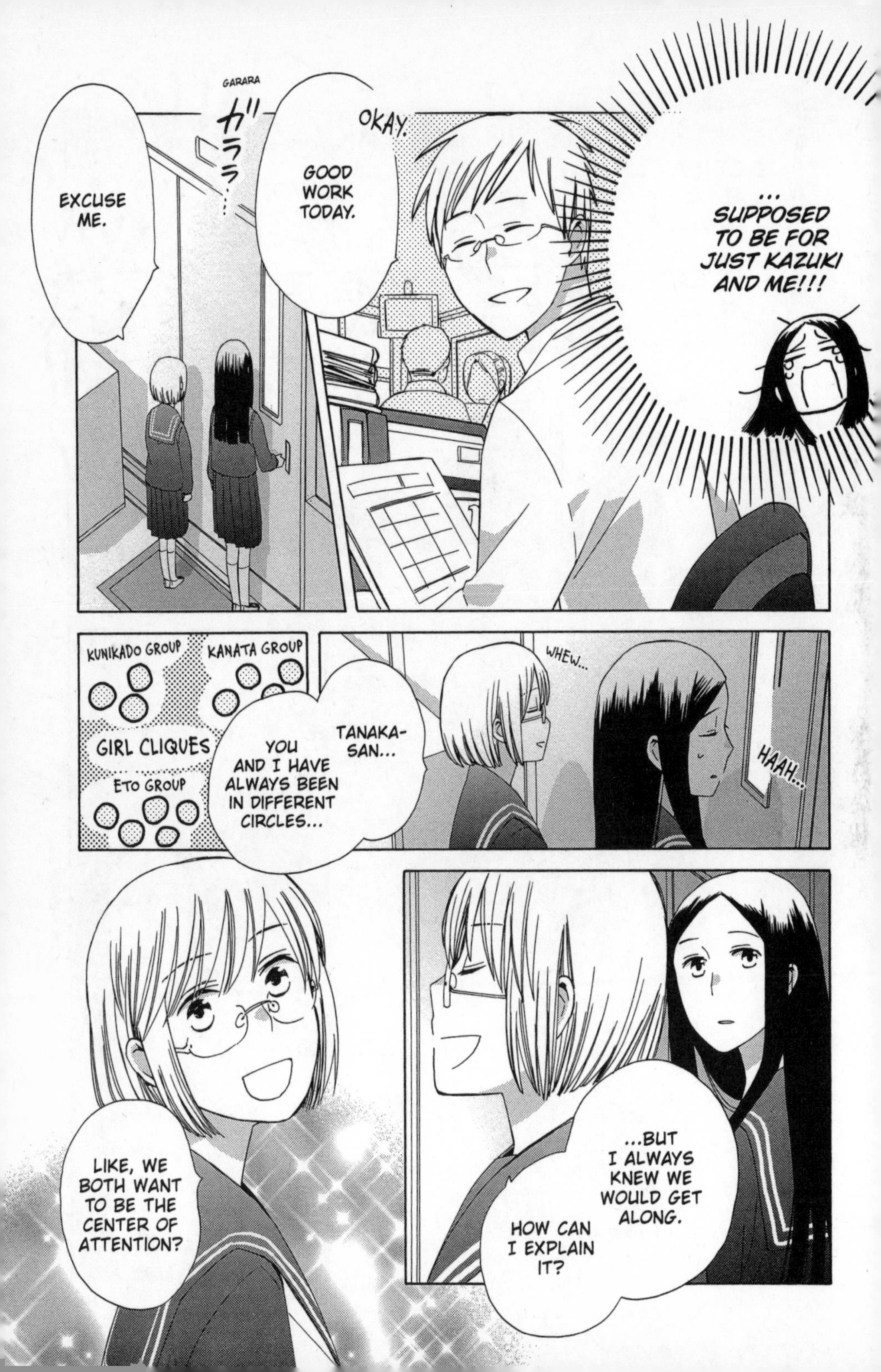
...SUPPOSED TO BE FOR JUST KAZUKI AND ME!!!
OKAY.
GOOD WORK TODAY.
GARARA
ガララ…
EXCUSE ME.
WHEW...
HAAH...
TANAKA-SAN...
YOU AND I HAVE ALWAYS BEEN IN DIFFERENT CIRCLES...
KUNIKADO GROUP
KANATA GROUP
GIRL CLIQUES
ETO GROUP
...BUT I ALWAYS KNEW WE WOULD GET ALONG.
HOW CAN I EXPLAIN IT?
LIKE, WE BOTH WANT TO BE THE CENTER OF ATTENTION?

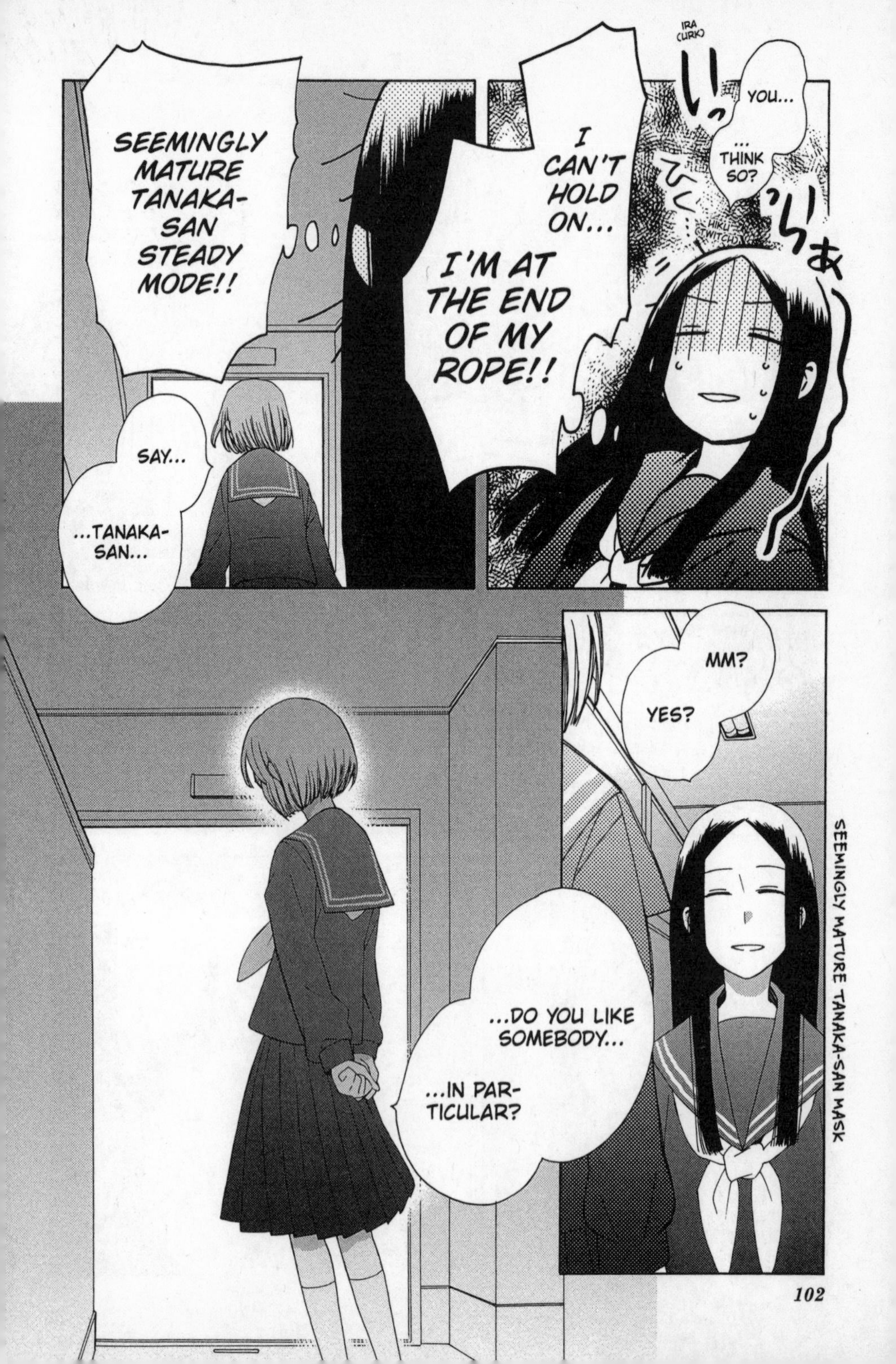
IRA (URK)
YOU... ...THINK SO?
HIKU (TWITCH)
I CAN'T HOLD ON...
I'M AT THE END OF MY ROPE!!
SEEMINGLY MATURE TANAKA-SAN STEADY MODE!!
SAY... ...TANAKA-SAN...
MM? YES?
SEEMINGLY MATURE TANAKA-SAN MASK
...DO YOU LIKE SOMEBODY... ...IN PARTICULAR?

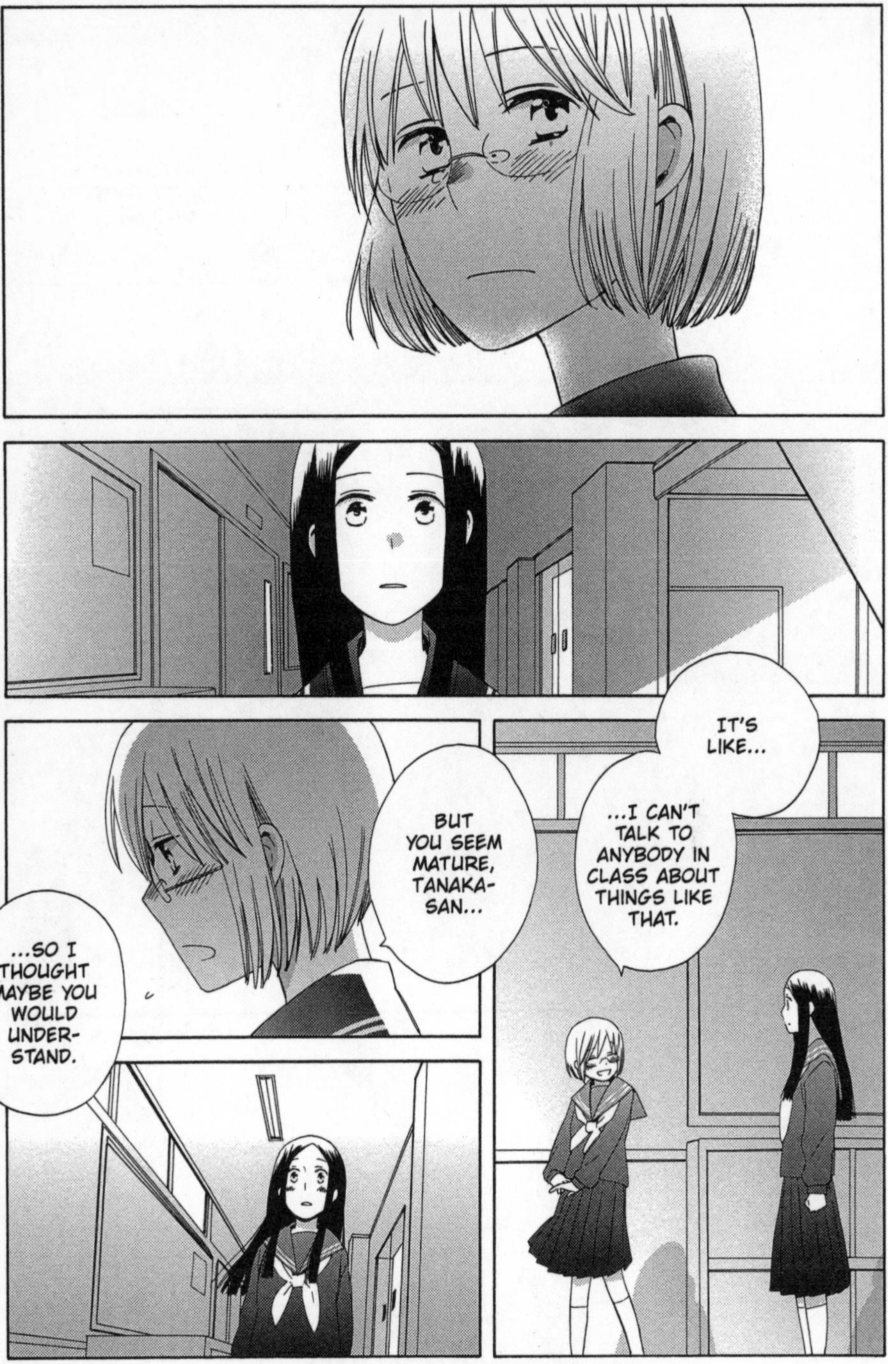
IT'S LIKE...
...I CAN'T TALK TO ANYBODY IN CLASS ABOUT THINGS LIKE THAT.
BUT YOU SEEM MATURE, TANAKA-SAN...
...SO I THOUGHT MAYBE YOU WOULD UNDER-STAND.

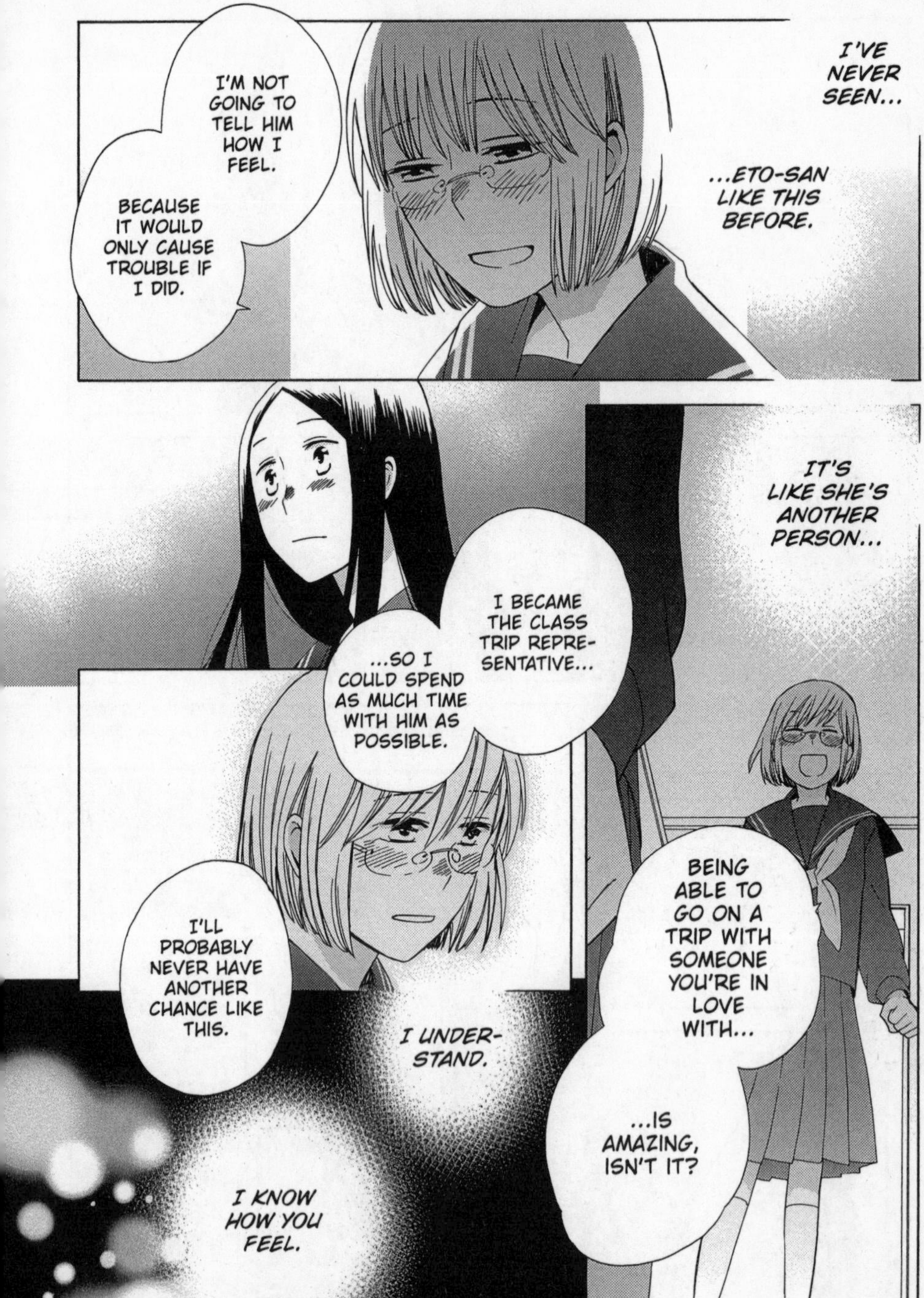
I'VE NEVER SEEN...
...ETO-SAN LIKE THIS BEFORE.
I'M NOT GOING TO TELL HIM HOW I FEEL.
BECAUSE IT WOULD ONLY CAUSE TROUBLE IF I DID.
IT'S LIKE SHE'S ANOTHER PERSON...
I BECAME THE CLASS TRIP REPRE-SENTATIVE...
...SO I COULD SPEND AS MUCH TIME WITH HIM AS POSSIBLE.
BEING ABLE TO GO ON A TRIP WITH SOMEONE YOU'RE IN LOVE WITH...
...IS AMAZING, ISN'T IT?
I'LL PROBABLY NEVER HAVE ANOTHER CHANCE LIKE THIS.
I UNDER-STAND.
I KNOW HOW YOU FEEL.

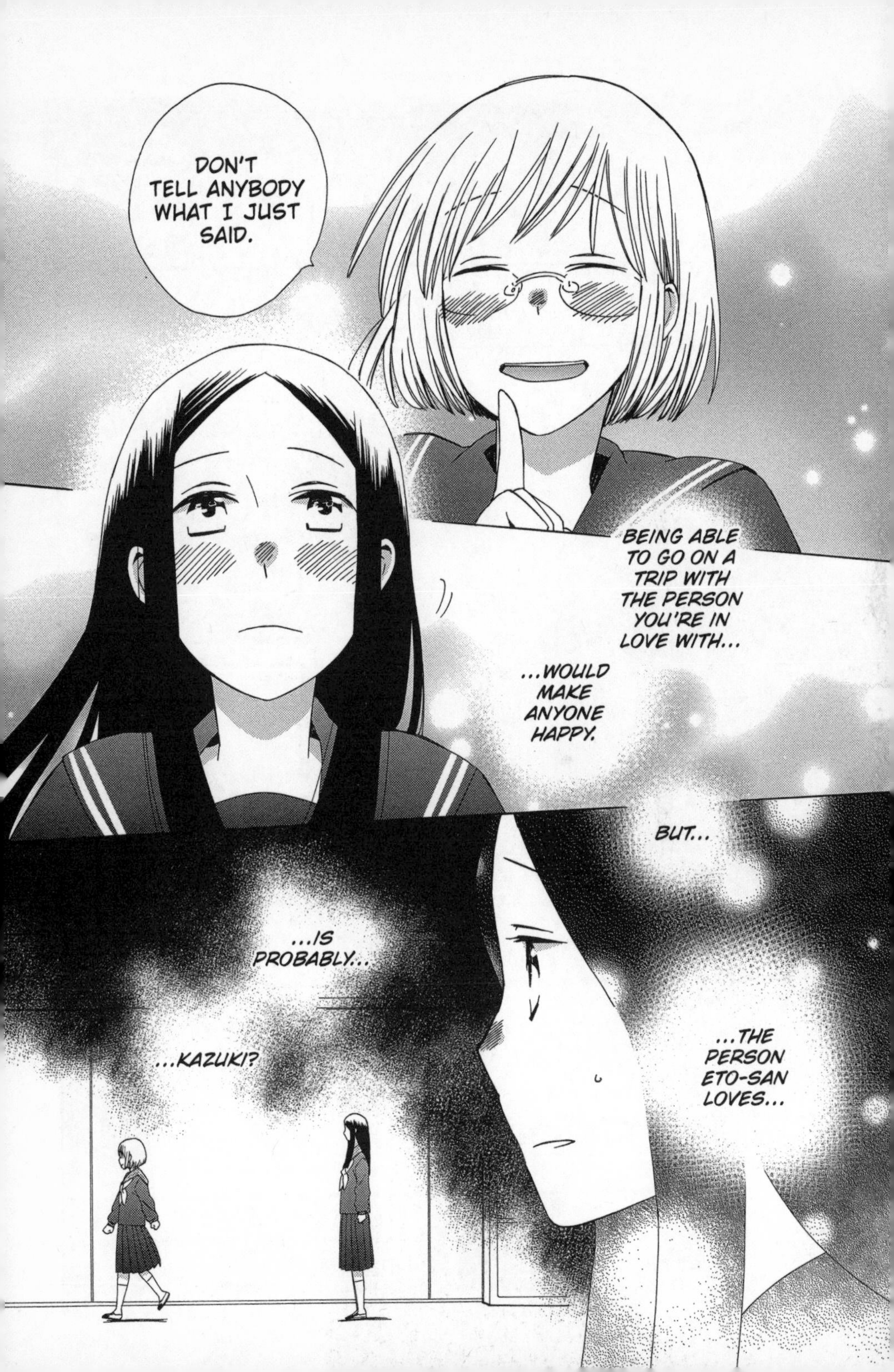
DON'T TELL ANYBODY WHAT I JUST SAID.
BEING ABLE TO GO ON A TRIP WITH THE PERSON YOU'RE IN LOVE WITH...
...WOULD MAKE ANYONE HAPPY.
BUT...
...THE PERSON ETO-SAN LOVES...
...IS PROBABLY...
...KAZUKI?

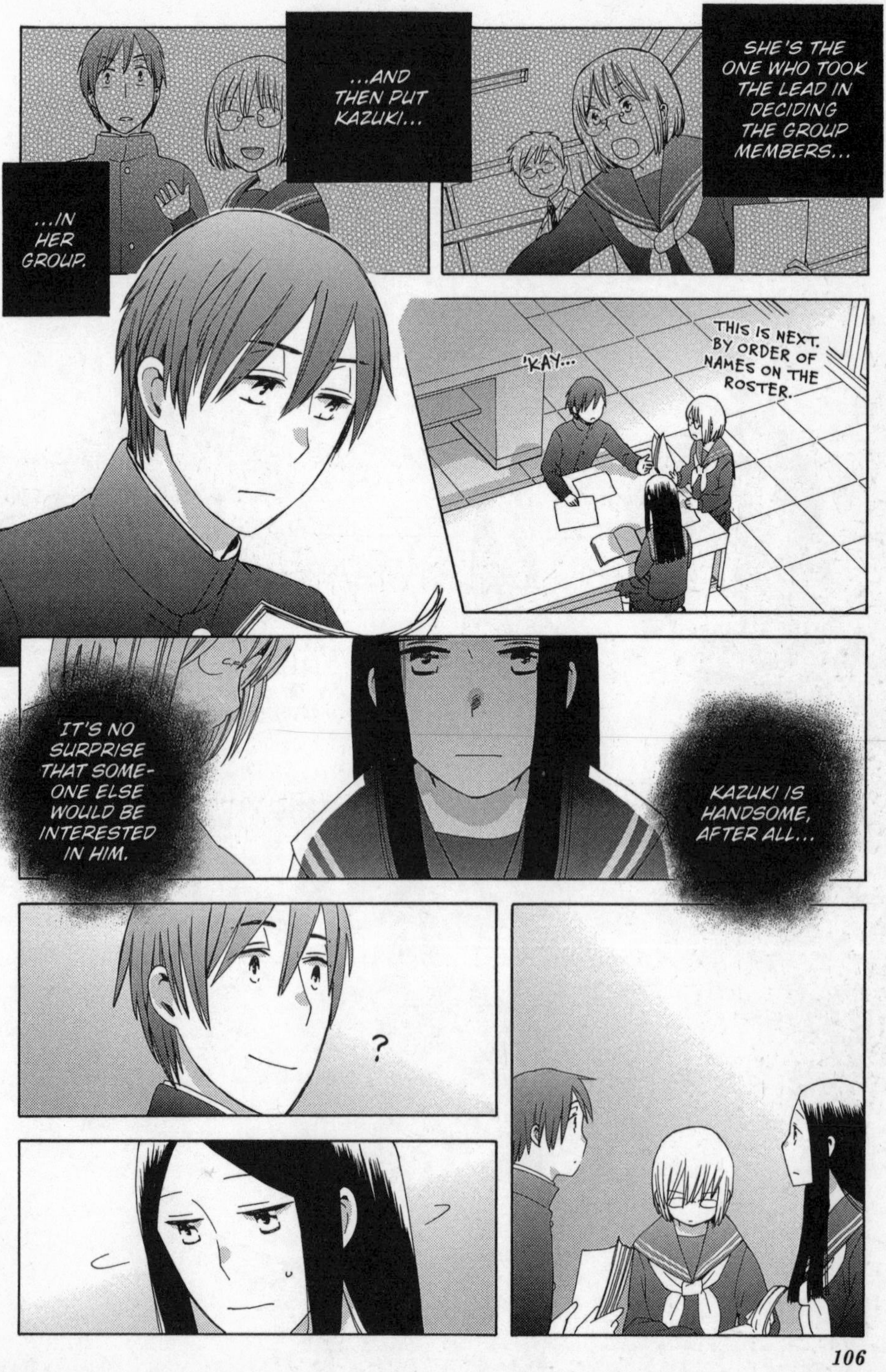
SHE'S THE ONE WHO TOOK THE LEAD IN DECIDING THE GROUP MEMBERS...
...AND THEN PUT KAZUKI...
...IN HER GROUP.
THIS IS NEXT. BY ORDER OF NAMES ON THE ROSTER.
'KAY...
KAZUKI IS HANDSOME, AFTER ALL...
IT'S NO SURPRISE THAT SOME-ONE ELSE WOULD BE INTERESTED IN HIM.
?

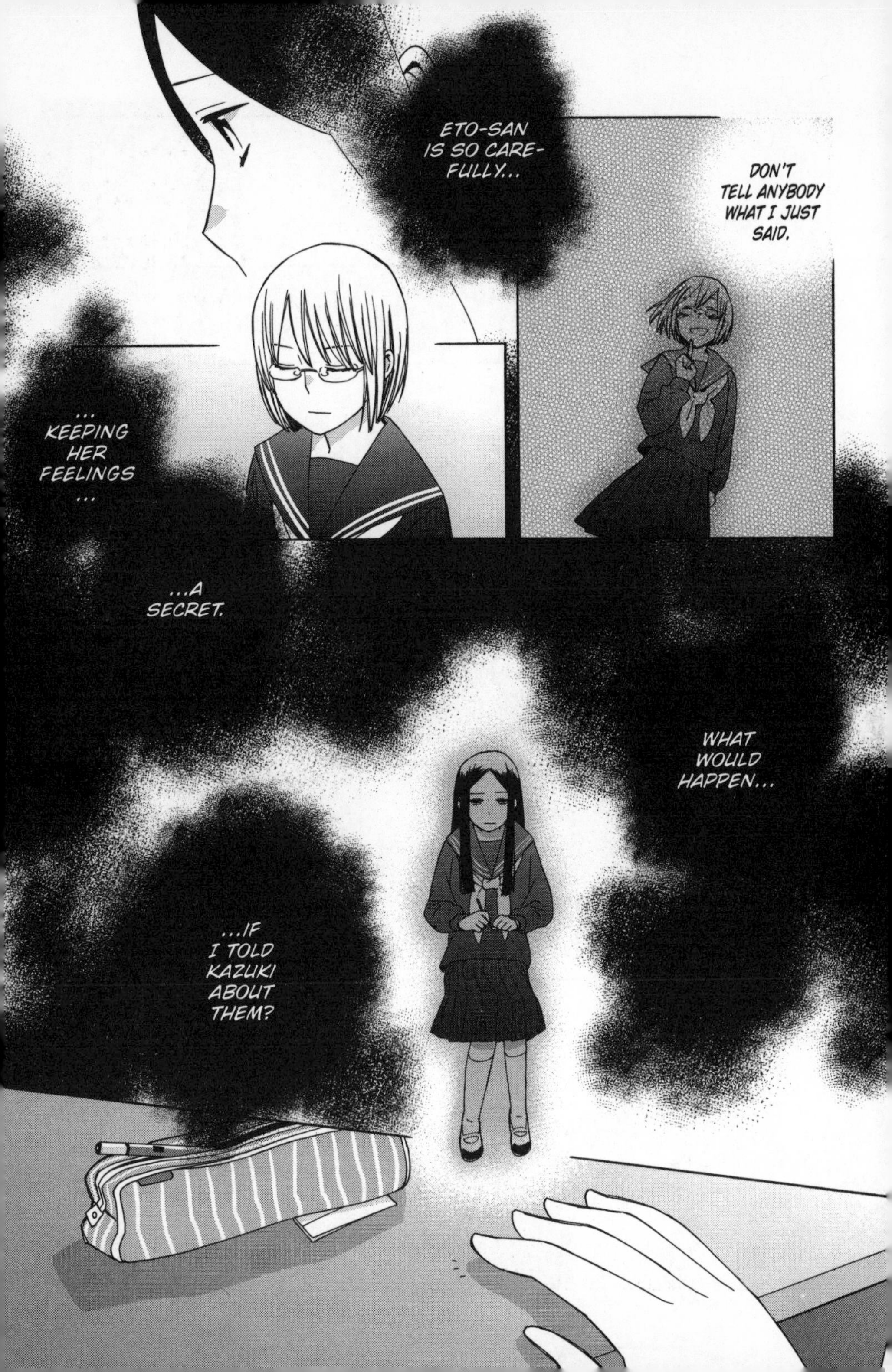
ETO-SAN IS SO CARE-FULLY...
DON'T TELL ANYBODY WHAT I JUST SAID.
...KEEPING HER FEELINGS...
...A SECRET.
WHAT WOULD HAPPEN...
...IF I TOLD KAZUKI ABOUT THEM?

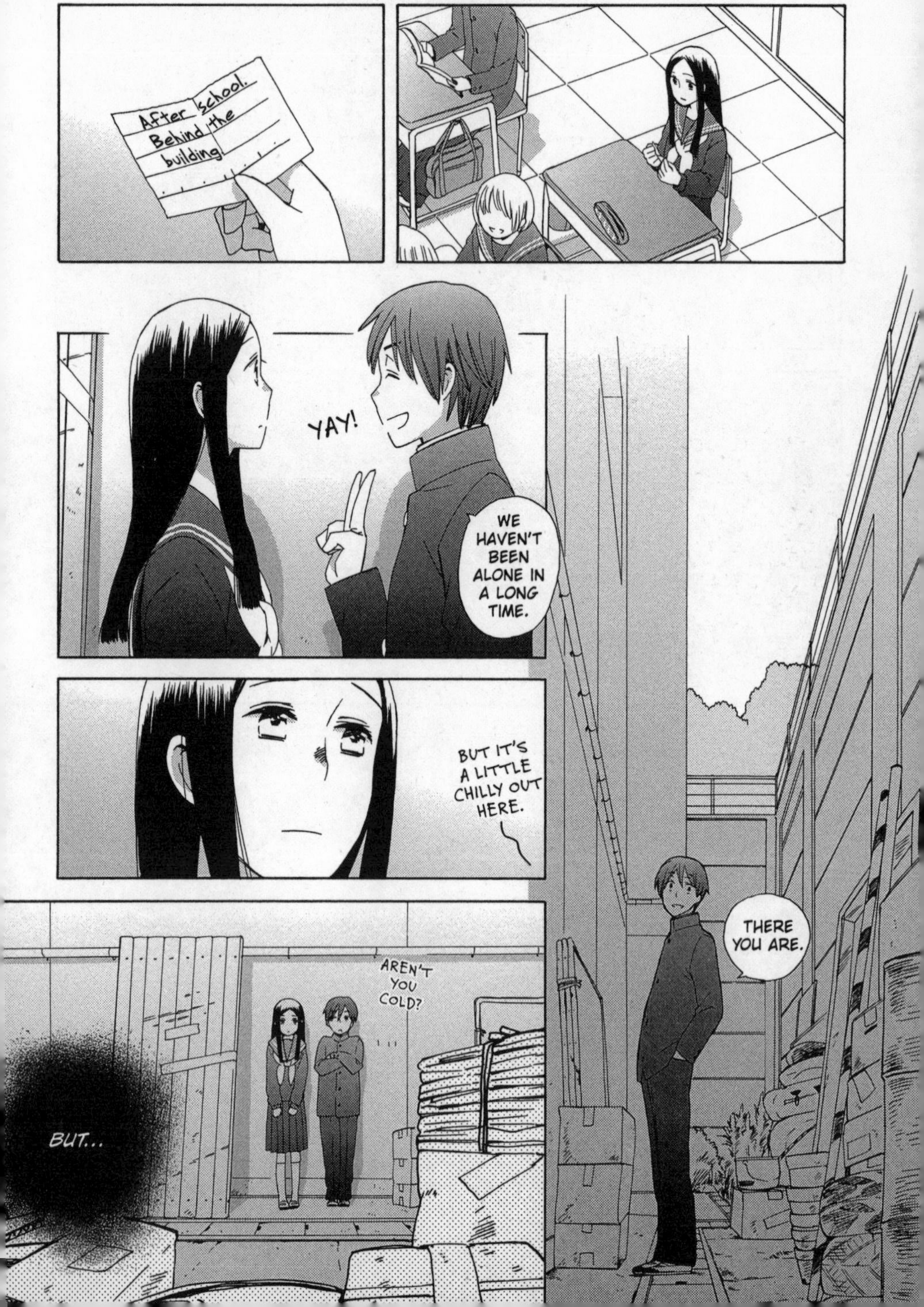
After school.
Behind the building
THERE YOU ARE.
YAY!
WE HAVEN'T BEEN ALONE IN A LONG TIME.
BUT IT'S A LITTLE CHILLY OUT HERE.
AREN'T YOU COLD?
BUT...

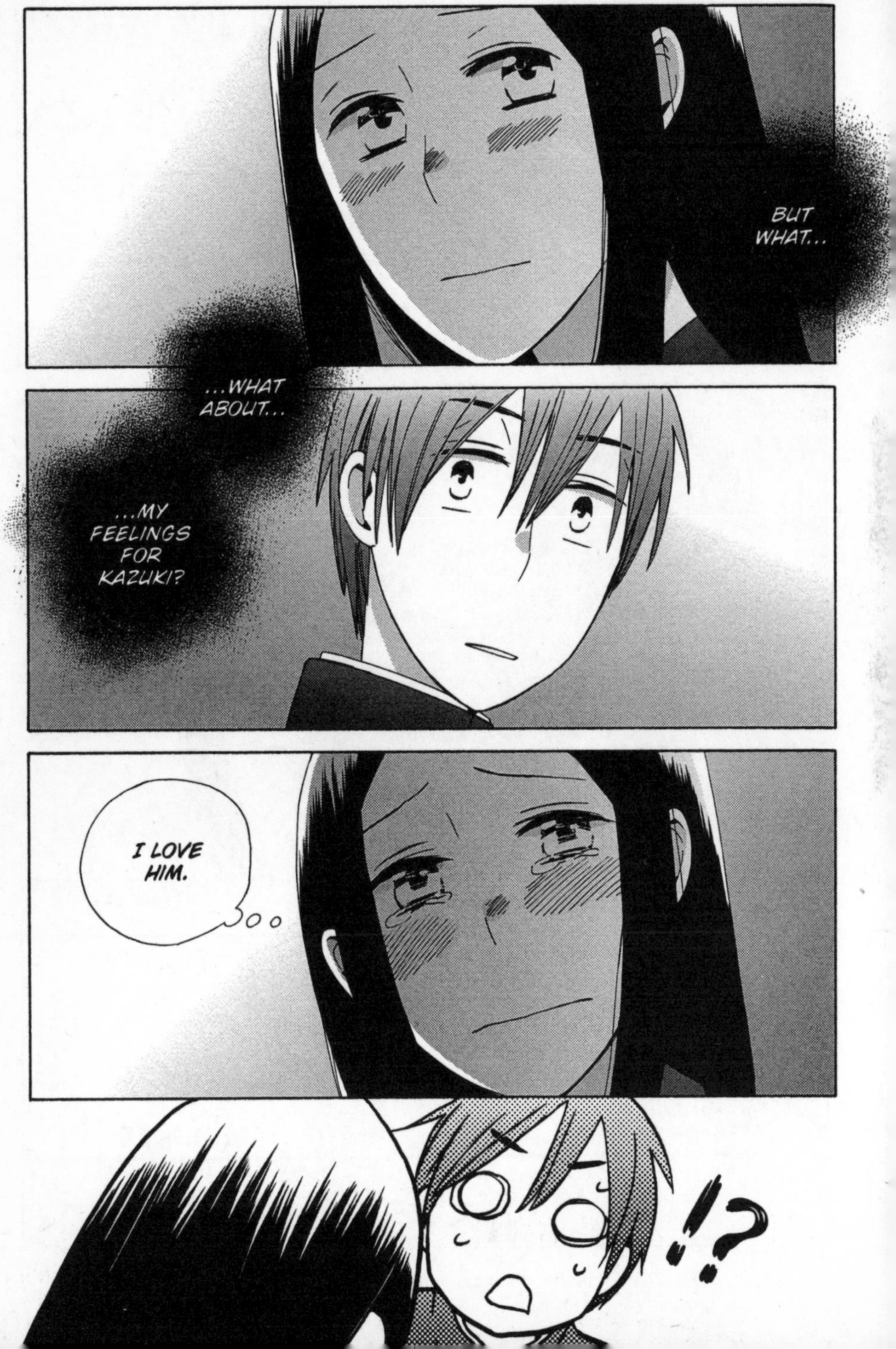
BUT WHAT...
...WHAT ABOUT...
...MY FEELINGS FOR KAZUKI?
I LOVE HIM.
!?

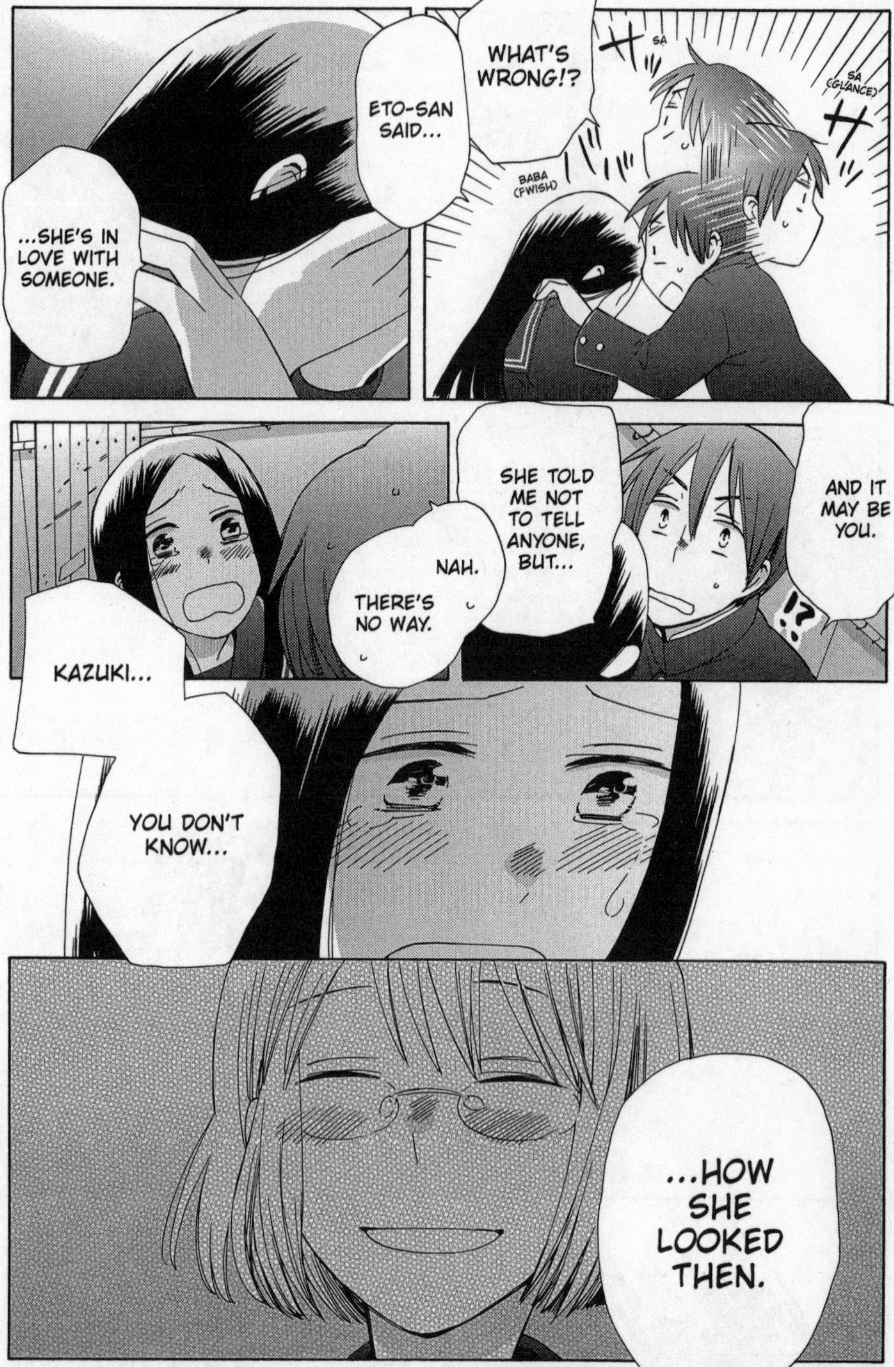
SA
SA (GLANCE)
BABA (FWISH)
WHAT'S WRONG!?
ETO-SAN SAID...
...SHE'S IN LOVE WITH SOMEONE.
SHE TOLD ME NOT TO TELL ANYONE, BUT...
AND IT MAY BE YOU.
!?
NAH.
THERE'S NO WAY.
KAZUKI...
YOU DON'T KNOW...
...HOW SHE LOOKED THEN.

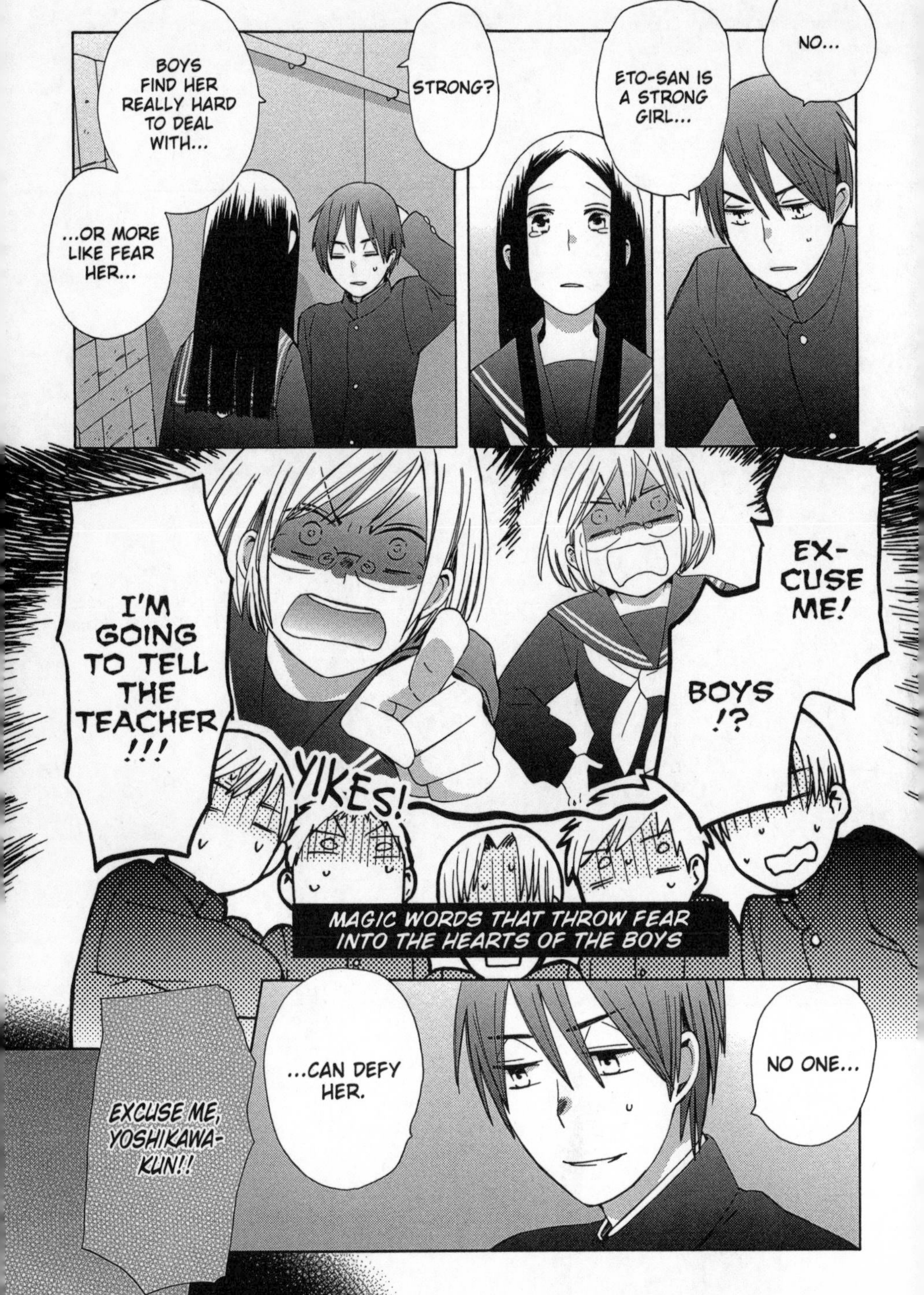
NO...
ETO-SAN IS A STRONG GIRL...
STRONG?
BOYS FIND HER REALLY HARD TO DEAL WITH...
...OR MORE LIKE FEAR HER...
EX-CUSE ME!
BOYS!?
I'M GOING TO TELL THE TEACHER!!!
YIKES!
MAGIC WORDS THAT THROW FEAR INTO THE HEARTS OF THE BOYS
NO ONE...
...CAN DEFY HER.
EXCUSE ME, YOSHIKAWA-KUN!!

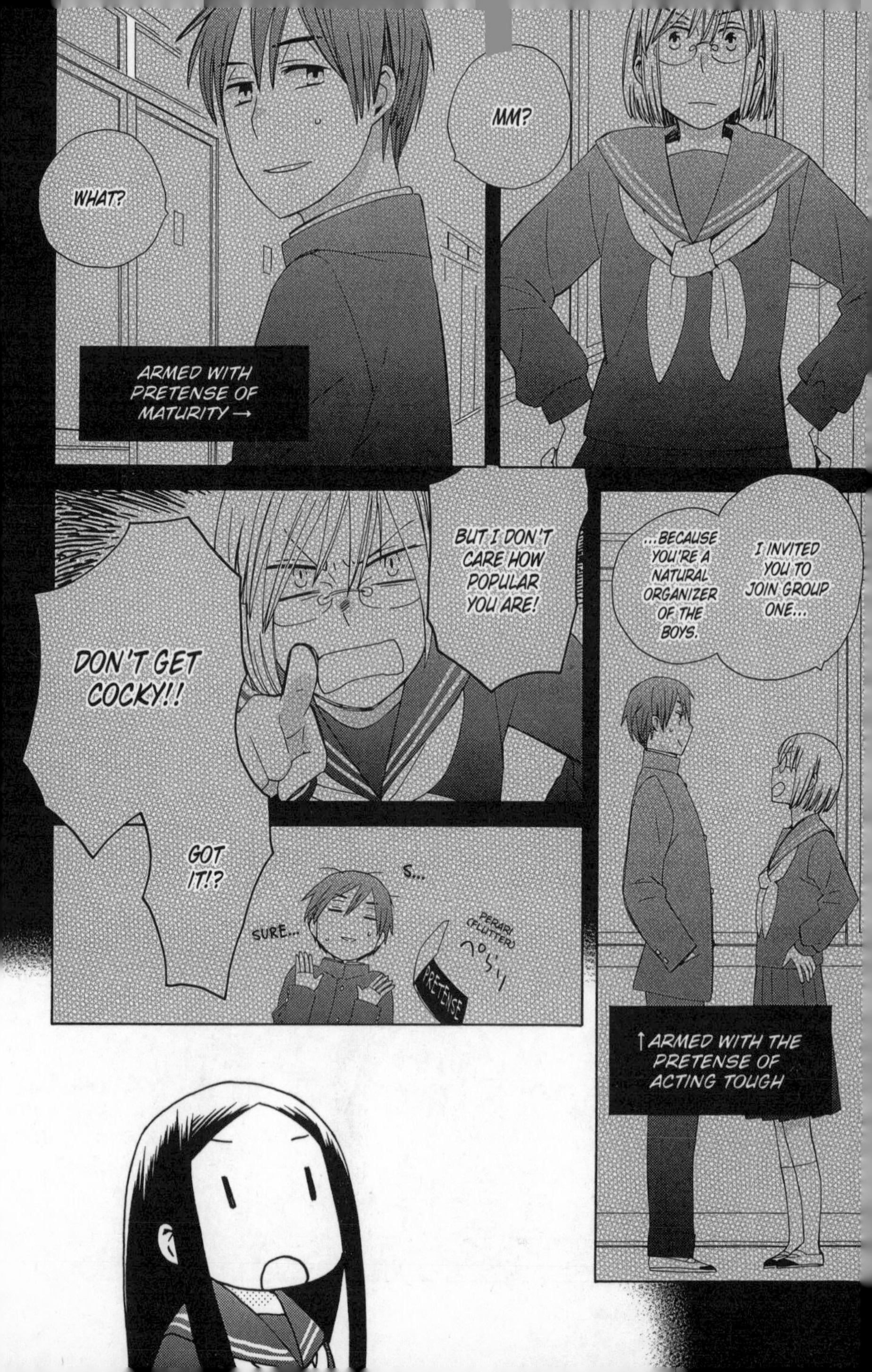
MM?
WHAT?
ARMED WITH PRETENSE OF MATURITY →
I INVITED YOU TO JOIN GROUP ONE...
...BECAUSE YOU'RE A NATURAL ORGANIZER OF THE BOYS.
↑ARMED WITH THE PRETENSE OF ACTING TOUGH
BUT I DON'T CARE HOW POPULAR YOU ARE!
DON'T GET COCKY!!
GOT IT!?
S...
SURE...
PERARI (FLUTTER)
PRETENSE

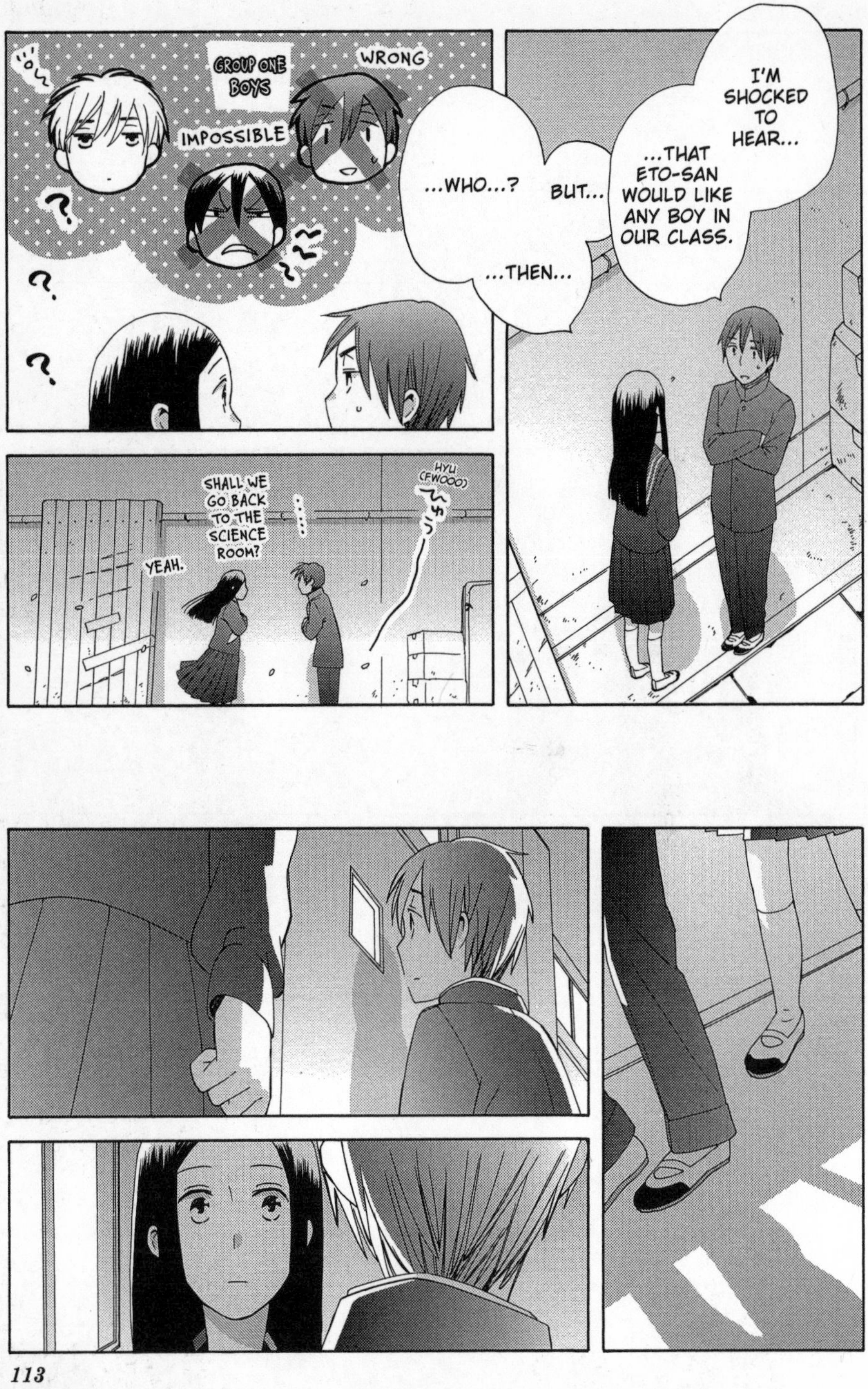
I'M SHOCKED TO HEAR...
...THAT ETO-SAN WOULD LIKE ANY BOY IN OUR CLASS.
BUT...
...THEN...
...WHO...?
WRONG
GROUP ONE BOYS
IMPOSSIBLE
HYU (FWOOO)
....
SHALL WE GO BACK TO THE SCIENCE ROOM?
YEAH.

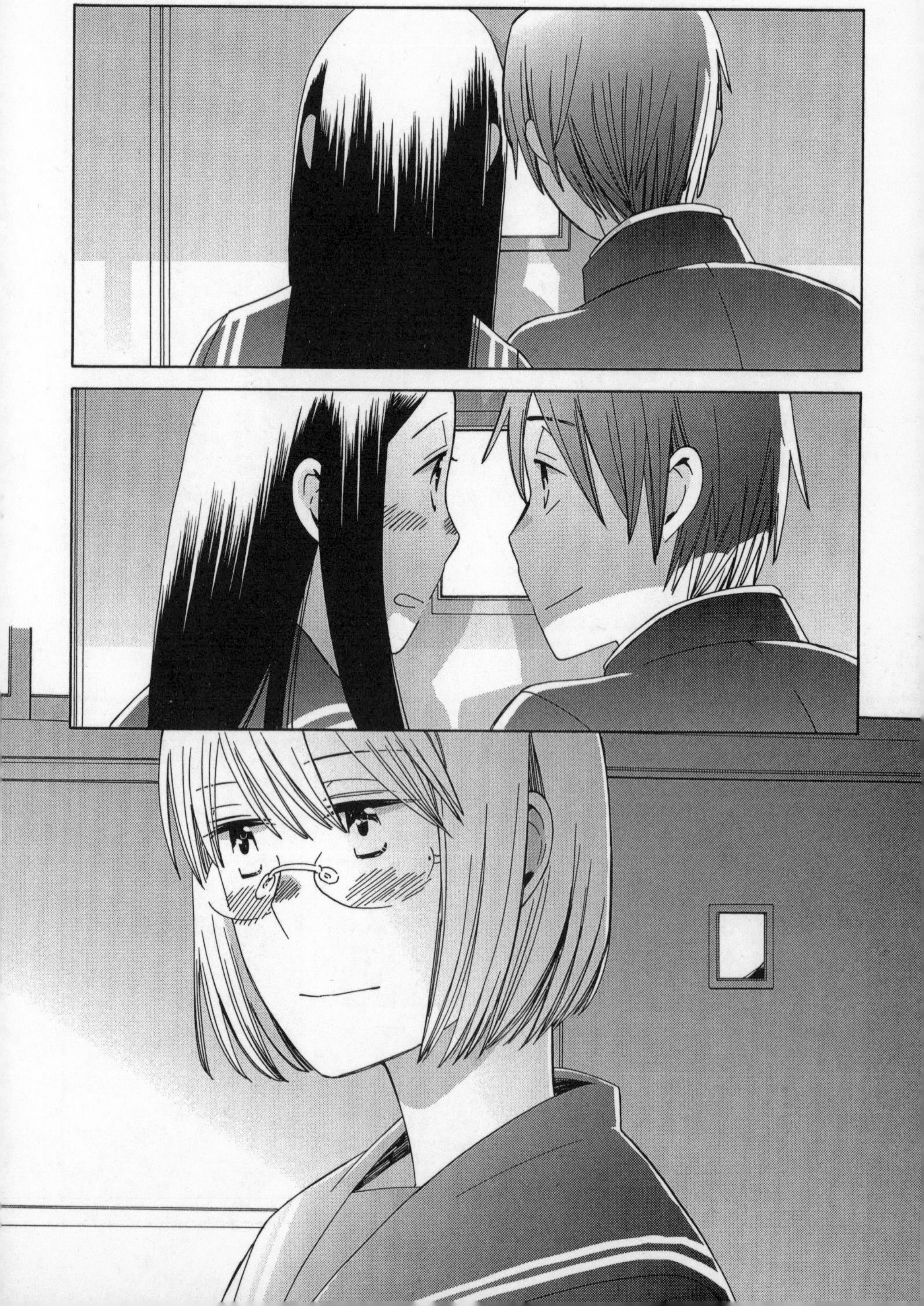

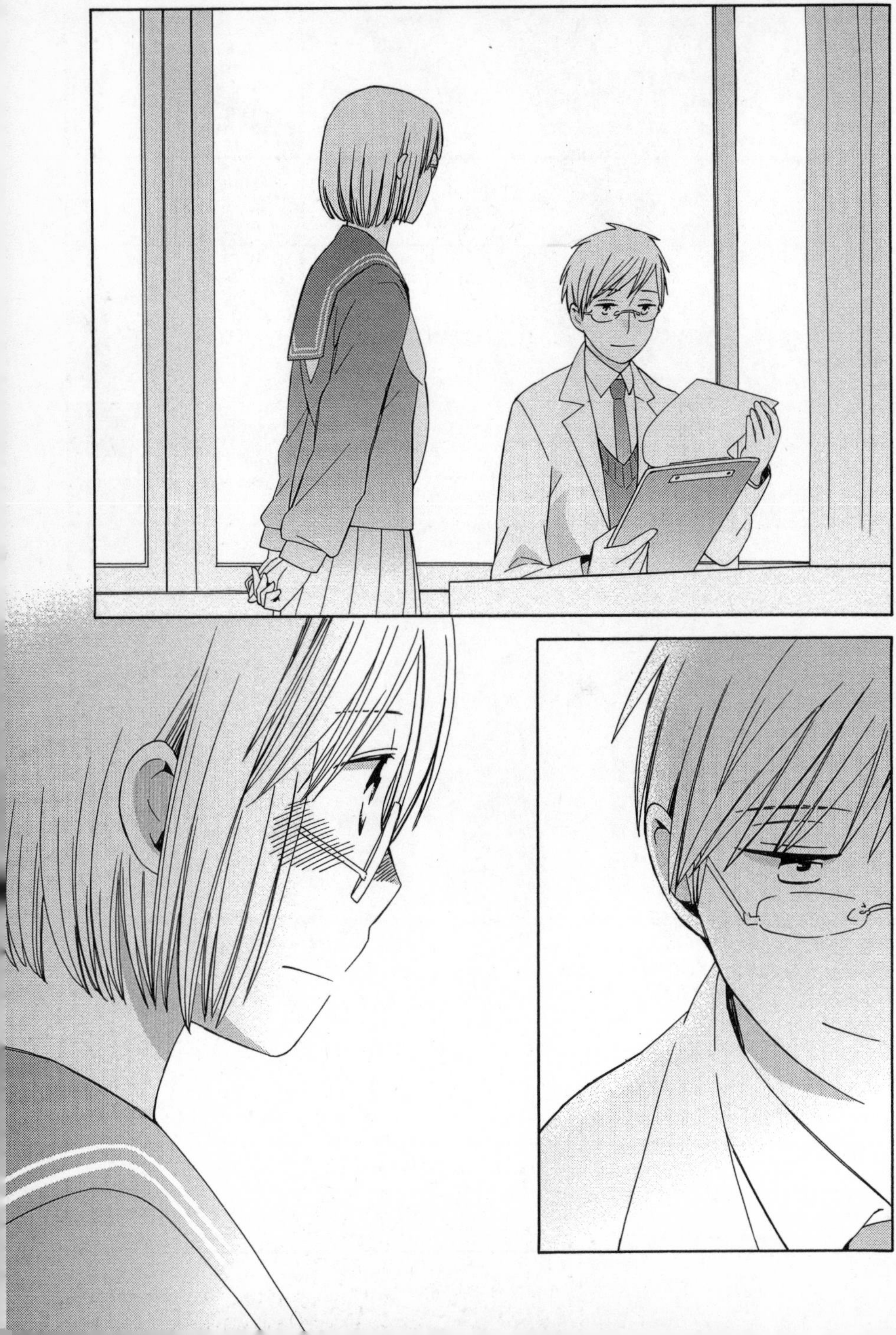

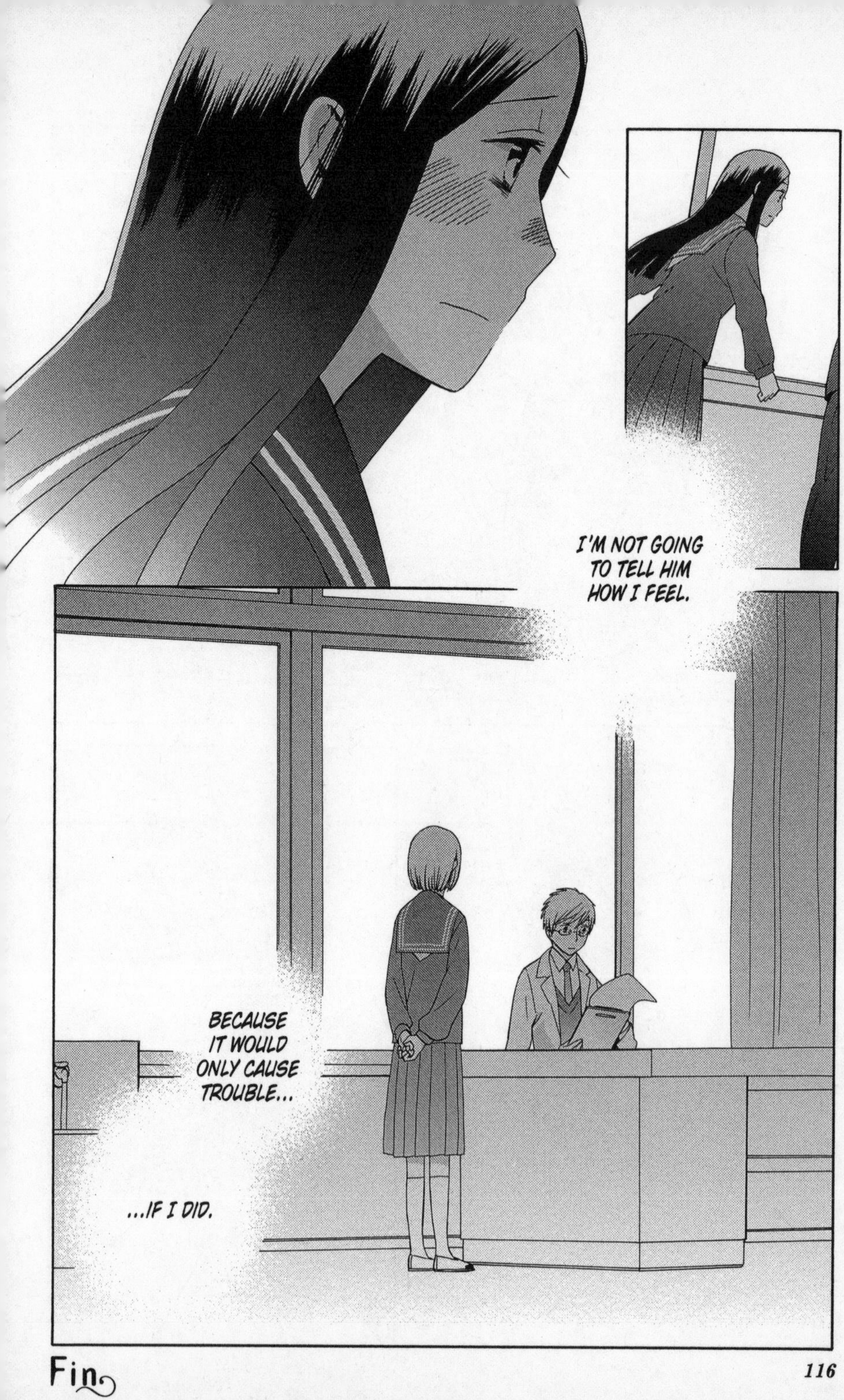
I'M NOT GOING TO TELL HIM HOW I FEEL.
BECAUSE IT WOULD ONLY CAUSE TROUBLE...
...IF I DID.

Fin

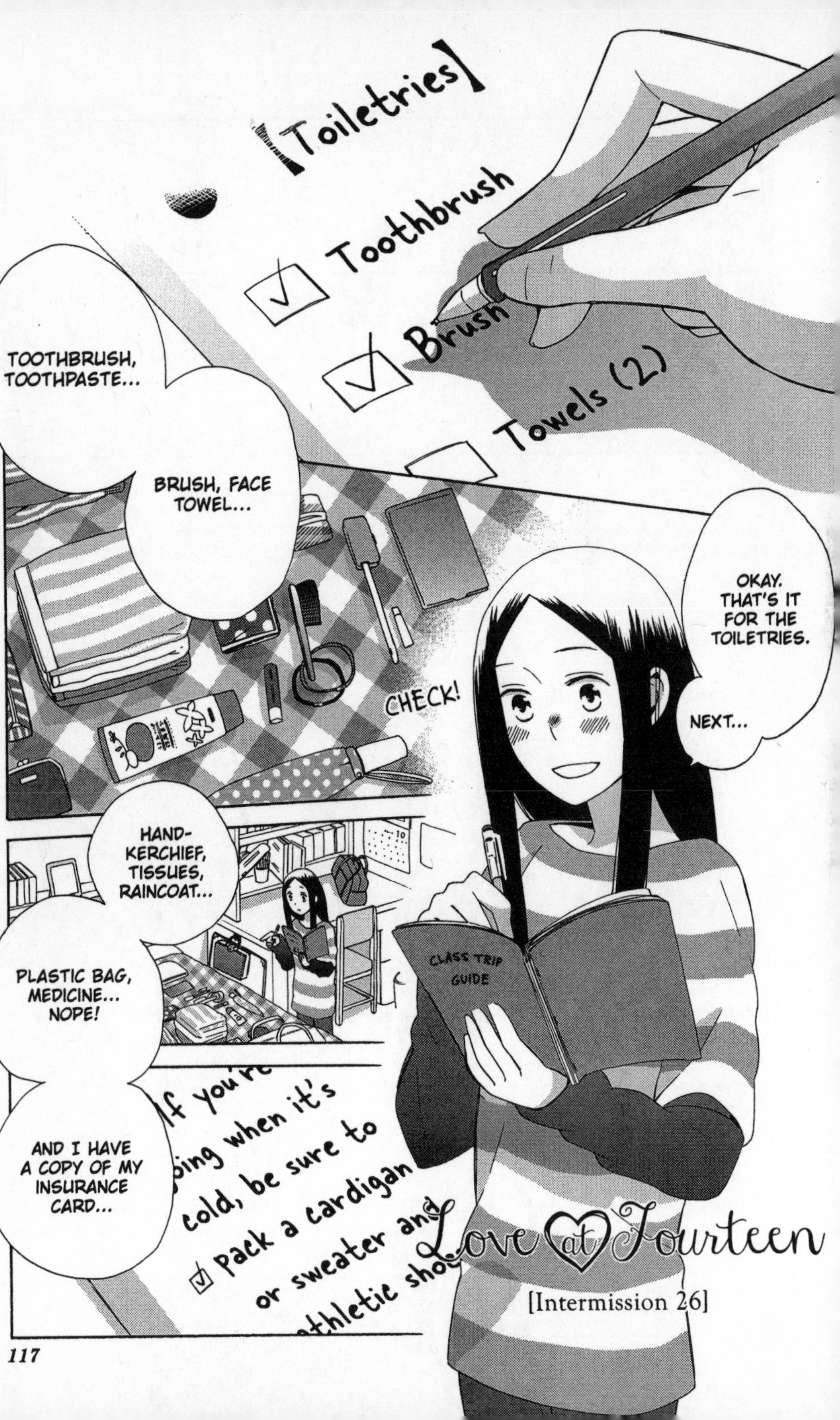
[Toiletries]
Toothbrush
Brush
Towels (2)
TOOTHBRUSH, TOOTHPASTE...
BRUSH, FACE TOWEL...
CHECK!
OKAY. THAT'S IT FOR THE TOILETRIES.
NEXT...
HAND-KERCHIEF, TISSUES, RAINCOAT...
PLASTIC BAG, MEDICINE... NOPE!
AND I HAVE A COPY OF MY INSURANCE CARD...
f you're
oing when it's
cold, be sure to
pack a cardigan
or sweater an
thletic sho
CLASS TRIP GUIDE
Love at Fourteen
[Intermission 26]

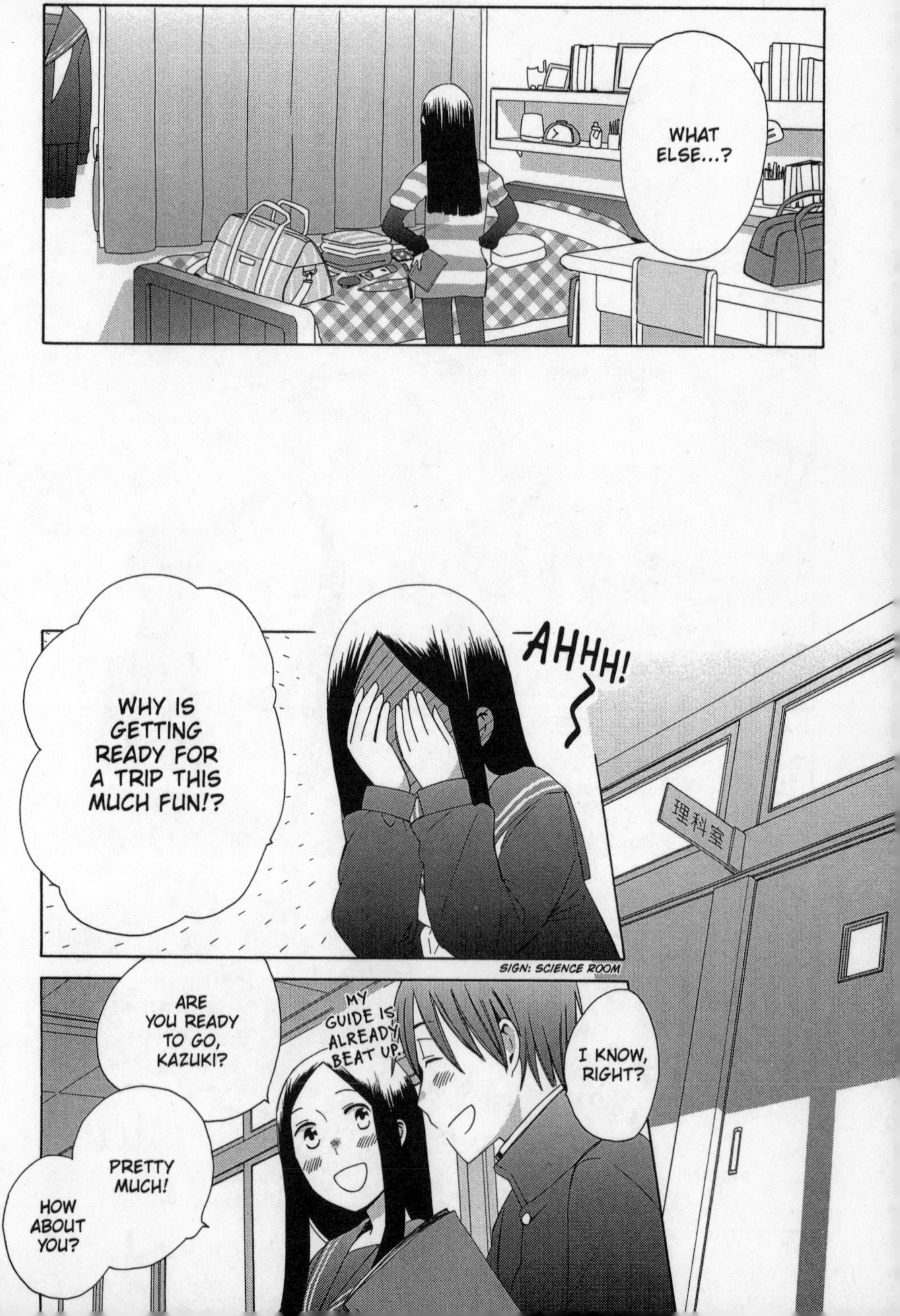
WHAT ELSE...?
AHHH!
WHY IS GETTING READY FOR A TRIP THIS MUCH FUN!?
理科室
SIGN: SCIENCE ROOM
ARE YOU READY TO GO, KAZUKI?
PRETTY MUCH!
HOW ABOUT YOU?
MY GUIDE IS ALREADY BEAT UP.
I KNOW, RIGHT?

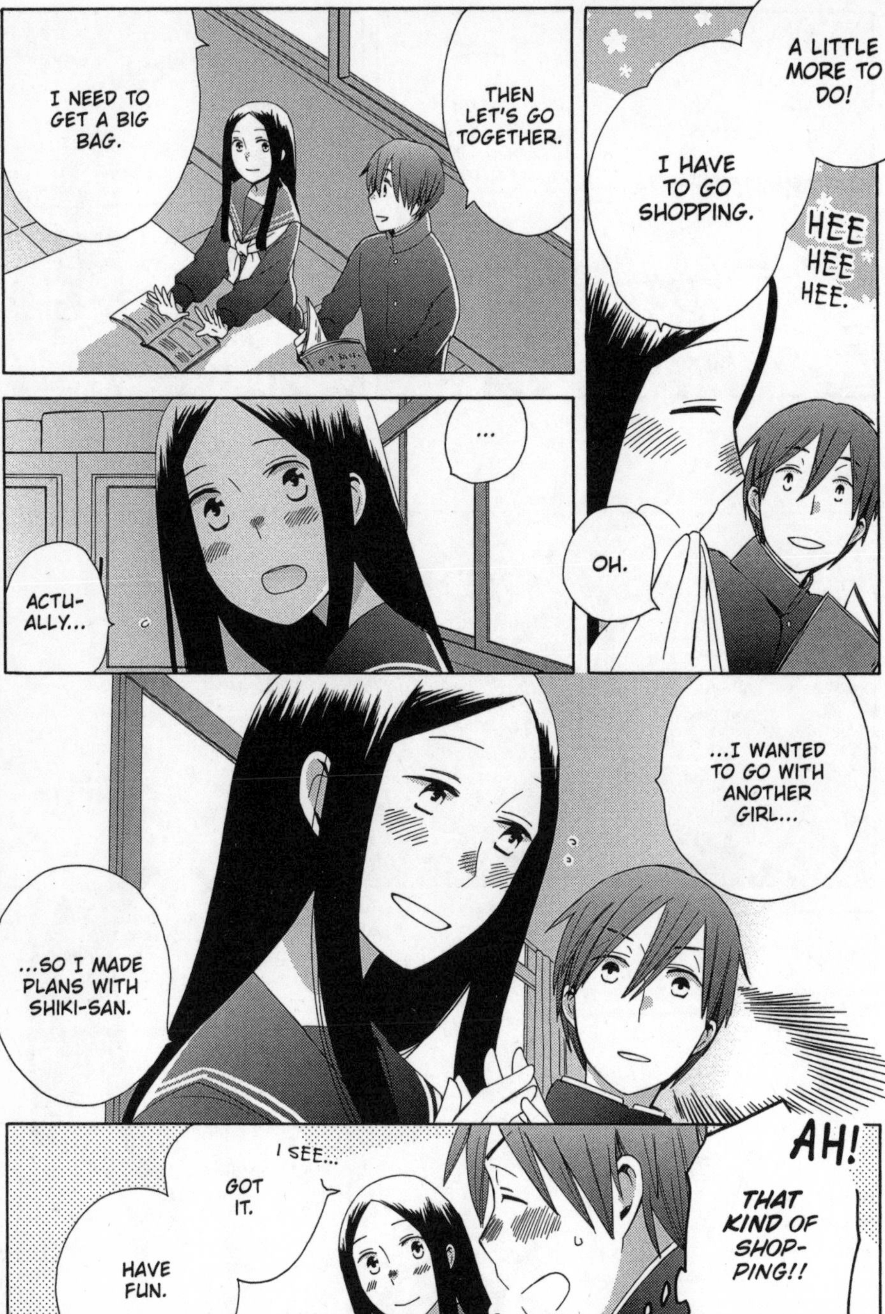
A LITTLE MORE TO DO!
I HAVE TO GO SHOPPING.
HEE HEE HEE.
THEN LET'S GO TOGETHER.
I NEED TO GET A BIG BAG.
OH.
...
ACTU-ALLY...
...I WANTED TO GO WITH ANOTHER GIRL...
...SO I MADE PLANS WITH SHIKI-SAN.
AH!
THAT KIND OF SHOP-PING!!
I SEE...
GOT IT.
HAVE FUN.

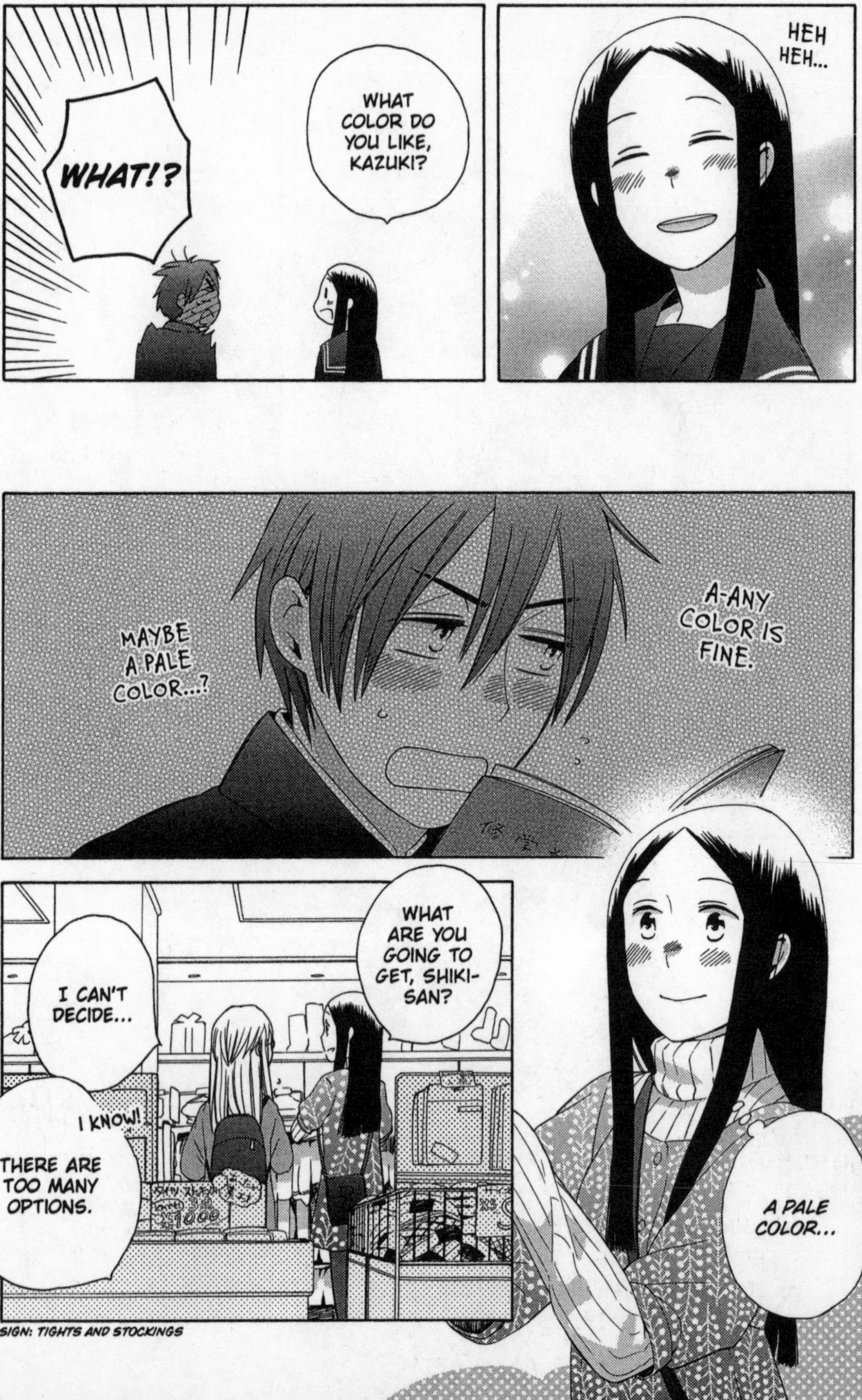
HEH HEH...
WHAT COLOR DO YOU LIKE, KAZUKI?
WHAT!?
A-ANY COLOR IS FINE.
MAYBE A PALE COLOR...?
A PALE COLOR...
WHAT ARE YOU GOING TO GET, SHIKI-SAN?
I CAN'T DECIDE...
I KNOW!
THERE ARE TOO MANY OPTIONS.

SIGN: TIGHTS AND STOCKINGS

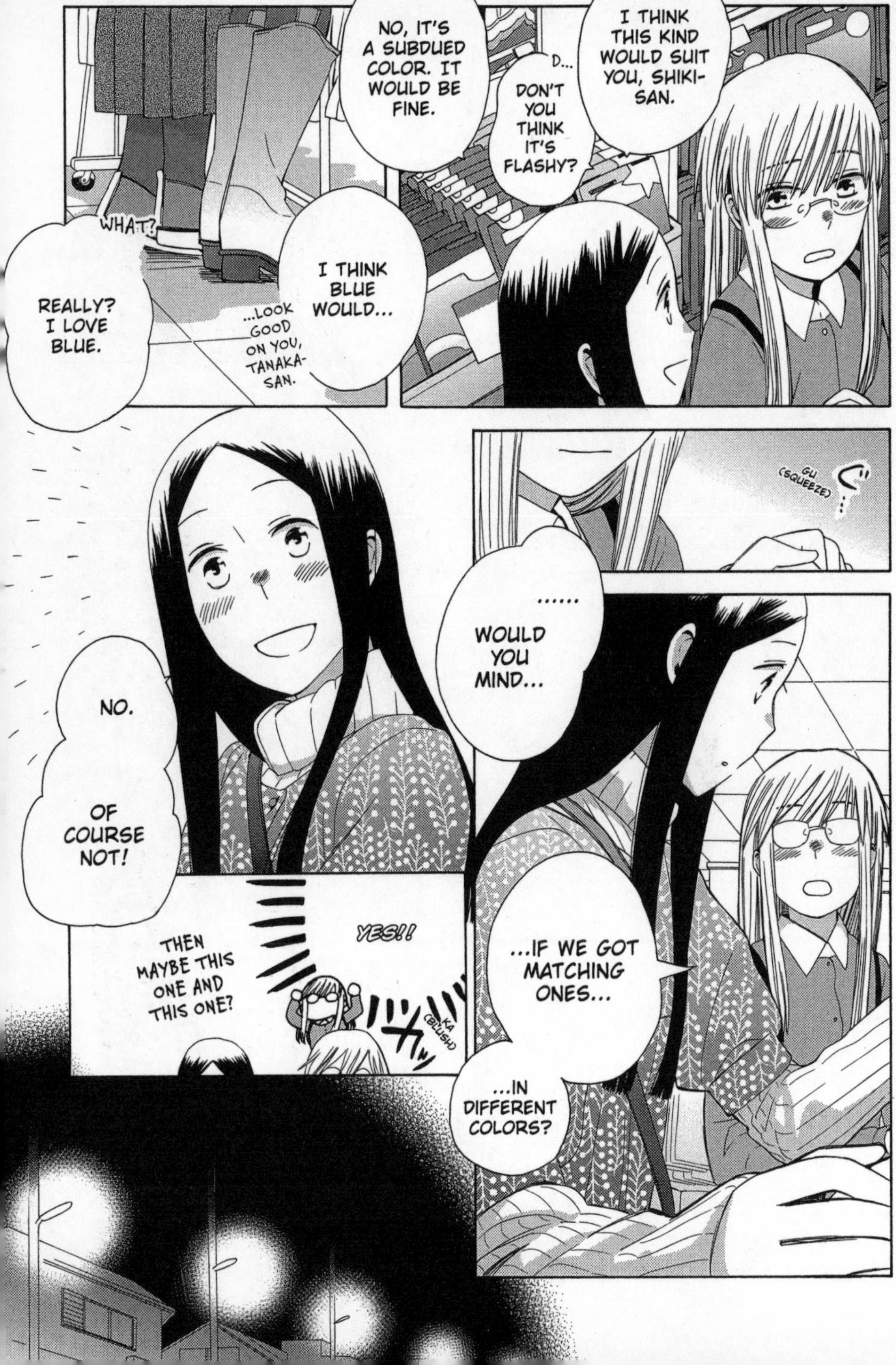
I THINK THIS KIND WOULD SUIT YOU, SHIKI-SAN.
D... DON'T YOU THINK IT'S FLASHY?
NO, IT'S A SUBDUED COLOR. IT WOULD BE FINE.
I THINK BLUE WOULD...
...LOOK GOOD ON YOU, TANAKA-SAN.
WHAT?
REALLY? I LOVE BLUE.
GU (SQUEEZE)
......
WOULD YOU MIND...
...IF WE GOT MATCHING ONES...
...IN DIFFERENT COLORS?
NO.
OF COURSE NOT!
YES!!
KA (BLUSH)
THEN MAYBE THIS ONE AND THIS ONE?

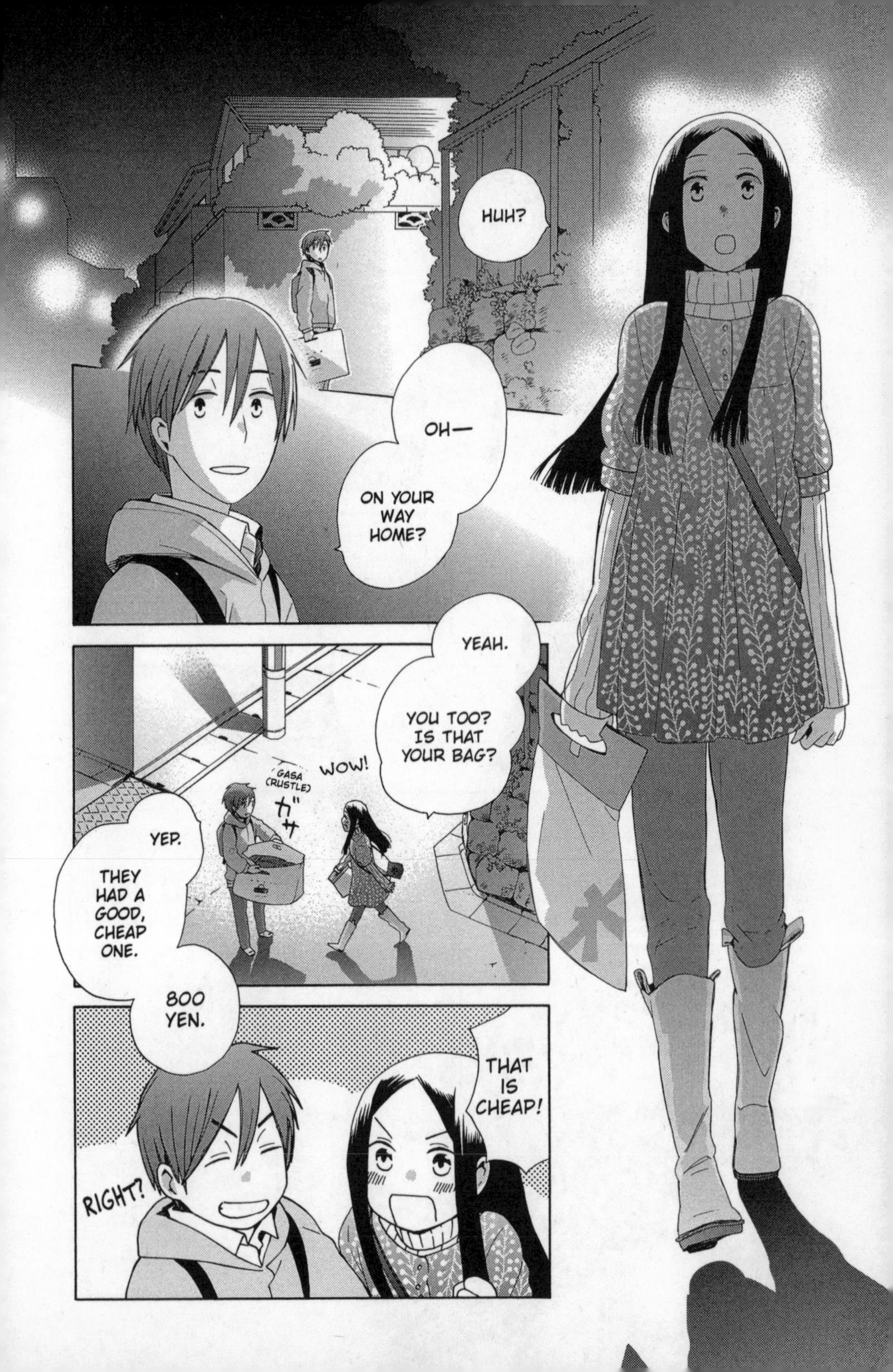
HUH?
OH—
ON YOUR WAY HOME?
YEAH.
YOU TOO? IS THAT YOUR BAG?
WOW!
GASA (RUSTLE)
ガサ
YEP.
THEY HAD A GOOD, CHEAP ONE.
800 YEN.
THAT IS CHEAP!
RIGHT?

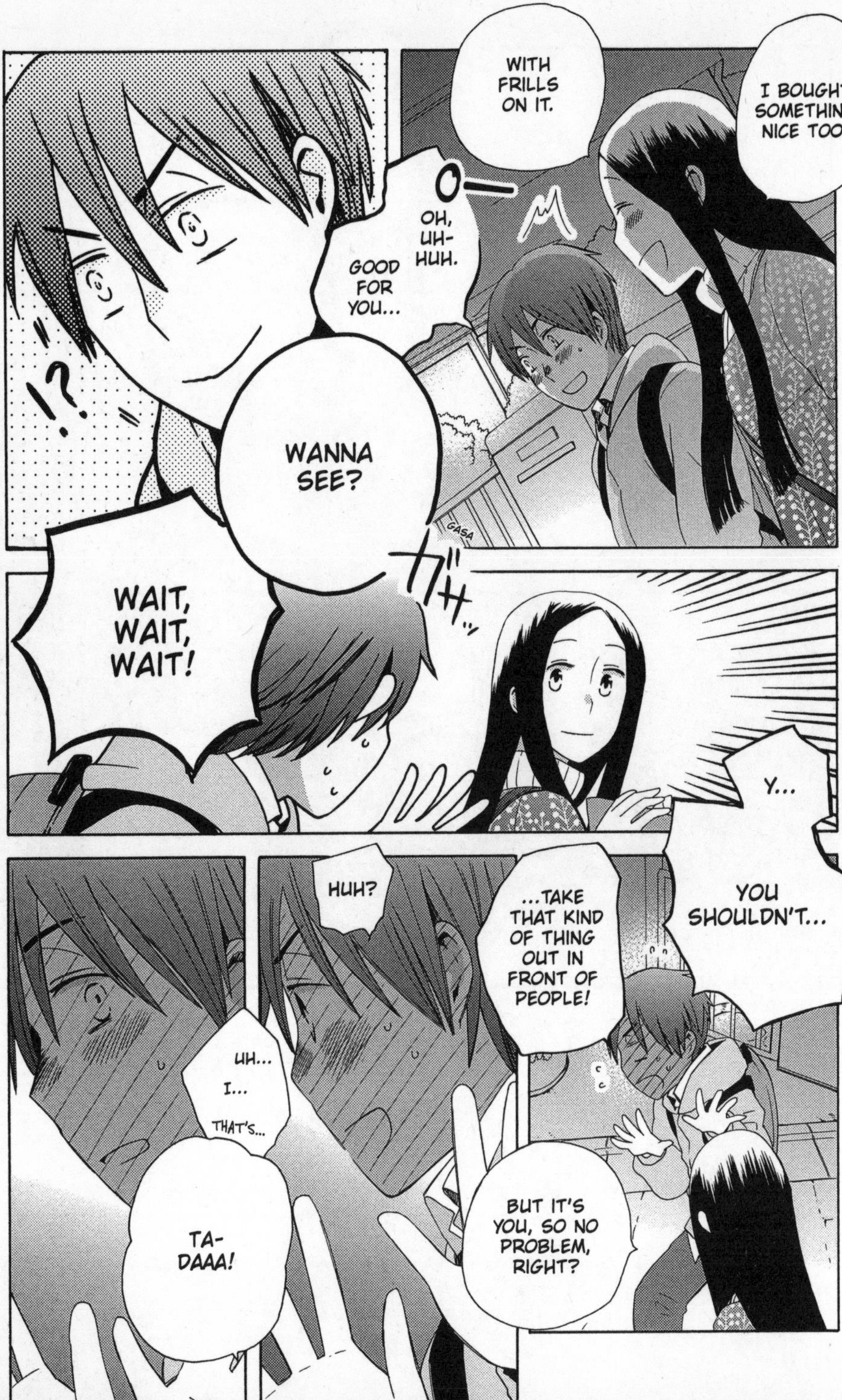
I BOUGHT SOMETHING NICE TOO.
WITH FRILLS ON IT.
O—
OH, UH-HUH.
GOOD FOR YOU...
!?
WANNA SEE?
GASA
WAIT, WAIT, WAIT!
Y...
YOU SHOULDN'T...
...TAKE THAT KIND OF THING OUT IN FRONT OF PEOPLE!
BUT IT'S YOU, SO NO PROBLEM, RIGHT?
HUH?
UH...
I...
THAT'S...
TA-DAAA!

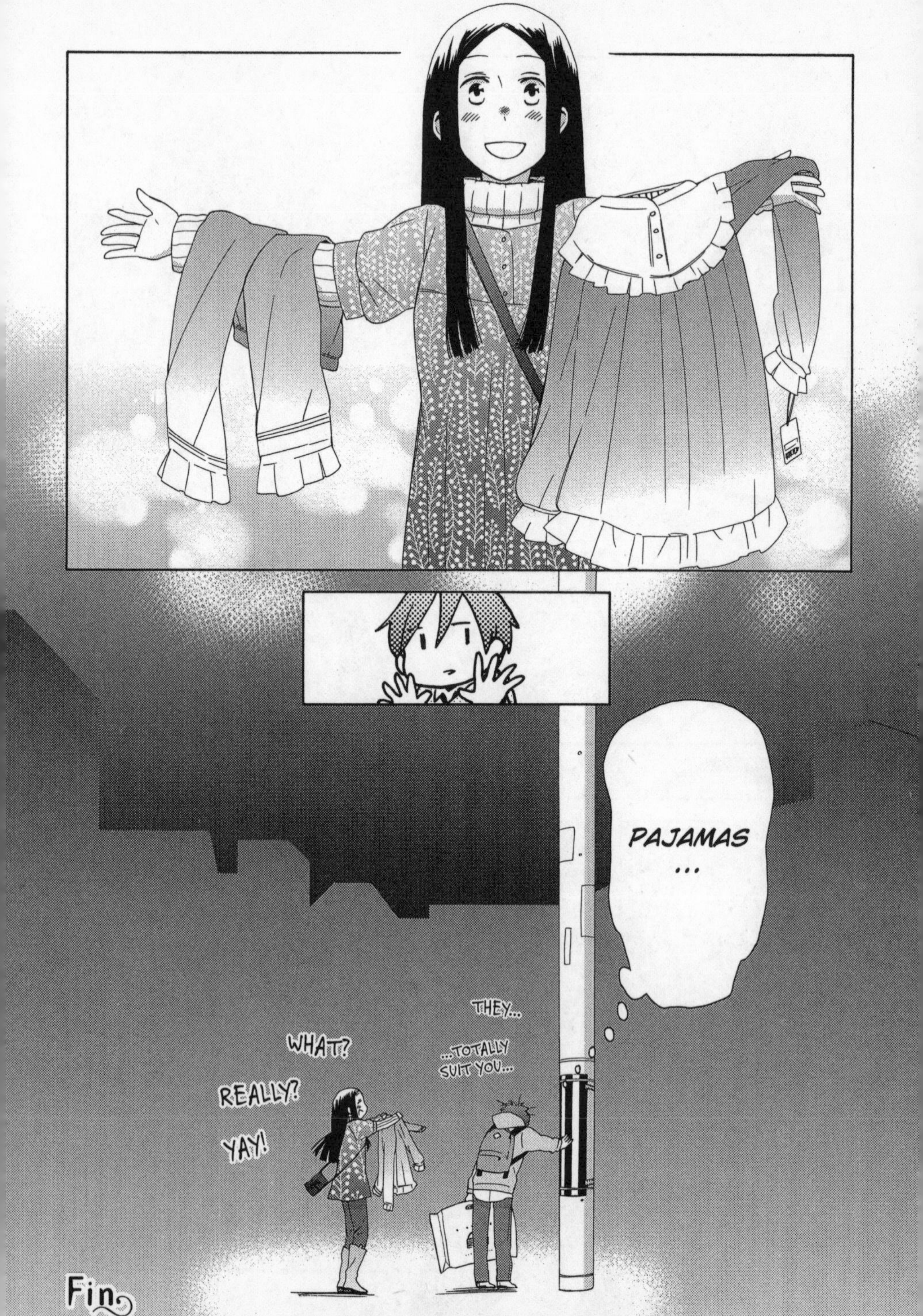
PAJAMAS
...
THEY...
...TOTALLY SUIT YOU...
WHAT?
REALLY?
YAY!
Fin.

Love at Fourteen

[Intermission 27]

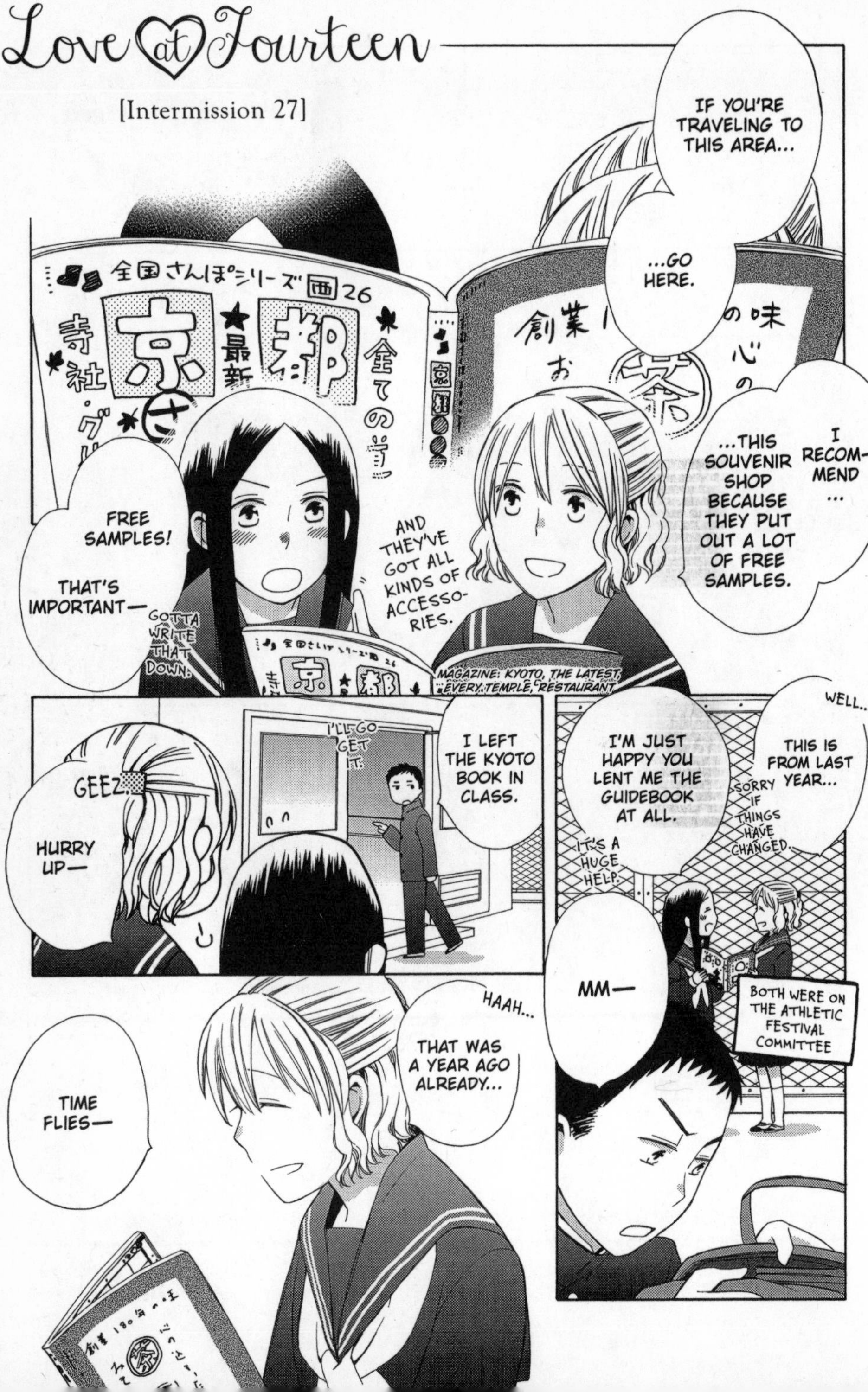
IF YOU'RE TRAVELING TO THIS AREA...
...GO HERE.
I RECOMMEND...
...THIS SOUVENIR SHOP BECAUSE THEY PUT OUT A LOT OF FREE SAMPLES.
AND THEY'VE GOT ALL KINDS OF ACCESSORIES.
FREE SAMPLES!
THAT'S IMPORTANT—
GOTTA WRITE THAT DOWN.
全国さんぽシリーズ 26
京都
MAGAZINE: KYOTO, THE LATEST, EVERY TEMPLE, RESTAURANT
WELL...
THIS IS FROM LAST YEAR...
SORRY IF THINGS HAVE CHANGED.
I'M JUST HAPPY YOU LENT ME THE GUIDEBOOK AT ALL.
IT'S A HUGE HELP.
MM—
BOTH WERE ON THE ATHLETIC FESTIVAL COMMITTEE
I LEFT THE KYOTO BOOK IN CLASS.
I'LL GO GET IT.
GEEZ.
HURRY UP—
HAAH...
THAT WAS A YEAR AGO ALREADY...
TIME FLIES—

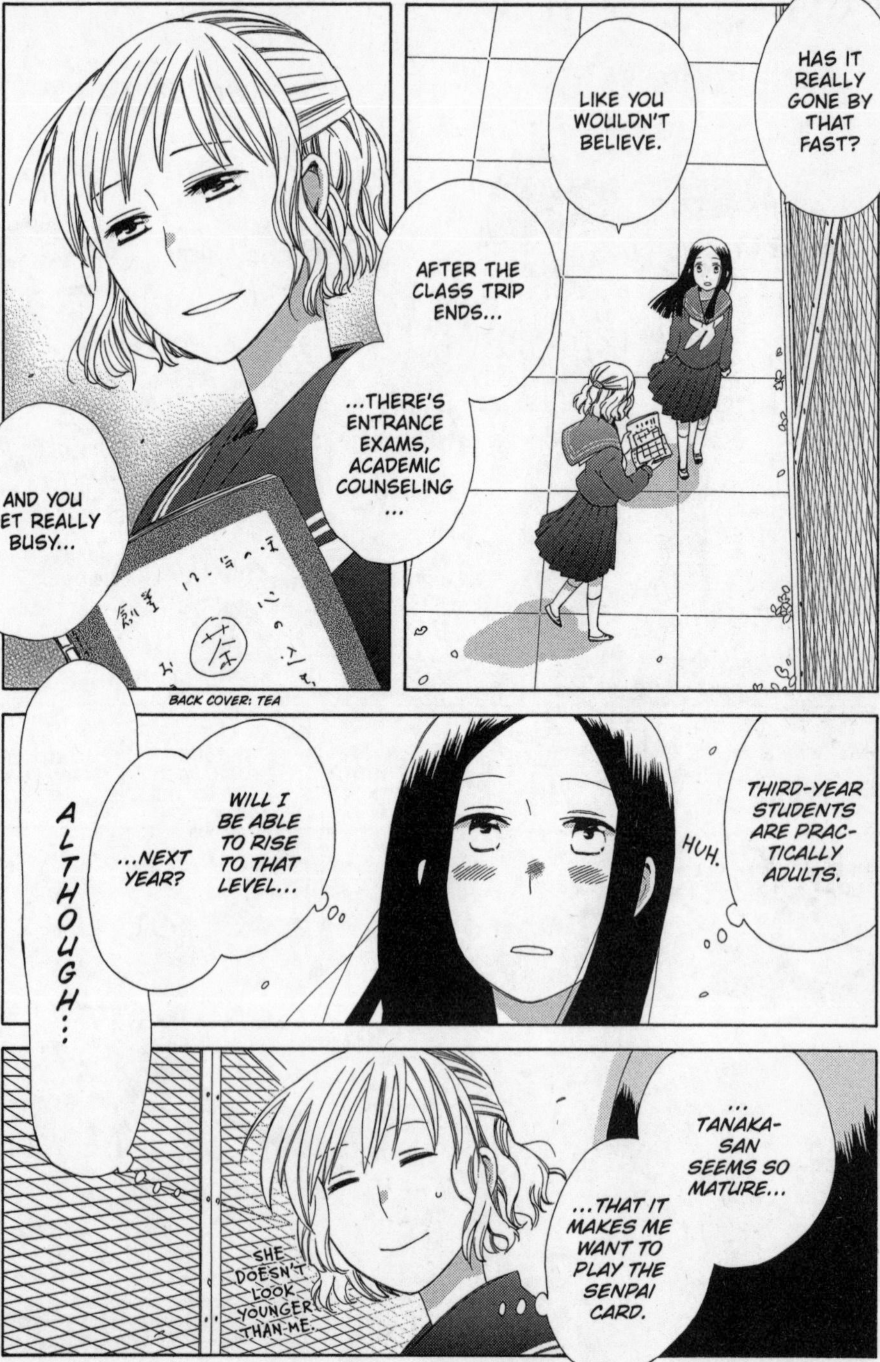
HAS IT REALLY GONE BY THAT FAST?
LIKE YOU WOULDN'T BELIEVE.
AFTER THE CLASS TRIP ENDS...
...THERE'S ENTRANCE EXAMS, ACADEMIC COUNSELING...
AND YOU GET REALLY BUSY...
BACK COVER: TEA
THIRD-YEAR STUDENTS ARE PRACTICALLY ADULTS.
HUH.
WILL I BE ABLE TO RISE TO THAT LEVEL...
...NEXT YEAR?
ALTHOUGH...
...TANAKA-SAN SEEMS SO MATURE...
...THAT IT MAKES ME WANT TO PLAY THE SENPAI CARD.
SHE DOESN'T LOOK YOUNGER THAN ME.

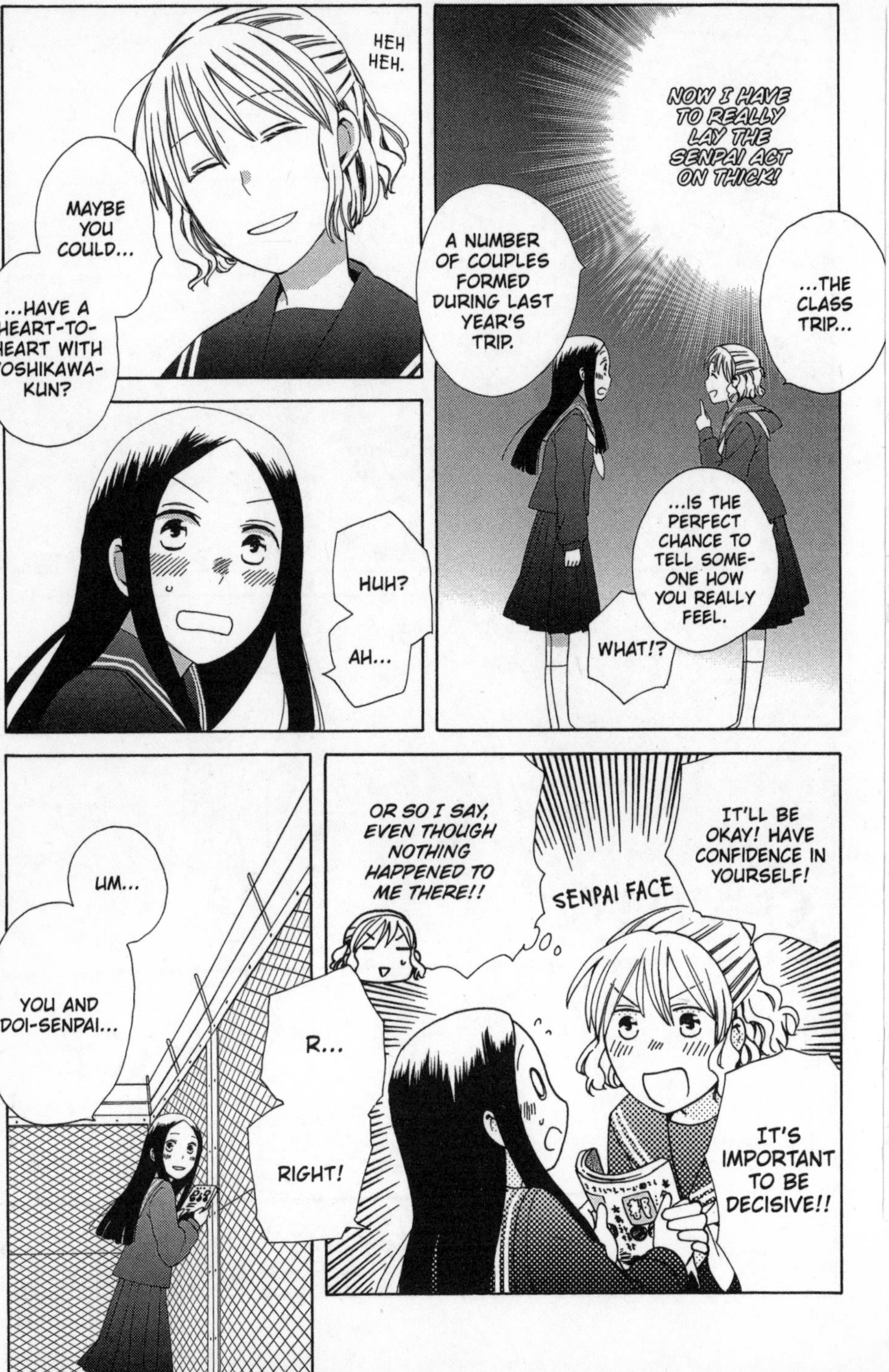
NOW I HAVE TO REALLY LAY THE SENPAI ACT ON THICK!
...THE CLASS TRIP...
A NUMBER OF COUPLES FORMED DURING LAST YEAR'S TRIP.
...IS THE PERFECT CHANCE TO TELL SOME-ONE HOW YOU REALLY FEEL.
WHAT!?
HEH HEH.
MAYBE YOU COULD...
...HAVE A HEART-TO-HEART WITH YOSHIKAWA-KUN?
HUH?
AH...
IT'LL BE OKAY! HAVE CONFIDENCE IN YOURSELF!
SENPAI FACE
OR SO I SAY, EVEN THOUGH NOTHING HAPPENED TO ME THERE!!
IT'S IMPORTANT TO BE DECISIVE!!
R...
RIGHT!
UM...
YOU AND DOI-SENPAI...

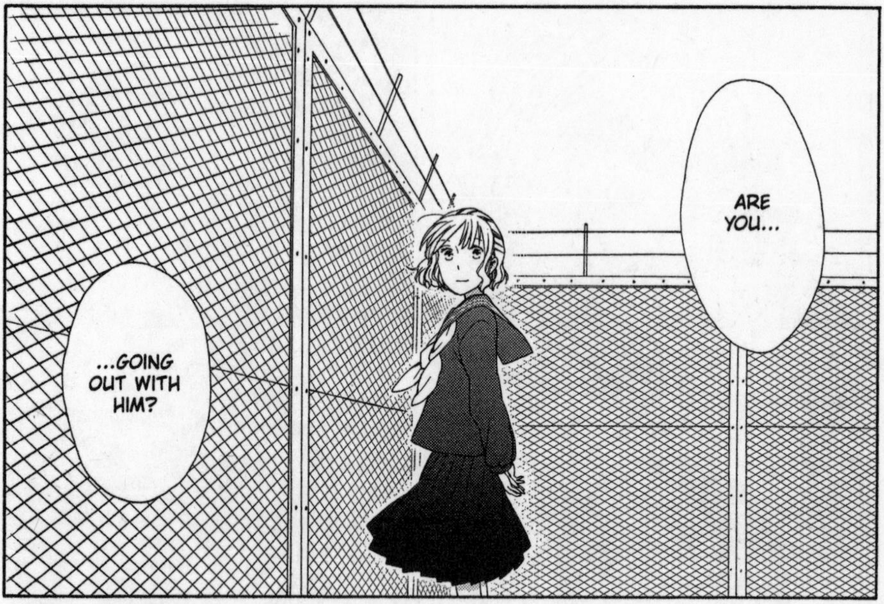
ARE YOU...
...GOING OUT WITH HIM?

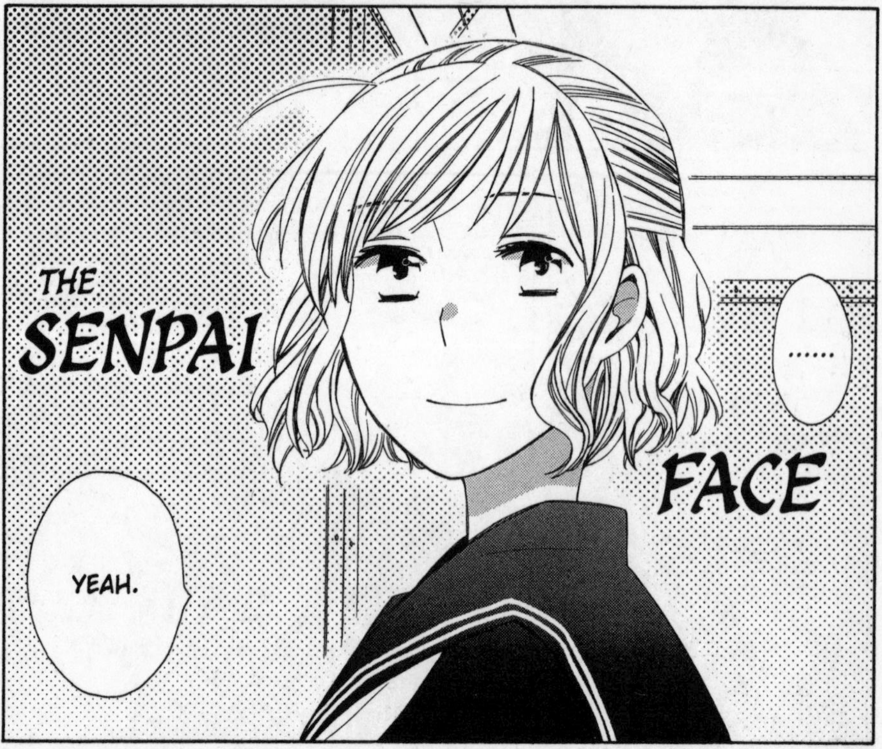
......
THE SENPAI FACE
YEAH.

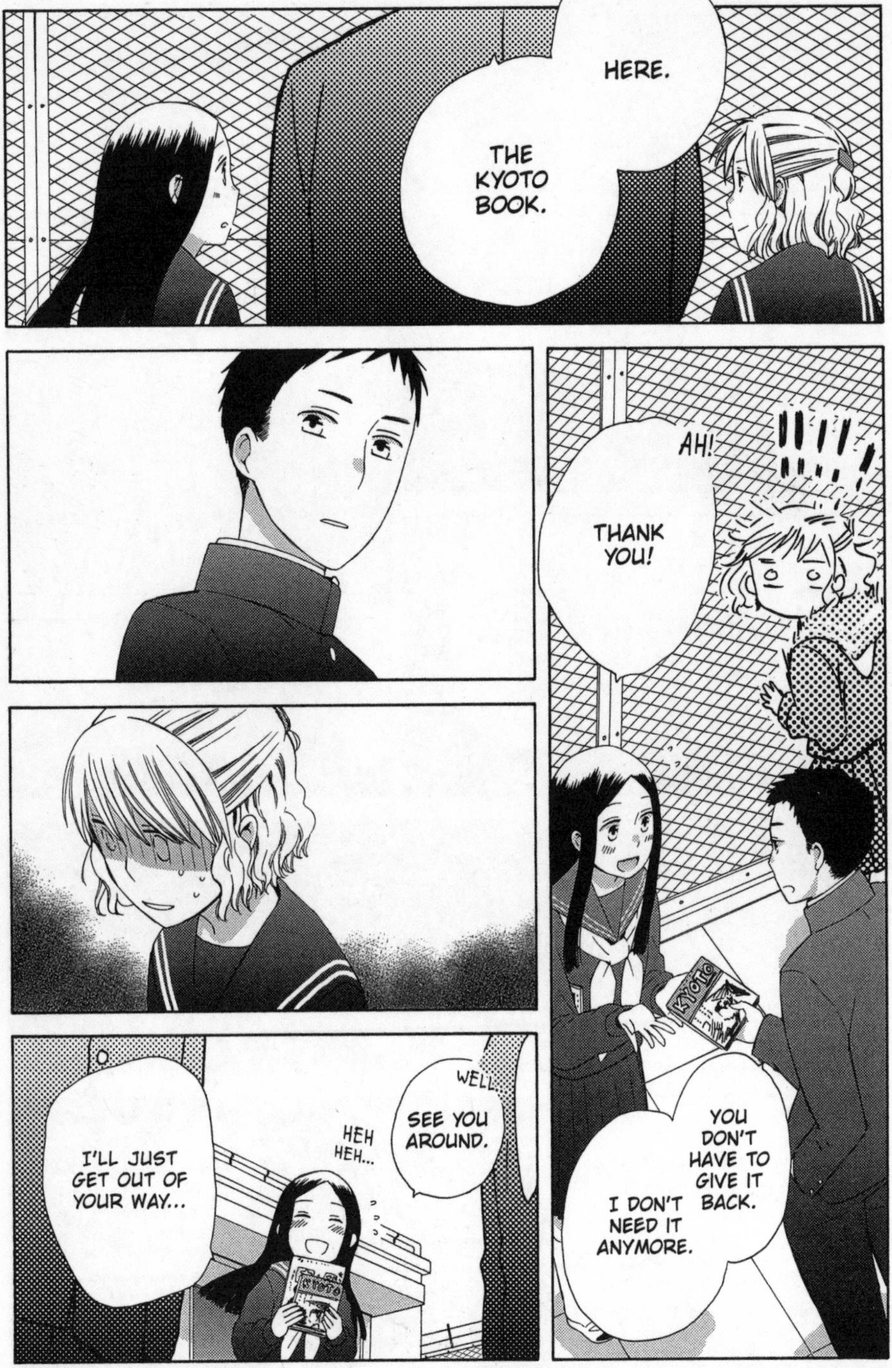
HERE.
THE KYOTO BOOK.
AH!
THANK YOU!
YOU DON'T HAVE TO GIVE IT BACK.
I DON'T NEED IT ANYMORE.
WELL.
SEE YOU AROUND.
HEH HEH...
I'LL JUST GET OUT OF YOUR WAY...

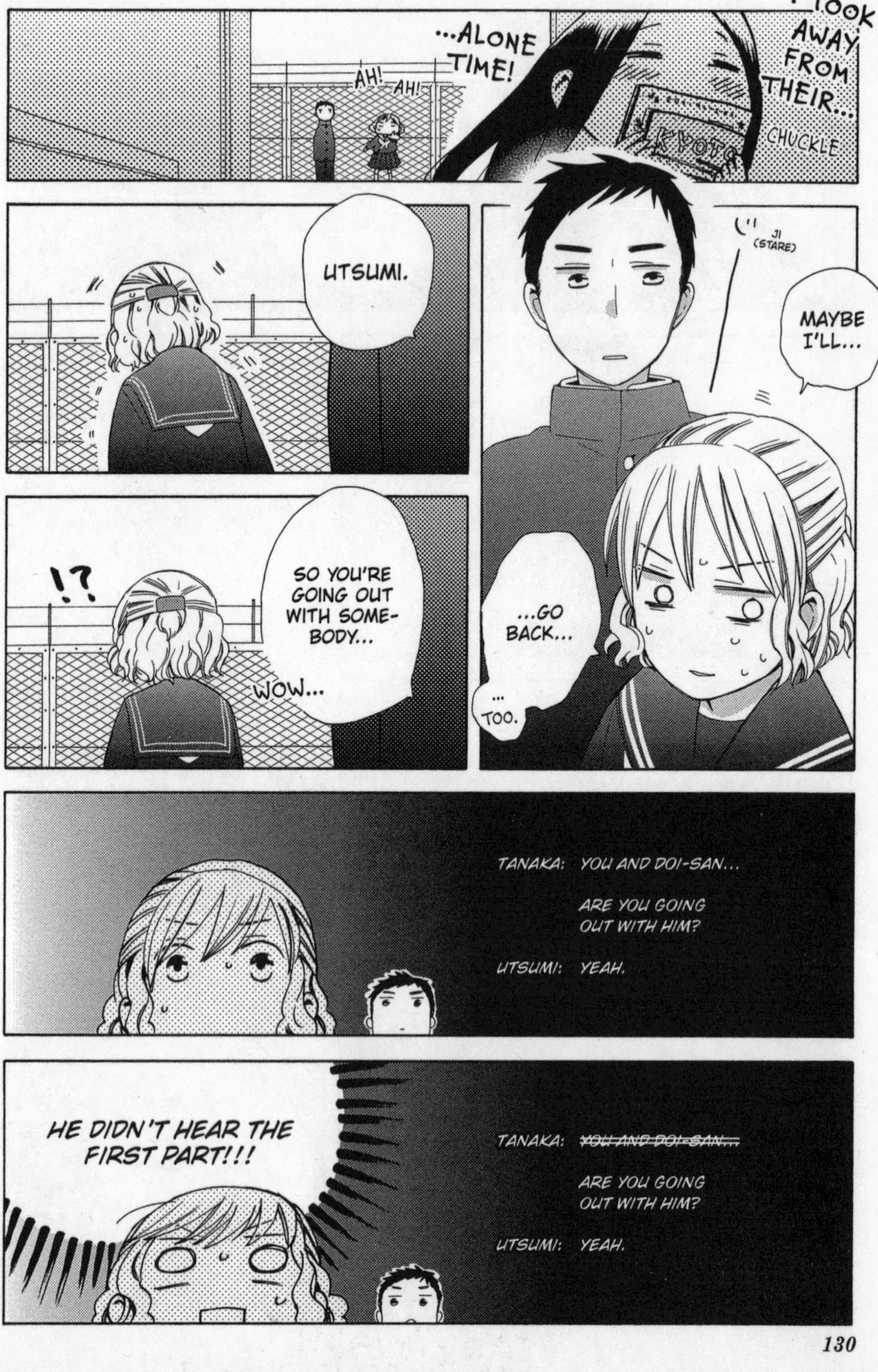
I TOOK AWAY FROM THEIR...
CHUCKLE
KYOTO
...ALONE TIME!
AH!
AH!
JI (STARE)
MAYBE I'LL...
...GO BACK...
... TOO.
UTSUMI.
SO YOU'RE GOING OUT WITH SOME-BODY...
!?
WOW...
TANAKA: YOU AND DOI-SAN...
ARE YOU GOING OUT WITH HIM?
UTSUMI: YEAH.
TANAKA: YOU AND DOI-SAN...
ARE YOU GOING OUT WITH HIM?
UTSUMI: YEAH.
HE DIDN'T HEAR THE FIRST PART!!!

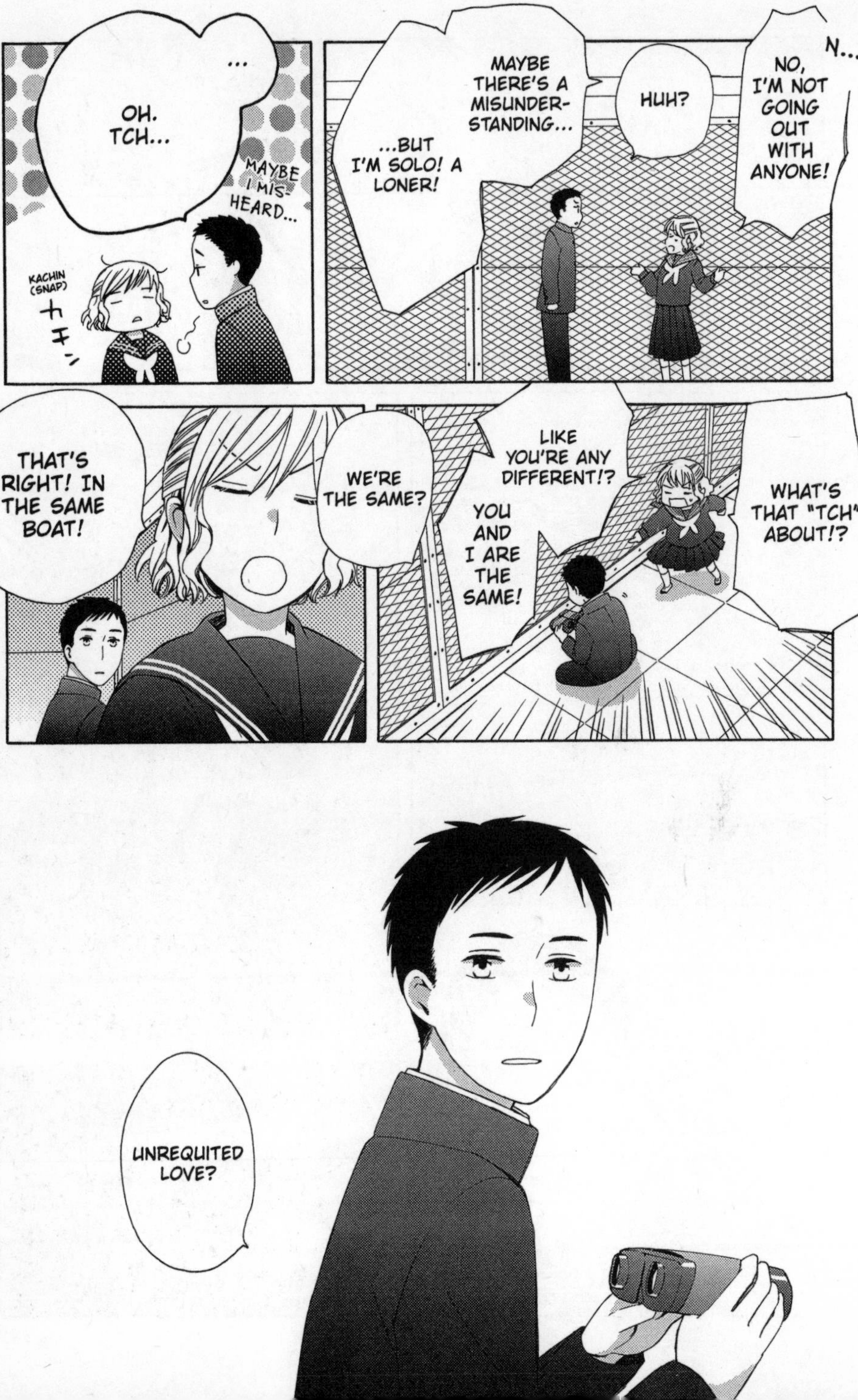
N...
NO, I'M NOT GOING OUT WITH ANYONE!
HUH?
MAYBE THERE'S A MISUNDERSTANDING...
...BUT I'M SOLO! A LONER!
...
OH. TCH...
MAYBE I MISHEARD...
KACHIN (SNAP)
WHAT'S THAT "TCH" ABOUT!?
LIKE YOU'RE ANY DIFFERENT!?
YOU AND I ARE THE SAME!
WE'RE THE SAME?
THAT'S RIGHT! IN THE SAME BOAT!
UNREQUITED LOVE?

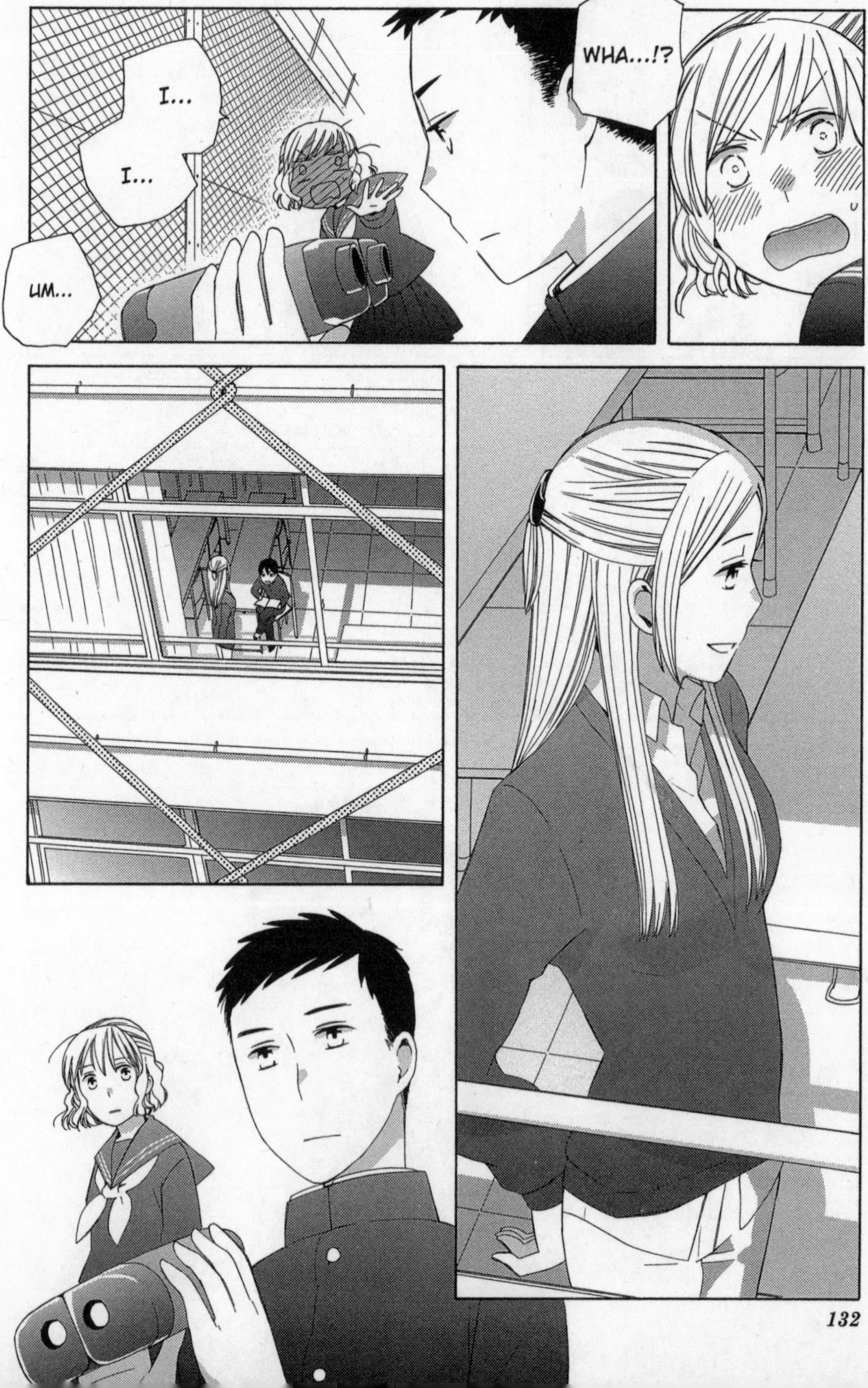
WHA...!?
I...
I...
UM...

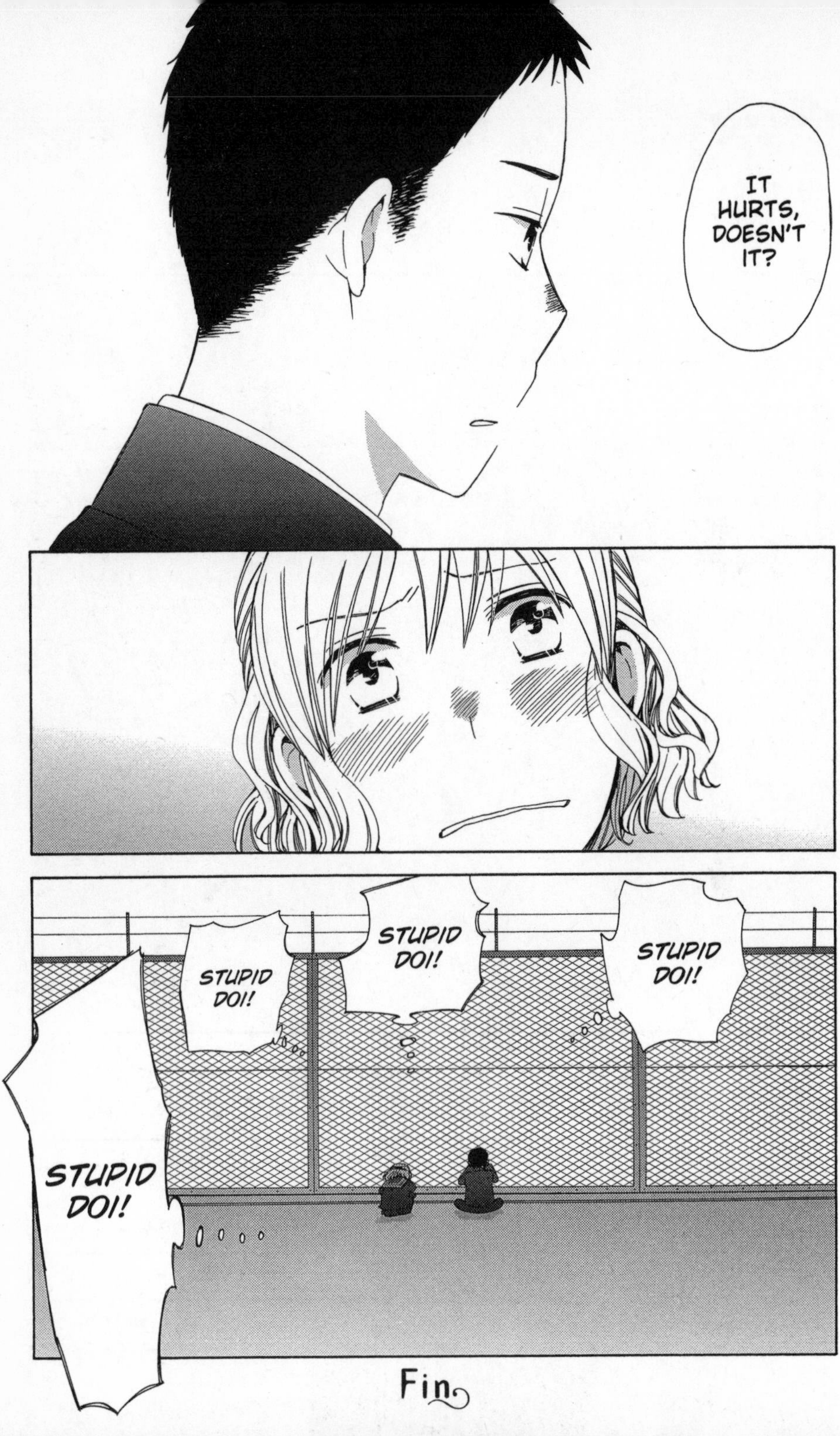
IT HURTS, DOESN'T IT?
STUPID DOI!
STUPID DOI!
STUPID DOI!
STUPID DOI!
Fin

Love at Fourteen

Fuka Mizutani

Love at Fourteen

[Intermission 28]

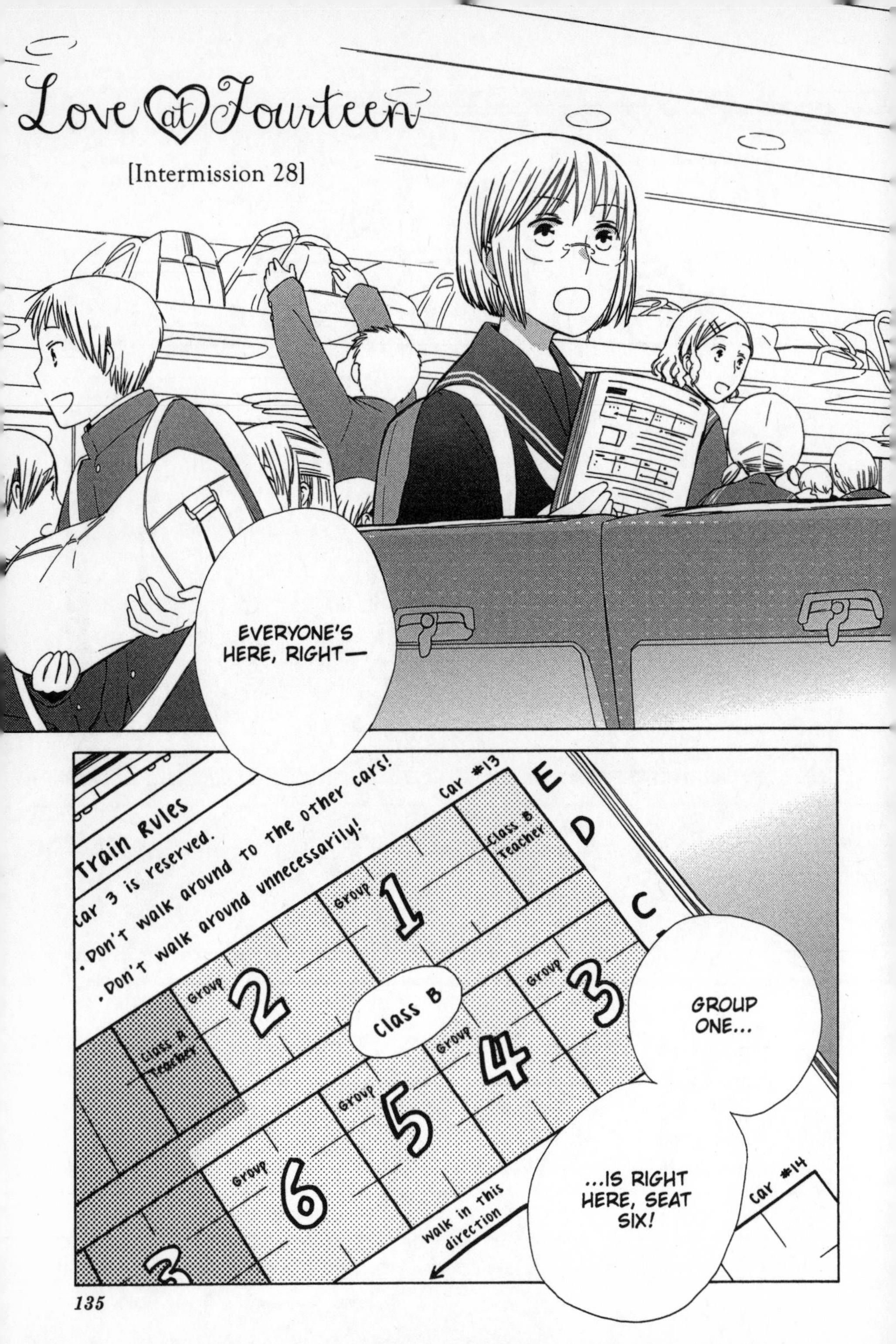
EVERYONE'S HERE, RIGHT—
Train Rules
ar 3 is reserved.
. Don't walk around to the other cars!
. Don't walk around unnecessarily!
Car #13
E
D
C
Class B Teacher
Group 1
Group 2
Group 3
Group 4
Group 5
Group 6
Class B
Class A Teacher
Car #14
Walk in this direction
GROUP ONE...
...IS RIGHT HERE, SEAT SIX!

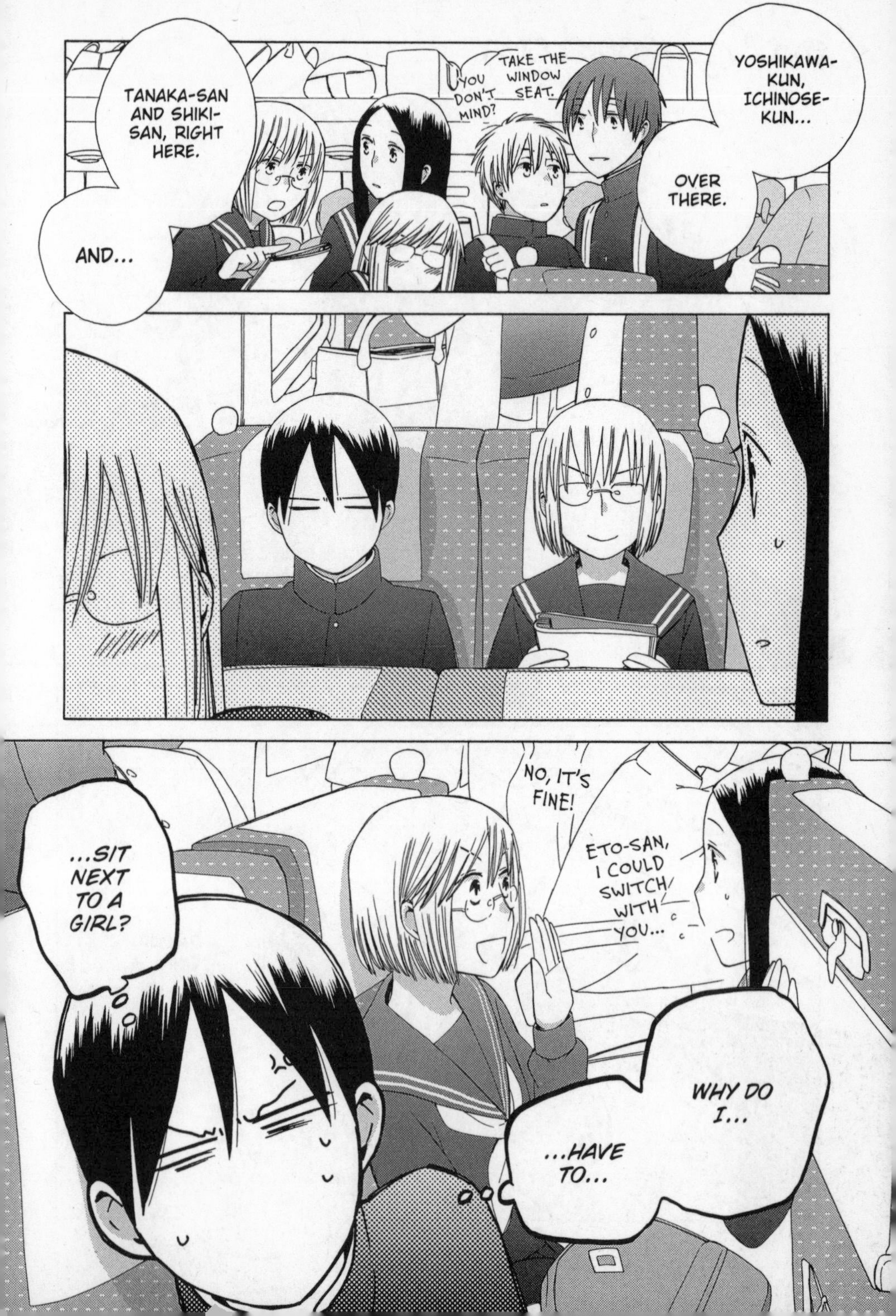
YOSHIKAWA-KUN, ICHINOSE-KUN...
OVER THERE.
TAKE THE WINDOW SEAT.
YOU DON'T MIND?
TANAKA-SAN AND SHIKI-SAN, RIGHT HERE.
AND...
ETO-SAN, I COULD SWITCH WITH YOU...
NO, IT'S FINE!
WHY DO I...
...HAVE TO...
...SIT NEXT TO A GIRL?

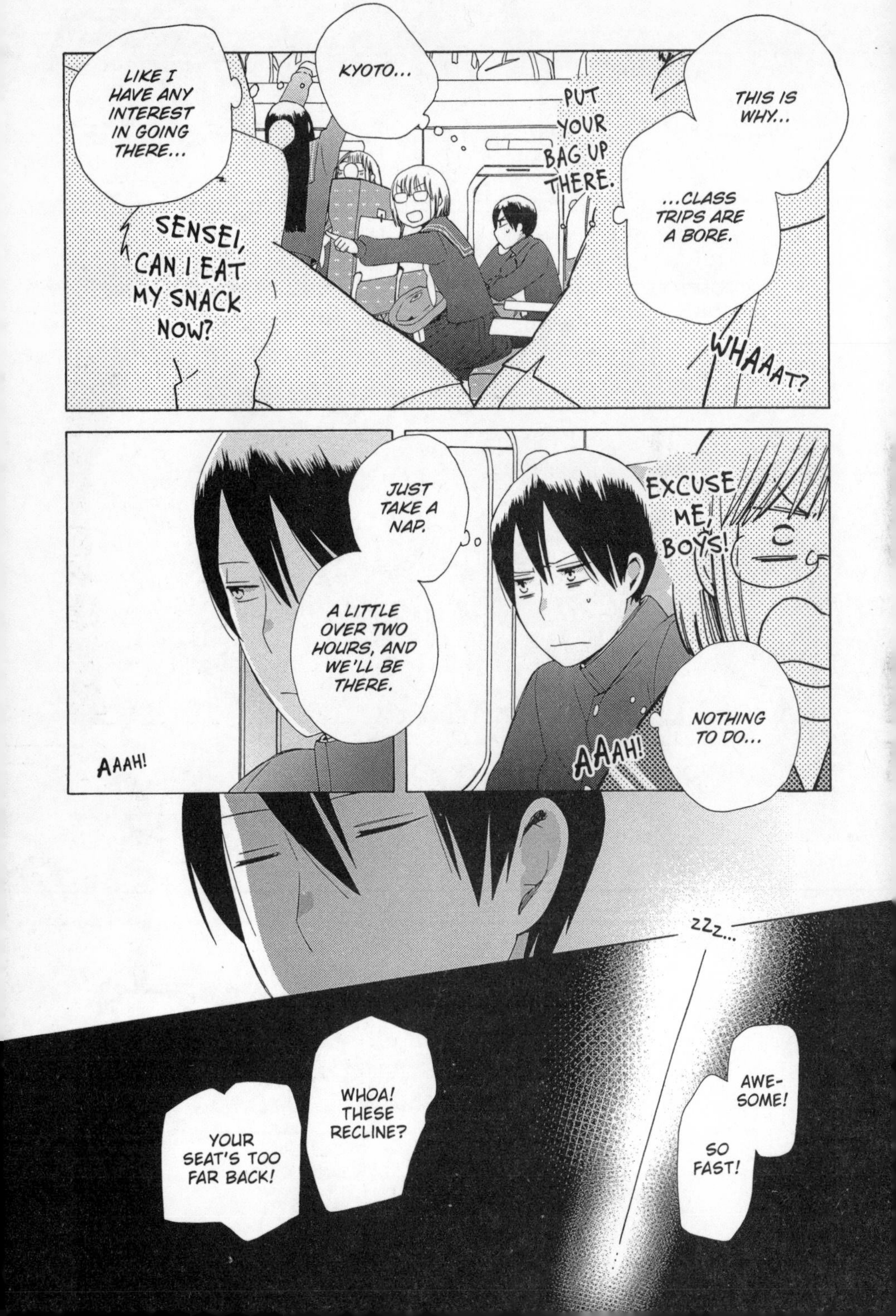
THIS IS WHY...
...CLASS TRIPS ARE A BORE.
WHAAAAT?
PUT YOUR BAG UP THERE.
KYOTO...
LIKE I HAVE ANY INTEREST IN GOING THERE...
SENSEI, CAN I EAT MY SNACK NOW?
EXCUSE ME, BOYS!
NOTHING TO DO...
AAAH!
JUST TAKE A NAP.
A LITTLE OVER TWO HOURS, AND WE'LL BE THERE.
AAAH!
ZZz...
AWE-SOME!
SO FAST!
WHOA! THESE RECLINE?
YOUR SEAT'S TOO FAR BACK!

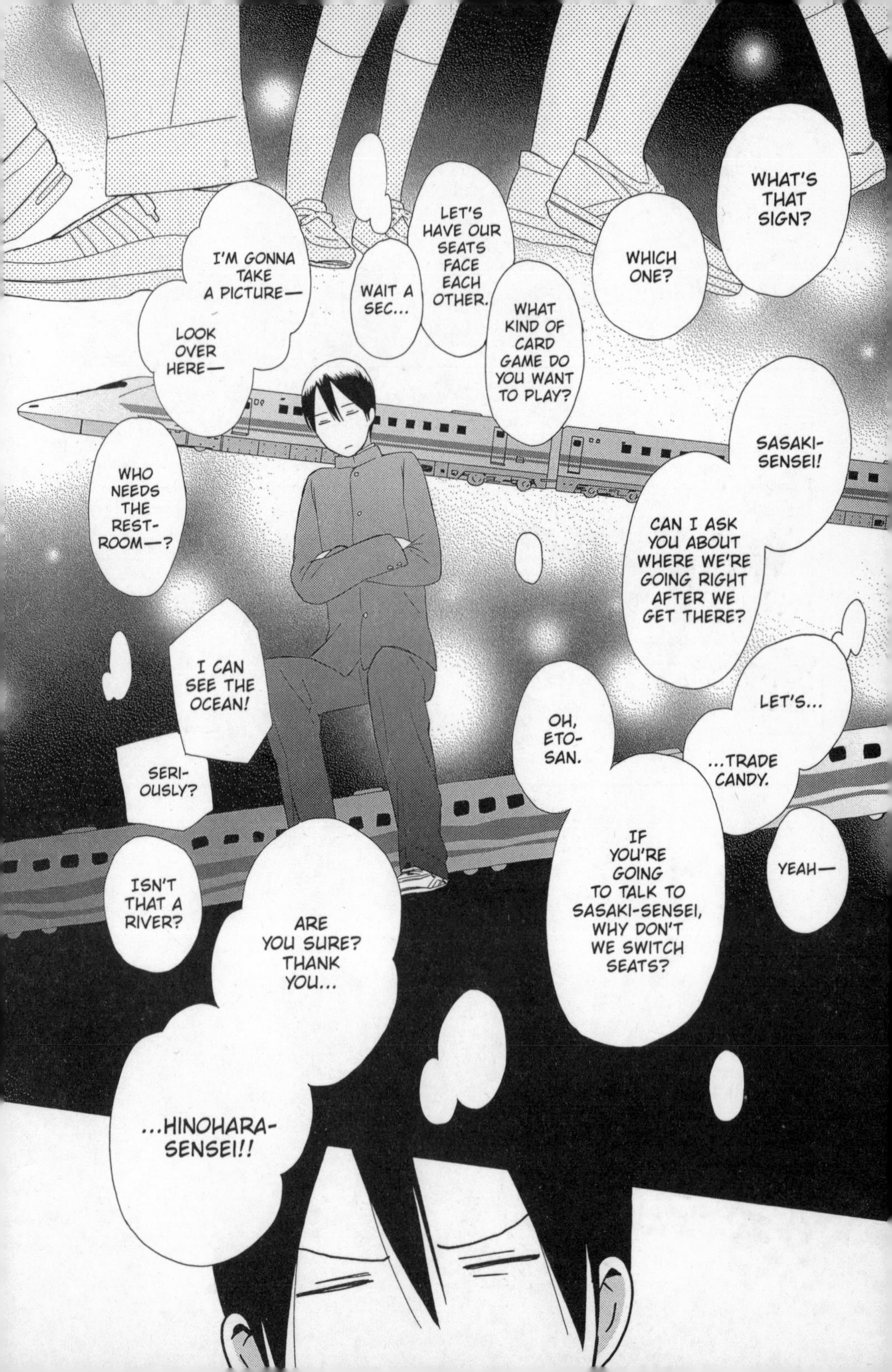
WHAT'S THAT SIGN?
WHICH ONE?
WHAT KIND OF CARD GAME DO YOU WANT TO PLAY?
LET'S HAVE OUR SEATS FACE EACH OTHER.
WAIT A SEC...
I'M GONNA TAKE A PICTURE—
LOOK OVER HERE—
SASAKI-SENSEI!
CAN I ASK YOU ABOUT WHERE WE'RE GOING RIGHT AFTER WE GET THERE?
WHO NEEDS THE REST-ROOM—?
LET'S...
...TRADE CANDY.
OH, ETO-SAN.
I CAN SEE THE OCEAN!
SERI-OUSLY?
YEAH—
IF YOU'RE GOING TO TALK TO SASAKI-SENSEI, WHY DON'T WE SWITCH SEATS?
ARE YOU SURE? THANK YOU...
ISN'T THAT A RIVER?
...HINOHARA-SENSEI!!

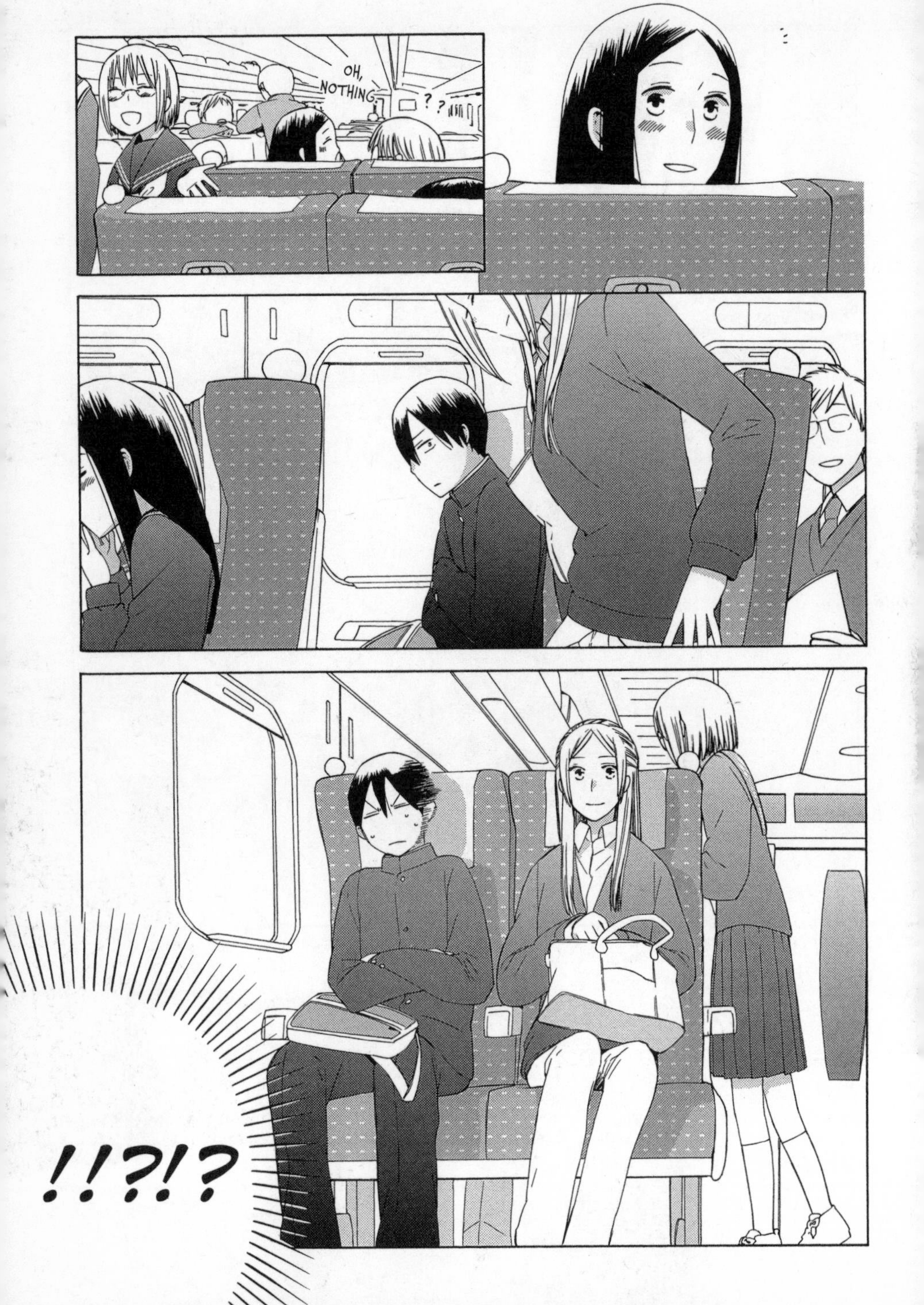
OH, NOTHING
? ?
!!?!?

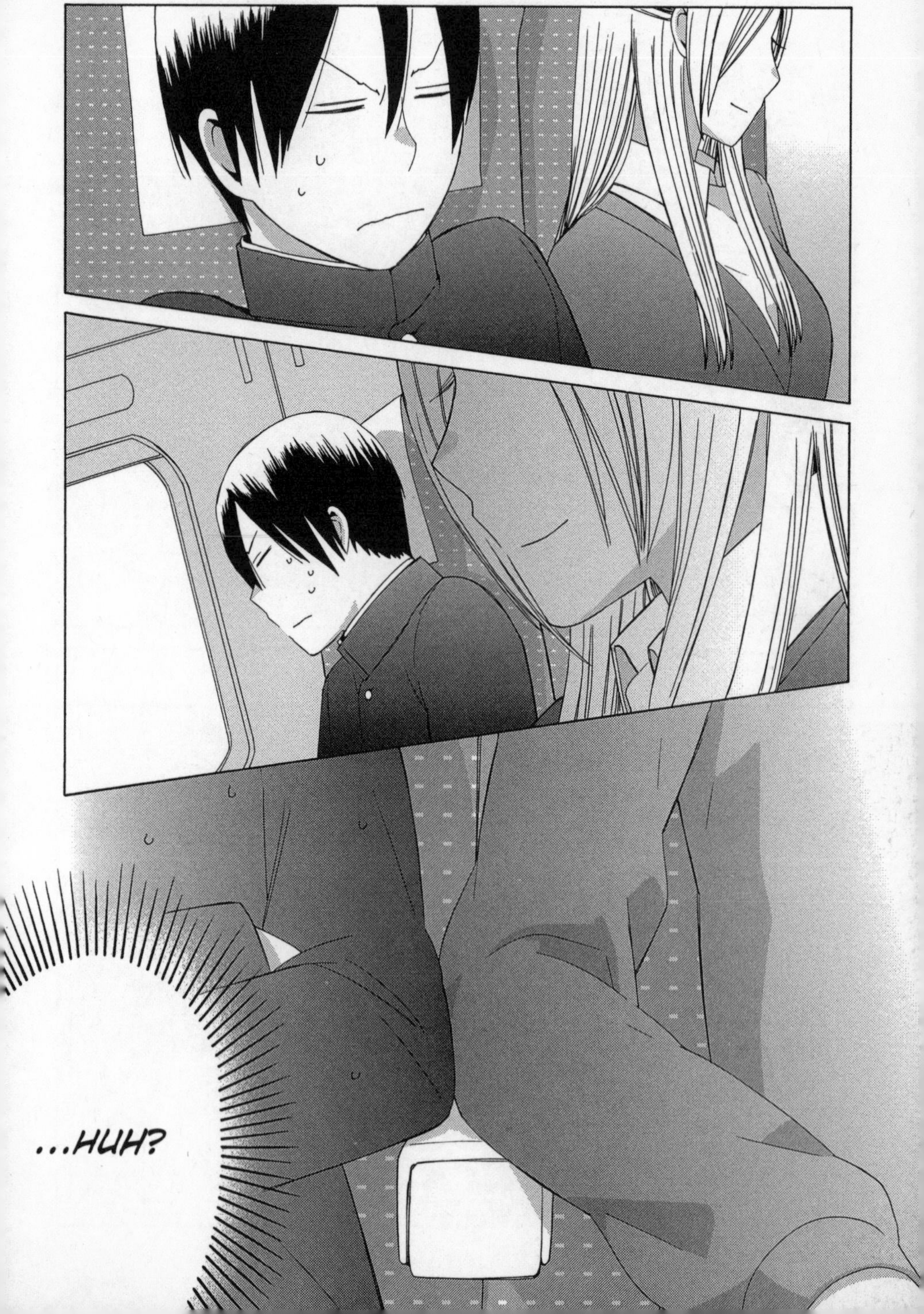
...HUH?

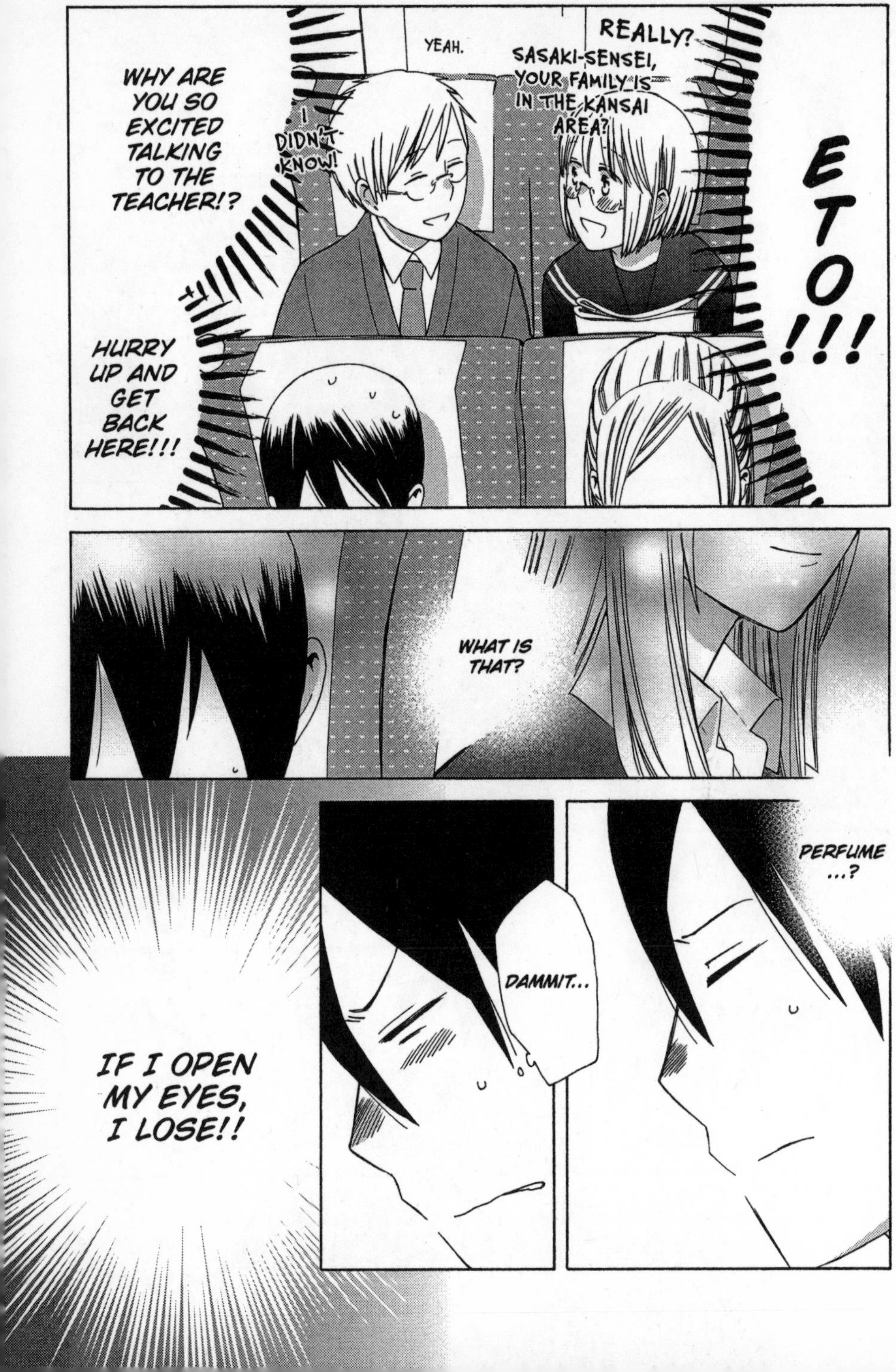
ETO!!!
REALLY?
SASAKI-SENSEI, YOUR FAMILY IS IN THE KANSAI AREA?
YEAH.
I DIDN'T KNOW!
WHY ARE YOU SO EXCITED TALKING TO THE TEACHER!?
HURRY UP AND GET BACK HERE!!!
WHAT IS THAT?
PERFUME ...?
DAMMIT...
IF I OPEN MY EYES, I LOSE!!

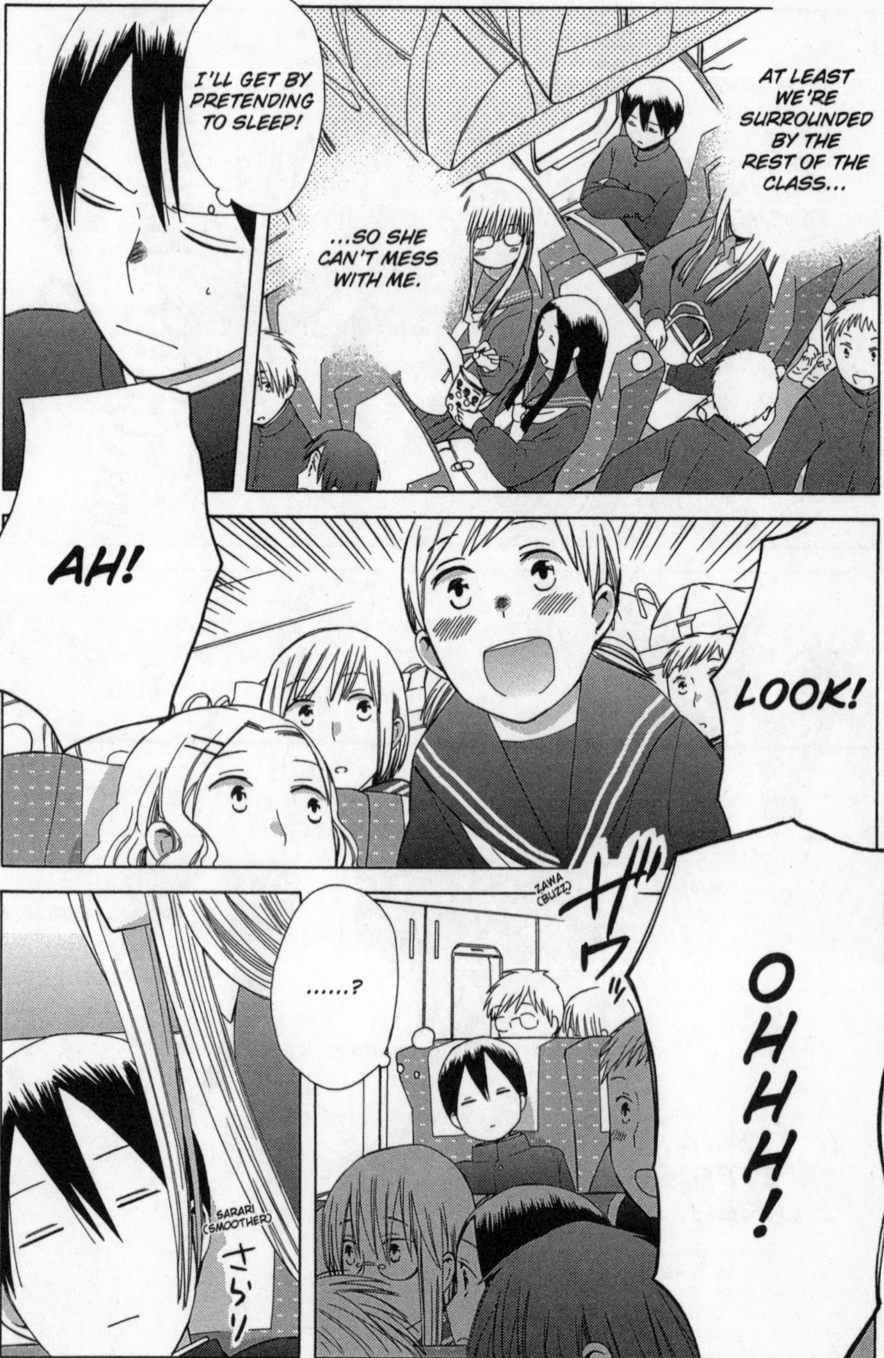
AT LEAST WE'RE SURROUNDED BY THE REST OF THE CLASS...
...SO SHE CAN'T MESS WITH ME.
I'LL GET BY PRETENDING TO SLEEP!
AH!
LOOK!
ZAWA (BUZZ)
ザワッ
OHHH!
......?
SARARI (SMOOTHER)
さらリ

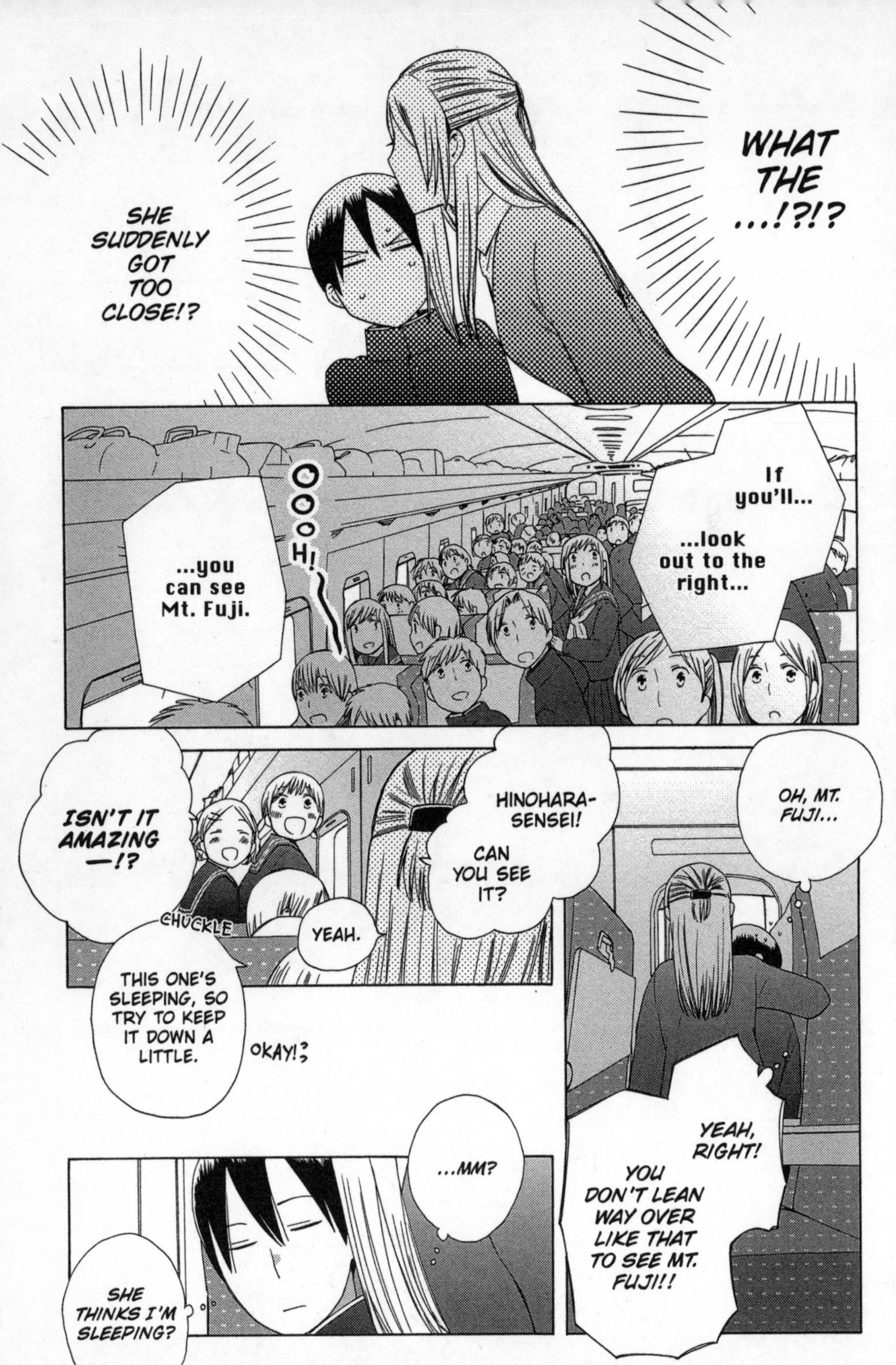
WHAT THE ...!?!?
SHE SUDDENLY GOT TOO CLOSE!?
If you'll...
...look out to the right...
OOOOH!
...you can see Mt. Fuji.
OH, MT. FUJI...
YEAH, RIGHT! YOU DON'T LEAN WAY OVER LIKE THAT TO SEE MT. FUJI!!
HINOHARA-SENSEI!
CAN YOU SEE IT?
YEAH.
ISN'T IT AMAZING—!?
CHUCKLE
THIS ONE'S SLEEPING, SO TRY TO KEEP IT DOWN A LITTLE.
OKAY!?
...MM?
SHE THINKS I'M SLEEPING?

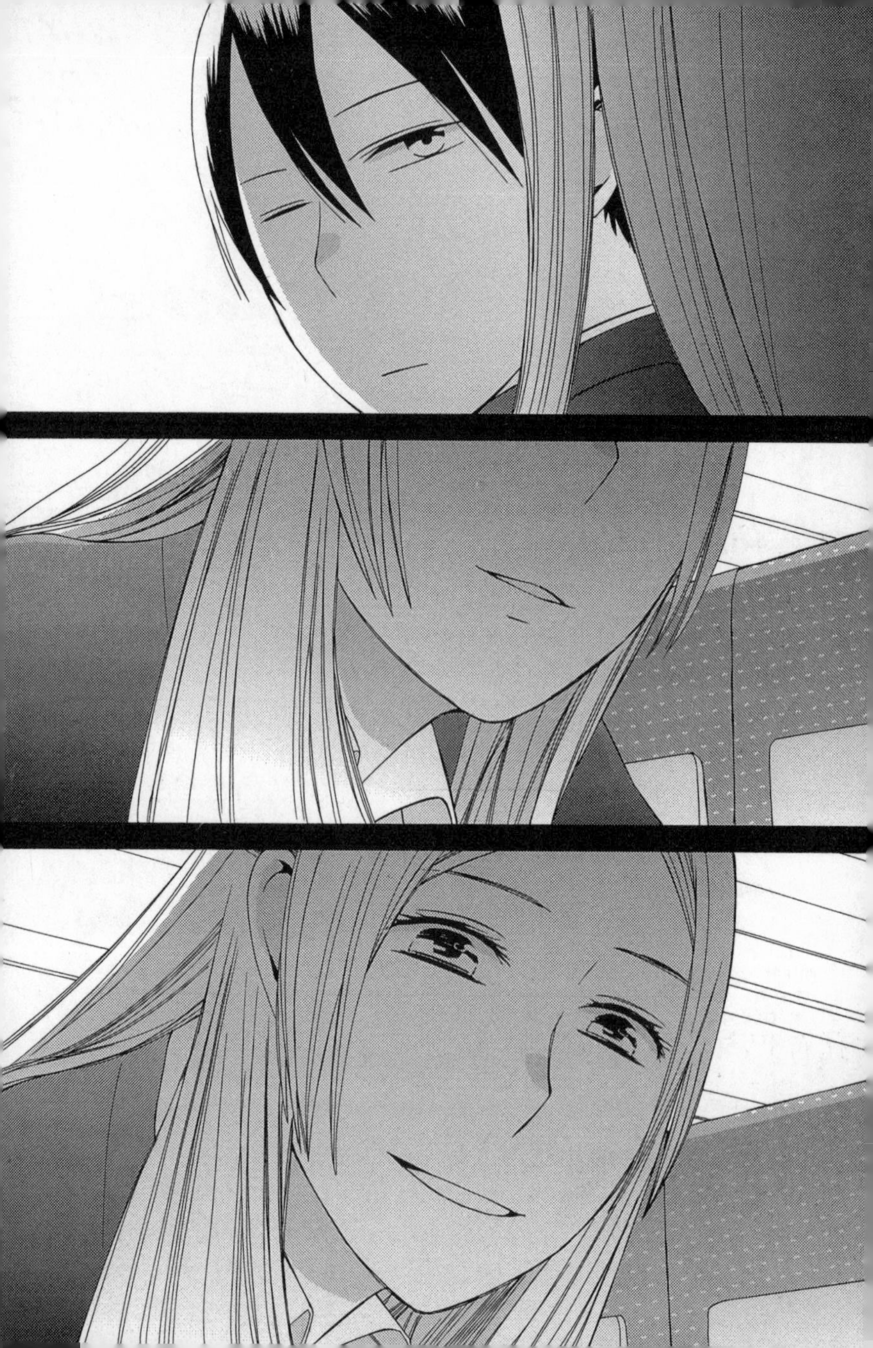

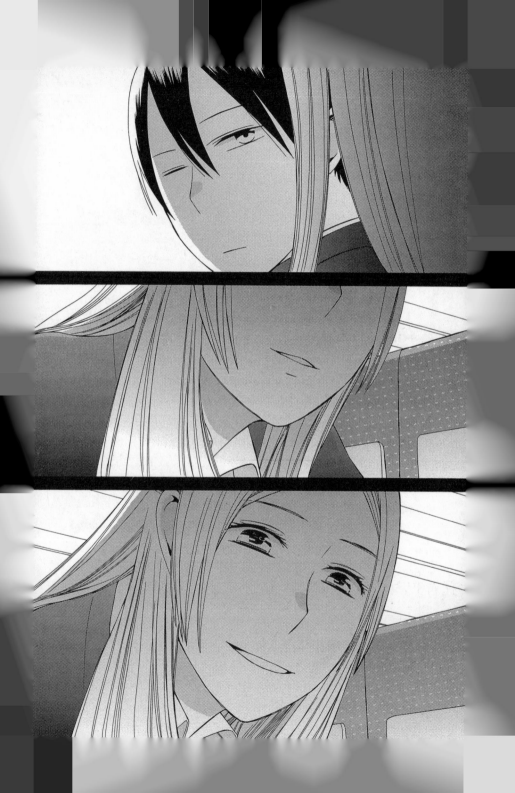

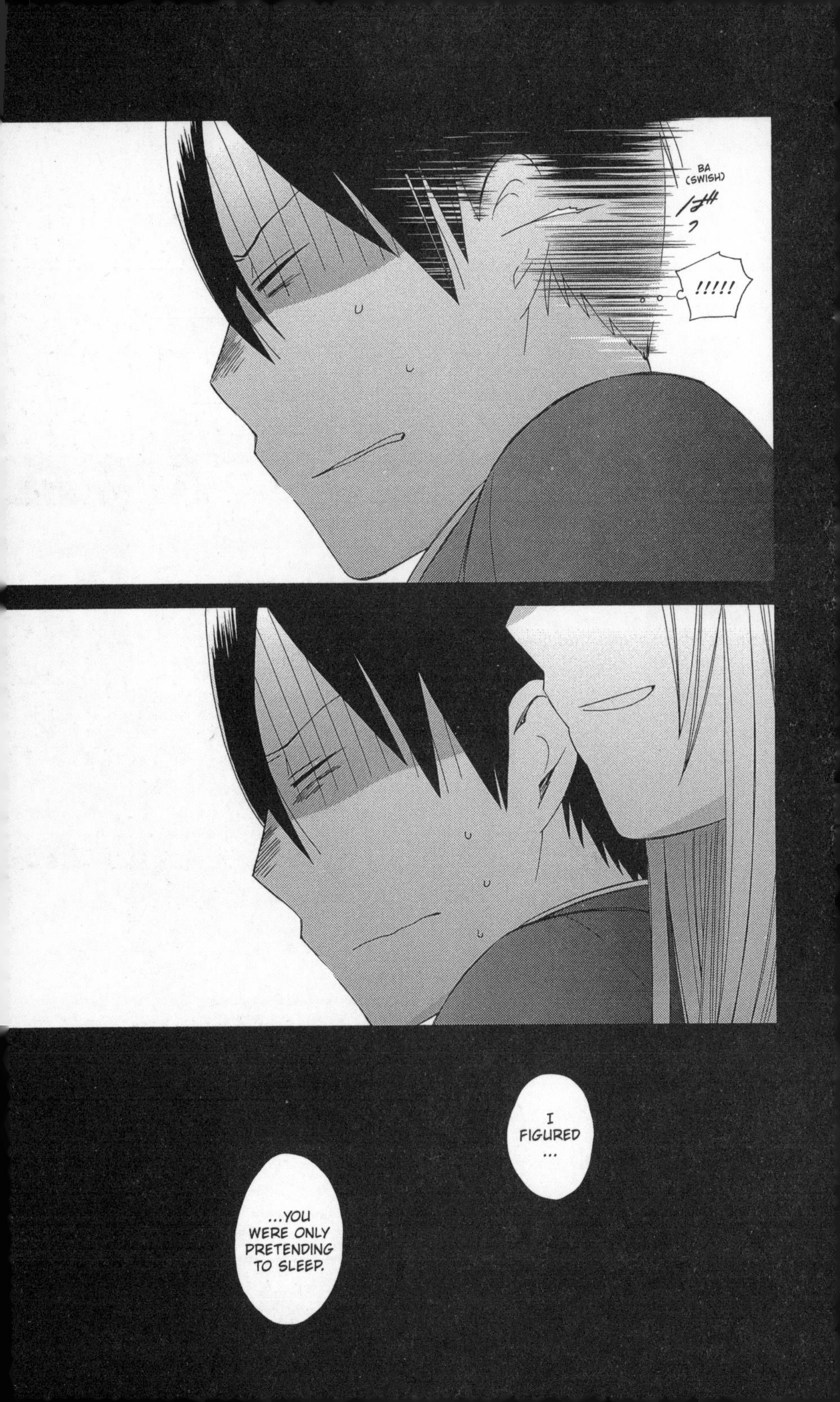
BA (SWISH)
ばっ
!!!!!
I FIGURED ...
...YOU WERE ONLY PRETENDING TO SLEEP.

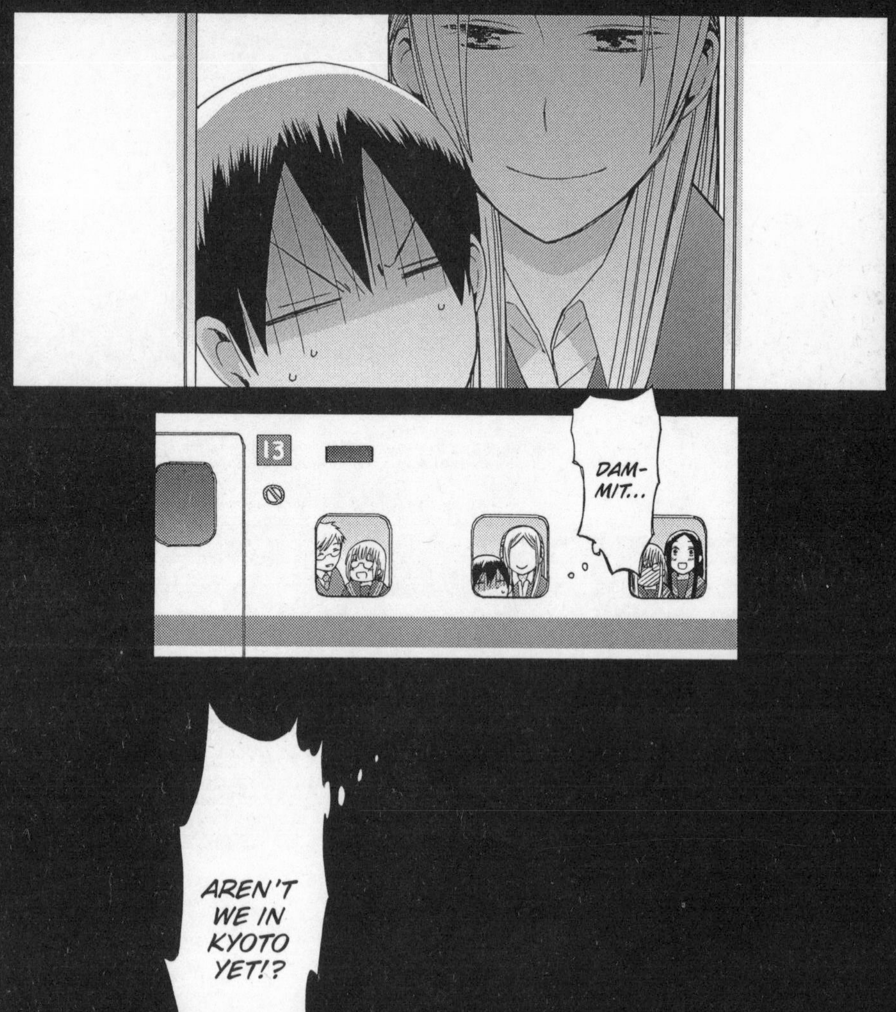
DAM-MIT...
AREN'T WE IN KYOTO YET!?

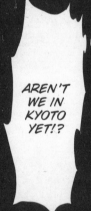

Fin

[Chapter 24]

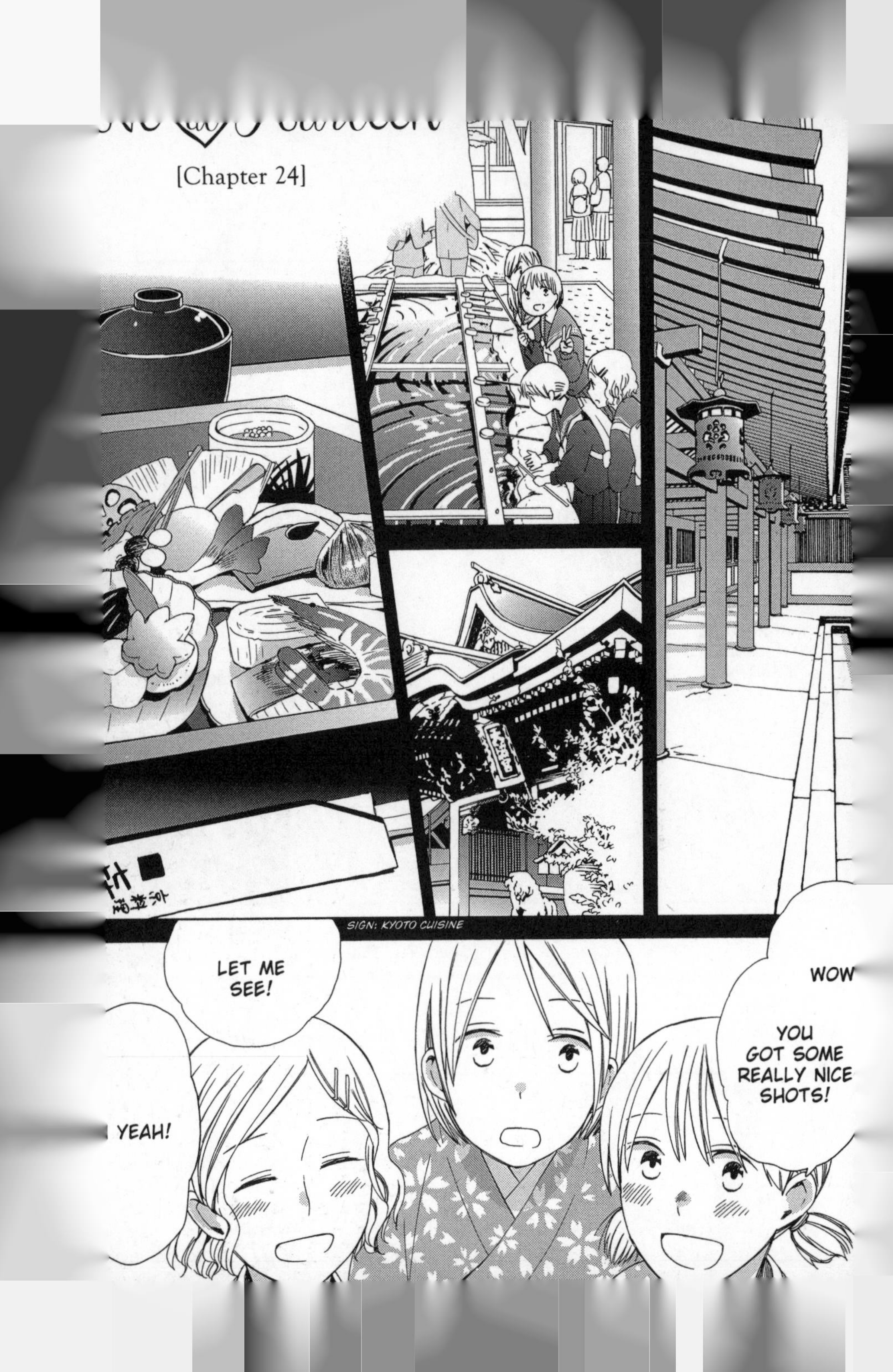
SIGN: KYOTO CUISINE
WOW
YOU GOT SOME REALLY NICE SHOTS!
LET ME SEE!
YEAH!

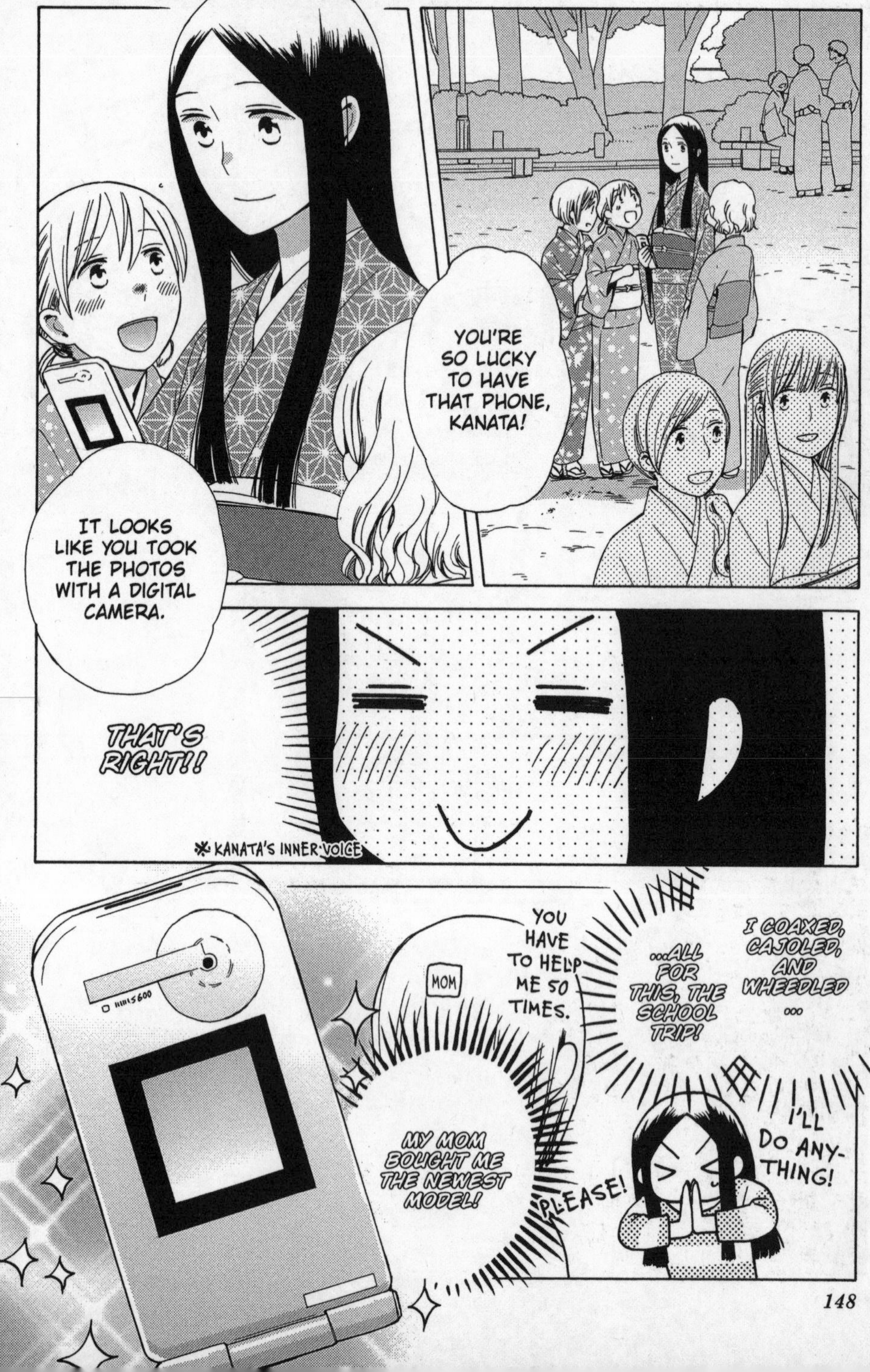
YOU'RE SO LUCKY TO HAVE THAT PHONE, KANATA!
IT LOOKS LIKE YOU TOOK THE PHOTOS WITH A DIGITAL CAMERA.
THAT'S RIGHT!!
※KANATA'S INNER VOICE
I COAXED, CAJOLED, AND WHEEDLED...
...ALL FOR THIS, THE SCHOOL TRIP!
YOU HAVE TO HELP ME 50 TIMES.
MOM
I'LL DO ANY-THING!
PLEASE!
MY MOM BOUGHT ME THE NEWEST MODEL!

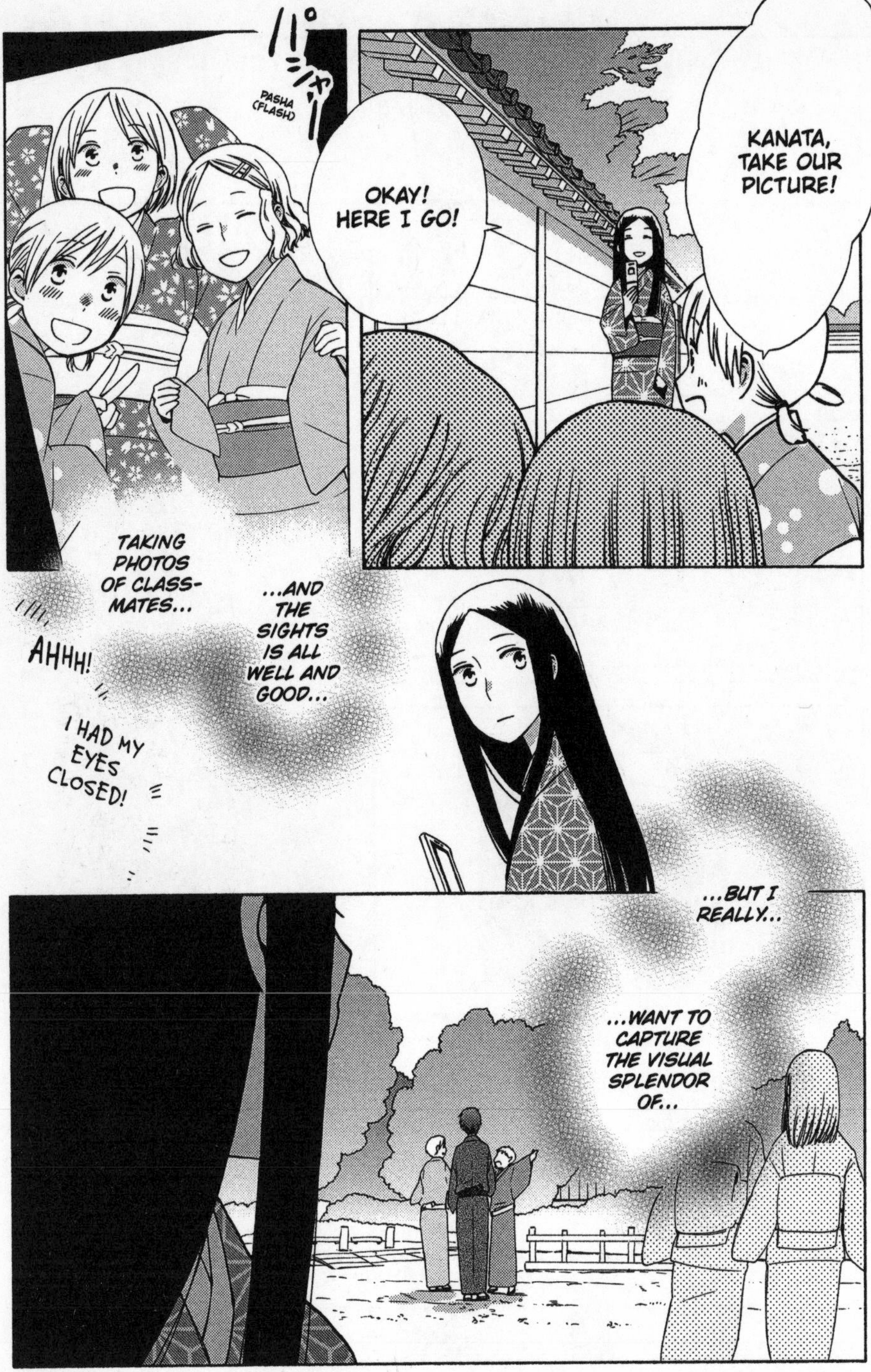
KANATA, TAKE OUR PICTURE!
OKAY! HERE I GO!
パシャ
PASHA (FLASH)
TAKING PHOTOS OF CLASS-MATES...
...AND THE SIGHTS IS ALL WELL AND GOOD...
AHHH!
I HAD MY EYES CLOSED!
...BUT I REALLY...
...WANT TO CAPTURE THE VISUAL SPLENDOR OF...

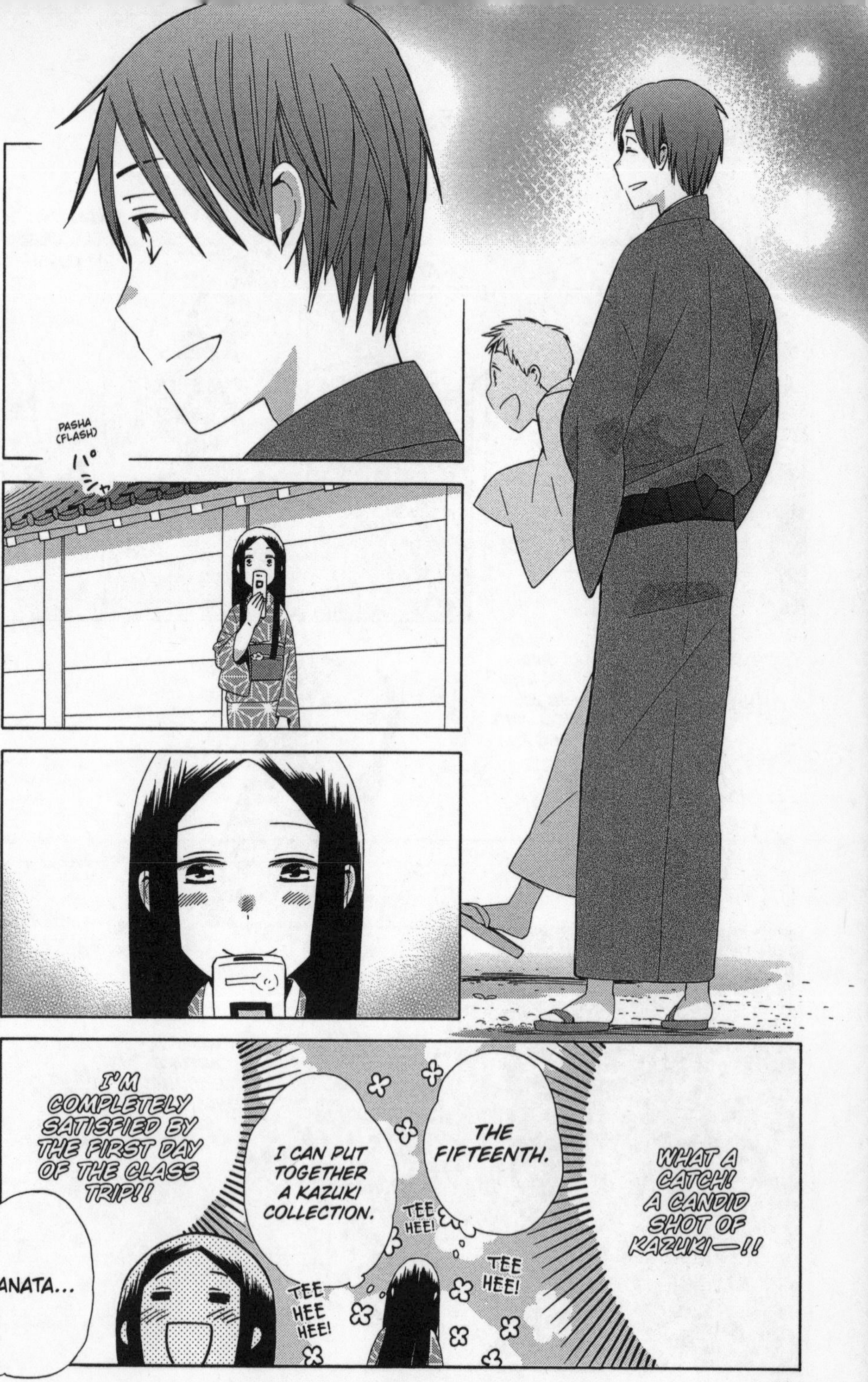
PASHA (FLASH)
パシャ
WHAT A CATCH! A CANDID SHOT OF KAZUKI—!!
THE FIFTEENTH.
TEE HEE!
TEE HEE!
I CAN PUT TOGETHER A KAZUKI COLLECTION.
TEE HEE HEE!
I'M COMPLETELY SATISFIED BY THE FIRST DAY OF THE CLASS TRIP!!
KANATA...

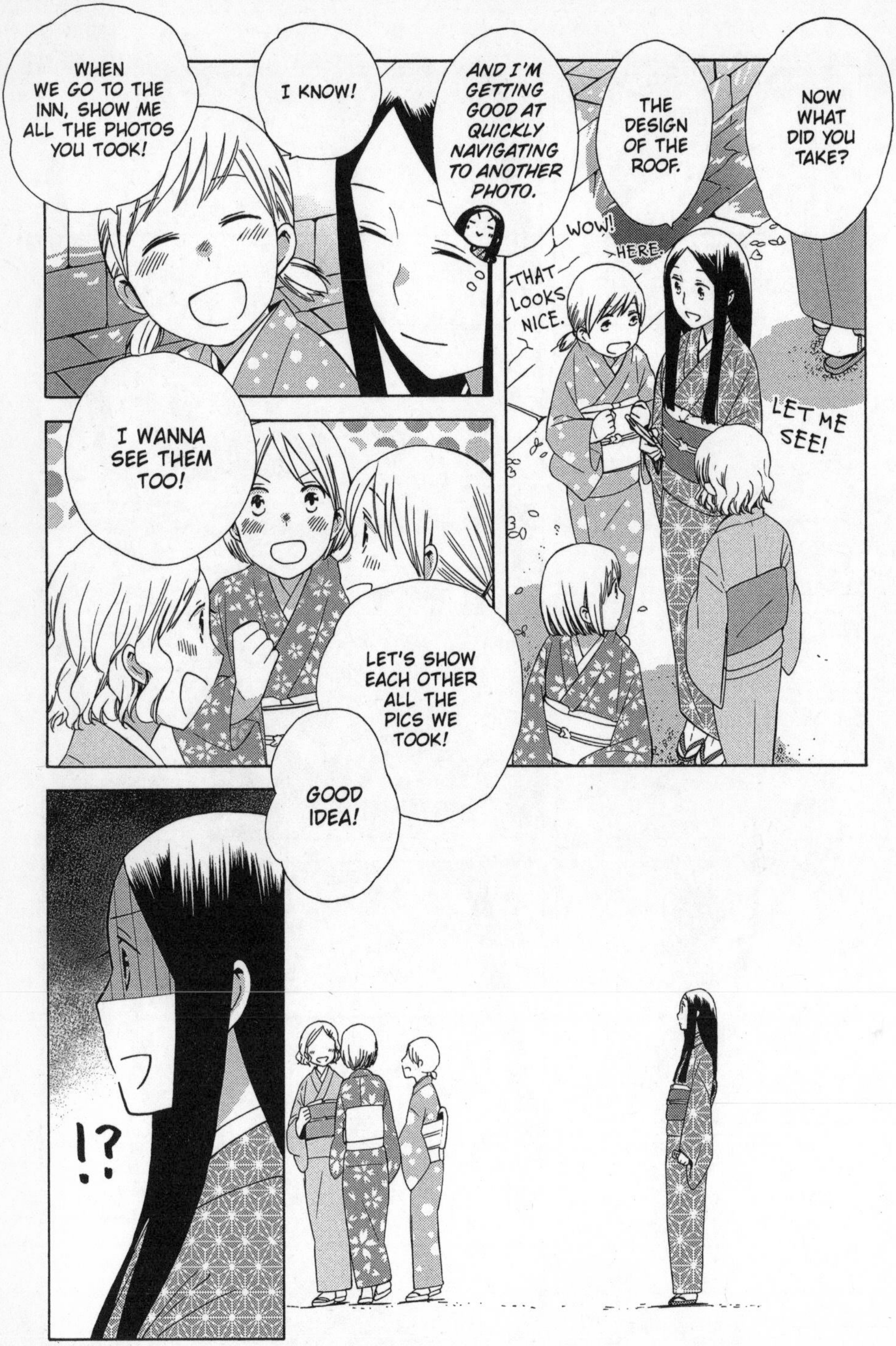
NOW WHAT DID YOU TAKE?
THE DESIGN OF THE ROOF.
HERE.
WOW!
THAT LOOKS NICE.
LET ME SEE!
WHEN WE GO TO THE INN, SHOW ME ALL THE PHOTOS YOU TOOK!
I KNOW!
AND I'M GETTING GOOD AT QUICKLY NAVIGATING TO ANOTHER PHOTO.
I WANNA SEE THEM TOO!
LET'S SHOW EACH OTHER ALL THE PICS WE TOOK!
GOOD IDEA!
!?

SIGN: WELCOME MIDDLE SCHOOL STUDENTS

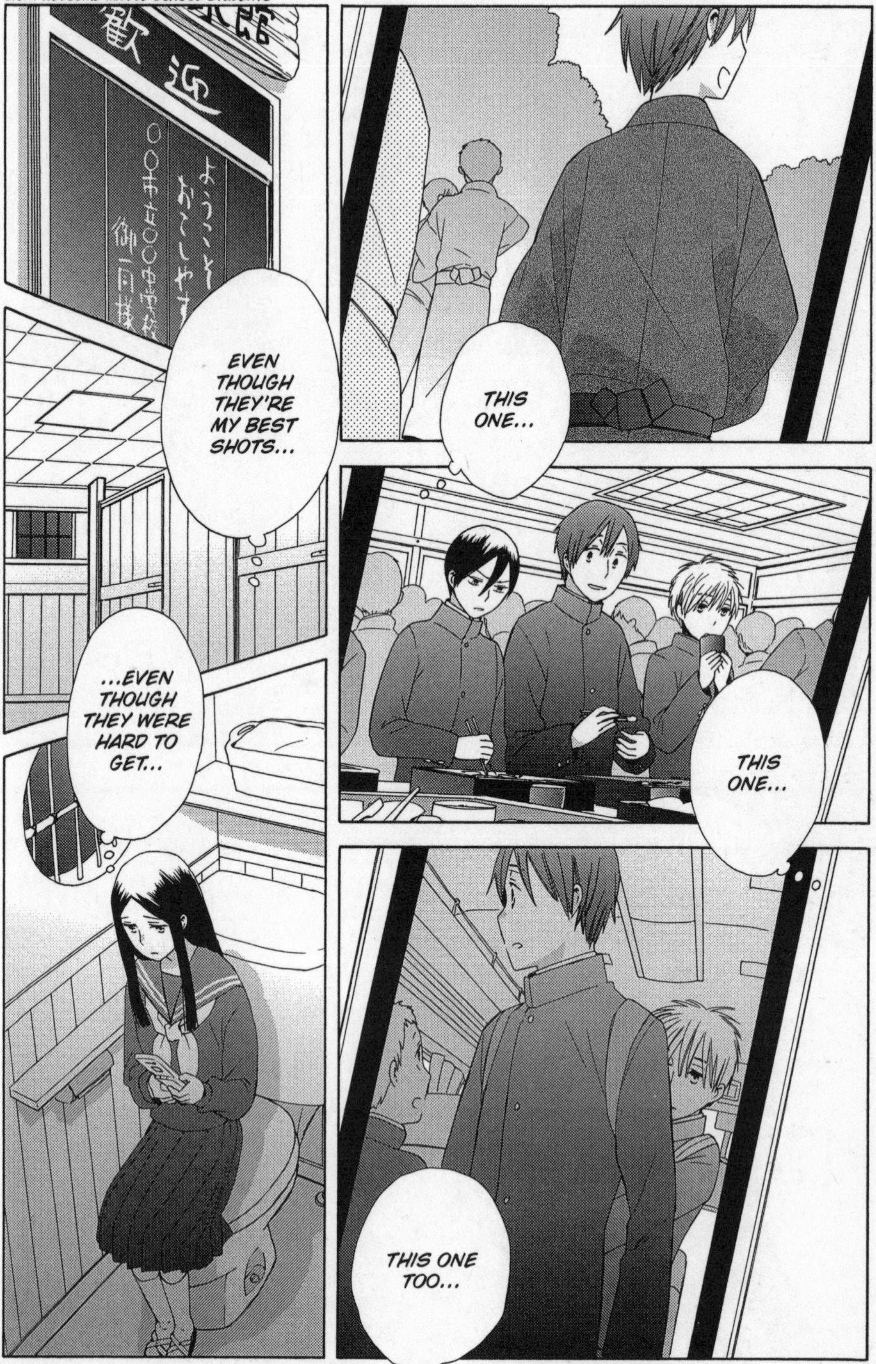
THIS ONE...
THIS ONE...
THIS ONE TOO...
EVEN THOUGH THEY'RE MY BEST SHOTS...
...EVEN THOUGH THEY WERE HARD TO GET...

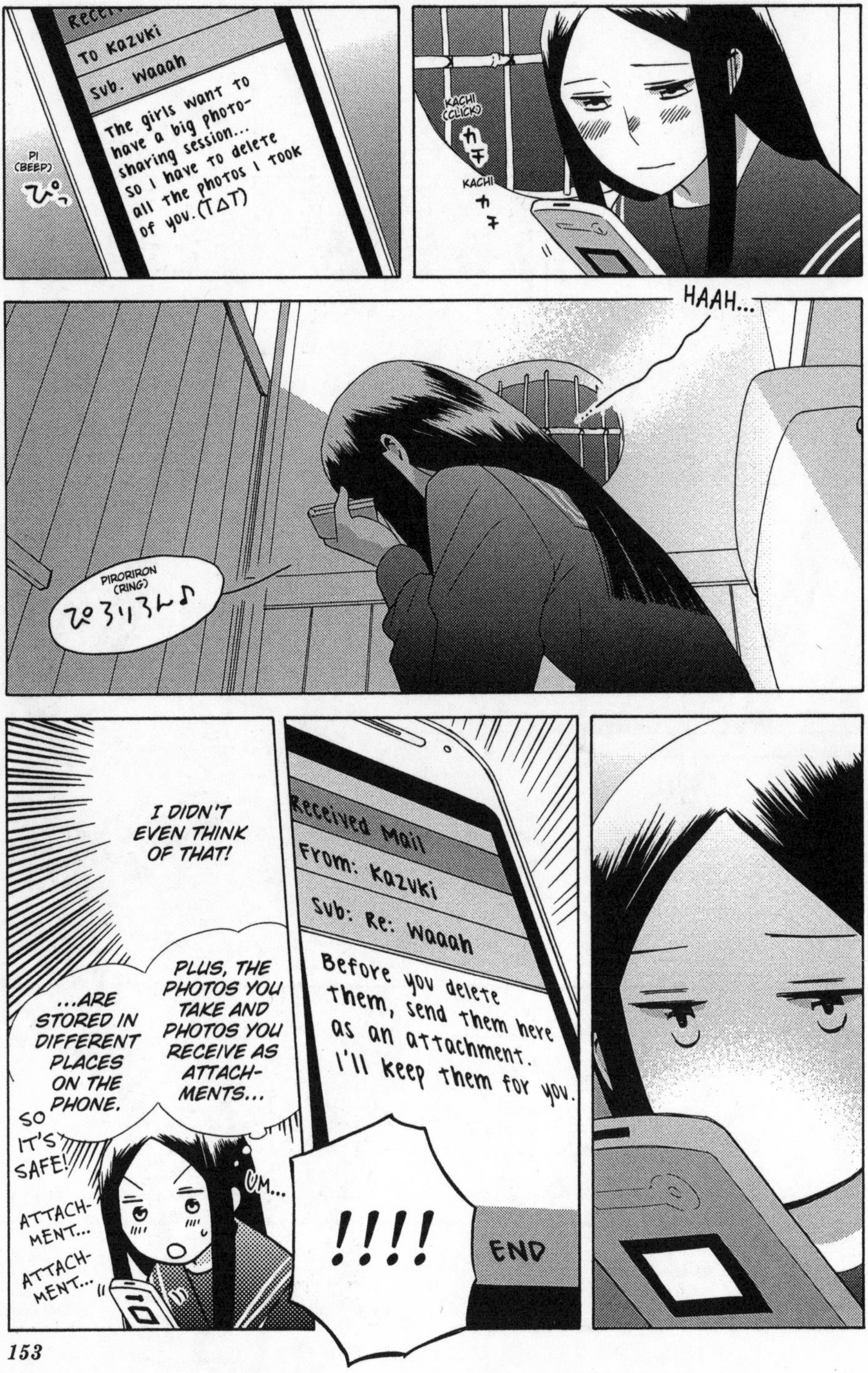
KACHI (CLICK)
カチ
KACHI
カチ
Received
To Kazuki
Sub. Waaah
The girls want to have a big photo-sharing session... so I have to delete all the photos I took of you. (T△T)
PI (BEEP)
ぴっ
HAAH...
PIRORIRON (RING)
ぴろりろん♪
Received Mail
From: Kazuki
Sub: Re: Waaah
Before you delete them, send them here as an attachment. I'll keep them for you.
END
I DIDN'T EVEN THINK OF THAT!
PLUS, THE PHOTOS YOU TAKE AND PHOTOS YOU RECEIVE AS ATTACHMENTS...
...ARE STORED IN DIFFERENT PLACES ON THE PHONE.
SO IT'S SAFE!
UM...
ATTACHMENT...
ATTACHMENT...
!!!!

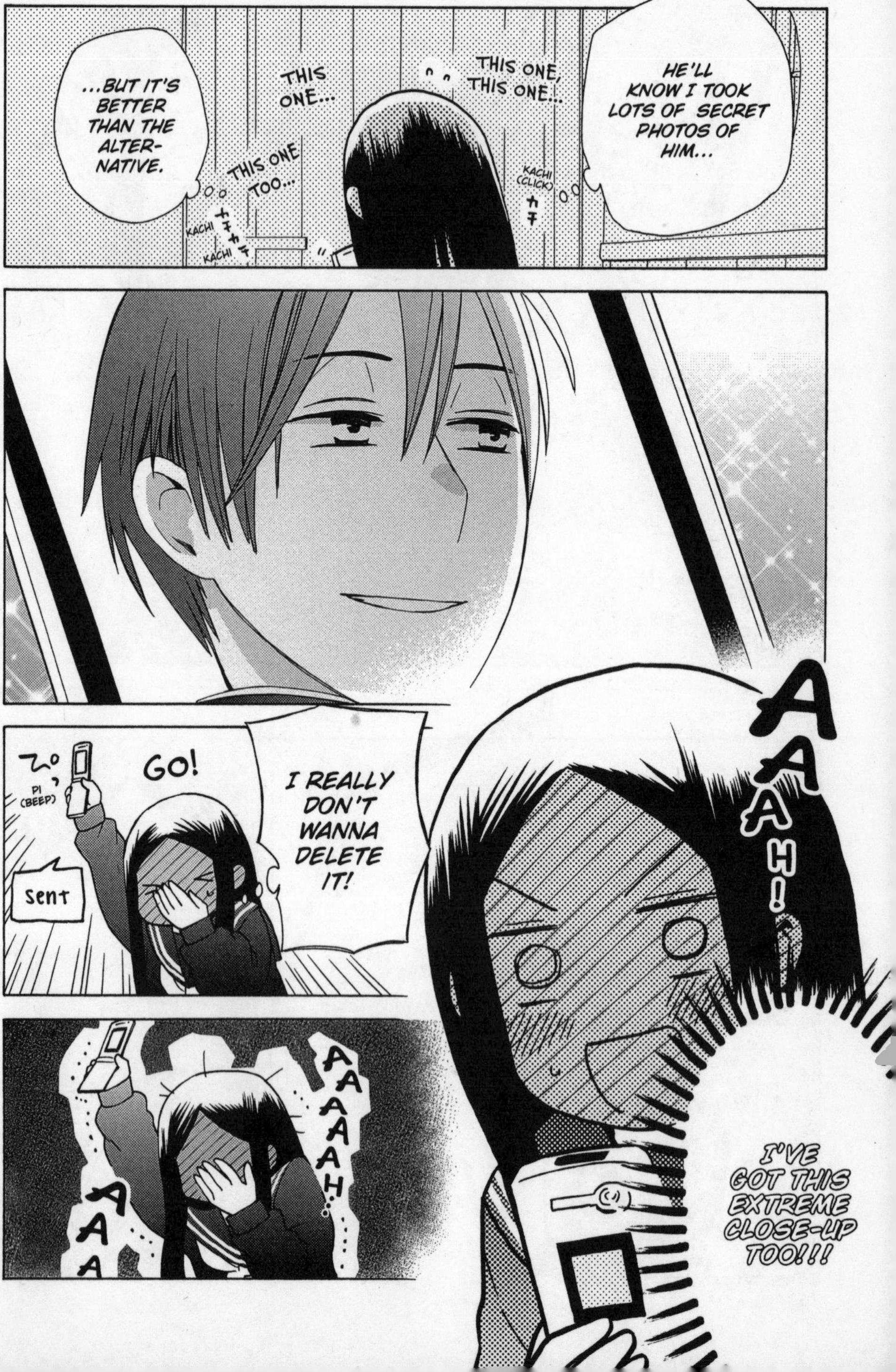
HE'LL KNOW I TOOK LOTS OF SECRET PHOTOS OF HIM...
THIS ONE, THIS ONE...
KACHI (CLICK)
THIS ONE...
THIS ONE TOO...
KACHI
KACHI
...BUT IT'S BETTER THAN THE ALTERNATIVE.
AAAH!
I'VE GOT THIS EXTREME CLOSE-UP TOO!!!
I REALLY DON'T WANNA DELETE IT!
GO!
PI (BEEP)
sent
AAAAAAH...
AAA

PIRORIRON (RING)

BIKU (TWITCH)

Received Mail

From: Kazuki

Sub: Me Too

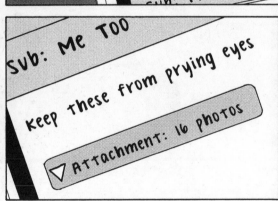

Sub: Me TOO

Keep these from prying eyes

▽ Attachment: 16 photos

open photos?

OK

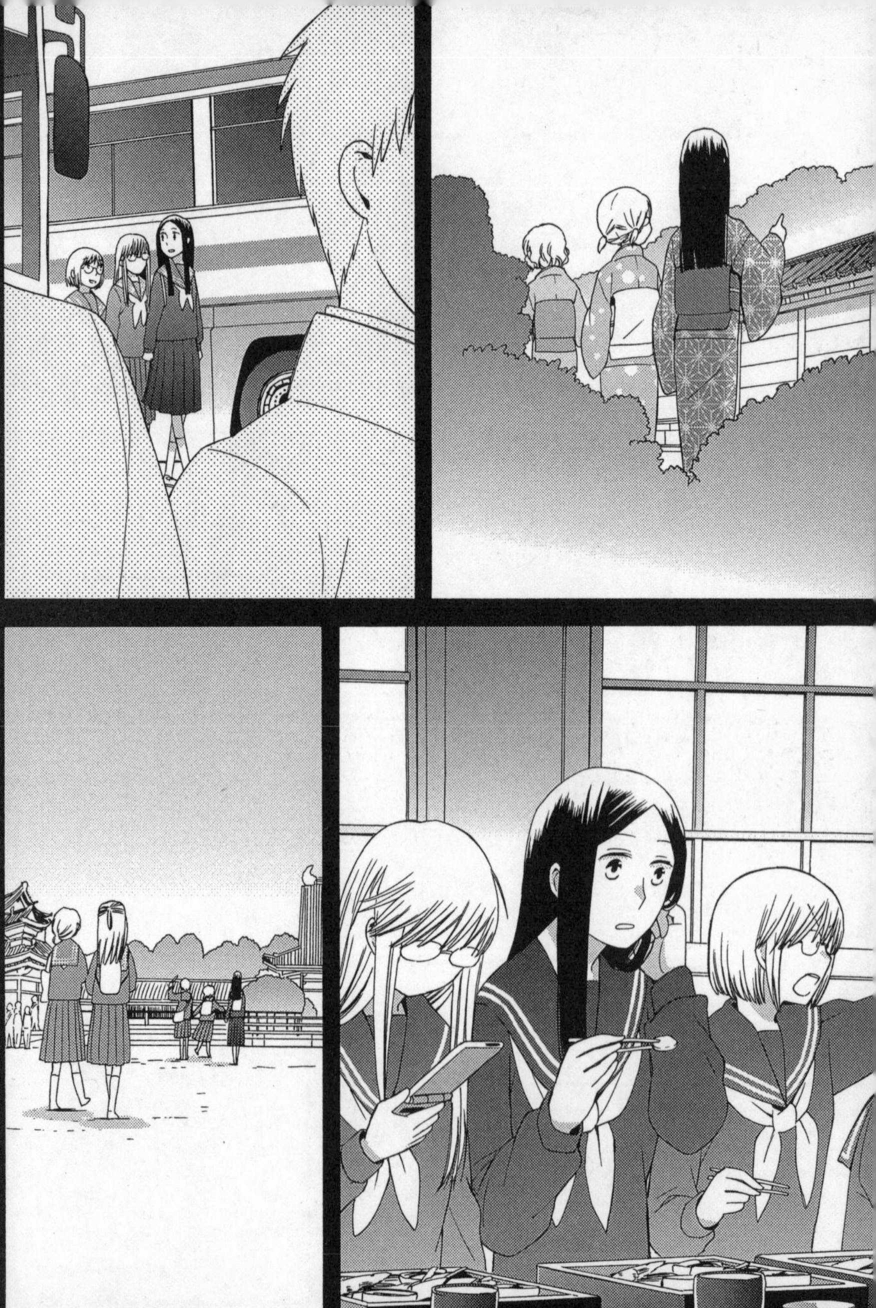

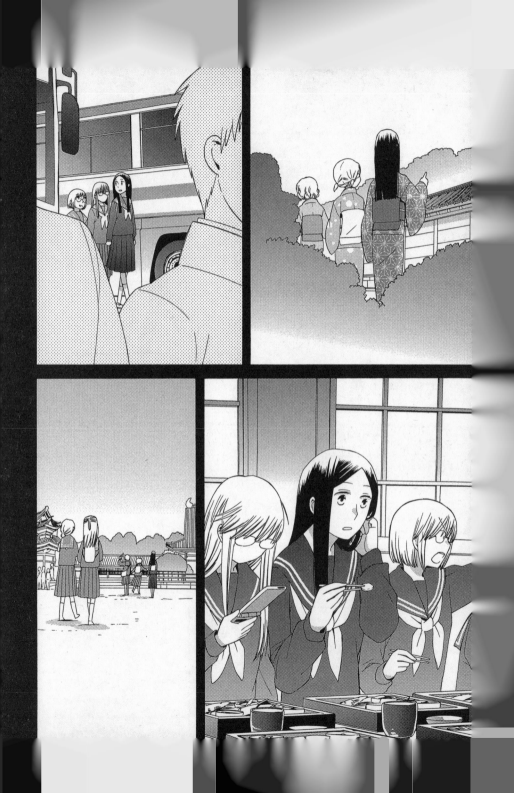

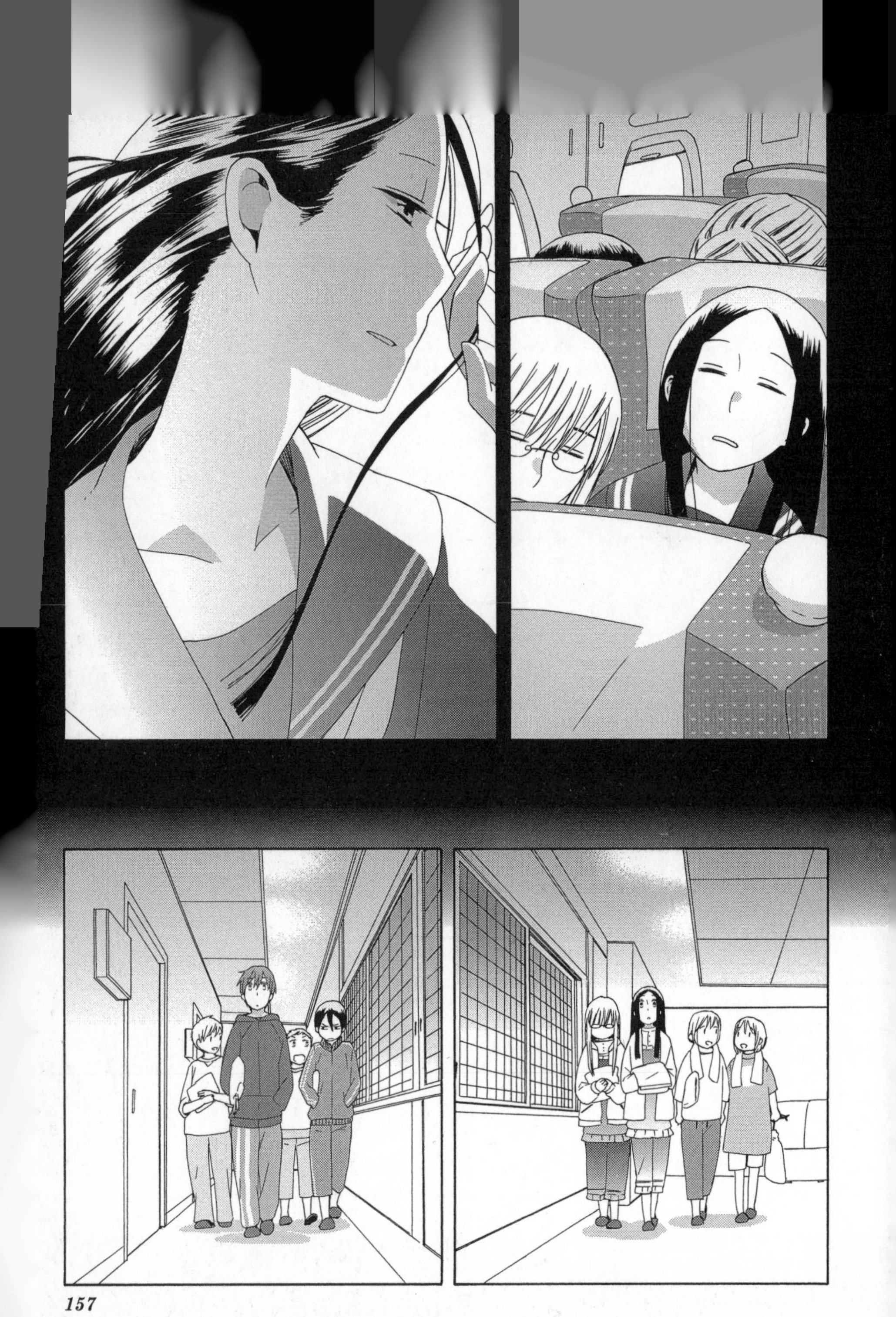

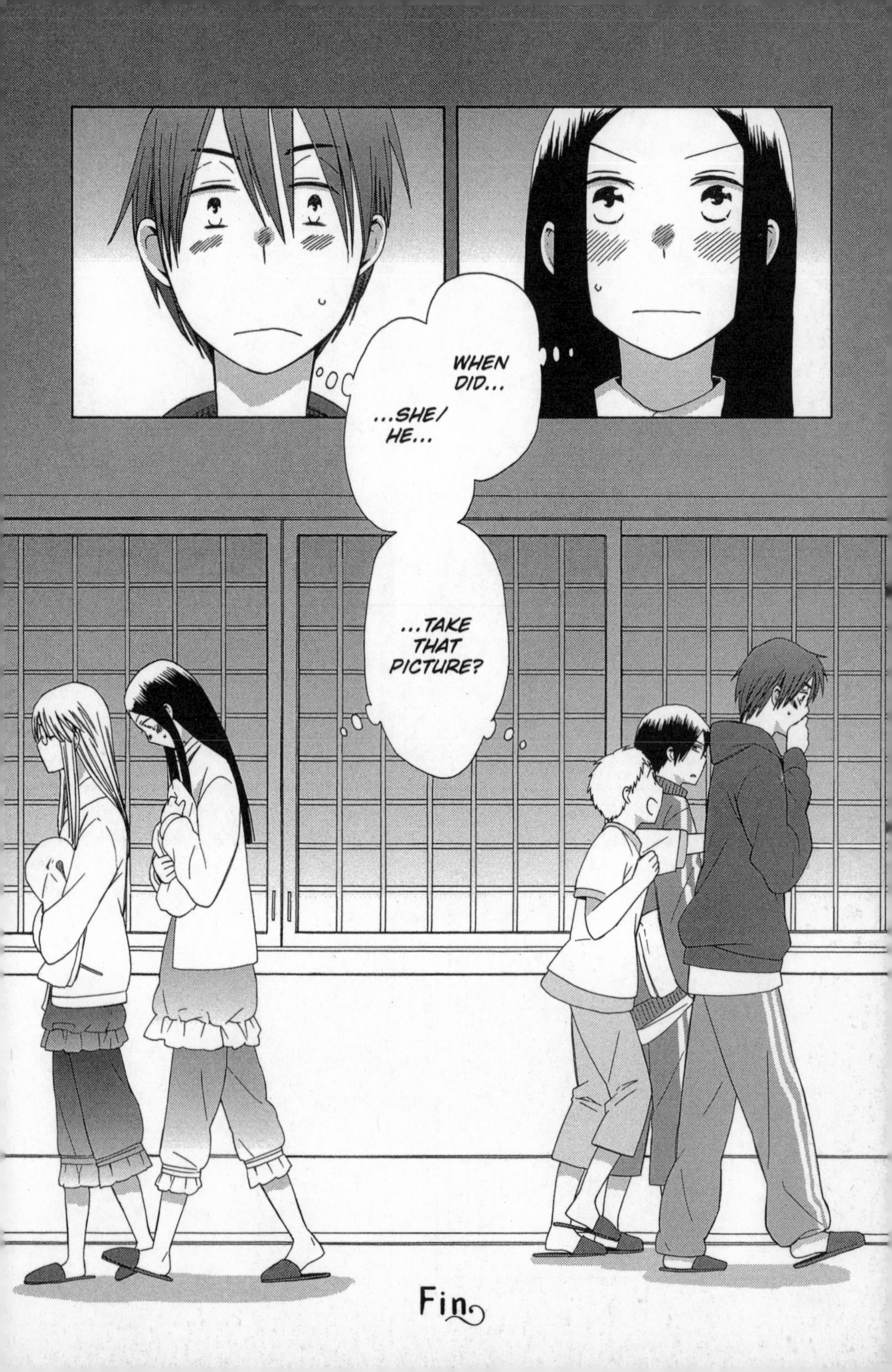
WHEN DID...
...SHE/ HE...
...TAKE THAT PICTURE?
Fin.

Love at Fourteen

[Chapter 25]

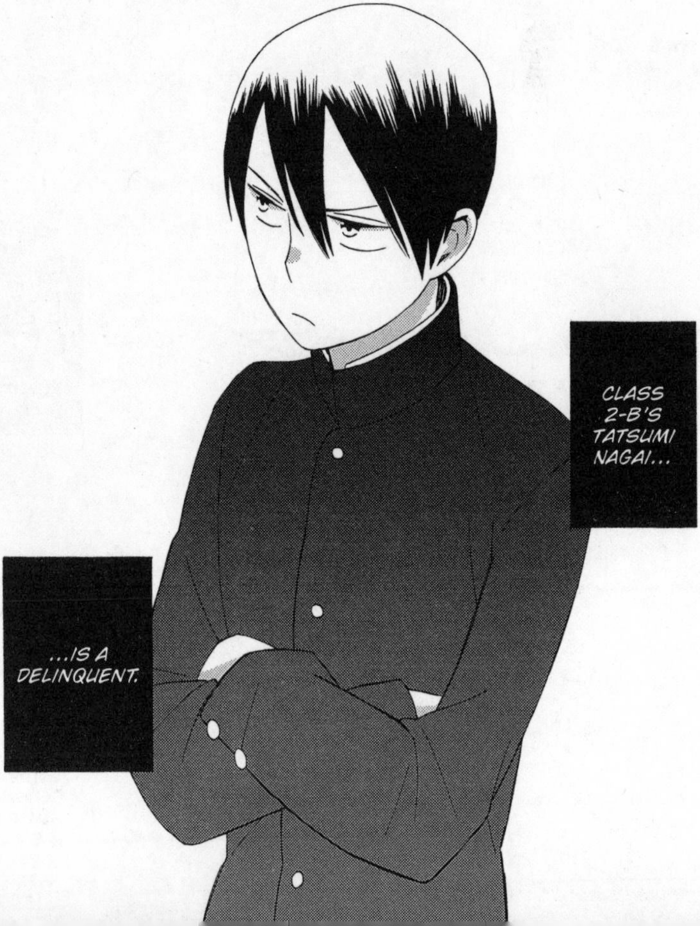
CLASS 2-B'S TATSUMI NAGAI...
...IS A DELINQUENT.

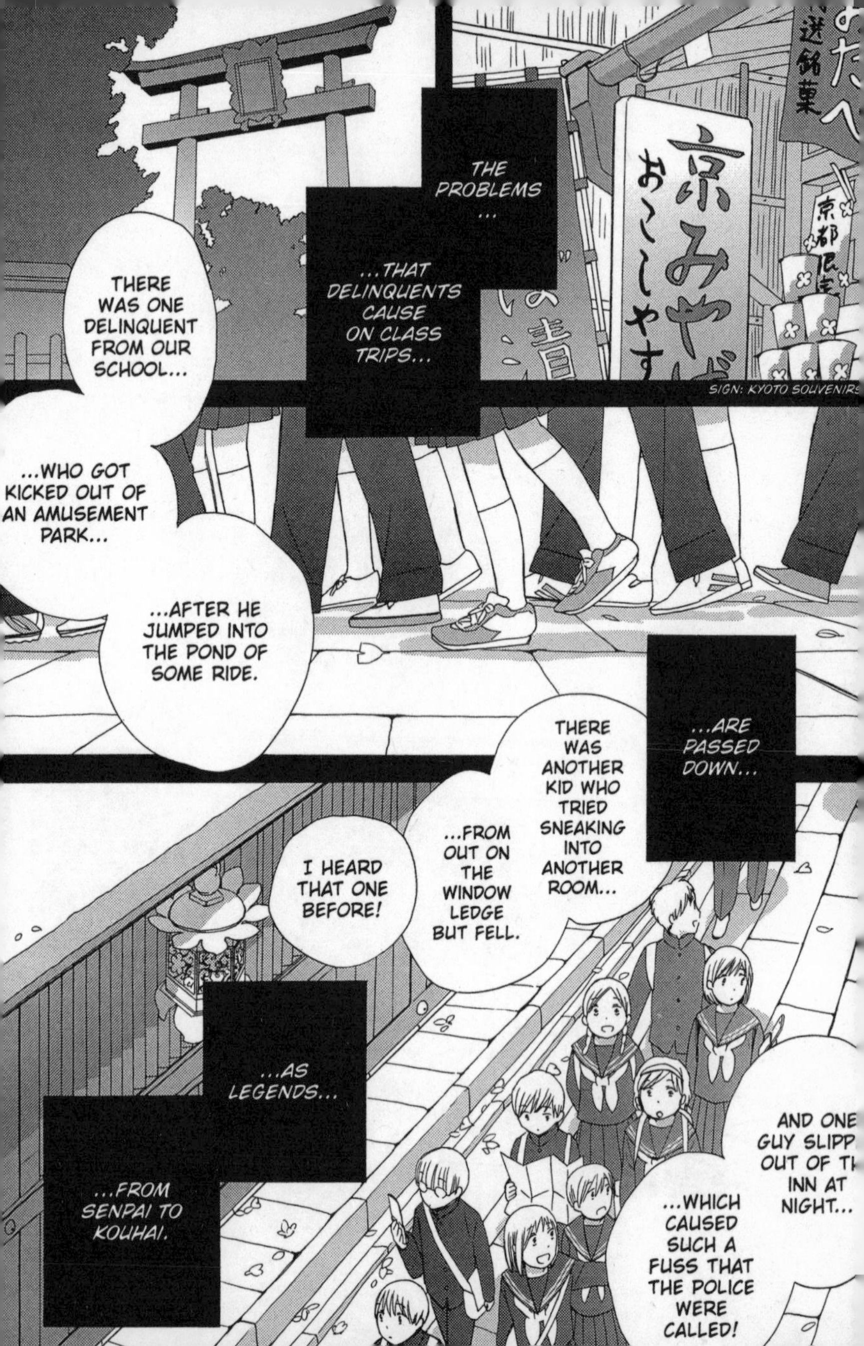
THE PROBLEMS ...
...THAT DELINQUENTS CAUSE ON CLASS TRIPS...
SIGN: KYOTO SOUVENIRS
THERE WAS ONE DELINQUENT FROM OUR SCHOOL...
...WHO GOT KICKED OUT OF AN AMUSEMENT PARK...
...AFTER HE JUMPED INTO THE POND OF SOME RIDE.
...ARE PASSED DOWN...
THERE WAS ANOTHER KID WHO TRIED SNEAKING INTO ANOTHER ROOM...
...FROM OUT ON THE WINDOW LEDGE BUT FELL.
I HEARD THAT ONE BEFORE!
AND ONE GUY SLIPP OUT OF TH INN AT NIGHT...
...WHICH CAUSED SUCH A FUSS THAT THE POLICE WERE CALLED!
...AS LEGENDS...
...FROM SENPAI TO KOUHAI.

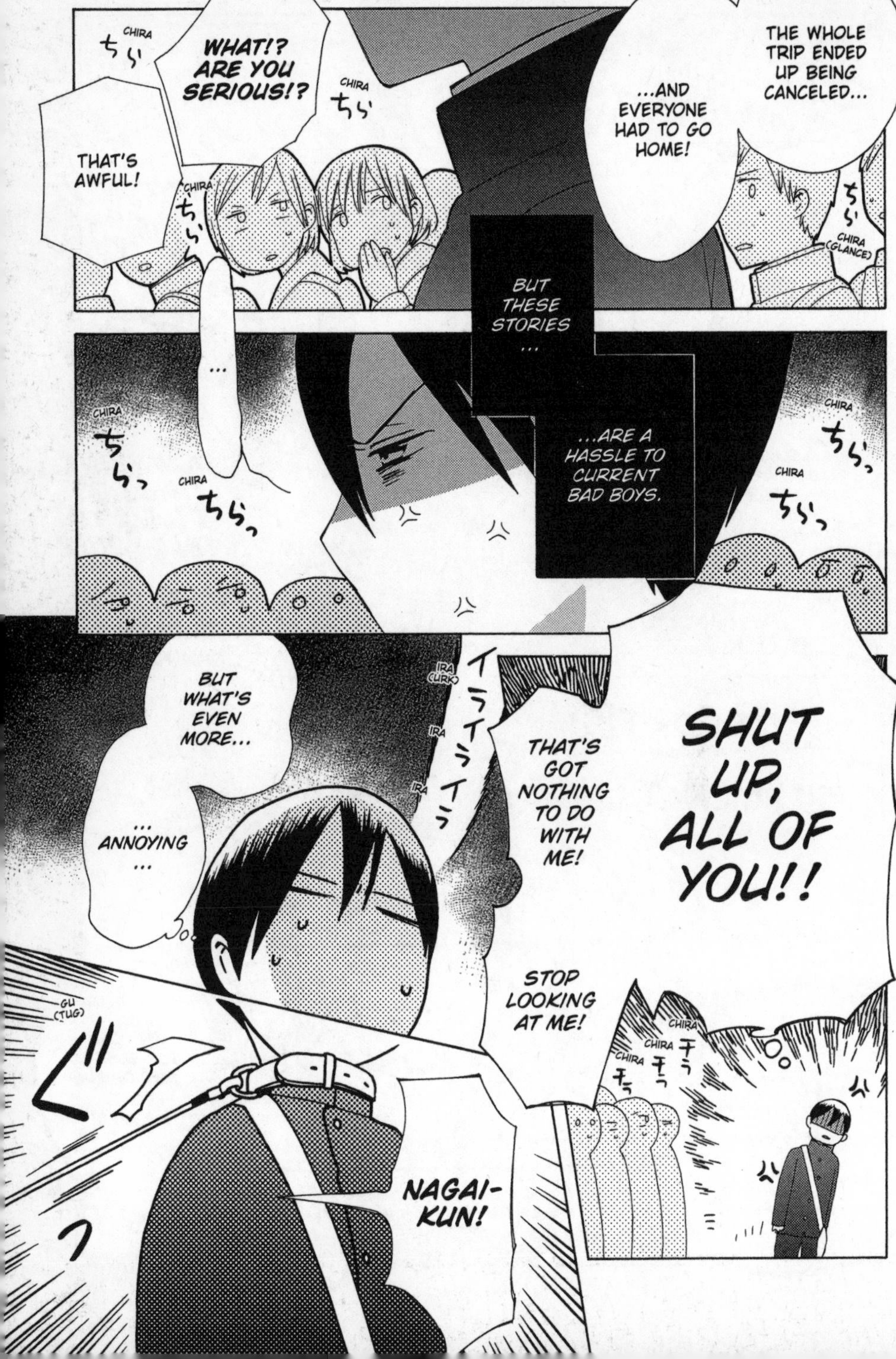
THE WHOLE TRIP ENDED UP BEING CANCELED...
...AND EVERYONE HAD TO GO HOME!
CHIRA (GLANCE)
CHIRA
WHAT!? ARE YOU SERIOUS!?
CHIRA
THAT'S AWFUL!
CHIRA
BUT THESE STORIES...
...ARE A HASSLE TO CURRENT BAD BOYS.
CHIRA
CHIRA
...
CHIRA
CHIRA
SHUT UP, ALL OF YOU!!
THAT'S GOT NOTHING TO DO WITH ME!
STOP LOOKING AT ME!
CHIRA
CHIRA
CHIRA
IRA (URK) IRA IRA
BUT WHAT'S EVEN MORE...
...ANNOYING...
GU (TUG)
NAGAI-KUN!

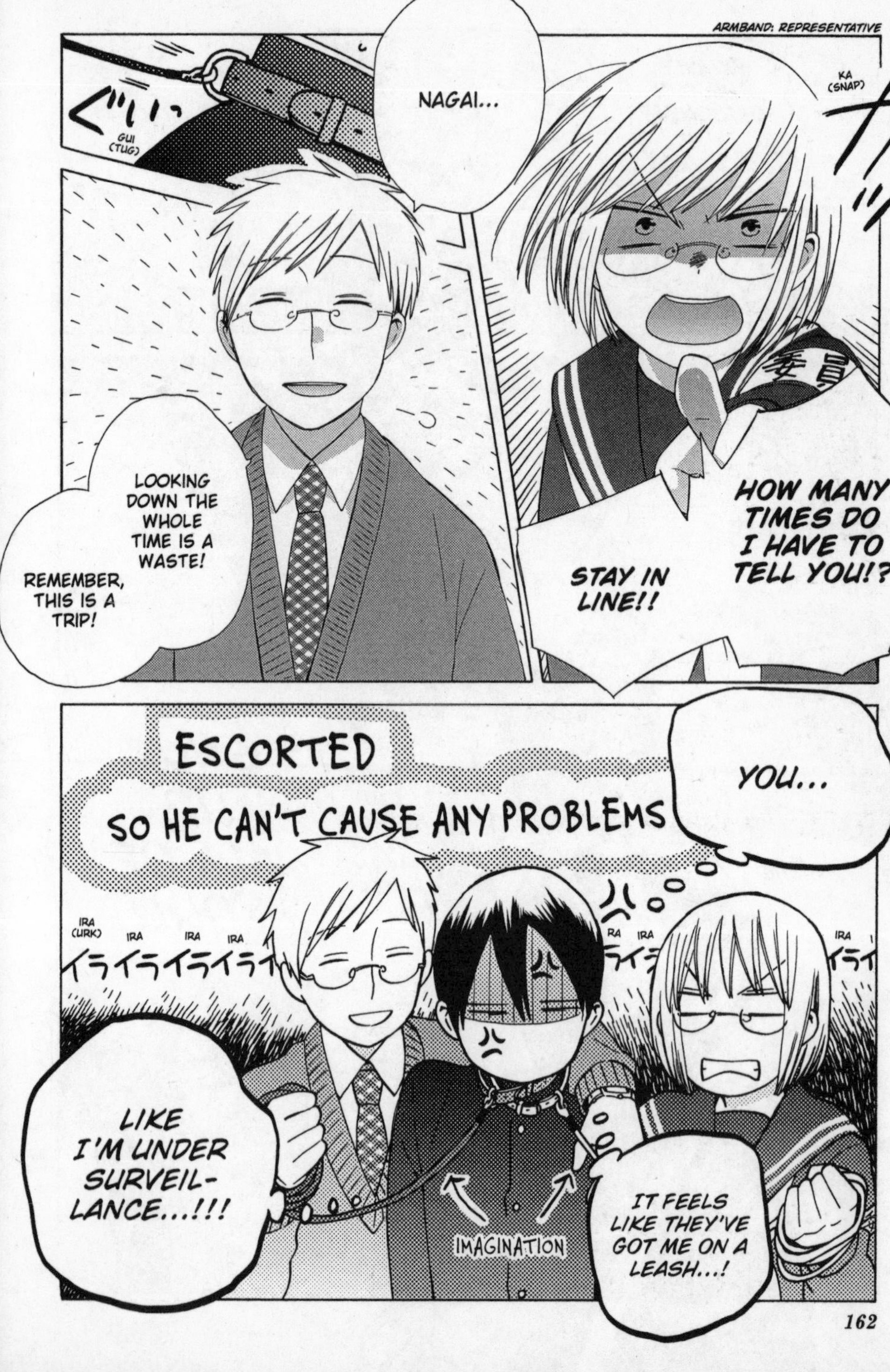

ARMBAND: REPRESENTATIVE
カッ
KA (SNAP)
HOW MANY TIMES DO I HAVE TO TELL YOU!?
STAY IN LINE!!
ぐいっ
GUI (TUG)
NAGAI...
LOOKING DOWN THE WHOLE TIME IS A WASTE!
REMEMBER, THIS IS A TRIP!
YOU...
ESCORTED
SO HE CAN'T CAUSE ANY PROBLEMS
IRA
イライ
RA IRA
イライ
IRA (IRK) IRA IRA IRA
イライライライライ
IT FEELS LIKE THEY'VE GOT ME ON A LEASH...!
IMAGINATION
LIKE I'M UNDER SURVEIL-LANCE...!!!

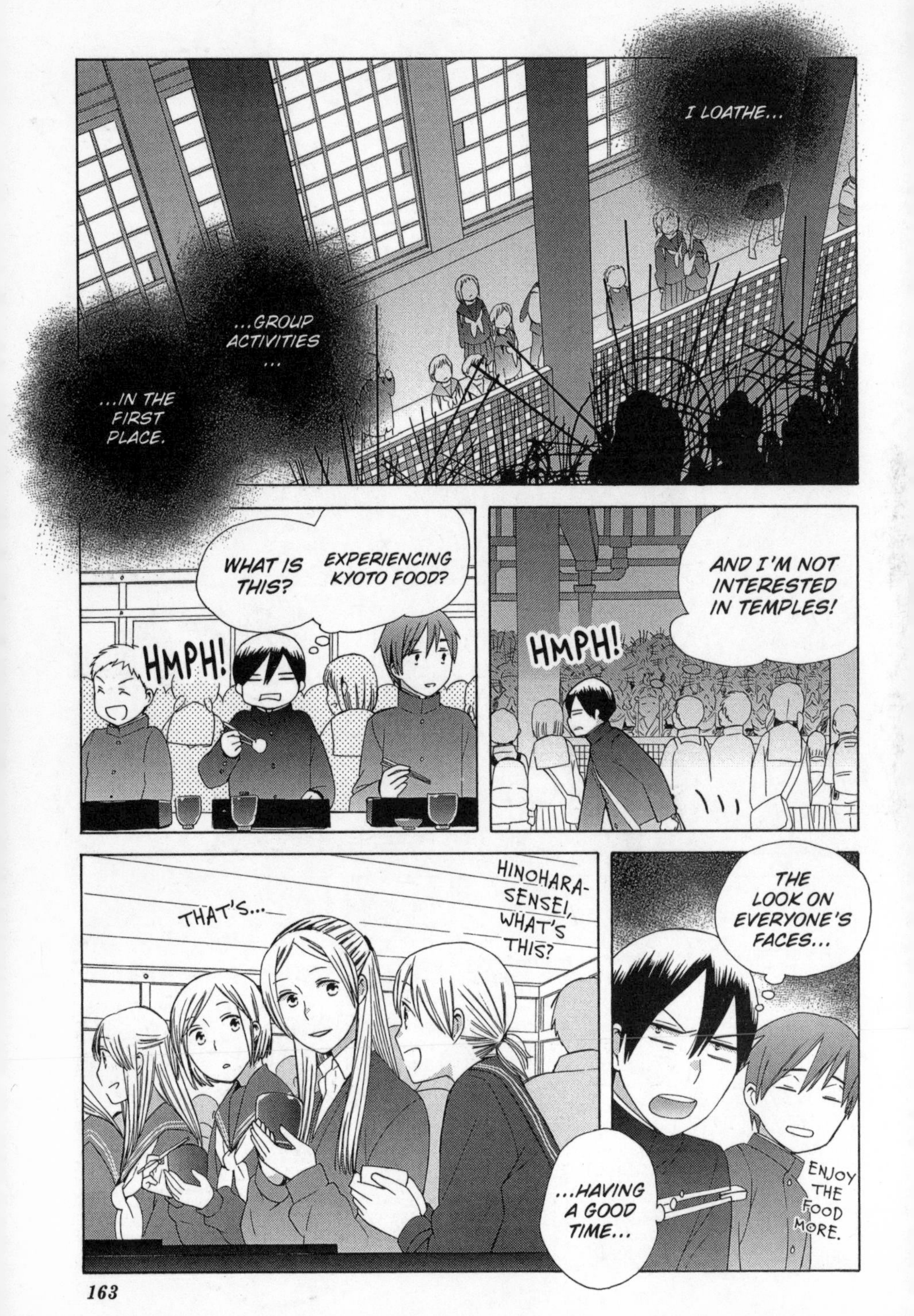
I LOATHE...
...GROUP ACTIVITIES ...
...IN THE FIRST PLACE.
AND I'M NOT INTERESTED IN TEMPLES!
HMPH!
WHAT IS THIS? EXPERIENCING KYOTO FOOD?
HMPH!
THE LOOK ON EVERYONE'S FACES...
ENJOY THE FOOD MORE.
...HAVING A GOOD TIME...
HINOHARA-SENSEI, WHAT'S THIS?
THAT'S...

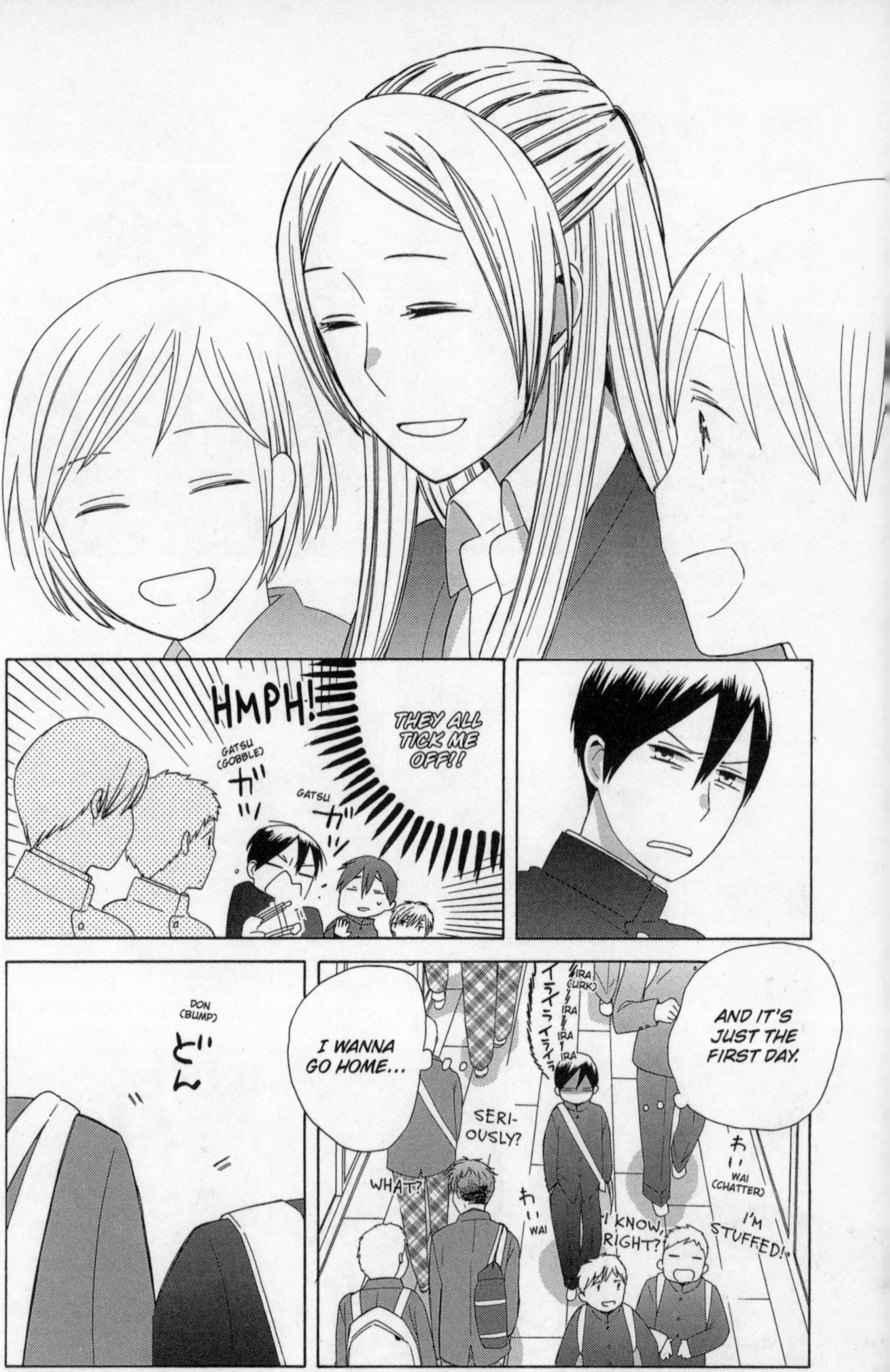
THEY ALL TICK ME OFF!!
HMPH!
GATSU
ガツ
GATSU (GOBBLE)
ガツ
AND IT'S JUST THE FIRST DAY.
IRA (URK) IRA IRA IRA
イライライライラ
I WANNA GO HOME...
SERI-OUSLY?
わい
WAI (CHATTER)
WHAT?
わい
WAI
I KNOW, RIGHT?
I'M STUFFED!
DON (BUMP)
どん

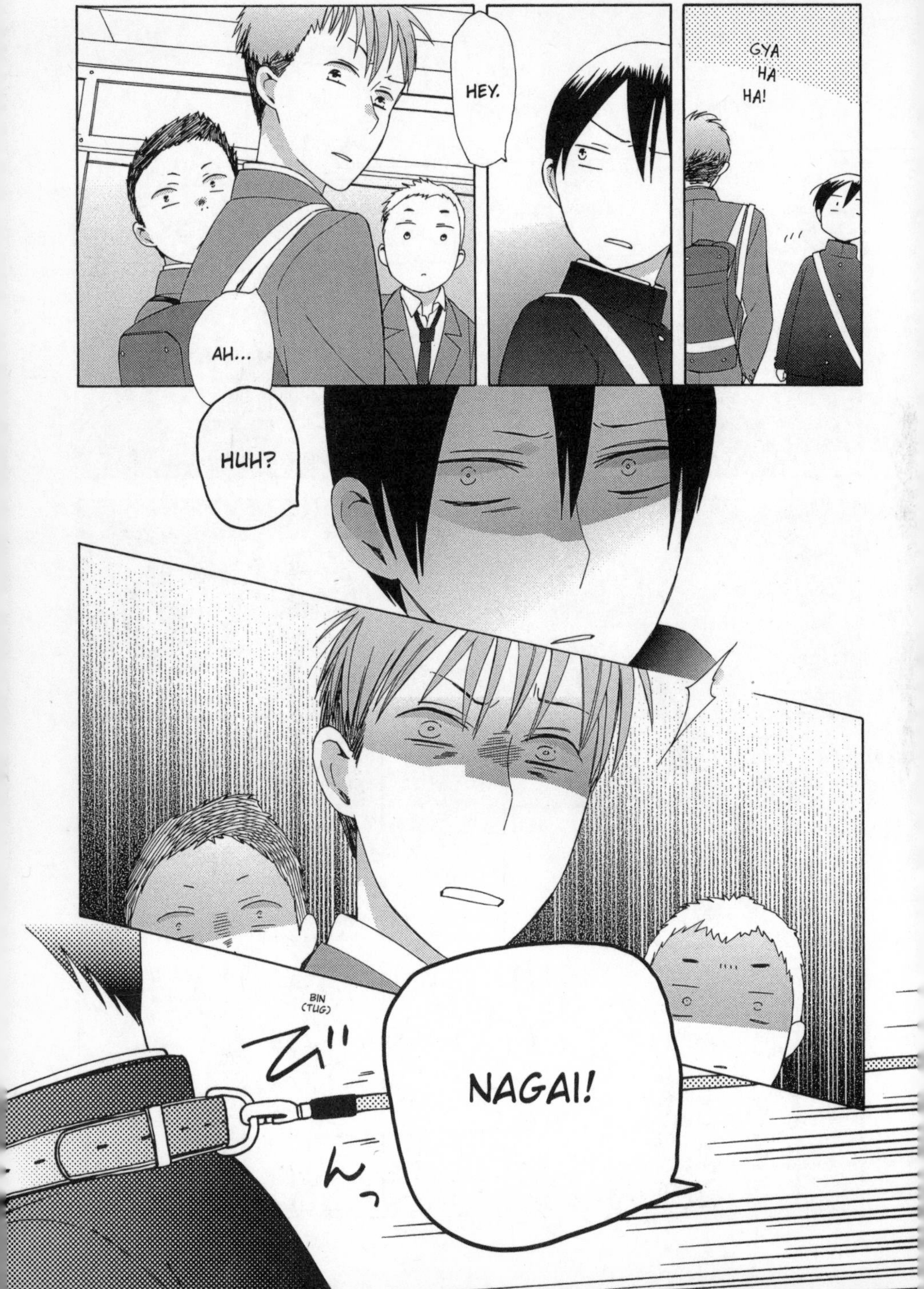
GYA HA HA!
HEY.
AH...
HUH?
BIN (TUG)
びんっ
NAGAI!

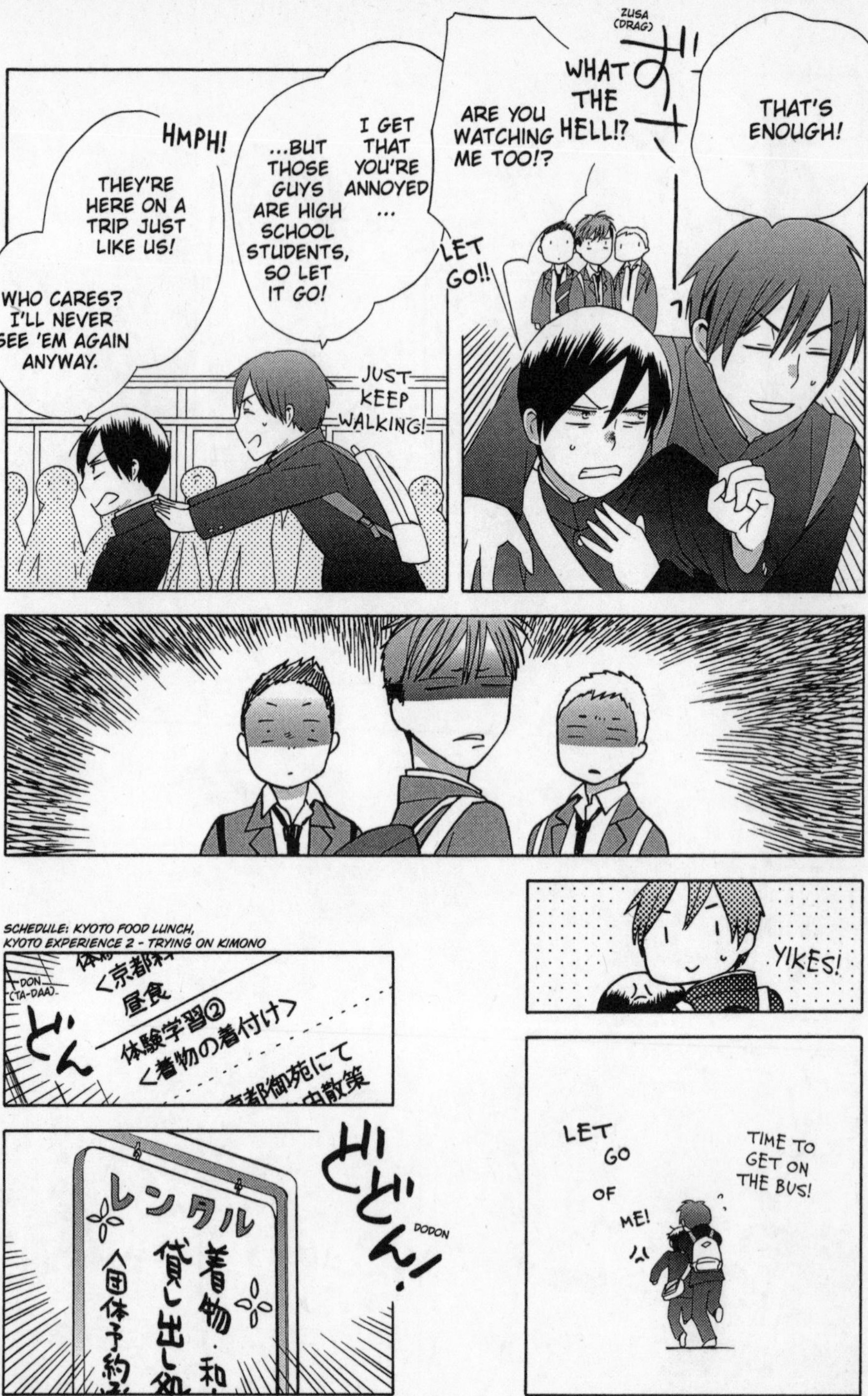
THAT'S ENOUGH!
ZUSA (DRAG)
WHAT THE HELL!?
ARE YOU WATCHING ME TOO!?
LET GO!!
I GET THAT YOU'RE ANNOYED ...
...BUT THOSE GUYS ARE HIGH SCHOOL STUDENTS, SO LET IT GO!
HMPH!
THEY'RE HERE ON A TRIP JUST LIKE US!
WHO CARES? I'LL NEVER SEE 'EM AGAIN ANYWAY.
JUST KEEP WALKING!
YIKES!
TIME TO GET ON THE BUS!
LET GO OF ME!
SCHEDULE: KYOTO FOOD LUNCH, KYOTO EXPERIENCE 2 - TRYING ON KIMONO
DON (TA-DAA)
どん
DODON
どどん!
SIGN: KIMONO RENTAL, GROUP RESERVATIONS

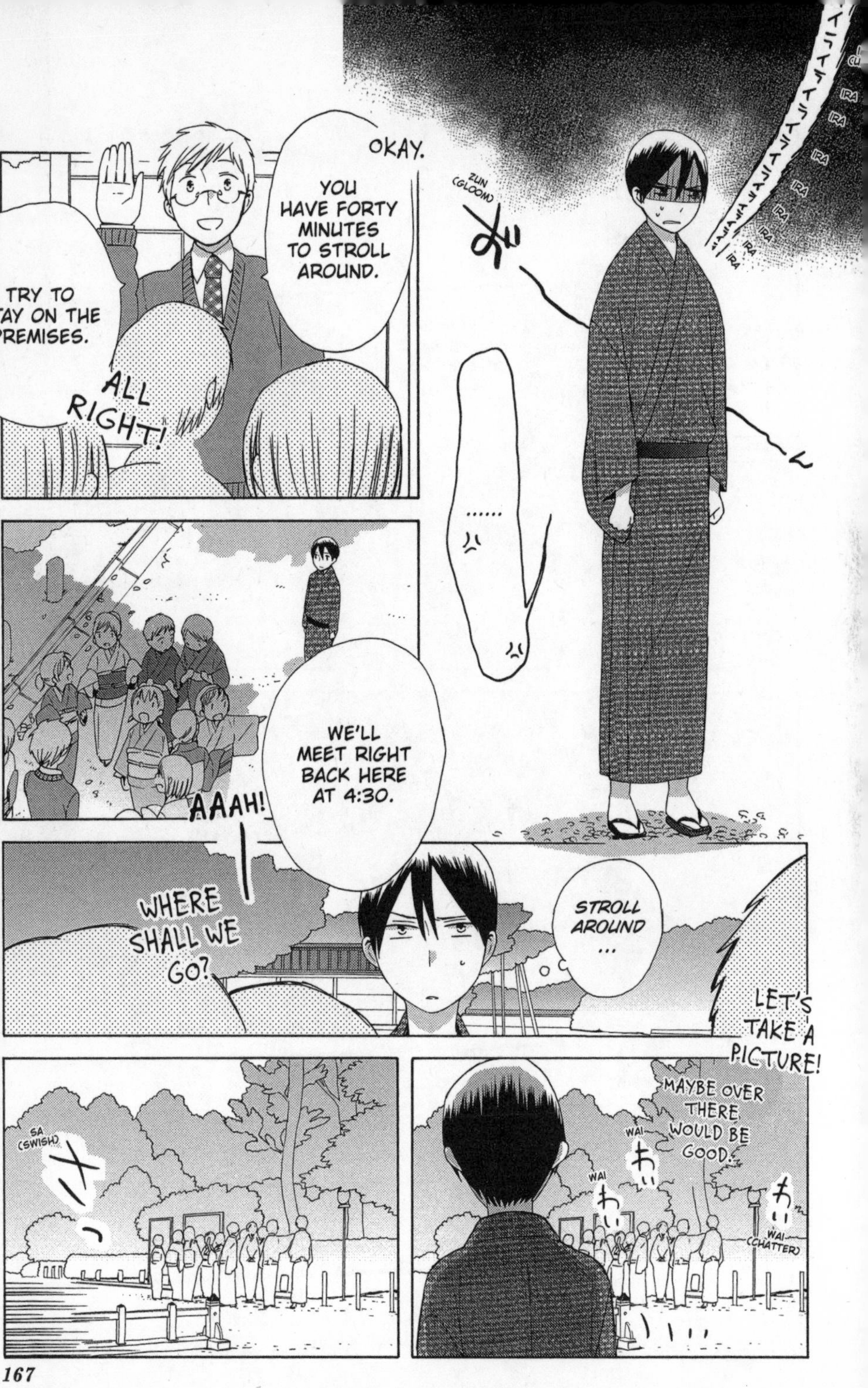

IRA IRA IRA IRA IRA IRA IRA
ZUN (GLOOM)
......
OKAY.
YOU HAVE FORTY MINUTES TO STROLL AROUND.
TRY TO STAY ON THE PREMISES.
ALL RIGHT!
WE'LL MEET RIGHT BACK HERE AT 4:30.
AAAH!
STROLL AROUND ...
LET'S TAKE A PICTURE!
WHERE SHALL WE GO?
MAYBE OVER THERE WOULD BE GOOD.
WAI
WAI
WAI (CHATTER)
SA (SWISH)

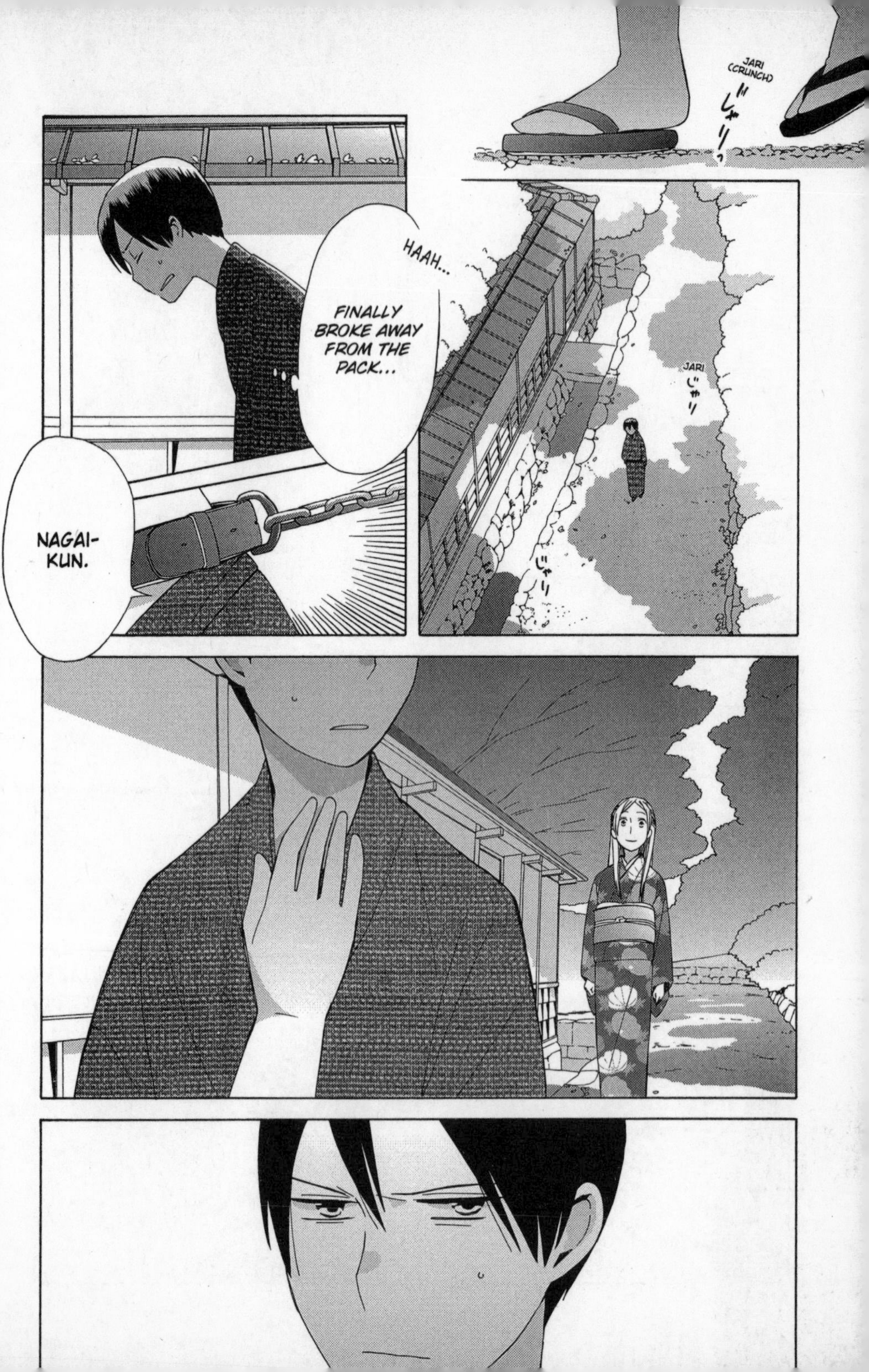
JARI (CRUNCH)
じゃりっ
JARI
じゃり
じゃり
HAAH...
FINALLY BROKE AWAY FROM THE PACK...
NAGAI-KUN.

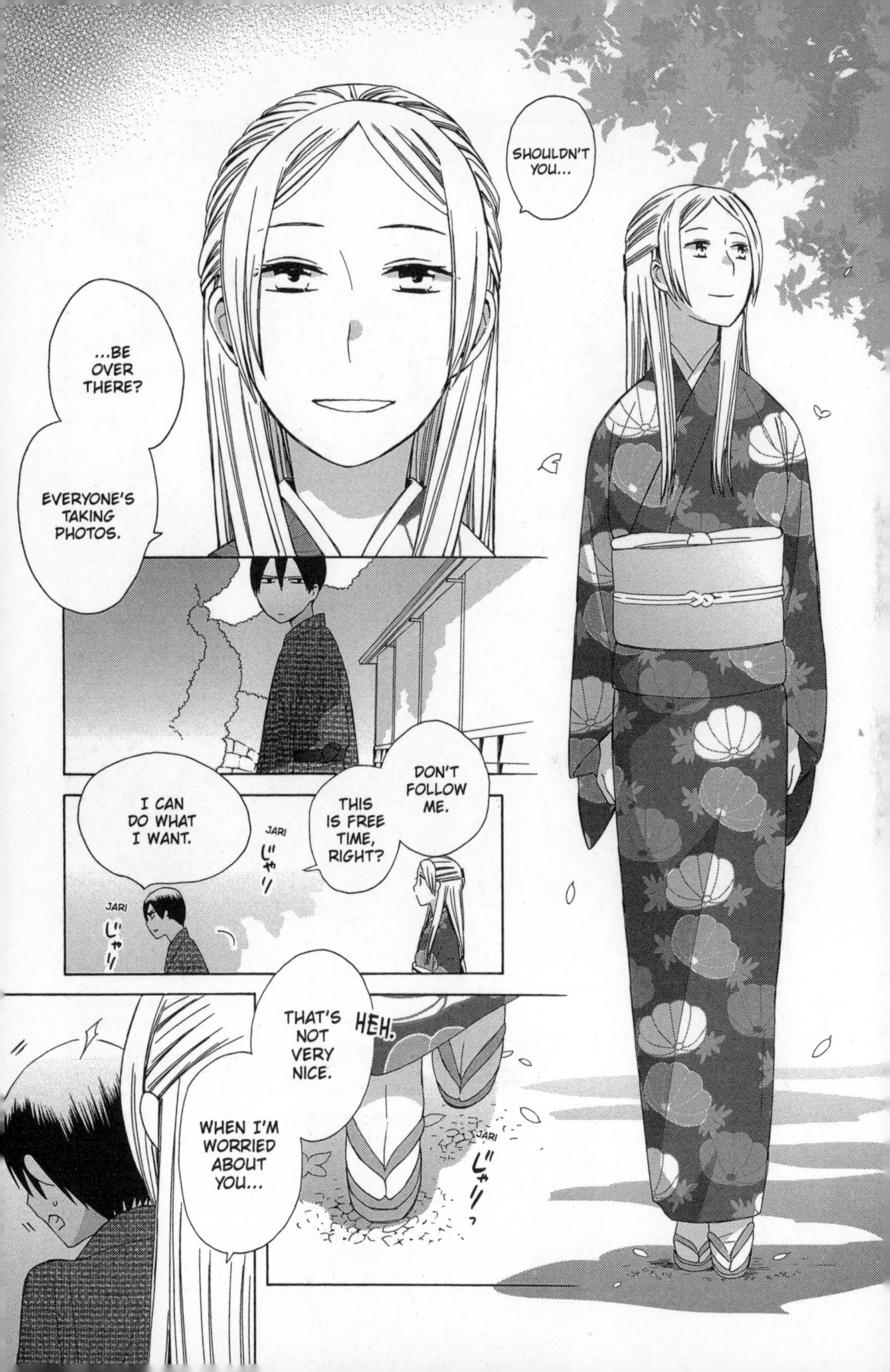

SHOULDN'T YOU...
...BE OVER THERE?
EVERYONE'S TAKING PHOTOS.
DON'T FOLLOW ME.
THIS IS FREE TIME, RIGHT?
JARI
じゃり
I CAN DO WHAT I WANT.
JARI
じゃり
JARI
じゃりっ
HEH.
THAT'S NOT VERY NICE.
WHEN I'M WORRIED ABOUT YOU...

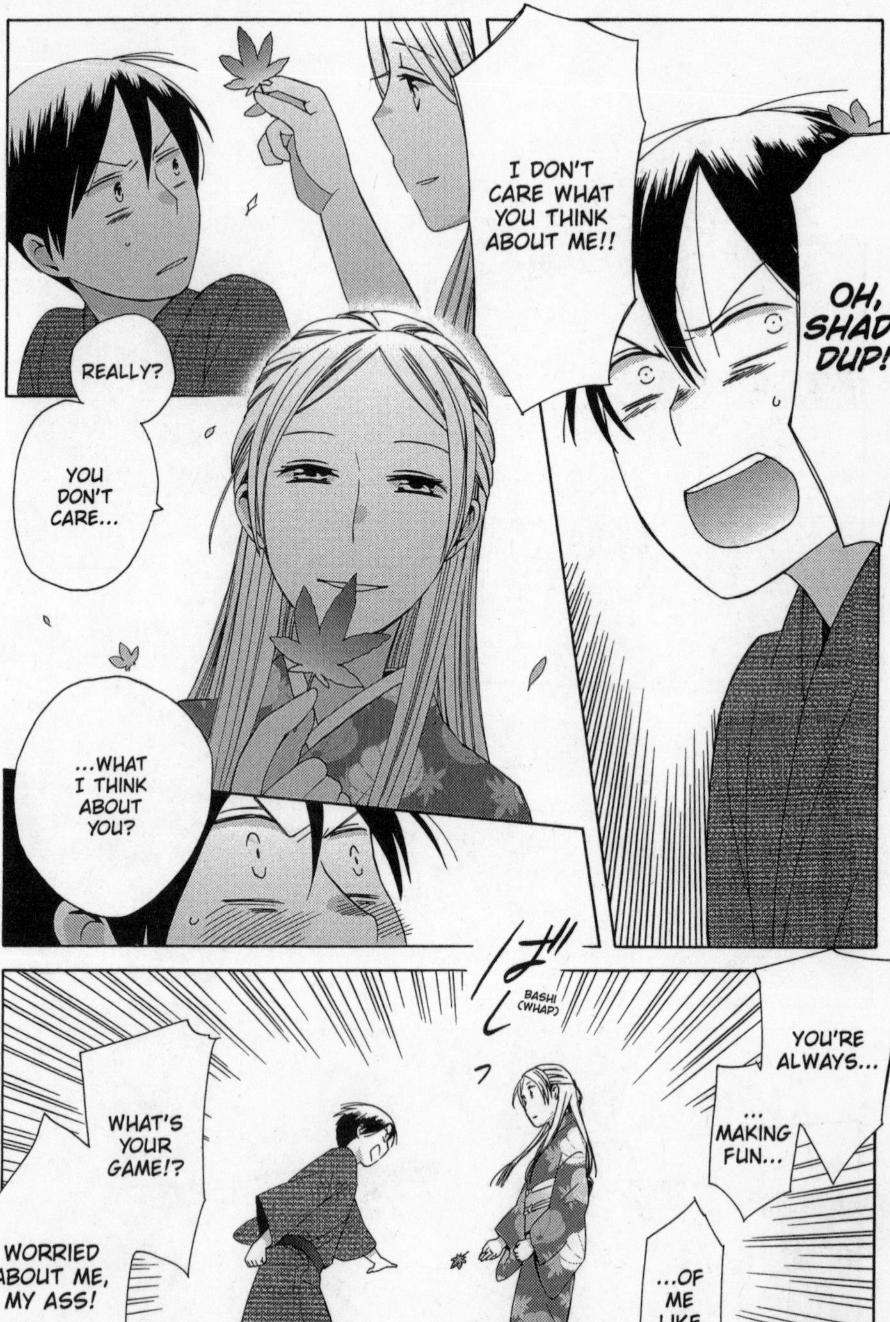
I DON'T CARE WHAT YOU THINK ABOUT ME!!
OH, SHAD-DUP!
REALLY?
YOU DON'T CARE...
...WHAT I THINK ABOUT YOU?
BASHI (WHAP)
YOU'RE ALWAYS...
...MAKING FUN...
...OF ME LIKE THIS!
WHAT'S YOUR GAME!?
WORRIED ABOUT ME, MY ASS!

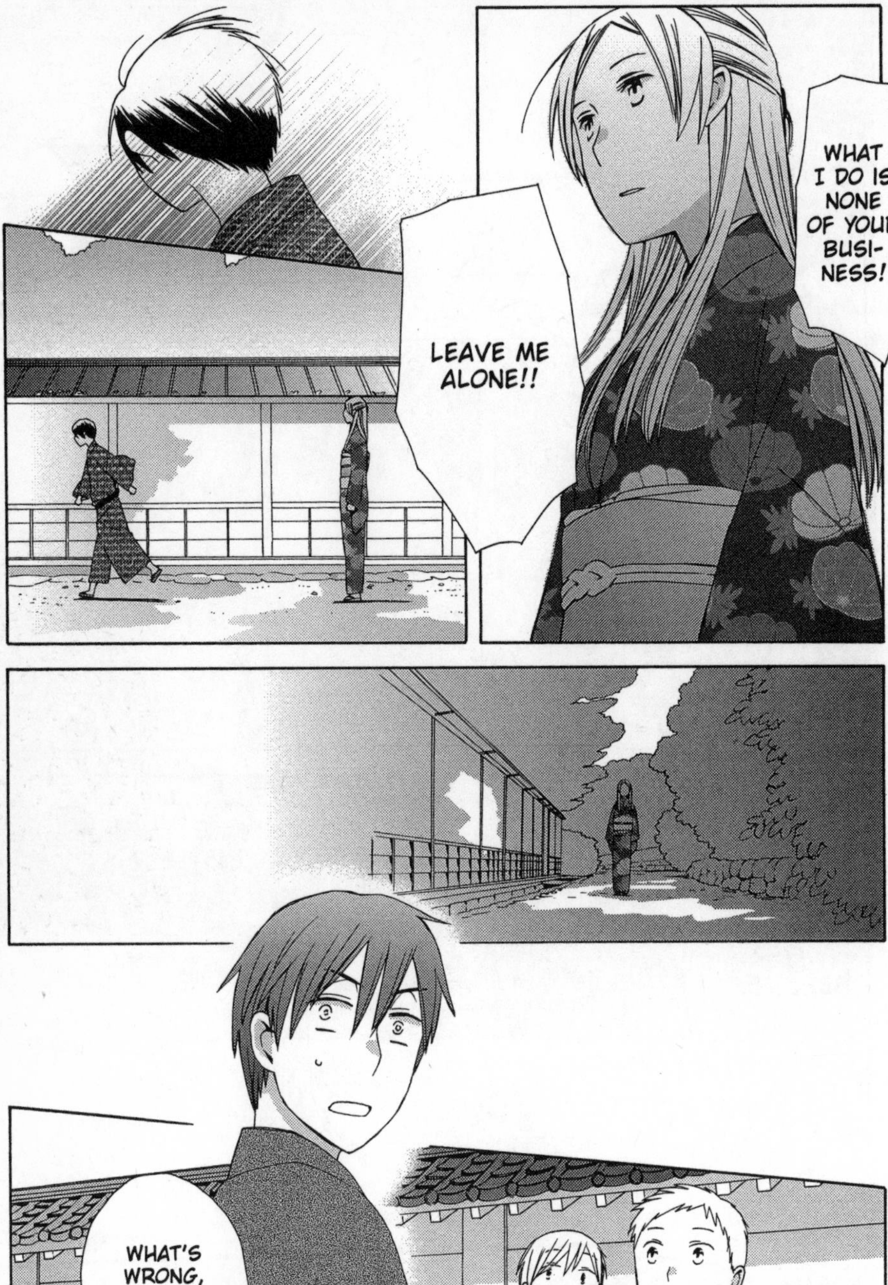
WHAT I DO IS NONE OF YOUR BUSI-NESS!
LEAVE ME ALONE!!
WHAT'S WRONG, YOSHIKAWA?

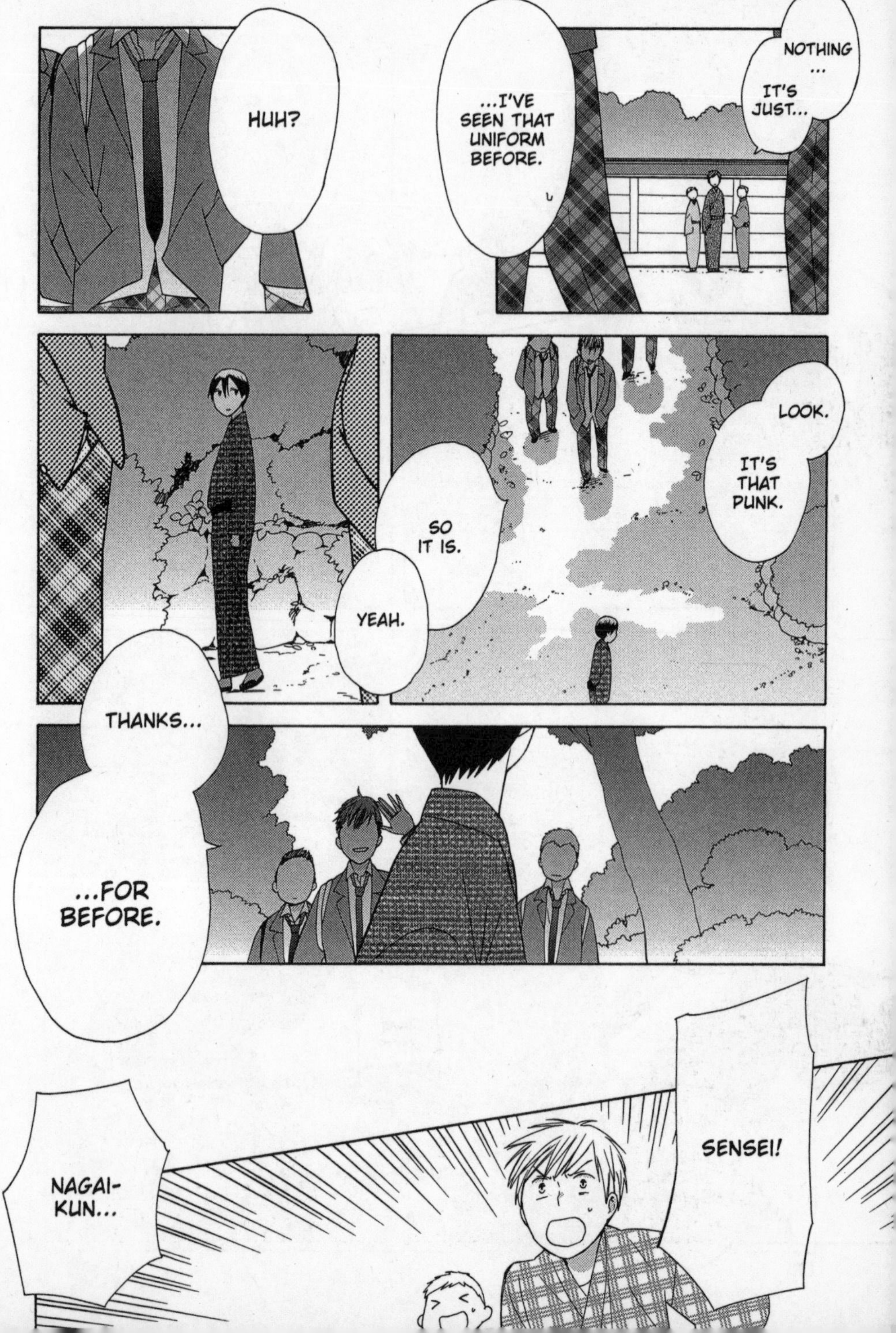
NOTHING ... IT'S JUST...
...I'VE SEEN THAT UNIFORM BEFORE.
HUH?
LOOK. IT'S THAT PUNK.
SO IT IS.
YEAH.
THANKS...
...FOR BEFORE.
SENSEI!
NAGAI-KUN...

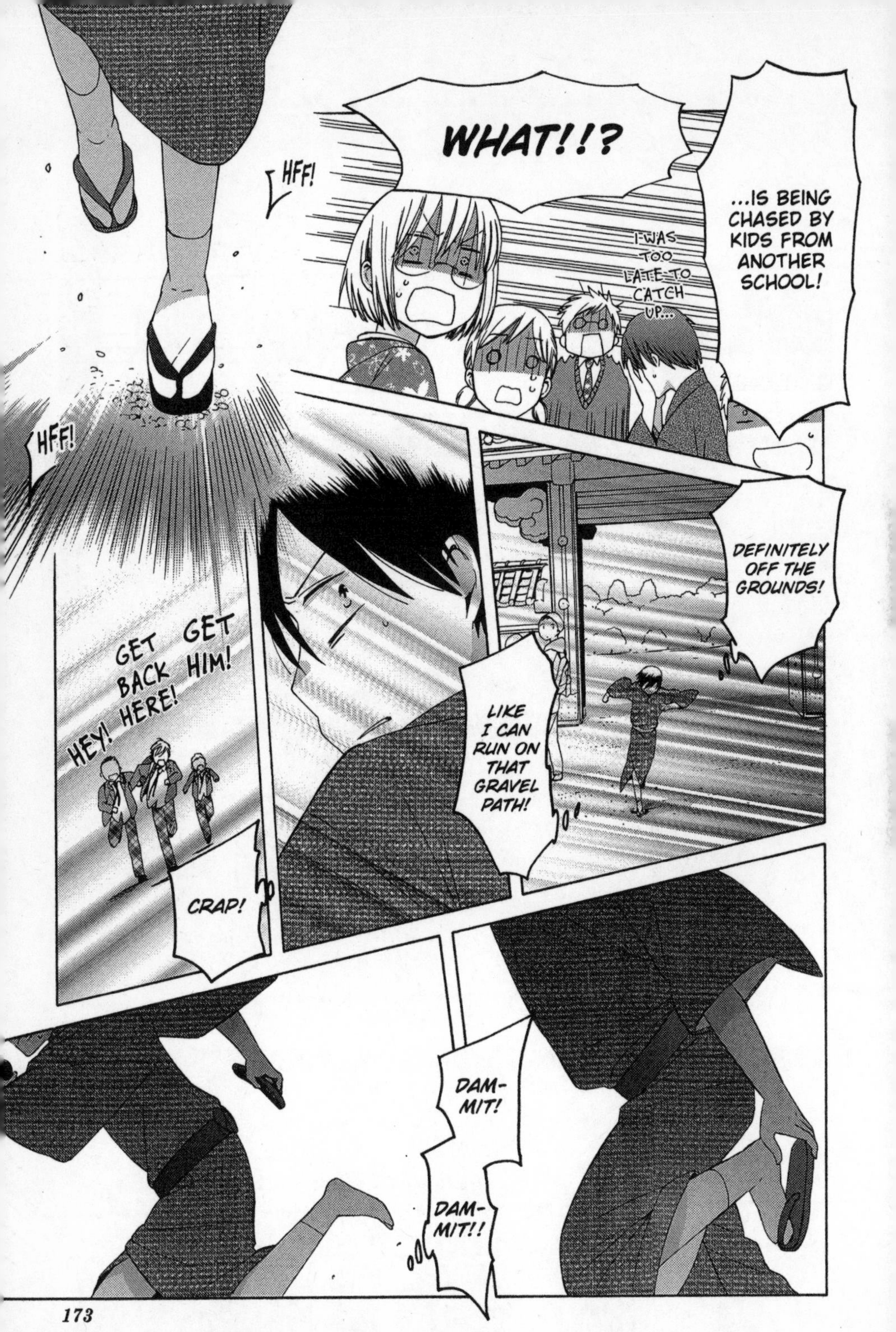
...IS BEING CHASED BY KIDS FROM ANOTHER SCHOOL!
WHAT!!?
I WAS TOO LATE TO CATCH UP...
HFF!
HFF!
DEFINITELY OFF THE GROUNDS!
LIKE I CAN RUN ON THAT GRAVEL PATH!
GET HIM!
GET BACK HERE!
HEY!
CRAP!
DAM-MIT!
DAM-MIT!!

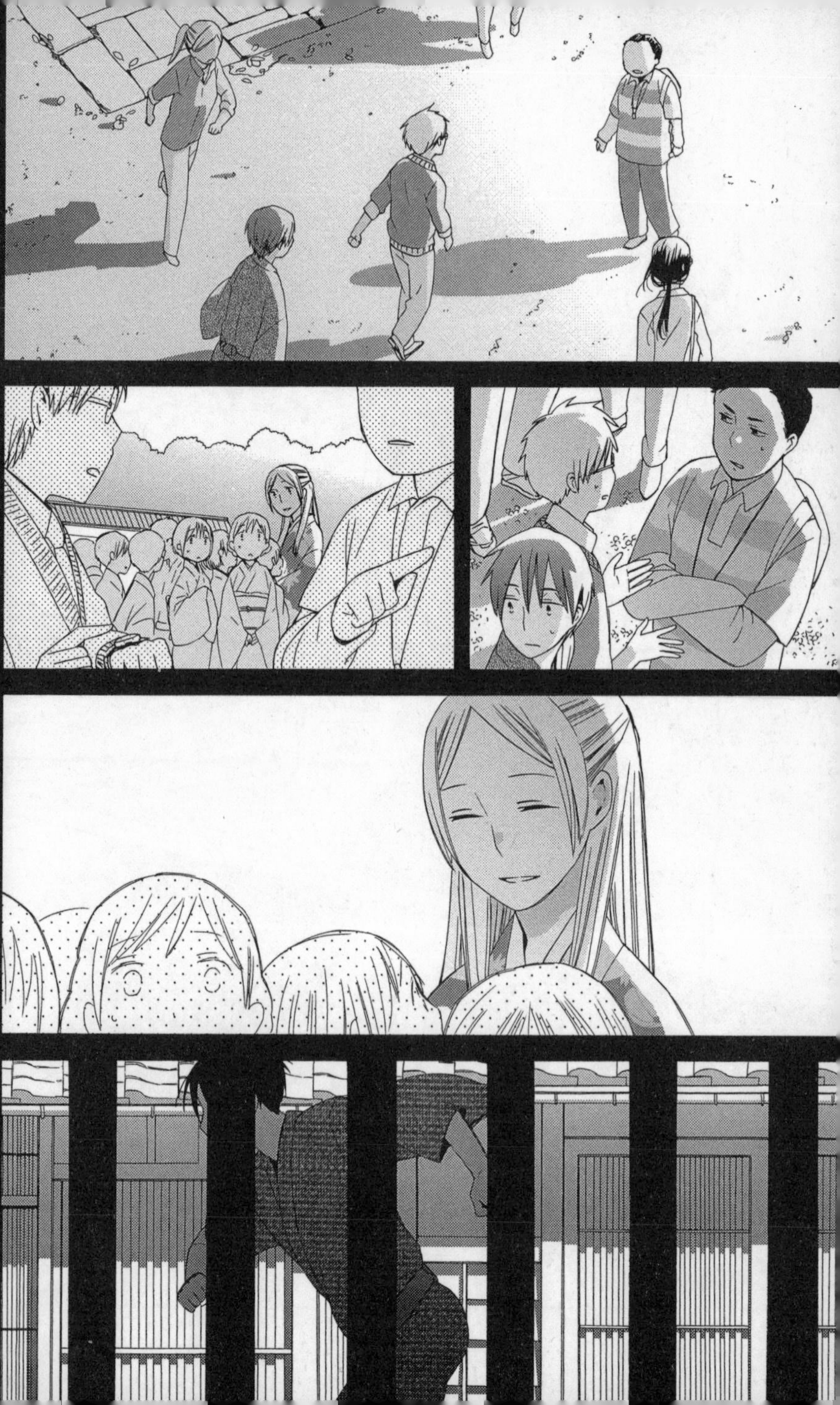

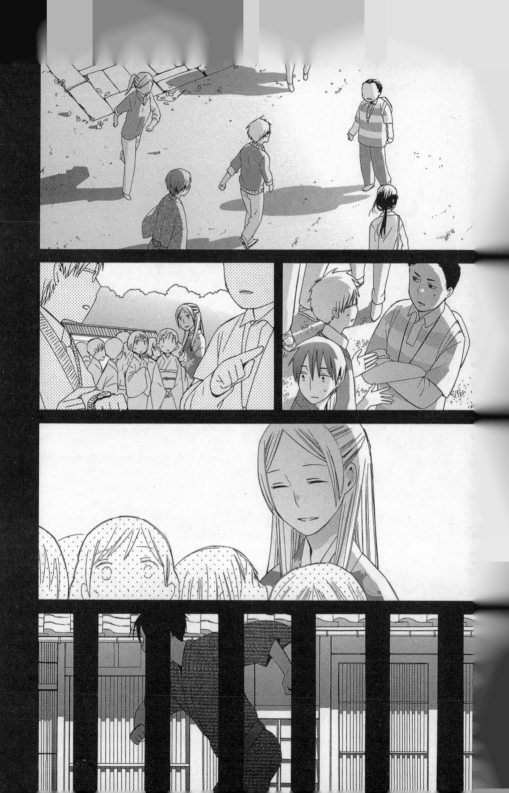

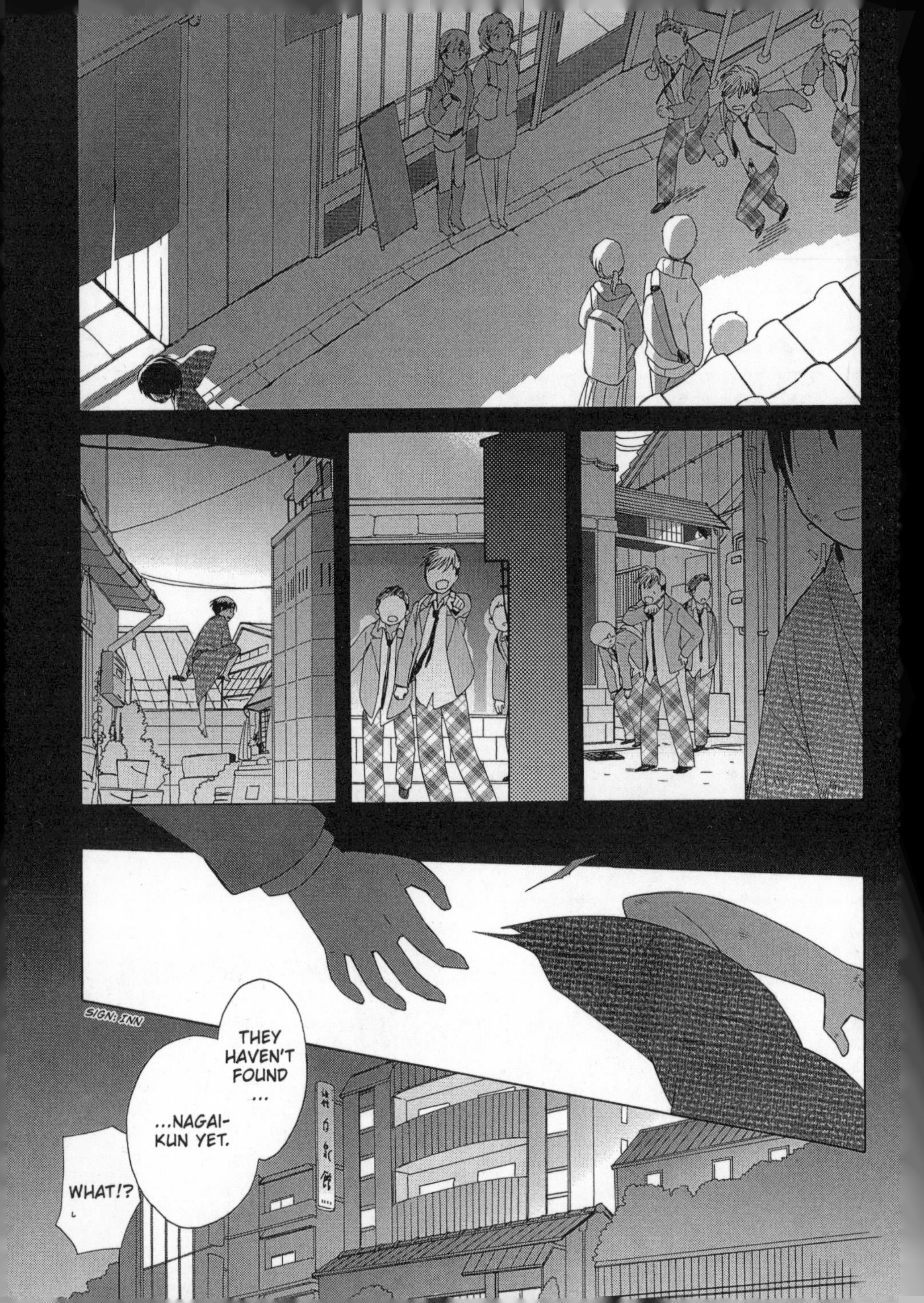
SIGN: INN
THEY HAVEN'T FOUND ...
...NAGAI-KUN YET.
WHAT!?

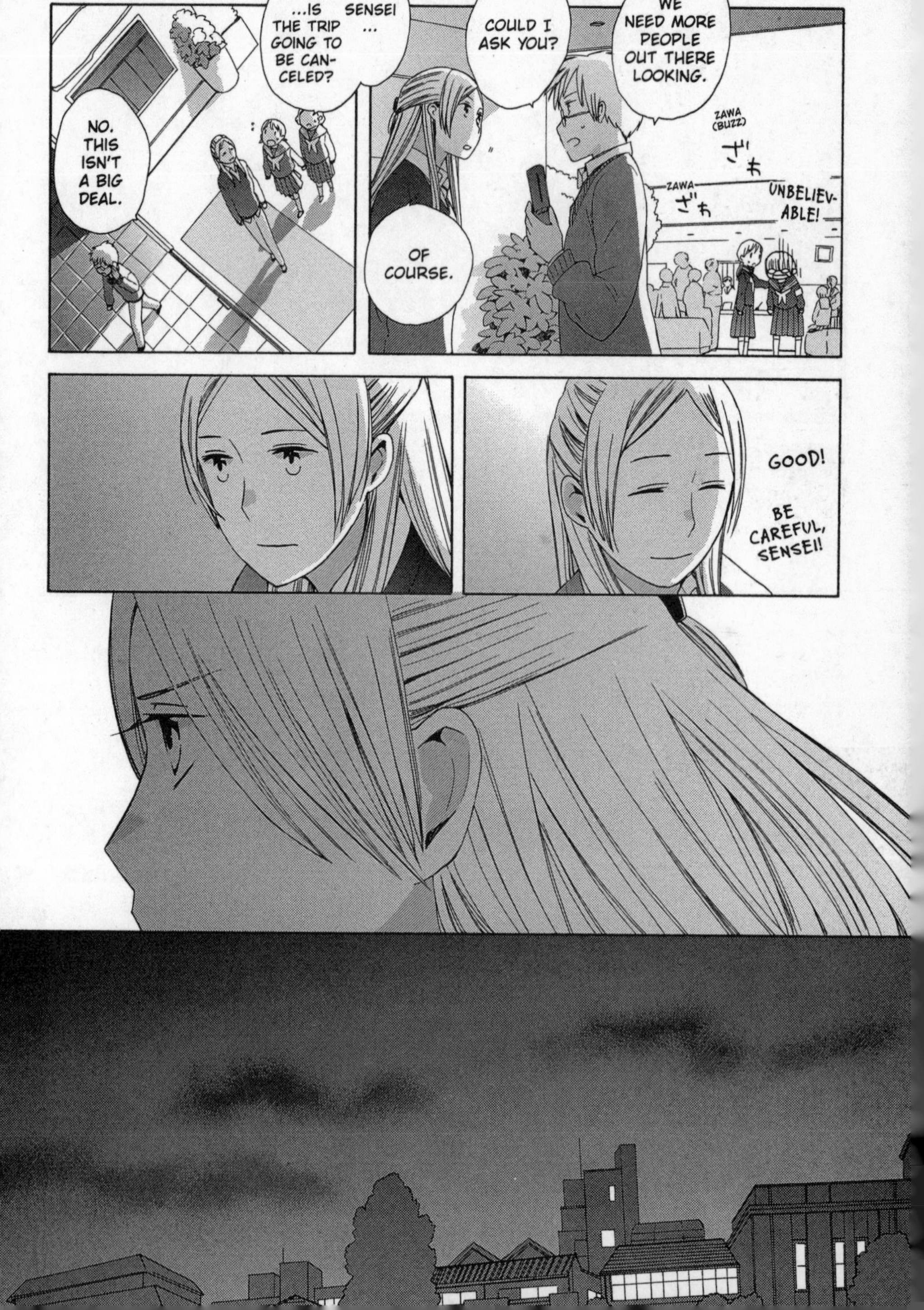
WE NEED MORE PEOPLE OUT THERE LOOKING.
COULD I ASK YOU?
ZAWA (BUZZ)
ざわ
ZAWA
ざわ
UNBELIEVABLE!
OF COURSE.
SENSEI...
...IS THE TRIP GOING TO BE CANCELED?
NO. THIS ISN'T A BIG DEAL.
GOOD!
BE CAREFUL, SENSEI!

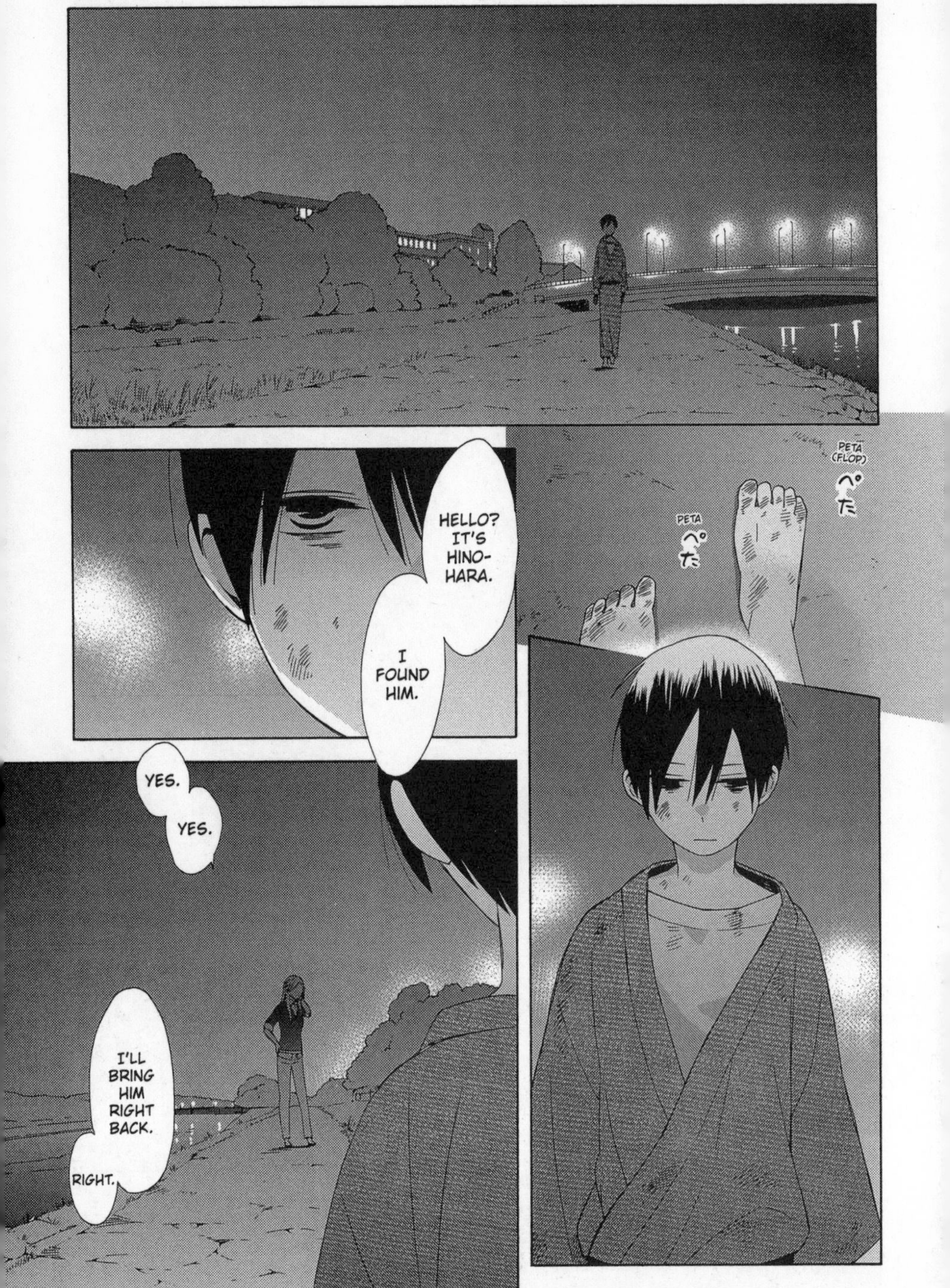
PETA (FLOP)
ぺた
PETA
ぺた
HELLO? IT'S HINO-HARA.
I FOUND HIM.
YES.
YES.
I'LL BRING HIM RIGHT BACK.
RIGHT.

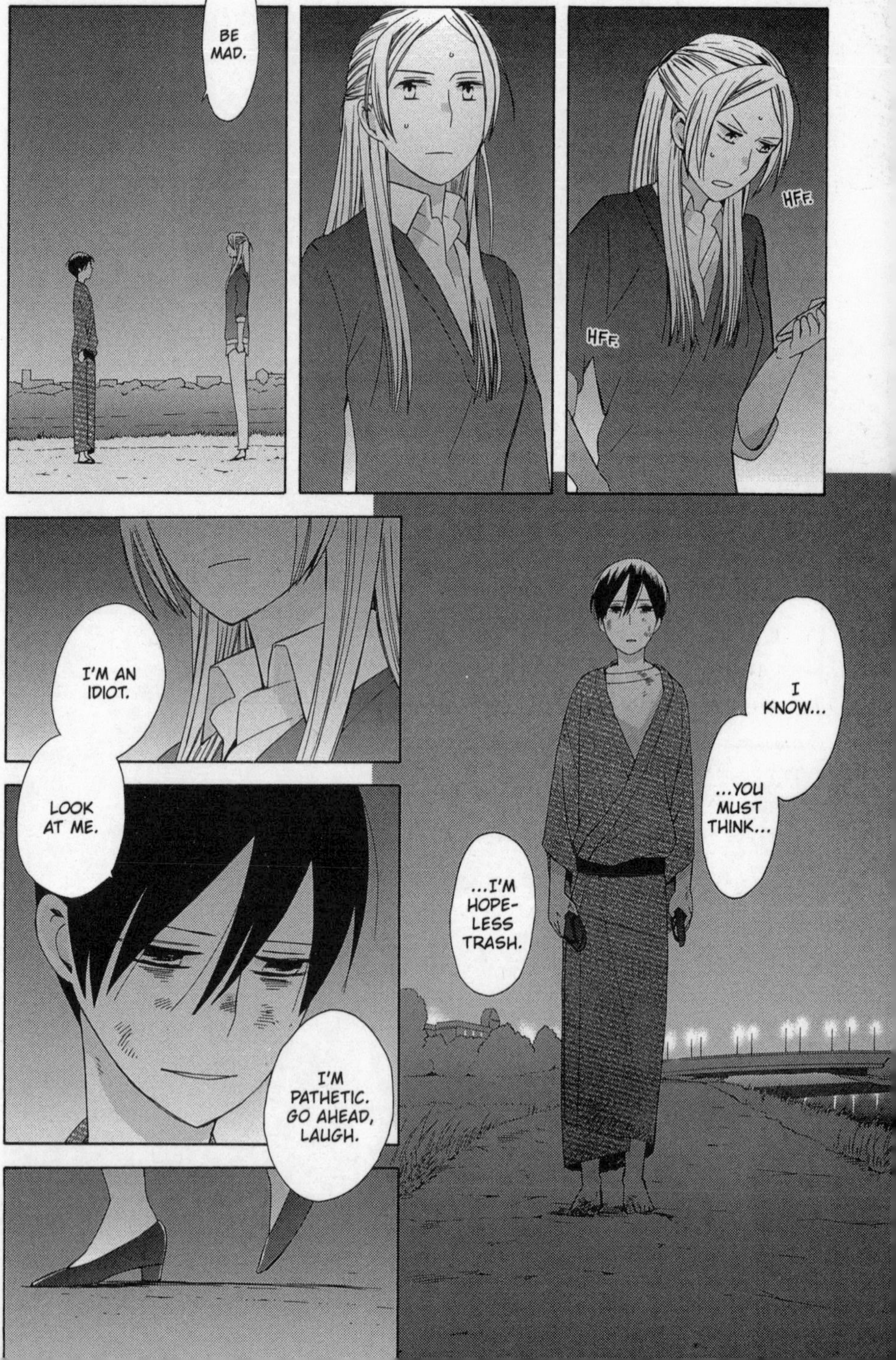
HFF.
HFF.
BE MAD.
I KNOW...
...YOU MUST THINK...
...I'M HOPELESS TRASH.
I'M AN IDIOT.
LOOK AT ME.
I'M PATHETIC. GO AHEAD, LAUGH.

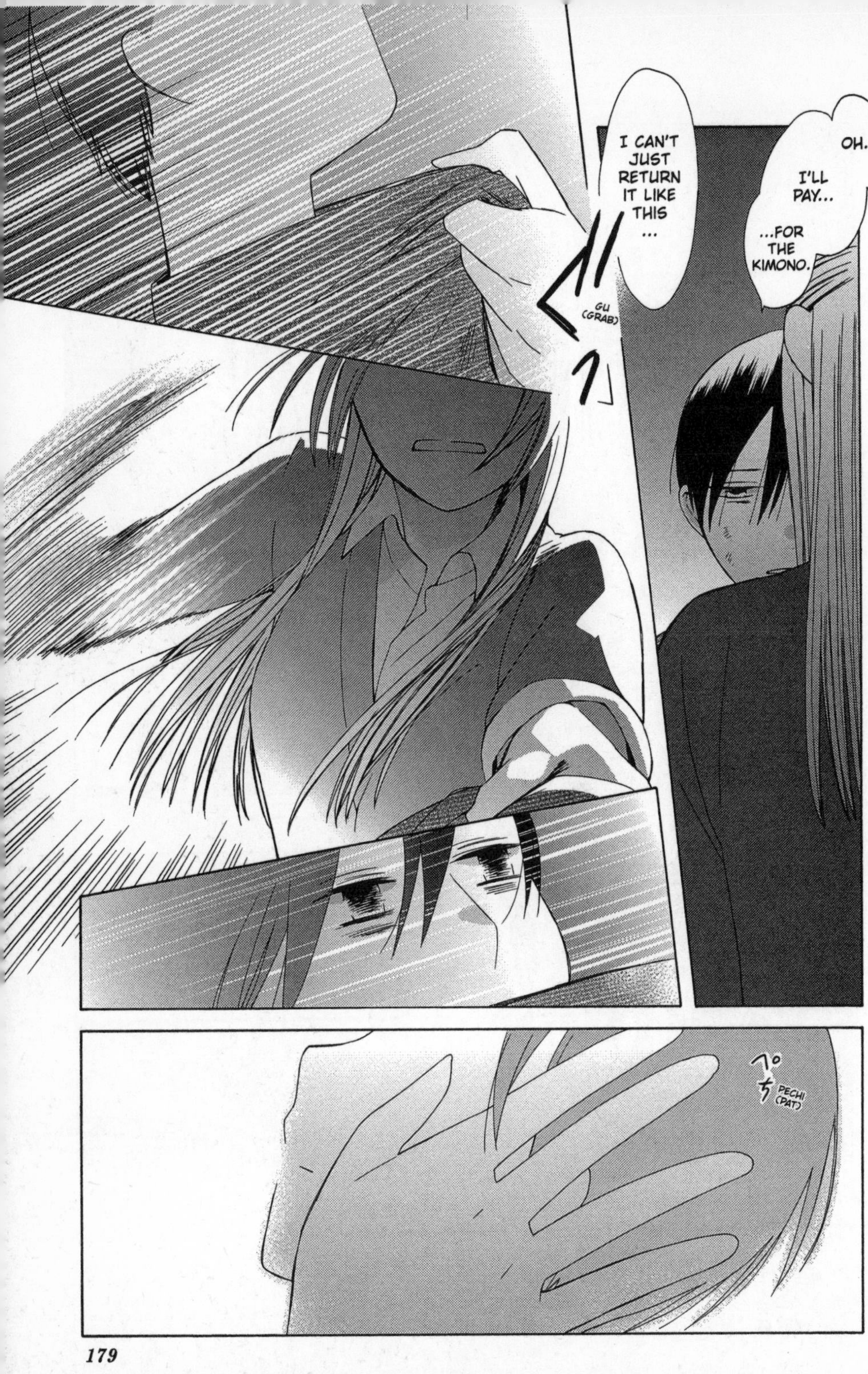
OH.
I'LL PAY...
...FOR THE KIMONO.
I CAN'T JUST RETURN IT LIKE THIS...
GU (GRAB)
ぺち
PECHI (PAT)

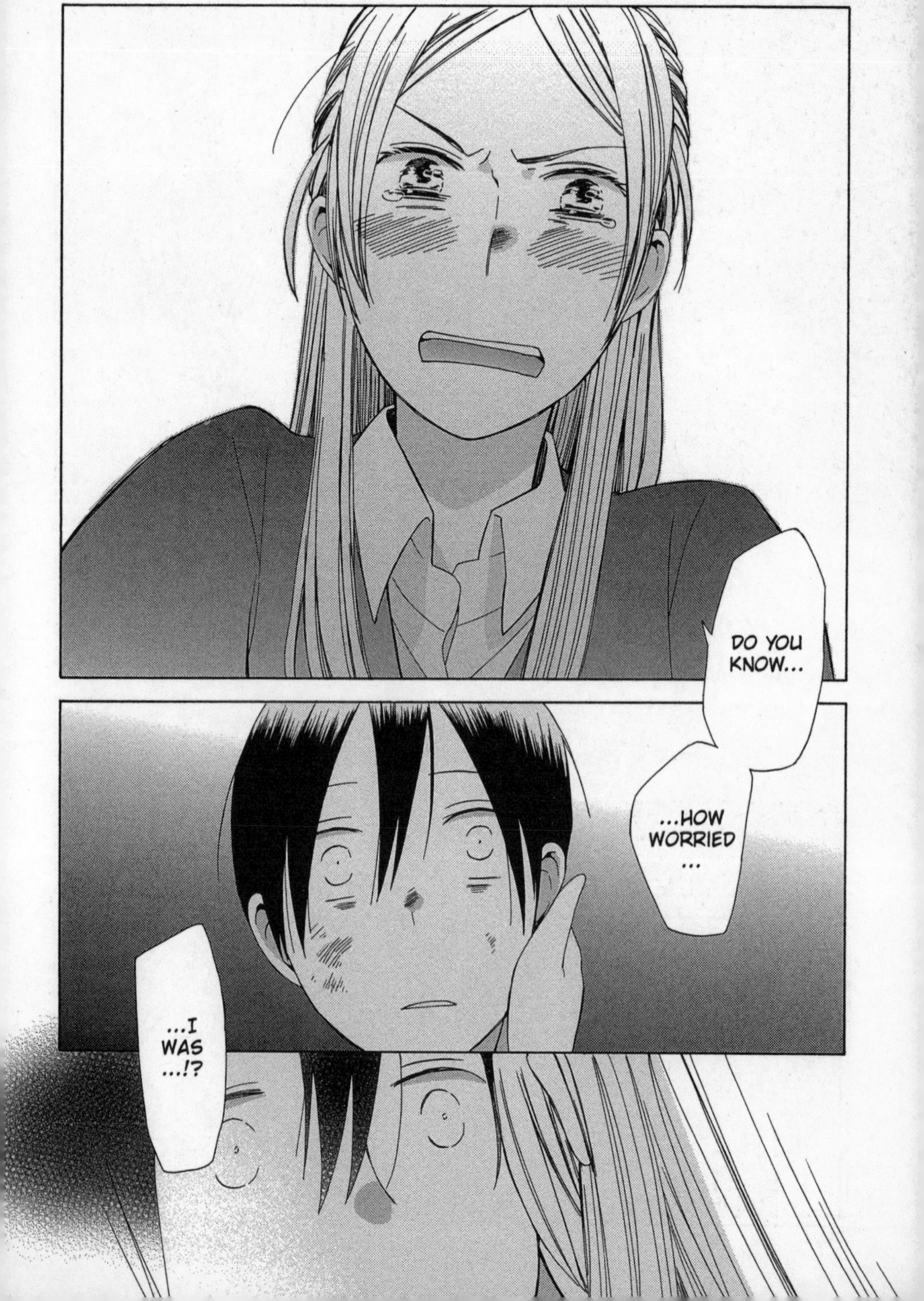
DO YOU KNOW...
...HOW WORRIED ...
...I WAS ...!?

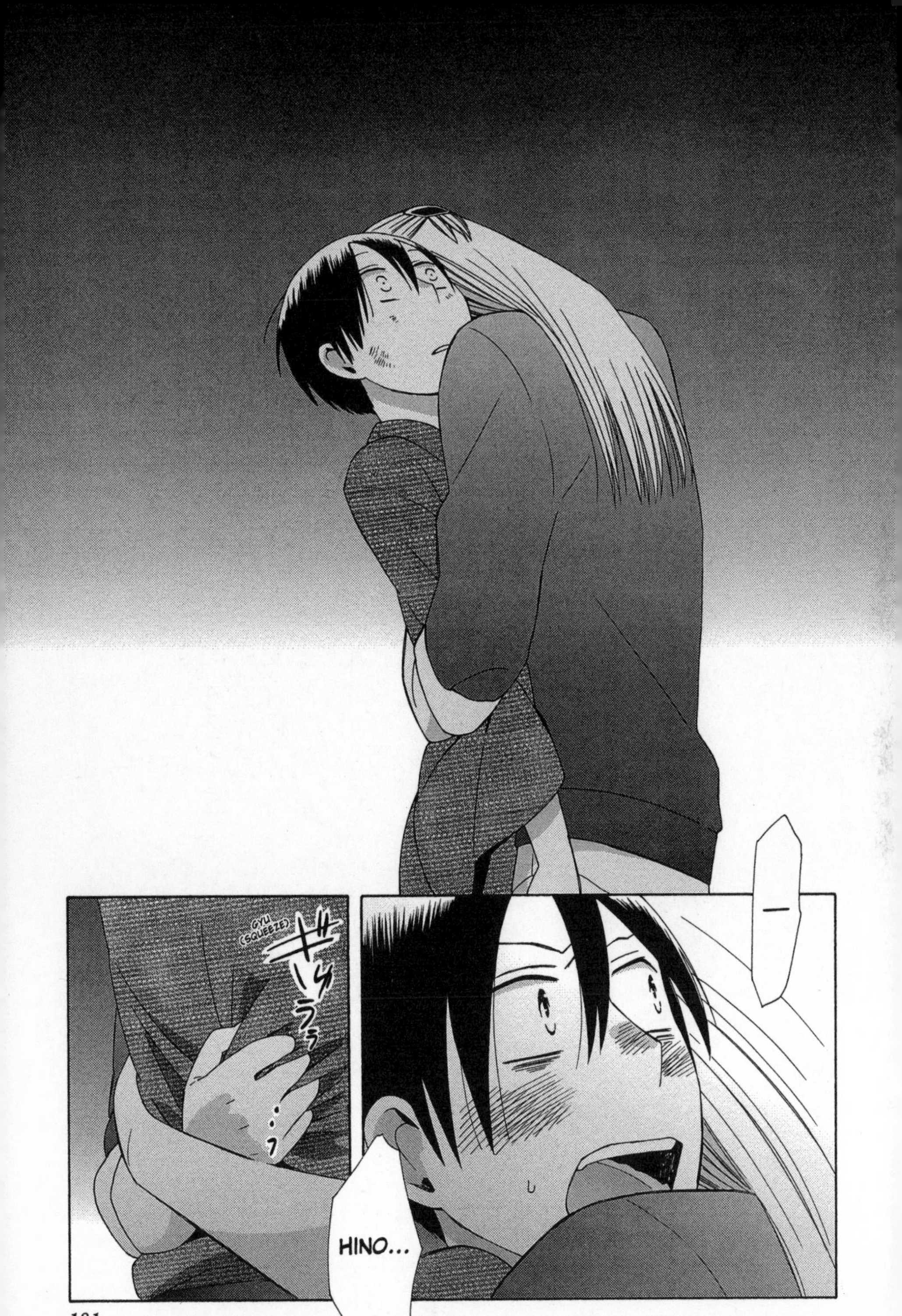

—
HINO...
GYU (SQUEEZE)

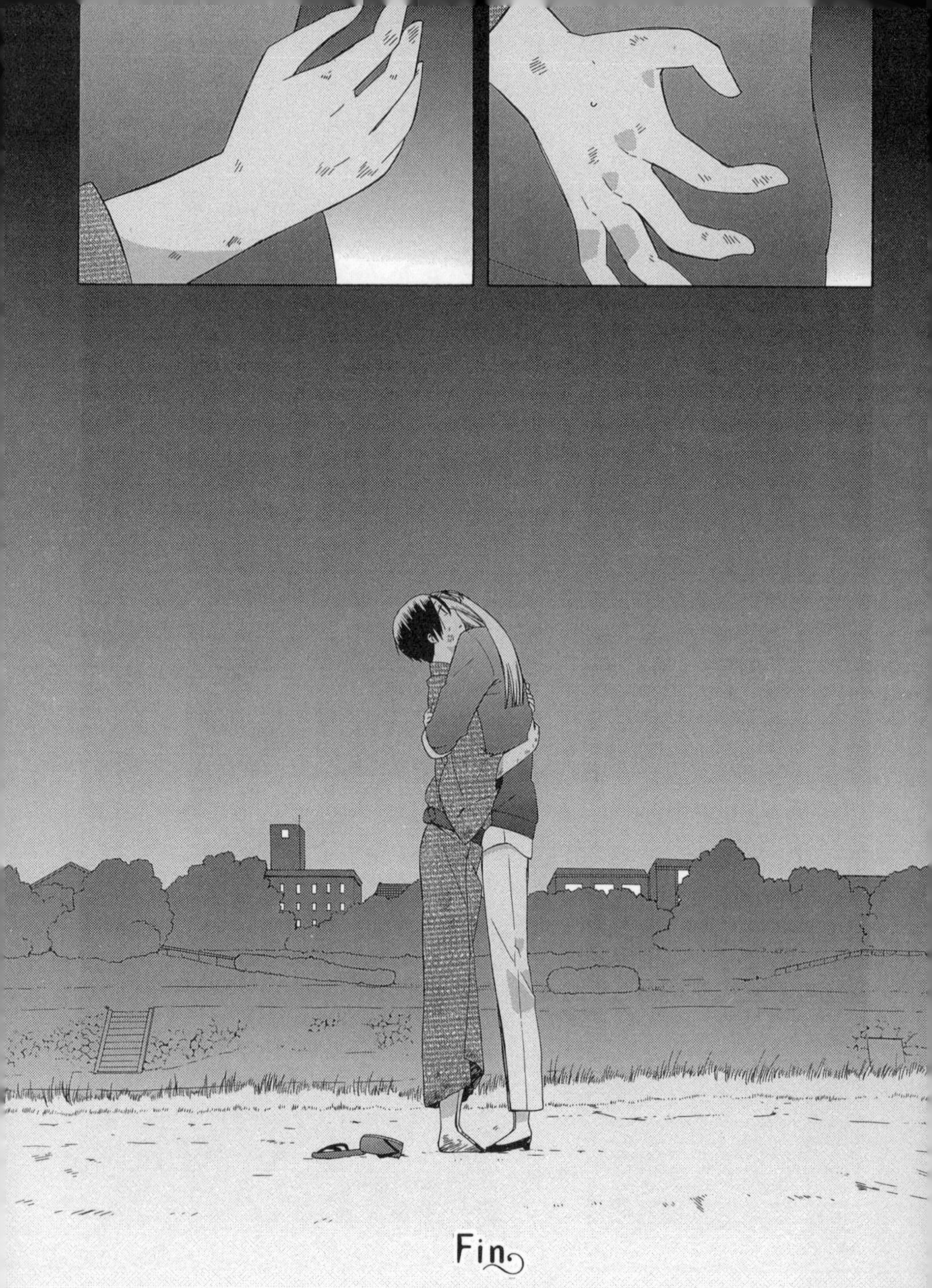
Fin

Love at Fourteen

Fuka Mizutani

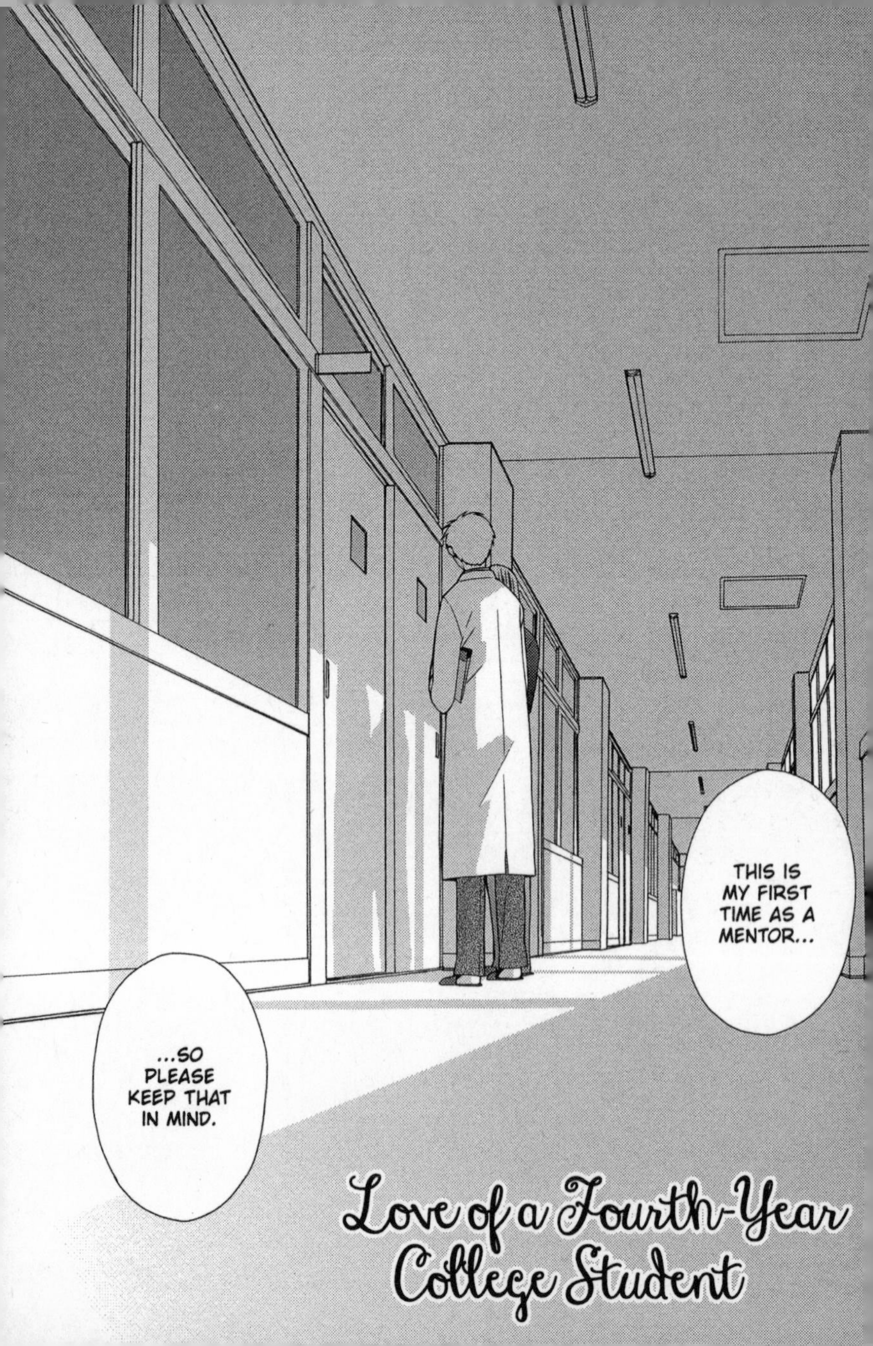
THIS IS MY FIRST TIME AS A MENTOR...
...SO PLEASE KEEP THAT IN MIND.
Love of a Fourth-Year College Student

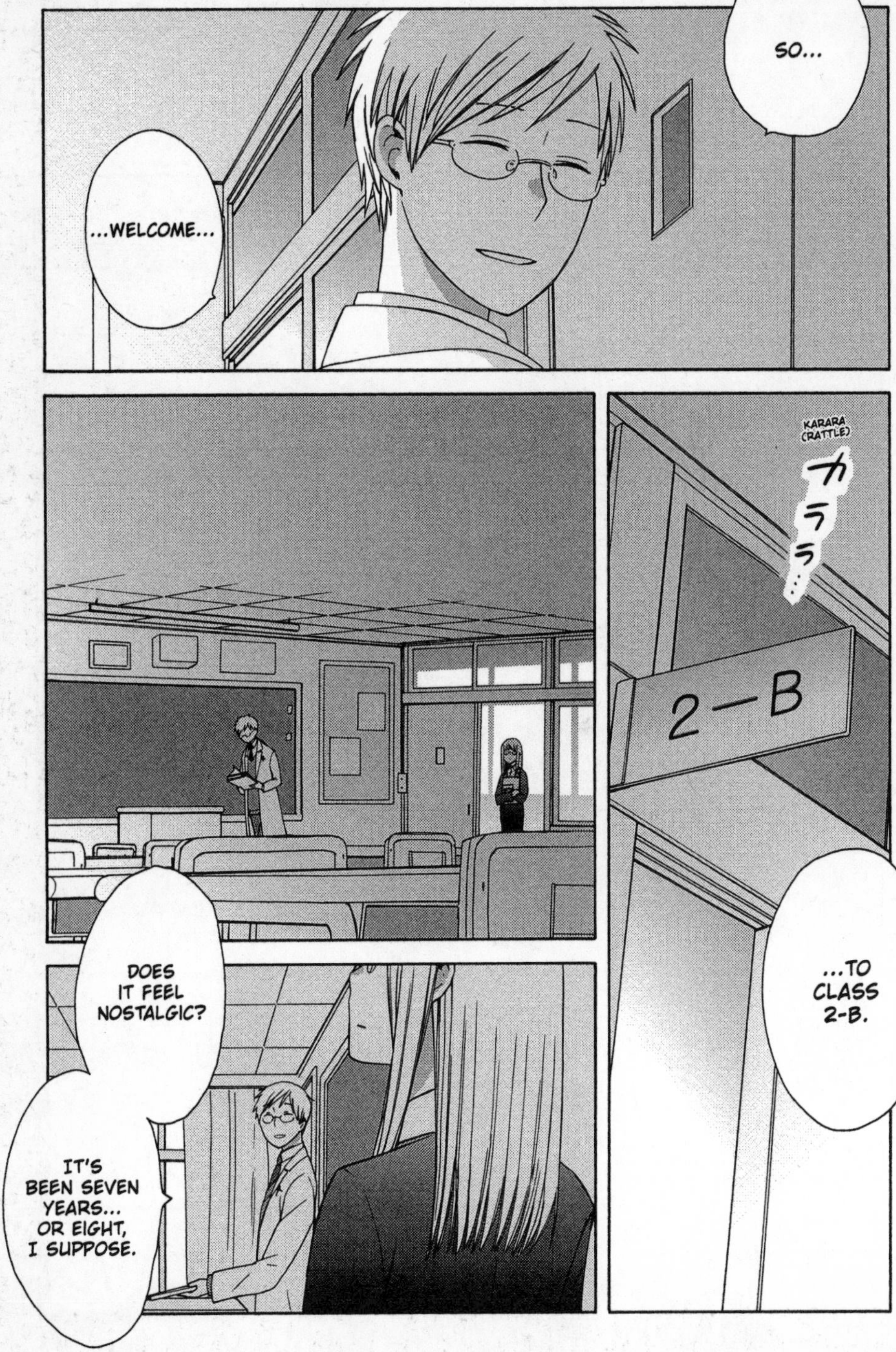
SO...
...WELCOME...
KARARA (RATTLE)
カララ…
2—B
...TO CLASS 2-B.
DOES IT FEEL NOSTALGIC?
IT'S BEEN SEVEN YEARS... OR EIGHT, I SUPPOSE.

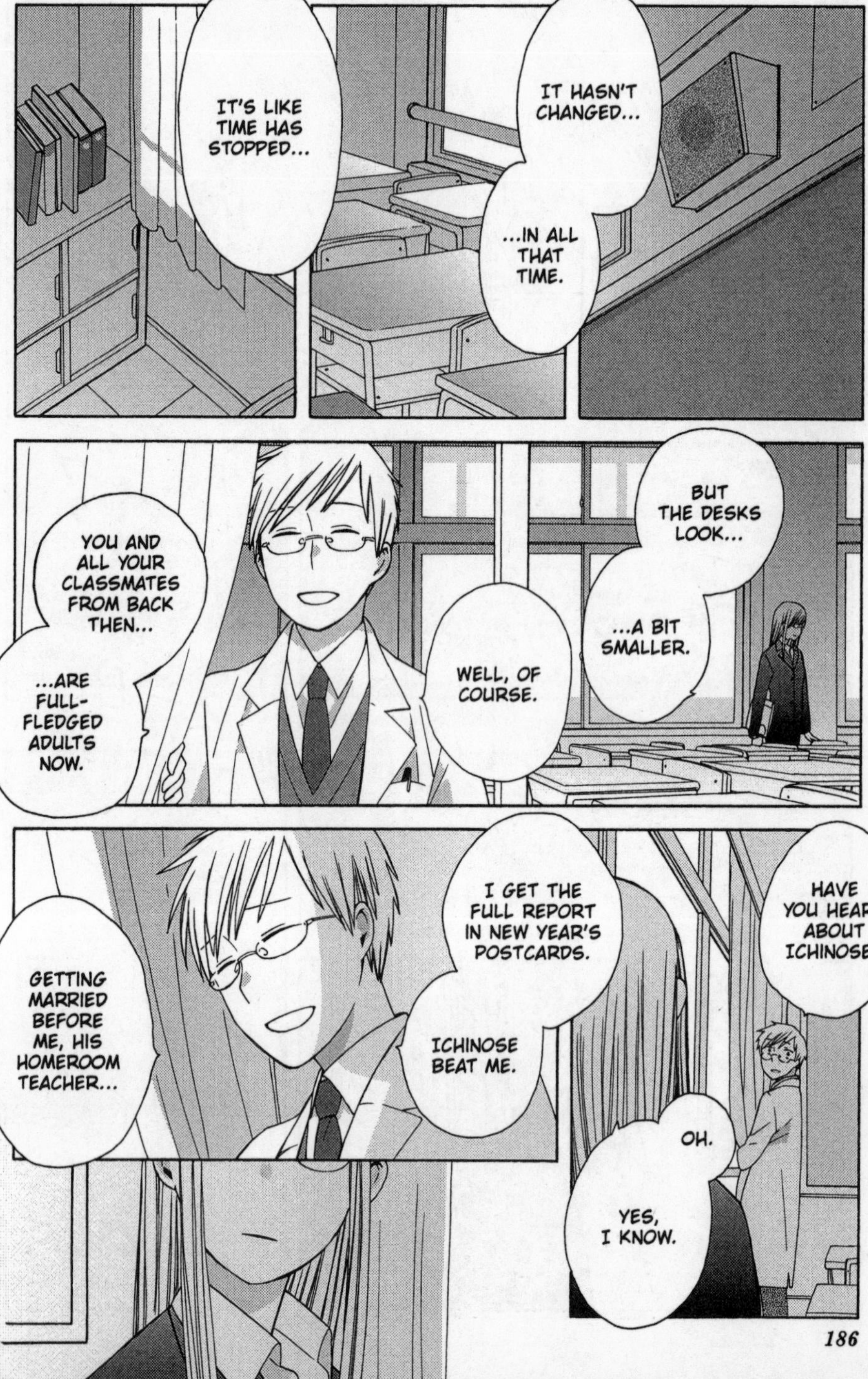

IT HASN'T CHANGED...
...IN ALL THAT TIME.
IT'S LIKE TIME HAS STOPPED...
BUT THE DESKS LOOK...
...A BIT SMALLER.
WELL, OF COURSE.
YOU AND ALL YOUR CLASSMATES FROM BACK THEN...
...ARE FULL-FLEDGED ADULTS NOW.
HAVE YOU HEARD ABOUT ICHINOSE?
I GET THE FULL REPORT IN NEW YEAR'S POSTCARDS.
ICHINOSE BEAT ME.
GETTING MARRIED BEFORE ME, HIS HOMEROOM TEACHER...
OH.
YES, I KNOW.

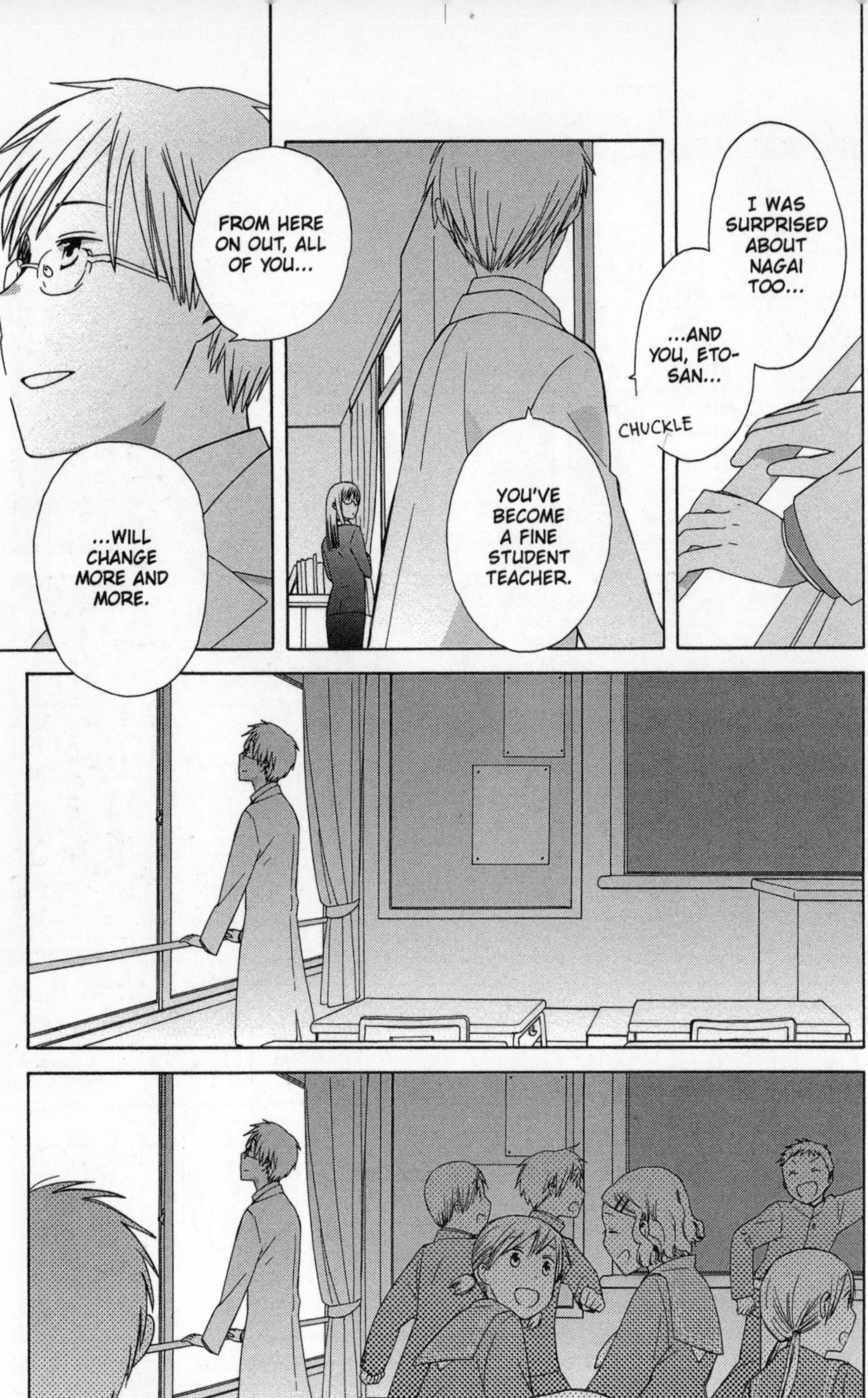
I WAS SURPRISED ABOUT NAGAI TOO...
...AND YOU, ETO-SAN...
CHUCKLE
YOU'VE BECOME A FINE STUDENT TEACHER.
FROM HERE ON OUT, ALL OF YOU...
...WILL CHANGE MORE AND MORE.

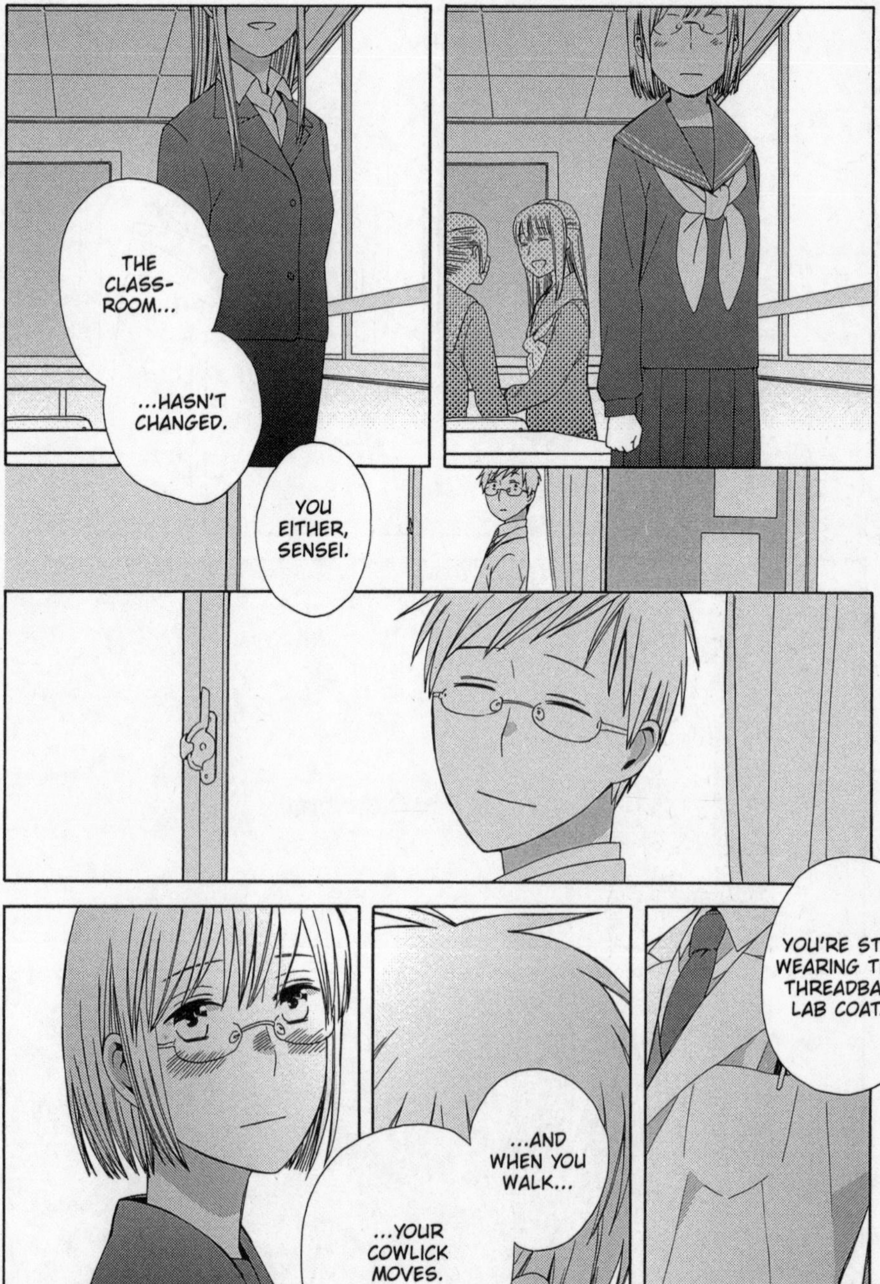
THE CLASSROOM...
...HASN'T CHANGED.
YOU EITHER, SENSEI.
YOU'RE STILL WEARING THAT THREADBARE LAB COAT...
...AND WHEN YOU WALK...
...YOUR COWLICK MOVES.

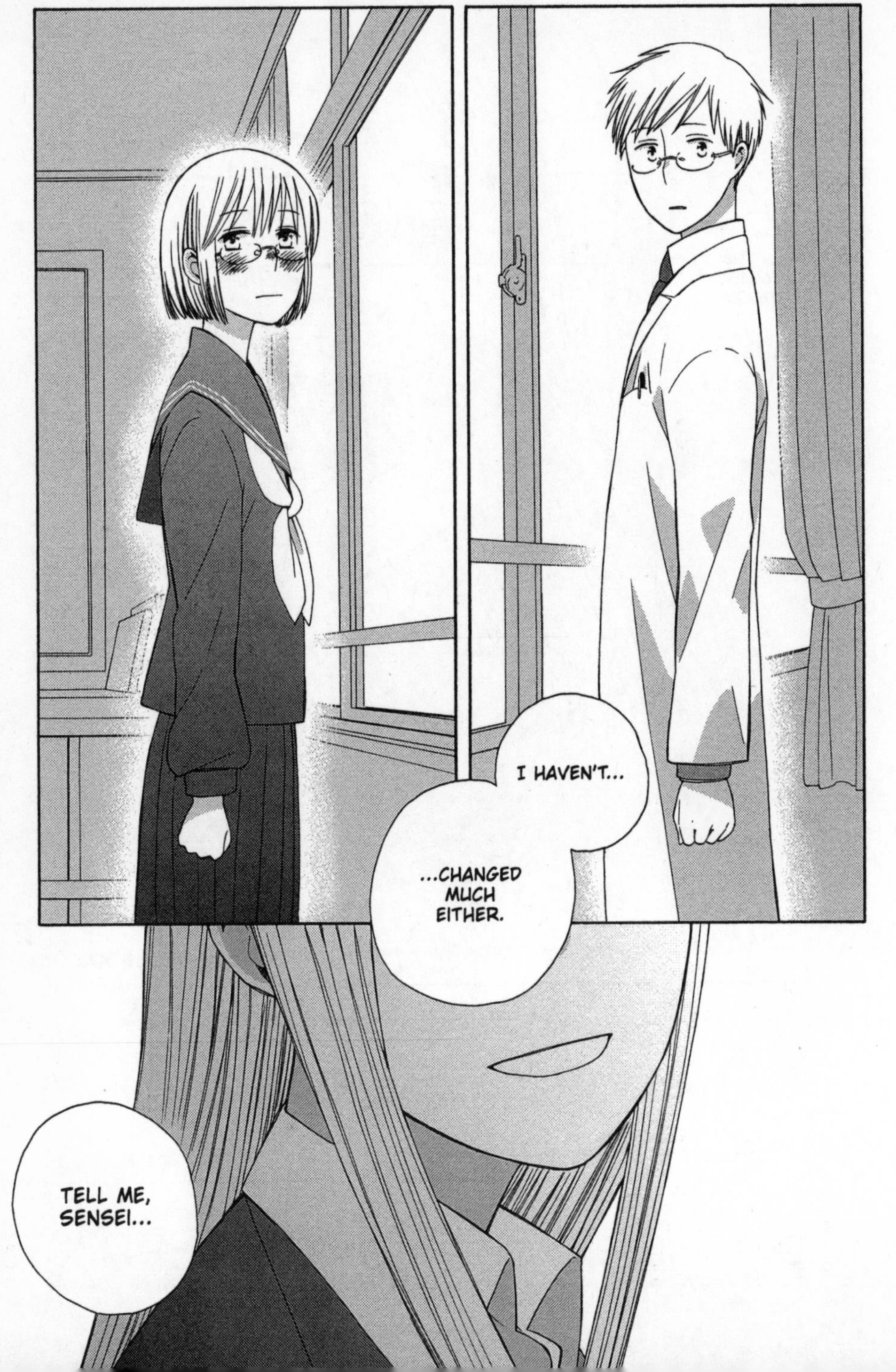
I HAVEN'T...
...CHANGED MUCH EITHER.
TELL ME, SENSEI...

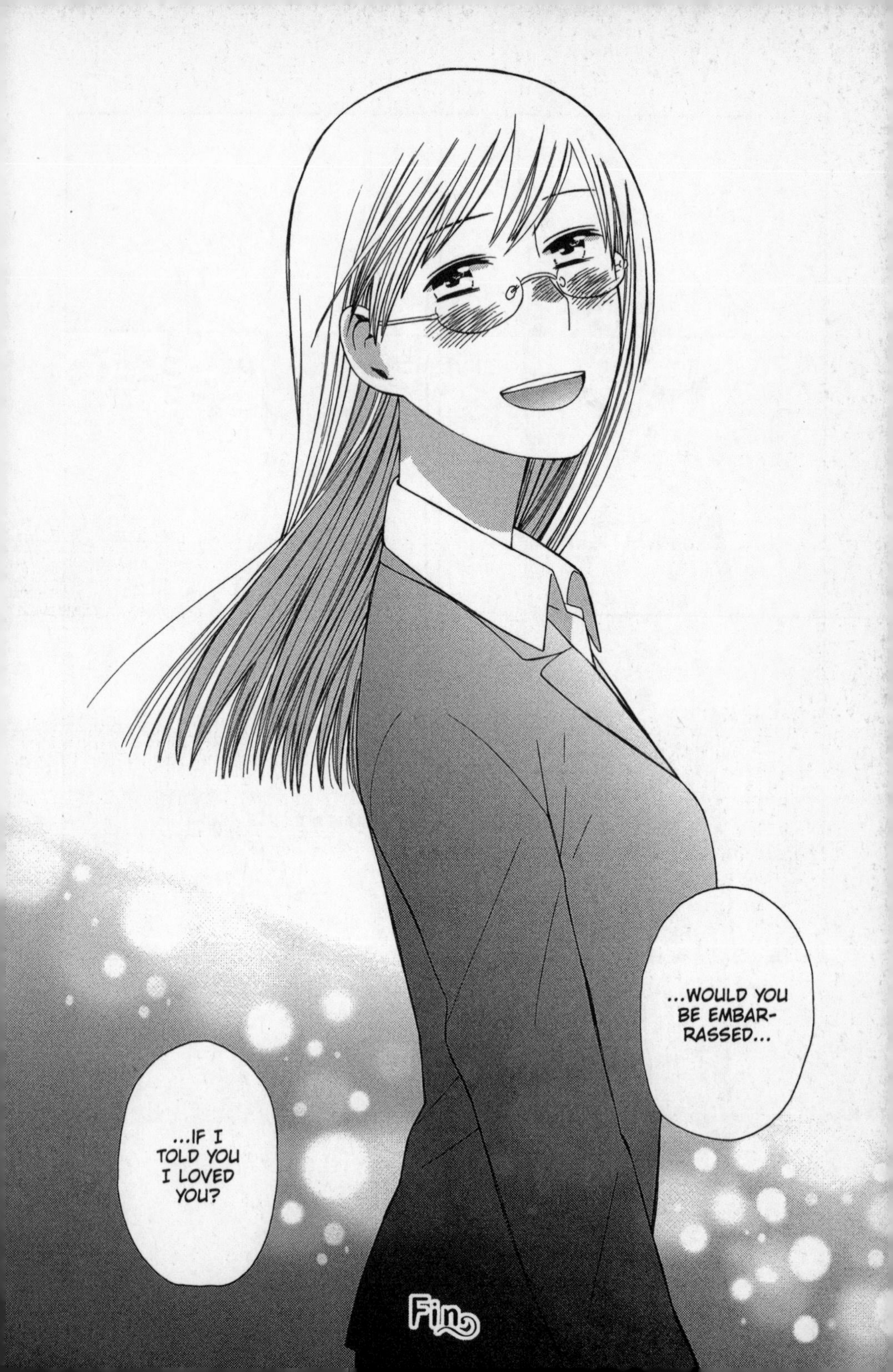
...WOULD YOU BE EMBAR-RASSED...
...IF I TOLD YOU I LOVED YOU?
Fin

AFTER-WORD
THANK YOU FOR BUYING THIS VOLUME.
I'M FUKA MIZUTANI.
UNRULY HAIR
THANKS TO YOU, THIS IS VOLUME 5.
I'M SO THANKFUL FOR BEING ALLOWED TO WORK ON THIS SERIES FOR SIX YEARS NOW.
5
5... WOW...
OH!
OOH!
THE MAIN STORY IN THIS VOLUME IS THE STANDARD CLASS TRIP TO KYOTO.
MY HOMETOWN! YOU CAN TRUST ME TO GET KYOTO RIGHT!!
WELCOME TO KYOTO
BORN AND RAISED IN KYOTO
BUT OF COURSE...
...I'VE NEVER COME TO KYOTO ON A CLASS TRIP.
I PEPPERED PEOPLE WITH QUESTIONS IF THEY ANSWERED YES TO "DID YOU GO TO KYOTO ON A CLASS TRIP?"
THANK YOU TO MY FRIENDS AND ACQUAINTANCES WHO SUPPORTED ME WITH THIS...!
DO YOU TAKE A BUS FROM PLACE TO PLACE?
UM...
WHAT FOOD DID THEY SERVE AT THE INN YOU STAYED AT?
WHAT DID YOU GET TO DO THERE?
IN ELEMENTARY SCHOOL, WE WENT TO HIROSHIMA...
MAPLE-LEAF SHAPED BEAN PASTE CAKE!
DENDERA RYUBA FINGER PLAY SONG!
...AND IN MIDDLE SCHOOL, WE WENT TO NAGASAKI.
HUH...
OH...
I HOPE WE'LL BE ABLE TO MEET AGAIN IN VOLUME 6.
THANK YOU FOR READING THIS FAR!

Special Thanks

Iida-sama of Hakusensha

Kohei Nawata Design

My family My great friends

Sayo Murata-chan

And all of you who are reading this now.

Spring 2015

水谷フーカ

Fuka Mizutani

TRANSLATION NOTES

COMMON HONORIFICS:

no honorific: Indicates familiarity or closeness; if used without permission or reason, addressing someone in this manner would constitute an insult.

-san: The Japanese equivalent of Mr./Mrs./Miss. If a situation calls for politeness, this is the fail-safe honorific.

-sama: Conveys great respect; may also indicate that the social status of the speaker is lower than that of the addressee.

-kun: Used most often when referring to boys, this indicates affection or familiarity. Occasionally used by older men among their peers, but it may also be used by anyone referring to a person of lower standing.

-chan: An affectionate honorific indicating familiarity used mostly in reference to girls; also used in reference to cute persons or animals of either gender.

-senpai: A suffix used to address upperclassmen or more experienced coworkers.

-kouhai: A suffix used to address underclassmen or less experienced coworkers.

-sensei: A respectful term for teachers, artists, or high-level professionals.

PAGE 77

OL: Short for "Office Lady," the general term for female office workers.

Love at Fourteen

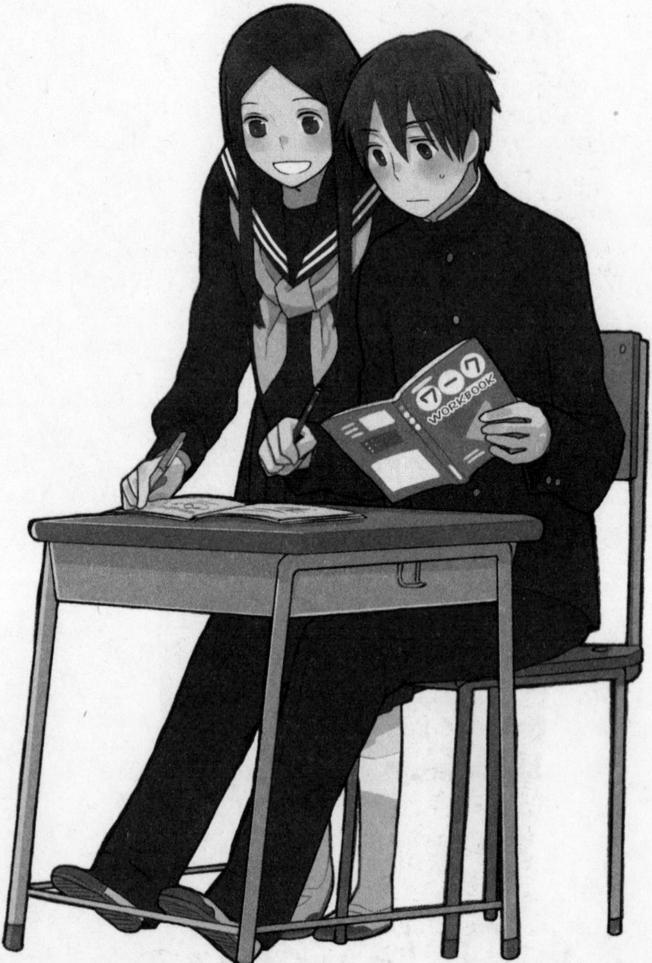
ワーク
WORKBOOK

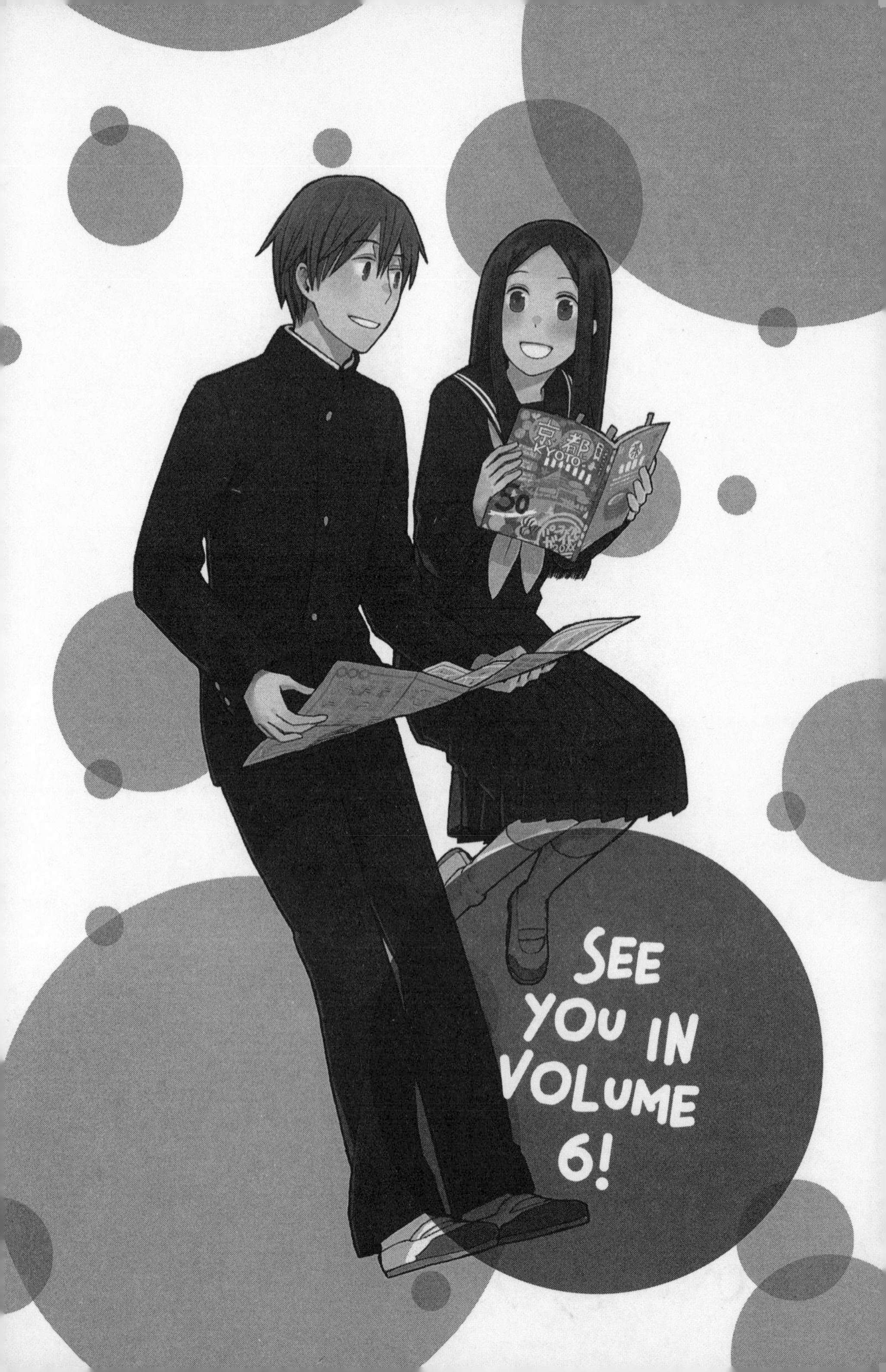
SEE YOU IN VOLUME 6!

Love at Fourteen

LOVE AT FOURTEEN ⑤

FUKA MIZUTANI

Translation: Sheldon Drzka

Lettering: Lys Blakeslee

JUYON-SAI NO KOI by Fuka Mizutani
© Fuka Mizutani 2015
All rights reserved.
First published in Japan in 2015 by HAKUSENSHA, INC., Tokyo.
English language translation rights in U.S.A., Canada and U.K. arranged with
HAKUSENSHA, INC., Tokyo through Tuttle-Mori Agency, Inc., Tokyo.

Yen Press
Hachette Book Group
1290 Avenue of the Americas
New York, NY 10104

www.HachetteBookGroup.com
www.YenPress.com

Yen Press is an imprint of Hachette Book Group, Inc.
The Yen Press name and logo are trademarks of Hachette Book Group, Inc.

The publisher is not responsible for websites (or their content) that are not owned by the publisher.

First Yen Press Edition: February 2016

Library of Congress Control Number: 2015952609

ISBN: 978-0-316-39054-5

10 9 8 7 6 5 4 3 2 1

BVG

Printed in the United States of America